More terrible
than
victory

More Terrible Than Victory

*North Carolina's Bloody
Bethel Regiment 1861–1865*

By Craig S. Chapman

BRASSEY'S

Washington • London

To my loving wife, Mary,

and my children,

Jennifer, Paul, & Thomas —

for their special contribution to this book

Brassey's Editorial Offices
22883 Quicksilver Drive
Dulles, Virginia 20166

Brassey's Order Department
P.O. Box 960
Herndon, Virginia 20172

Brassey's books are available at special discounts for bulk purchases for sales promotions, premiums, fund-raising, or educational use.

Library of Congress Cataloging-in-Publication Data
Chapman, Craig S.
      More terrible than victory : North Carolina's bloody Bethel
            Regiment,1861–65 / by Craig S. Chapman.
            p.   cm.
      Includes bibliographical references (p.) and index.
      ISBN 1-57488-129-9
            Confederate States of America. Army. North Carolina Infantry Regiment, 11th.
      2. United States — History — Civil War, 1861–1865 — Regimental histories.   3. North
      Carolina — History — Civil War, 1861–1865 — Regimental histories.   I. Title.
      E573.5 11th. C48   1998
      973.7'456 — dc   97-27207
                                                                            CIP

10 9 8 7 6 5 4 3 2 1

Printed in the United States of America

"But one thing is
more terrible than victory
and that is defeat."

First Lieutenant Benjamin Huske, after the Battle of Bethel,
paraphrasing a quote by the Duke of Wellington
following the Battle of Waterloo.

Contents

List of Maps

Map Legend

TERRAIN SYMBOLS

HILL/RIDGE

WOODS/FOREST

SWAMP

CREEK/RIVER

ROAD

RAILROAD

BREASTWORKS

BUILDING

CITY/URBAN AREA

MILITARY SYMBOLS

CONFEDERATE UNIT

UNION UNIT

CAVALRY UNIT

ARTILLERY

III
REGIMENT

X
BRIGADE

XX
DIVISION

XXX
CORPS

Acknowledgments

Abook may have a single author, but it is never the result of a solitary effort. In the years spent researching and writing this history, I have benefited from the help and support offered by many people.

My friends in the National Guard played a critical role by inspiring me to prepare a history of the unit in which I served. I particularly wish to mention Deanie Walker, my commander at the time I began this endeavor, for encouraging and guiding me in the initial stages of my work. During the first few months on the project, Alan Litehizer helped me research the topic and made several important discoveries. Jerry Parker, Paul Vivian, and some of my other "buddies" assisted me with useful advice and constructive criticism. To all of my fellow soldiers, many of whom share this military heritage, I hope this history proves worthy of the unit it portrays.

Many professional historians and writers helped me along the way. Without their helpful hints, encouragement, and practical suggestions I could not have completed this project. Wilson Angley of the North Carolina Department of Archives and History took an early interest in my work and got me started at the state's archives. Al Featherstone and Greg Mast helped me find sources in the research libraries around North Carolina and the rest of the country. Robert Downing, director of the Regiment Band of the 11th North Carolina Troops, provided material and insights into the history of the regiment, its band, and the Bethel flag. My brother, Bruce Chapman, helped improve the quality of my writing with his objective analyses and useful suggestions.

Finally, I want to thank all of the thoughtful archivists and librarians in the places where I conducted my research. The staffs at the North Carolina State Archives, the Southern Historical Collection at the University of North Carolina, the Special Collections Library at Duke University, the Library of Congress, the staff of the Gettysburg National Military Park, and the Virginia Historical Society earned my undying thanks for their kind consideration of my requests for help and information. Their care of the letters, diaries, manuscripts, and memorabilia of the people who experienced the Civil War has preserved the facts about this great conflict that writers, such as myself, use in producing our accounts of what has preceded us.

Craig S. Chapman
Raleigh, North Carolina

Introduction

July 14, 1863

Captain Francis Bird led the exhausted troops of the 11th North Carolina as they scrambled over the pontoon bridge to the southern shore of the Potomac River, just before the Union cavalry closed in for the kill. The Tar Heel soldiers were among the last of the Army of Northern Virginia to cross the bridge at Falling Waters, after a swirling rear guard engagement. They barely made it. Their hurried crossing marked the end of the Gettysburg campaign. A month earlier, the Confederates had invaded the North in the hope of winning the war. For General Lee and the Army of Northern Virginia, the Gettysburg campaign had been a bloody setback and a great disappointment. For the 11th N.C., Gettysburg had been a catastrophe. Only three men out of ten returned from Pennsylvania. The rest? Wounded . . . missing . . . captured . . . dead. The huge losses reduced the regiment to a shell — a mere remnant — of its former self.

But they still had their colors. The survivors marched under the only flag in the entire brigade that had been saved from the carnage on Cemetery Ridge. The citizens of North Carolina, by vote of the legislature, had specially inscribed their flag to commemorate the regiment's victory at Bethel, the war's first land battle. The men drew hope from their colors. They would rebuild their fractured outfit. Younger leaders would step forward to replace some of the fallen officers. The wounded would return to duty. Prisoners would be exchanged. Recruits would join the ranks alongside the veterans. Bit by bit, the regiment would restore the qualities that distinguished it; it would march to other battlefields and more victories under its proud banner.

Yet, there was another catastrophe looming in the future — a tragedy that would reduce the regiment and its colors to a mere remnant. The rest? Consumed by the flames of war.

The Civil War produced many examples of notable military units. The Stonewall Brigade, the 54th Massachusetts, and the Iron Brigade, to name a few, emerge from a long list of organizations to earn a prominent place in America's history, either through their fighting prowess or their special role. North Carolina's "Bethel Regiment" merits its place in history both as a first class fighting unit and as a body of soldiers destined to play a poignant part in the savage conflict.

The Bethel Regiment, like all fine military units, filled its ranks with men fully committed to its cause. Mustered into service at the very beginning of the war, the 1st North Carolina Volunteers (later redesignated as the 11th Regiment N.C. Troops) was recruited completely from the state's citizen volunteers. Most enlisted directly from existing volunteer militia companies; none came directly from the U.S. Army. The regiment was a product of the volunteer military system used by the United States in the nineteenth century, before the nation adopted a professional military structure. Yet, the Bethel Regiment has ties to America's current army. The combat battalions of today's North Carolina National Guard trace their lineage from the regiment formed in 1861. The concept of the citizen-soldier provides the common thread between these Civil War volunteers and the guardsmen of today.

The specific motivation of the Confederate soldier is more difficult to understand for the modern reader. After all, it is hard to imagine two less worthy causes than the perpetuation of slavery or the breakup of the Union. Obviously, the typical Carolina volunteer did not see the issues of the time from a modern perspective. The Tar Heel soldier grew up in a society that had known and tolerated slavery for generations. Although most white families in the state did not own slaves, they knew their economy depended on the institution and few had any moral misgivings about it. The poor mountain farmer reacted to the slavery debate in much the same way as the coastal planter; they felt indignant over northern abolitionist preachings. The secessionists convinced the common farmers and laborers that the northern assault against slavery threatened the rights of all southerners. The acceptance of this line of reasoning represents the great political triumph of the secessionist movement. Defending slavery did not arouse most Confederate soldiers, but preserving their property and rights did. In 1861, the Confederate volunteers answered the call to arms believing that they served a noble cause. Unburdened by draftees and bounty-soldiers, the regiment performed faithfully under cruelly harsh conditions.

These volunteers had the good sense to elect highly qualified leaders who proved to be very capable field commanders. The men looked for bravery, decisiveness, and forcefulness in their leaders, rather than popularity. The political hacks who squandered the lives of so many fine soldiers did not become leaders in the regiment. Their senior officers in the Army of Northern Virginia were competent combat leaders, although far from the best in the Confederate army. Lacking the resources of the Union side, the Confederate leadership showed a greater tendency to employ sound tactics to defeat the enemy rather than bludgeoning their opponents by sheer force of arms. Only once did their leaders depend on brute force to win. The results of that battle (Gettysburg) caused them to rely on tactics to preserve the South's dwindling strength.

These leaders also deserve credit for imbuing the Bethel Regiment with discipline. Strict discipline binds the actions of soldiers to a common purpose and to orderly conduct. Held to exacting standards and drilled to perfection, these North Carolina volunteers learned to control their actions and accomplish their mission in the face of daunting odds and miserable circumstances. The regiment, under several different leaders, adhered to a strong code of discipline and most highly valued those commanders who most rigidly enforced it. With enthusiasm, competent leadership, and discipline the men quickly developed an aggressive fighting spirit that served them well through their first trial. Call it boldness, confidence, or killer instinct, this fighting spirit gave the troops the ability to throw themselves into the battle with the determination to either win or die. Thorough training and experience helped to nurture this feeling of indomitability that so often delineates the victors from the vanquished. Head to head against Union soldiers, the Bethel Regiment almost never flinched. Given its unique status as the state's first regiment and the boost in morale from its early victory, the Bethel Regiment acquired a strong *esprit de corps*—a sense about themselves that they were special. This *esprit de corps* held the regiment together in many tense situations that would have caused other units to fold. The regimental flag embodied that spirit and became a treasured symbol. The Bethel Regiment never surrendered its colors, even when the cause died.

Indeed, the regiment was special. It suffered the South's first battlefield death only three weeks after the state seceded and was still serving proudly when the end came at Appomattox. Frequently caught in the center of the action, its combat journey characterized the final twenty-two months of the Army of Northern Virginia's struggle. It won the acclaim of the army, yet bore the blame of a scapegoat. It triumphed in many battles, endured grueling hardships, survived the fiercest clashes, and escaped near brushes with destruction, but it could not evade a terrible fate. In the last week of the war, it suffered annihilation at the hands of an overwhelming enemy force. Then, in its final moments, the regiment exchanged salutes with its victorious enemy—a parting tribute to the fighting qualities of the Confederate soldier.

1

Marching to the Field of Blood

SECESSION

One of the remarkable ironies of the Civil War is the fact that North Carolina, the southern state most reluctant and nearly last to break from the Union, gave more troops and shed more blood for the South than any other state. Despite its aversion to secession, North Carolina suffered the South's first battlefield death a mere three weeks after leaving the Union. Over the next four years, forty thousand more men from the ranks of its regiments gave their lives in bloody conflicts or to the ravages of disease. The state's uncertain path to secession gave no clue to the ardor the Tar Heel soldiers would bring to the southern struggle for independence. Rabid sectional politics did not dominate North Carolina's political scene in the antebellum years. The state's demographics leaned heavily toward the yeoman farmer and common laborer who cared more about political representation within the state than issues such as nullification. Certainly, the state had a large slave population — more than three hundred thousand — and sympathized with the planters over the issue of slavery. North Carolinians, like their brethren in the deep south, resented northern moralistic complaints that slavery "is a social and political evil and a sin." Most agreed with Democrat John W. Ellis "that it is a system of labor eminently well adapted to our climate and soil . . . one of the providences of God for civilizing and christianizing that benighted race." Those feelings of sympathy, however, lacked the passion to force a split with the federal government.[1]

Politically, North Carolina split more along party than sectional lines. The national debates over slavery did not excite the state's voters nearly so much as internal political issues. Not until the 1850s did North Carolina's Democrats, who favored a stronger prosouthern stance, wrest control of the state house and governor's office from the Whigs, which they did by riding the issue of equal suffrage for all whites. North Carolina only fell in line with the southern sectional alliance during the election of 1856, when it threw its support to Democrat James Buchanan rather than Millard Fillmore because Buchanan seemed more likely to defeat the Republicans. A common fear of the newly formed Republican party pulled the state into the fold of the southern Democrats just as it pulled apart the national Whig party. The abolitionist leanings of the Republican party worried southern voters who feared the Republicans wanted to deny the South "those equal rights and privileges to which all the States in the Union are entitled." The poor farmers from the western mountains may not have owned any slaves, but they supported the planters' rights. For them, slavery was a fact of life — not a moral issue.[2]

North Carolina's qualified support of Buchanan proved that the state supported slave interests, but it hardly demonstrated a willingness to secede. Party politics still suppressed strong sectional loyalties and separated the plantation owners from the small farmers. The state's Whigs even staged a political comeback near the end of the decade over the issue of an *ad valorem* tax that would shift more financial burdens to the large planters. Lacking a secure political base, the state's Democrats could not afford to push a prosecessionist platform and risk alienating the crucial voting bloc of nonslave-owning farmers. Something beyond the extension of slavery into new territories was needed to stimulate the secessionist passions of the Old North State.

An odd, tragic event inflamed those passions in North Carolina and the other southern states. On October 17, 1859, John Brown, a fanatic abolitionist, led a small militant band in the seizure of the federal arsenal at Harpers Ferry, Virginia. Brown intended to destroy the institution of slavery violently, by igniting and arming a slave revolt. John Brown failed, but his legacy persisted, especially in the South. John Brown embodied two of the worst fears of southerners: forcible subjugation of "southern liberties" by northerners and the armed insurrection of slaves. These twin fears united all white southerners, regardless of social standing or economic condition. Having witnessed an abolitionist taking violent measures to destroy slavery, North Carolinians began to think of taking arms against northerners whom they viewed with suspicion. Even Whig supporter William S. Pettigrew proclaimed, "We can only keep these people back by showing them we are prepared to defend ourselves when attacked by their lawless bands."[3]

In cities and towns throughout the state, old established volunteer militia companies began training in greater earnest. Community-minded citizens had previously enlisted in the volunteer companies to march at civic events and publicly demonstrate their patriotism. These volunteers had always felt a strong sense of loyalty and displayed it by parading in uniforms they purchased at their own expense. However, many volunteer militia companies were noted more for their resplendent uniforms and distinctive headgear than for rigorous training or discipline. After John Brown's raid, the existing companies lured more venturous volunteers who showed more concern for defending the state than the Union. James C. MacRae, who belonged to the Fayetteville Independent Light Infantry, described the mood of these times. "Portents of war thickened the air, and men who had heretofore taken pride in their organization as an ornament and a thing of pomp and pleasure, now began more minutely to examine their arms and more earnestly to apply themselves to perfection in the drill of the soldier."[4]

The organized companies of volunteers filled a void left by the state's ineffective militia system which, theoretically, included every able-bodied white citizen but, actually, afforded no security against a military threat. Across North Carolina, entirely new volunteer companies sprang into existence in response to worries about the state's security. In Tarboro, a citizens' committee gathered at the court house and called for the formation of a local volunteer company to be called the Edgecombe Guards. John L. Bridgers, a noted Democrat, accepted the appointment as captain of the company and delivered a patriotic speech about defending the South, not the United States. His enthusiastic words prompted fifty-six Edgecombe County citizens to join the fledgling outfit.[5] Other volunteer militia companies, such as the Enfield Blues and Buncombe Riflemen, formally organized and began training young men within their respective communities. The state welcomed the volunteer companies as an important augmentation to the state's meager military preparations. Though lacking any formal military training, the volunteer companies offered the state organized bodies of men who were eager to serve.

Others began deliberate preparations for war. In 1859, Daniel Harvey Hill, a West Point graduate and Mexican War veteran, resigned from the faculty of Davidson College to become the superintendent of the newly founded North Carolina Military Institute in Charlotte. D. H. Hill took on the mission of preparing future Tar Heel officers for the approaching war between the states. Hill attended the duties of a soldier with stiff professionalism and firm self-assurance. A physically spare, deeply religious man, Hill was contemptuous of those who lacked self-discipline or indulged too heavily in drink. On one occasion during the Mexican War, he accosted his intemperate commanding general with a sword after receiving a verbal reprimand he thought was too insulting. Hill gained a wide reputation for his deep prejudices and his acerbic wit in expressing those prejudices. He had developed an intense dislike for "Yankees" during his years in the U.S. Army and zealously used his position to impart those animosities to the cadets. He wanted North Carolina to have a pool of motivated and trained officers when the war against the North finally arrived.[6]

The 1860 elections created much worry and anxiety in North Carolina. The thought of northern antislavery interests gaining control over the Congress and White House fueled fears of federal intervention in state affairs (that is, the abolition of slavery). Across party lines, Carolinians vehemently opposed the "Black Republican" candidate, Abraham Lincoln, though they still remained deeply divided politically. Radicals and conservatives still fought over the issues of fair taxes and representation. The vote favored the Democrats who still could not push for outright secession, but felt heartened by the election results nonetheless. The state elected a prosecessionist governor, John W. Ellis, by a narrow margin. On the national level, Lincoln's election to the presidency drove a deep wedge between the country's sections and fanned radical rhetoric. Lincoln won the election over the unified opposition of southern politicians who suddenly realized that the election had turned them into a political minority. Northern states now had the political clout to attack slavery directly. Six southern states seceded from the Union before Lincoln could even take office.

The secession crisis profoundly changed the dynamics of party politics in the state. The Democratic party splintered between those who advocated secession (mostly from the coastal region and southwest piedmont) and those who wanted to preserve the union. The Democratic coalition of slave-owning planters and poor white farmers fell apart once the latter perceived the proslave position of the party. Pro-union Democrats joined former Whigs to create a "Union" party that gained strength in the central piedmont and western mountains. "Old party lines are forgotten, as if they had never existed." Even William Woods Holden, the champion of the Democratic resurgence in the 1850s, abandoned the party to campaign against disunion.[7]

The elected politicians adopted a "wait and see" attitude rather than push for secession on the heels of the deep south states. They recognized the popular sentiments for compromise and peace that existed in the state. "We perceive in the fact of [Lincoln's] election no sufficient cause for the subversion and abandonment of the Government of our Fathers," declared a conservative citizens' committee from Hillsborough. "There is but a remote probability of a successful encroachment on our rights during the limited period of his administration." Even avowed secessionists knew the state would not break from the Union solely because of the slavery issue. "You cannot unite the masses of any southern State much less those of N. C. against the Union & in favor [of] slavery alone." The wiser secessionists redirected their argument toward the issue of upholding southern honor and rights against federal oppression. "If the Pres. adopts the doctrine of coercion . . . then farewell to this union. North Carolina can't be held in it. Why? The issue will have been changed from the Negro to that of a question of popular liberty." This line of reasoning found a more receptive audience. Nearly everyone, unionist or secessionist, rallied around the idea of preserving southern rights and resisting federal intervention. The same conservative Hillsborough committee reassured the radicals on their support of southern rights. "We recognize in its full extent the right of resistance by force, to unauthorized injustice and oppression." William W. Holden used his pro-Union newspaper, the *North Carolina Standard,* to affirm his support of southern honor. "There is only one evil greater than disunion, and that is the loss of honor and Constitutional right. *That evil the people of the South will never submit to.*"[8]

Political discord confounded any consensus on the touchy issue of secession, but prudence dictated that the state take some steps to prepare for military contingencies while the threat of war hung over the country. Everyone recognized the deplorable condition of the state's loosely organized militia. Politicians—Whig and radical—agreed that something had to be done to improve the state's defenses. At the time, the local volunteer companies represented the only available defensive force. That winter, the legislature passed a bill to reorganize the militia and sanction the volunteer companies as the state's first line of defense. The act established a volunteer citizen army, commanded by officers elected by their companies, armed with modern weapons, and trained according to the regulations of the U.S. Army. To oversee the state's military system, the law re-created the office of the adjutant general. John F. Hoke, a Mexican War veteran from Lincoln County, won the election to this vital post and started measures to field a citizen army almost from scratch. The legislature helped him by authorizing the purchase of three hundred thousand dollars worth of weapons to arm the volunteer companies and by commissioning D. H. Hill to advise the governor on the best use of military appropriations. Accordingly, one of Hill's associates, Charles C. Lee, traveled north to order rifles and other weapons from northern arms manufacturers.[9]

The prosecessionist *Wilmington Journal* reflected the sentiments of many citizens in an editorial praising these moves. "The strength of a nation in time of need and danger is its army, and at such time we all instinctively turn to it for protection. But as a large standing army is thought to be unsuited to a Republican Government like ours, our chief dependence must rest, as heretofore, upon the volunteer citizen soldiery." Meanwhile, the ranks of volunteer companies continued to swell as young men signed up. In several communities, more companies, such as the Hornet's Nest Riflemen and the LaFayette Light Infantry, formally organized under corporate by-laws. By this time, the volunteer companies concentrated more on training for field operations instead of their customary parade duties. "In the winter of 1860 and the spring of 1861, drills were had almost every night, and the martial spirit of the corps was fully aroused." The Edgecombe Guards added assault tactics and target practice to their drill routines.[10]

While the state advanced its military preparations, Governor Ellis tried to push the legislature forward on the issue of secession, but the elected officials equivocated. The Assembly agreed to send three commissioners to attend the Confederate States convention in Montgomery, Alabama, to consult with the seceded states. Of the three men appointed, only John L. Bridgers favored secession.[11] At the same time, the legislators sent another delegation to the National Peace Conference called by the state of Virginia. At the governor's urging, the legislature debated calling for a state convention to consider secession, but the unionists argued against the idea. In late January, the Assembly, against the governor's wishes, decided to put the issue of a convention before the electorate on a special referendum rather than vote on the issue directly.

The convention vote set off an intense political struggle across North Carolina. The secessionists campaigned for delegates who would support breaking away from the Union and joining the "nation of the south." North Carolina unionists split themselves over the convention vote; some wanted to vote down the convention to prevent the possibility of secession, while others preferred electing pro-Union delegates to reaffirm North Carolina's tie with the United States. The political conflict fueled passions on both sides and tempers flared as the public debated. An incident in Bertie County showed how far the strife had pushed emotions by the time of the election. William G. Parker, a slave holder and ardent secessionist, returned to his home after casting his vote for the convention. As he approached the gate of his small plantation, a rifle shot whizzed past his head. When the votes were tabulated the election results disheartened the secessionists. The electorate narrowly defeated the call for a state convention on February 28, 1861. Oddly enough, of the delegates elected to attend the convention, two-thirds advocated remaining in the Union; 60 percent of the ballots went to union delegates. The voters of North Carolina had spoken. Sectional ties and the threat to slavery took a back seat to the citizens' bond with the nation. North Carolina refused to leave the Union without some provocation from the federal government or overt threat to the state's "rights and institutions."[12]

Despite the reassuring vote, the entire state felt uneasy over the widening sectional split across the country. North Carolina and the other border states paid close attention to Lincoln's inaugural address on March 4, 1861, for signs of his intent. The new president's speech sounded sufficiently conciliatory, but the principal confrontation between the South and his administration remained. Lincoln refused to recognize the independence of the seceded states, which left the troublesome question of what he intended to do "to preserve, protect and defend the Constitution of the United States." North Carolina may have decided to stay in the Union, but the Confederate States and the Lincoln administration appeared to be on a collision course. One pro-union man wrote to Whig Congressman Zebulon B. Vance from Buncombe County suggesting that "a little delay is all that is needed." Congressman Vance and his friends hoped for a gradual cooling of tensions between the Confederate States and the federal government. "Let this crisis pass. Let the Union seem quietly to settle down with the free states and border slave states." The North Carolina Unionists hoped that the seceded states would eventually return to the fold; if only hostilities could be avoided. That was not to be.[13]

On April 13–14, 1861, Confederate military commanders bombarded Fort Sumter in Charleston harbor and forced the U.S. Army garrison to surrender. On April 15, President Lincoln responded by calling for seventy-five thousand volunteers to suppress the armed rebellion. Lincoln's call for troops finally settled the issue of secession in North Carolina. His action conjured up the image of John Brown rising from the grave to lead northern abolitionists in a campaign to subdue the South and its institutions (that is, slavery). Unionist sentiment collapsed. "All hope is now extinguished . . . there is a United North against a United South, and both are marching to the field of blood." The thought of Union troops marching against the South legitimized the Confederacy in North Carolina far more than the arguments for secession. Now the citizens felt justified in taking arms against the northern "invaders" with a spirit similar to that of 1776. For Zebulon Vance, Lincoln's call for troops became the defining moment of his conversion to secession. "I was addressing a large and excited crowd, large numbers of whom were armed, and literally had my arm extended upward in pleading for peace and the Union of our Fathers, when the telegraphic news was announced of the firing on

Sumter and the President's call for seventy-five thousand volunteers. When my hand came down from that impassioned gesticulation, it fell slowly and sadly by the side of a secessionist." The editor of the formerly unionist *North Carolina Standard,* William W. Holden, publicly joined ranks with the secessionists. "We are all states' rights men now . . . let us stand together and act together as one people until our rights and liberties are fully established and secured."[14]

When Lincoln's secretary of war telegraphed Governor Ellis to provide two regiments for federal service, Ellis coldly rebuffed the request. "I regard the levy of troops made by the administration for the purpose of subjugating the States of the South as in violation of the Constitution and a gross usurpation of power . . . You can get no troops from North Carolina."[15] Instead of helping the federal government, Governor Ellis issued a proclamation for a special session of the legislature to convene on May 1 to start the legal process of secession.

The governor, satisfied that the issue of secession was settled in the public's mind, quickly proceeded to take military action. The federal government maintained five properties within the state: Forts Caswell, Johnston, and Macon, the Charlotte Mint and, most important of all, the Fayetteville Arsenal. The governor employed prominent volunteer militia companies in a preemptive campaign against the federal installations. A Wilmington company seized forts Caswell and Johnston on April 16. Three days later, the Hornets Nest Rifles traveled from Charlotte to garrison Fort Caswell. Captain Bridgers led the Edgecombe Guards toward the coast to occupy Fort Macon, an important post controlling Beaufort Inlet that local militiamen had already taken. On April 20, the Charlotte Greys took control of the Charlotte Mint. Next came the big prize. In the early hours of April 22, a large throng of militia gathered around Fayetteville's two volunteer companies, the Fayetteville Independent Light Infantry and the LaFayette Light Infantry. The force of eleven hundred armed men marched to the Fayetteville Arsenal to demand the surrender of the forty-two soldiers defending the federal works. Warren Winslow, acting on behalf of the governor, negotiated with the arsenal's officers. The two senior officers of the Fayetteville Independent Light Infantry, Wright Huske and Benjamin Huske, stood beside Winslow during the negotiations to emphasize the force ready to attack the post. The intimidating numbers of militia and the isolated position of the arsenal "rendered surrender a military necessity." The departure of the garrison, under generous terms, cleared North Carolina of all federal troops and left the state with a windfall of thirty-seven thousand muskets and other weapons.[16]

A furious martial spirit swept across North Carolina during the following days. The *Wilmington Daily Herald* printed one patriotic plea from "A Warsaw Lady." "The war-cry sounds from every valley and hill top . . . Brave, noble hearted youth! hopes of your country! stand up dauntless at the cannon's mouth, filled with the same spirit which animates you, resolve to conquer or die!" With a chorus of war cries ringing in their ears, the "noble hearted youths" flocked to the recruiting stations to perform their patriotic duties. Doctors, lawyers, editors, professors, and students enlisted, along with farm boys and laborers. Pvt. Lewis Warlick and one of his four brothers, Portland, joined the Burke Rifles in response to the call for volunteers. Warlick expressed the sentiments of many of the eager volunteers in a letter to his girlfriend. "When his country is invaded with thieves and lawless persons, then every man should do all in his power for the protection of his much loved country and fireside." Warlick intended his letters to do more than proclaim his belief in the cause; he also had to explain to his sweetheart why he left her to go off to war. The young lovers would carry on a troubled courtship during Warlick's enlistment. Egbert A. Ross, one of the cadets of the North Carolina Military Institute in Charlotte, had a more political rationale behind his enthusiasm for the upcoming conflict. "How could we do otherwise than march boldly to the cannon's mouth to defend what we assert . . . that we ought and should be a free and independent people. I am in the *war*."[17]

The adjutant general, J. F. Hoke, faced the formidable challenge of organizing and arming a competent military force from these willing, though inexperienced, volunteers. The seizure of the arsenal provided the arms, and plenty of men had signed up, but, more than anything else, the state needed trained soldiers. The military situation did not afford the state the time to prepare the large number of volunteers before cries for help interceded. By this time, Virginia urgently needed forces from other states to defend itself from the now hostile federal government. The adjutant general decided to form the volunteer companies into regiments so that North Carolina could put troops into the field quickly. On April 19 Hoke sent a letter to Col. D. H. Hill.

"You are hereby commanded to organize . . . a regiment, to be designated the 'First Regiment of North Carolina Volunteers' . . . The seat of war is the designation of the regiment, and Virginia, in all probability, will be the first battle-ground. The services of this regiment will not exceed six months, but the men should be prepared to keep the field until the war is ended . . . Arms are now in Raleigh for the use of the regiment, and the men will be furnished with them promptly. The regiment will be moved into Virginia as soon as possible, but will not be led into battle until the field officers are of the opinion that the men are fit for duty . . . The cause of Virginia is the cause of North Carolina. In our first struggle for liberty she nobly and freely poured out her blood in our defence. We will stand by her now in this our last effort for independence."[18]

Three days after Colonel Hill received his instructions, the governor received a formal request from the Confederate secretary of war to help defend Virginia. "Virginia needs our aid. I therefore request you to furnish one regiment of infantry without delay to rendezvous at Richmond, Va." Governor Ellis replied on April 24, "You shall have from one to ten thousand volunteers in a few days, with arms, and I wish them to go as state troops. Many of our men will enlist in Confederate Army. Will have a regiment ready in four days . . . Our legislature will meet in few days. I will not await, however."[19] General Hoke quickly ordered the volunteer companies to move to a "Camp of Instruction" that D. H. Hill had established in Raleigh. The volunteers could train for the approaching combat under the supervision of the veteran officer.

In hometowns across the state, the officers and enlisted men of the volunteer companies bade farewell to their friends and families. The townspeople turned out to pay their respects and to wish the troops success on the battlefield. While preparing to leave Asheville, the Buncombe Riflemen received new Confederate colors, a gift from six young ladies of Asheville. The daughters of militia Col. Nicholas Woodfin and four of their friends stitched the flag, using material from their own silk dresses. Miss Anna Woodfin and her father presented the flag to Capt. W. W. McDowell and the Riflemen in a public ceremony that moved "the stoutest heart to sympathy and tears." The Buncombe Riflemen later became the color company for the state's first regiment and carried this flag on the first battlefield of the Civil War. The Charlotte Greys, who had been recruited from the corps of cadets of the Military Institute, held a similar ceremony on April 24. Miss Hattie Howell presented the Greys with a company flag and words of praise. Then she reminded them, "You are the sons of Mecklenburg! Your sires have written the brightest pages of history with their blood; in achieving the Independence and Equality in government which you are called upon to defend!" The Greys left for Raleigh on the Thursday morning mail train. The state's martial zeal helped lift the recruits' spirits as the volunteer companies converged on Raleigh. Lt. Frank M. Parker felt overwhelmed by the greeting the Edgecombe Guards received on their march. "All along the road every man, woman, child and little negro seemed brim full of [enthusiasm]: shouting, hurrahing, and waving secession flags met us everywhere." Louis Leon, a Jewish store clerk who had joined the Charlotte Greys, described the public passion during their journey. "Our trip was full of joy and pleasure, for at every station where our train stopped the ladies showered us with flowers and Godspeed. We marched to the [Raleigh] Fair Grounds. The streets were lined with people, cheering us."[20]

The mood changed when the jaunty volunteers got their first taste of a soldier's camp life. "When we got there our company was given quarters, and, lo and behold! horse stables with straw for bedding is what we got. I know we all thought it a disgrace for us to sleep in such places with our fine uniforms — not even a washstand, or any place to hang our clothes on. They didn't even give us a looking-glass." Some of the volunteer companies had to discard their gaudy uniforms and feathered hats after arriving to comply with the adjutant general's newly prescribed state uniform. Many of them did not know the first thing about soldiering. Under Colonel Hill's scrutiny, the Camp of Instruction forged ahead with the serious business of turning volunteers into soldiers. D. H. Hill had the right qualities to instruct the men. He strongly sympathized with the southern cause and set a good example of personal conduct by praying daily, avoiding liquor, and never swearing. Of course, his biting sarcasm hardly needed any embellishment. After serving in the U.S. Army during the Mexican War, Hill had returned to North Carolina abhorring two things: Yankees and volunteers. Now, with an entire camp of volunteers under his charge, he labored to convert the men into regular soldiers. Hill, a stickler for discipline, kept the troops busy with six hours of drill each day. One of the local newspapers noted the pace of Hill's instruction, "The drilling is energetically, though not laboriously conducted." He even took time to teach the finer points of guard duty to the troops. One private in the Orange Light Infantry, John T. Jones, had a memorable confrontation with him. "Col. Hill tried to pass me and came very near getting day light poked through him . . . He told me who he was & I knew him at first sight but I told him he could not pass; after trying me a while he told me I would do & gave the countersign & I let him pass." By May 4, Harvey Hill had the companies ready to march in a grand review for the governor and state legislators.[21]

Not all the volunteers adapted well to a life of discipline. One of the Randalsburg Riflemen from Mecklenburg County became so frustrated that he tried to shoot his captain. Another soldier deflected the assailant's hand at the last moment, but the captain was wounded in the thigh, nonetheless. The adjutant general had listed the company in the 1st N.C. Volunteers, but the incident prevented the Randalsburg Rifles from joining the regiment. One other incident disturbed the encampment. An accidental pistol discharge wounded a Buncombe Rifleman in the arm, though not seriously. The time spent at the Camp of Instruction seemed like an eternity to the anxious young men in uniform. After only a short time in Raleigh the youthful Egbert Ross complained, "We are still in this detestable hole." He noted that the patriotic enthusiasm of the state capital did not dissuade the local merchants from a little price gouging on fresh food used to supplement the soldiers' skimpy rations. Ross had different feelings toward the young women of Raleigh who came each evening to watch dress parade. "I must admit that the ladies are very kind indeed to us. They come to cheer us with their smiles and when they leave us in the evening you can hear a simple 'God bless them' escape from the lips of all our men."[22]

Fortunately, boredom did not subdue spirits within the camp. The majority of soldiers could write and they took the time to correspond with family and friends back home. Lewis Warlick wrote to his sweetheart in the western mountains, regularly. Both of them valued the other's letters, although their correspondence sometimes caused problems. Once Warlick insinuated that she was partly responsible for his enlistment because "If we had [gotten] married last winter . . . I would not have left my 'sweetie' under any considerations." Warlick had to back-pedal deftly after he got her anguished and angry response. His young lover could not bear the thought that she had anything to do with his serving in the army. Most of the men managed to pass the time by amusing themselves with music and other entertainment. "We have lively times in the camp. A fiddle and banjo are going all day by some one except when we drill." "Large numbers engage in the social dance. Here they miss their lively partners in the dance, but still the fun goes on. Others again . . . engage in singing songs." The camp commander made sure that the troops received proper religious instruction during off-duty hours in addition to their other diversions. One visiting minister "delivered a very appropriate sermon; warning the soldiers against the vices of the camp, and telling them that they were engaged in a holy and just cause."[23]

Spirits in the camp soared when the troops learned of the adjutant general's decision to send the regiment to Virginia. The volunteers "rent the air with cheers for Virginia, and every man of them seemed to appreciate the honor of being in the First Regiment ordered to the post of danger."[24] The soldiers' response provides some insight into their sense of duty and loyalty. Although the volunteers often expressed their motivation to defend their homes from invasion, the reaction to the news proved that the men in the regiment felt honored to fight for the South, not only for North Carolina. The coming years presented several situations when the defensive needs of the state differed from those of the Confederate government. Raleigh and Richmond would exchange many angry words over the deployment of North Carolina's regiments, especially when Union forces threatened the state. The soldiers in the regiment did not care about the official squabbling between the two capitals. At times they asked to deploy to Virginia, at other times to North Carolina. In each case, the men wanted to go where they could fight.

While the soldiers trained and Virginia begged for help, the state's politicians moved to break away from the federal government. Meeting in special session on May 1, the legislature enacted a bill to call a constitutional convention — the delegates to be elected on May 13th — to decide whether or not to remain as one of the United States. Political sentiments had changed so drastically that the legislature overturned the February referendum with almost no dissent. The legislators then turned to military affairs. On May 10, they passed a measure permitting the governor to call volunteers for Confederate service and specifying how these units would muster into the Confederate army. The volunteers would serve twelve months — a term that matched the numerous enlistments that had already been signed. The Assembly passed another bill authorizing the governor to send the First Regiment of North Carolina Troops to Virginia for the duration of the volunteers' enlistments and sanctioning the election of its officers.[25]

Adjutant General Hoke formally organized the 1st N.C. Volunteers and directed that an election of field grade officers be held on May 11. The troops cast their ballots for the regimental colonel, lieutenant colonel, and major. As expected, D. H. Hill won the election for colonel, Charles C. Lee earned the rank of lieutenant colonel, and James H. Lane became the regiment's major. All three came from the cadre of the North Carolina Military Institute in Charlotte. Lieutenant Colonel Lee mustered the regiment on May 15, marking the official start of the regiment's six-month term of service. Since the day the adjutant general had first written to D. H. Hill, the regiment had experienced several changes in the ten volunteer companies assigned to it because some units could not muster the minimum of sixty troops. Hoke finalized the regiment's organization with the following companies that each averaged eighty men:[26]

Company	Volunteer Unit	Commander
A	Edgecombe Guards	Captain Bridgers
B	Hornets Nest Rifles	Captain Williams
C	Charlotte Greys	Captain Ross
D	Orange Light Infantry	Captain Ashe
E	Buncombe Riflemen	Captain McDowell
F	LaFayette Light Infantry	Captain Starr
G	Burke Rifles	Captain Avery
H	Fayetteville Independent Lt. Inf.	Captain W. Huske
I	Enfield Blues	Captain Bell
K	Southern Stars	Captain W. J. Hoke

The companies in the regiment represented the cream of North Carolina's volunteer militia. The Fayetteville Independent Light Infantry, the oldest military unit in the state, had formed in 1793 during the Citizen Genet turmoil. The company had maintained its organization ever since, including service in two wars. Four other companies, the Lafayettes, Hornets, Greys, and Guards, had already helped seize federal property. Although several companies had organized years before, a few had formed spontaneously after Lincoln's call for troops. Students and faculty from the University of North Carolina signed up together to form the Orange Light Infantry. However, the most remarkable unit had to be C Company, the Charlotte Greys. According to popular rumor, not a single soldier in the company, not even its commander, Capt. Egbert Ross, had reached the age of twenty-one. This distinction earned it the nickname, the "Boy Company."[27]

The distribution of the regiment's troops demonstrated the unity of North Carolina's military effort, which encompassed the state's geographic, political, and economic factions. Each region of the state provided companies for the state's first organized regiment. The Edgecombe Guards represented the heart of the slaveholding coastal region. A wealthy planter, John Bridgers, commanded the company along with several other prominent secessionists. A cotton broker and several well-to-do planters led the Enfield Blues. The western counties contributed half the companies and all of the field grade officers. The Burke Rifles came from a western county where fewer than 18 percent of the households owned any slaves. They demonstrated political consensus in their election of company officers. The westerners chose Clark M. Avery, a secessionist delegate in the February convention vote, to command the company. The Rifles then split the lieutenant positions between two Whigs and another Democrat. Both Buncombe and Orange Counties had been strongly unionist before Lincoln's call for troops, while the Charlotte companies and Southern Stars came from secessionist country. Once formed, the regiment put past political differences aside and prepared to move to Richmond to fulfill Governor Ellis' promise to the Confederate government.[28]

While the 1st N.C. Volunteers organized, the citizens voted for their delegates to the State Convention on May 13. This time the radicals garnered the majority of seats, although everyone appeared ready to secede. The Convention agreed to meet in Raleigh on May 20 to vote on the matter. The date selected for the Convention had special significance for North Carolina; it marked the 86th anniversary of the Mecklenburg Declaration of Independence. That declaration by the patriotic citizens of Mecklenburg County had preceded the nation's vote for independence by thirteen months. The state took great pride in the spirit shown by its forefathers. Obviously, the Convention wanted to link itself symbolically to the spirit of the "First War of Independence."

The governor, thoroughly confident about the Convention's vote, proceeded to dispatch the 1st N.C. Volunteers to Richmond. The military situation dictated haste, but North Carolina and the Confederate government had yet to agree upon procedures for incorporating volunteer units into the Confederate army. The state and the Confederate secretary of war haggled for months over terms of service, appointment of officers, transfer dates for pay, deployment restrictions, and so forth. Despite the disagreements, both governments allowed the regiment to deploy while the details of acceptance into Confederate service were negotiated. By the time the State Convention met on May 20, Colonel Hill, along with F, H, and K companies, had already departed for Richmond as an advance detachment for the regiment. The rest of the regiment was scheduled to depart May 21, the day after the Convention met.

The delegates set quickly to work on a secession act. They voted down one bill modeled after the Declaration of Independence proposed by Judge George Badger, a former unionist. Badger sought to justify the act of secession by citing the reasons for North Carolina's break from the United States, but the Convention's radicals rejected the idea. The former Whig politician could not bear the triumph of his old political rivals, so he left the Convention in a depressed mood. In the end, the delegates simply passed an act rescinding North Carolina's 1789 ratification of the Constitution, a tacit affirmation of the state's sovereign right to secede from the United States. When the secession ordinance passed the capital city burst into celebration. "The artillery thundered forth, every bell in the city rang a peal." Hearing the bells from his dinner table, a somber Judge Badger lifted his hand and prophesied that it was "the death knell of slavery."[29]

The advance detachment of the regiment learned of the secession vote via the Richmond telegraph office. The H Company troops reacted emotionally to the news. "Then there was a mass meeting of the citizen soldiery: many and stirring were the speeches made; but of all these speeches we remember with most affection and pride the address of our own First Lieutenant [Benjamin Huske]. It was no secret to us, the deep and earnest attachment he had for the Union, the strong struggle he had made against the tide of passion which was sweeping over the land, the sorrow of his heart when the old ties were broken; and we well knew the steady strength of resolution with which . . . he went forth where honor and conscience told him was the way . . . and how faithfully he trod it to the end."[30] In a way, Benjamin Huske articulated the sentiments of the entire state. He still had sincere and loyal feelings toward the United States. Only when forced to choose between his homeland and the Union did he, reluctantly, bear arms against his former countrymen. Once he had made that choice, though, he gave his strength and his life, wholeheartedly, to the South. The state's commitment to the South became complete when the pro-unionists finally transferred their patriotism to the Confederacy. Former American patriots from the old volunteer companies, ardent secessionists, and men who simply served to defend their native soil stood together in the ranks of North Carolina's premier regiment. North Carolina ended its long, contentious political struggle over secession with a united will to fight.

The following day the rest of the 1st N.C. Volunteers gathered at the Raleigh rail station to embark on their journey to Virginia. North Carolina had accomplished a major feat to have organized, equipped, and fielded a regiment in the five weeks since Fort Sumter. There had been very little time to prepare for combat operations — a mere six days since the regiment mustered into service. The officers could only hope that the peacetime training of the volunteer companies and the past month's drills would suffice. Despite the minimal training time, the regiment had to leave immediately for Virginia. A correspondent for the *Western Democrat* described the scene at the rail station as the 1st N.C. Volunteers headed off to war. "A large number (mostly the acquaintances of the members of the different companies) assembled at the Raleigh depot to see the regiment off. Among the spectators there were thirty patriotic Raleigh ladies, who showered bouquets into the ranks of the soldiers and cheered with all their might. The gallant soldiers all seemed to have lighter hearts than their friends who bid them farewell; there were tears in the eyes of many of the spectators, but not one in the eye of a soldier. They left firmly resolved to do their duty, and every man appeared anxious to get nearer the scene of war. In the day of battle we are confident this regiment will prove an honor to the old North State and to themselves."[31]

BIG BETHEL

May—June 1861, Eastern Virginia

The Virginia citizens cheered the 1st N.C. Volunteers as their train pulled into Petersburg. A correspondent with the regiment described their greeting. "Although it was night-time when we arrived at Petersburg, the ladies thronged the streets, shook us by the hand, gave us snacks nicely done up in paper, strewed our path with flowers, and called down the blessings of God upon us. Our advance into Virginia was a constant ovation." Virginia, home to the Confederate capital in Richmond, lay dangerously exposed to military action from the North. The appearance of the Tar Heels helped ease the tension by proving that the rest of the South would not abandon Virginia to the northern army. In addition, the 1st N.C. Volunteers made an impressive showing as they disembarked. "The remainder of the First Regiment of North Carolina Volunteers, numbering seven companies and over seven hundred men, reached this city last night [May 21, 1861], in extra trains, about 8 o'clock," the *Petersburg Express* wrote. "We must say that this is the best equipped regiment which has yet made its route through our city." The cities of Virginia made an equally strong impression on some of the young troops from rural North Carolina. "I have to laugh at part of our company when they get into a city," wrote Lewis Warlick, one of the Burke Rifles from the western mountains. "They look at everything and in every direction and their fingers [point] at every curiosity, which their eyes behold. It shows at once they never travelled a great ways from their native place."[32]

The regiment's main body linked up with the advance party at Howard's Grove before dawn on May 22. The tired troops only got a short rest from their journey; the military situation dictated an early movement. Union forces occupied Fort Monroe at the tip of the peninsula between the James and York rivers, only eighty miles from Richmond. The Confederates needed troops to fortify a defensive line across the Virginia peninsula near Yorktown. The site of Washington's victory over Cornwallis in the Revolutionary War seemed to be an appropriate place to defend the South. On May 24, the regiment crowded aboard another train bound for West Point, Virginia. At West Point, the men transferred to the steamboat *Logan* and sailed down the York River, arriving at the Yorktown fortifications on May 25. An unfortunate accident during the trip took the life of one of the regiment's soldiers. Pvt. Julius Sadler fell asleep on a rail car, then fell off to his death. The fatal accident and the proximity of the Union forces, twenty-six miles away, sobered the troops. The dizzying pace of events had distracted them from the serious business at hand. Suddenly, the five-week veterans found themselves on the front line in Virginia, where they got their first glimpse of enemy ships patrolling the Chesapeake Bay. One of the troops noted, "This is not playing soldier now; it is a stern reality."[33]

Upon arrival, the men attended to the needs of the camp's defenses. "The day after we got here our company was sent out with spades and shovels to make breastworks—and to think of the indignity! We were expected to do the digging," wrote a disillusioned Pvt. Louis Leon.[34] Leon's surprise at the onerous duties of a soldier shed some light on the lack of experience within the ranks. Although much of the regiment had been drawn from the organized militia companies, many soldiers had just enlisted and had no military training. Even the men with years of service in the volunteer militia had much to learn about soldiering. Veterans like Colonel Hill knew that the officers and men needed far more training before they would be ready to face an enemy in battle. As events turned out, the regiment received precious little before their baptism of fire.

A short time later, a Union force under the command of Maj. Gen. Benjamin Butler reinforced the Union troops at Hampton, Virginia. Butler's appearance caused alarm at Yorktown. Twice the troops marched from camp to meet an enemy movement but made no contact. While tensions mounted, Harvey Hill kept the men busy working on the fortifications and rehearsing for battle. In early June, Butler's men finally took an aggressive step. They moved up the peninsula and occupied Bethel Church, a small church at a crossing site over the northwest branch of the Back River. General Butler withdrew his troops, but not before they had defaced the church with painted slogans such as "Death to the Traitors."[35]

Col. J. Bankhead Magruder, commander of the Yorktown defenses, decided to stop further Union forays by posting a force at the Bethel Church bridge. He ordered Hill to move the 1st N.C. to Bethel along with seven artillery pieces of Maj. George Randolph's Virginia Battery. On June 6, Hill's men trudged over the Virginia back roads on a ten-mile march to Bethel. "It was a trying one, as it was made in heavy marching order, with knapsacks, haversacks, canteens, loaded cartridge boxes, often a Bible in the knapsack, and with a tin cup and extra pair of shoes dangling from either corner of this boxy affair." They had much to learn about forced marching. The heavily laden soldiers reached their objective after dark under a drizzling rain. For the first time, the green troops slept on wet ground and cooked in the field. They may have felt miserable, but the move to Bethel allowed D. H. Hill to get away from the immediate presence of Magruder. Hill had already expressed his distaste for Magruder in a letter to his wife. "Col. Magruder in command is always drunk and giving foolish and absurd orders."[36] Fortunately, Hill managed to suppress his animosity when he later had to fight under Magruder's command.

Hill reconnoitered the terrain the next day and closely examined the approaches to Bethel. The road coming over the bridge from Hampton presented an obvious threat because of an open field to the front where "masses of the enemy might be readily deployed." At this stage of the war, most soldiers carried muskets, not rifles, so a massed infantry attack could only be repelled at close range. "Presuming that an attempt would be made to carry the bridge across the stream, a battery was made for its special protection, and Major Randolph placed his guns so as to sweep all the approaches to it." Hill did not have enough troops to block all routes over the Back River, so he provided for all around security. "The nature of the ground determined me to make an inclosed work." The regiment's perimeter defense on the northern (Richmond) side of the branch blocked the crossing site but lay exposed to fire from "two commanding eminences beyond the creek and on our right." Wisely, Hill fortified one of these hills on the south side and positioned a howitzer there to keep any enemy artillery from gaining an advantageous firing point that would allow them to fire down into the regiment's perimeter.[37] Once Hill and Lt. Col. Charles Lee laid out the defensive lines, the troops began constructing the breastworks.

The closeness of Bethel Church to Butler's forces — only eight miles — made a clash between the two armies inevitable, although no field combat had yet occurred. The next day, June 8, a Union foraging party came within a few miles of Bethel. Hill dispatched a small party from F Company, with Charles Lee in charge, to drive them off. Lee's party surprised the marauders with an artillery round, chased the Union troops back to the New Market bridge and captured one prisoner. No sooner had Lee returned than another Union raiding party appeared. This time Major Lane with a howitzer and E Company sortied. Lane's advance guard, led by 2d Lt. George Gregory, confronted the larger Union force near the New Market bridge. Both sides appeared reluctant to open fire, and an uneasy interlude settled over the confrontation. Gregory cautiously approached within thirty-five yards of the Union party's lead element that indicated a desire to parley. As the antagonists questioned each other, a "stout, ugly fellow" blurted out to Gregory, "I know you are friends! I belong to the Second New York Regiment." Gregory surprised the New Yorker by drawing his pistol, pointing it at the soldier's head and shouting, "Drop your musket or I'll blow your brains out! You are my prisoner." E Company immediately fired a volley into the Union ranks, killing and wounding several of them. The New Yorkers returned fire, without effect, then fell back to Hampton. Lane, Gregory, and E Company returned to Bethel with the prisoner. Sensing that a conflict would soon erupt at Bethel, Colonel Magruder "came up that evening and took command."[38]

Union intelligence brought in reports of the Confederate encampment to General Butler but mistakenly identified Little Bethel Church, a few miles farther south on the Hampton Road, as the primary position. Butler, thoroughly irritated by the skirmishes, decided to roust the offending enemy force. "Having learned that the enemy had established an outpost of some strength at a place called Little Bethel . . . I had determined to send up a force to drive them back and destroy their camp." Butler's decision would lead to the first field battle between the Union and Confederate armies in the Civil War. Butler committed three New York regiments, a mixed battalion of Vermont and Massachusetts men, and a battery of the 2d U.S. Artillery, all under the immediate command of Brig. Gen. Ebenezer Pierce. Butler had two more regiments in reserve, ready to reinforce Pierce. Pierce's force included the 5th N.Y. Regiment of Zouaves, led by Col. Abram Duryea and Lt. Col. Gouverneur K. Warren, his deputy. The Zouaves wore a distinctive uniform of bright red baggy pants in the fashion of Algerian warriors and trained using special assault tactics that emphasized intense physical conditioning. Butler's plan called for Duryea's Zouaves to infiltrate between Little Bethel and Big Bethel churches in the predawn hours of June 10. Colonel Townsend's 3d N.Y. would follow on the road from Hampton while Col. Bendix's 7th N.Y. and the mixed New England Battalion under Lieutenant Colonel Washburn advanced from Newport News. "Bendix's and Townsend's regiments should effect a junction at a fork of the road leading from Hampton to Newport News, something like a mile and a half from Little Bethel. I directed the march to be so timed that the attack should be made just at daybreak, and that after the attack was made upon Little Bethel, Duryea's regiment and a regiment from Newport News should follow immediately upon the heels of the fugitives, if they were enabled to get off, and attack the battery on the road to Big Bethel."[39]

Butler sent General Pierce's force into battle with inaccurate intelligence and an overly elaborate plan. The Union soldiers soon paid a stiff penalty for their own and their general's inexperience. Colonel Townsend and his men neared the rendezvous point in the early morning twilight. "On approaching a defile through a thick wood, about five or six miles from Hampton, a heavy and well-sustained fire of canister and small arms was opened upon the regiment while it was marching in a narrow road . . . wholly unsuspicious of an enemy." After a brisk exchange of fire, the Union leaders discovered, to their horror, that Bendix's 7th N.Y. had been the ones firing at Townsend's men. Butler seethed when he learned about the fratricide. "By this almost criminal blunder two men of Townsend's regiment were killed, and eight (more or less) wounded."[40]

The incident forfeited the element of surprise and tangled Pierce's march columns. Pierce tried to straighten out matters with his regimental commanders. "Leaving the rest to collect the wounded and refresh the tired men, I had an interview with the commanding officers present." Significantly, Duryea and Washburn strongly recommended a retreat because they feared that the Confederates would reinforce Little Bethel from Yorktown. Butler's aides-de-camp, Maj. Theodore Winthrop and Captain Hagerty, urged Pierce to follow through on Butler's orders. Apparently, Pierce felt that a withdrawal before making contact with the enemy would be dishonorable, so he decided to continue toward the two Bethels. Nevertheless, the Union commanders on the scene had already lost their fighting spirit.[41]

A long roll of the drums—the signal for an alarm—jarred the Confederate troops at Bethel from their sleep at 3:00 A.M. The men scrambled to their feet and quickly donned their gear for a night march. "The whole camp was in arms within three minutes." The Confederate commanders had gotten wind of the Union movement and aroused the troops "for a general advance upon the enemy." As Lieutenant Benjamin Huske wrote, "After proceeding three miles . . . a lady, whose husband had been taken prisoner, [ran] up the road and informed Col. Magruder that the enemy was advancing. Our scouts of course had seen a portion of them but it was through her coolness that their large number [about 3,500 men] was learned." Magruder and Hill listened carefully as Hannah Tunnel described the approaching Union force. The two colonels prudently decided to march the 1st N.C. back to the fortifications at Big Bethel. They preferred to fight the larger opponent from their prepared defensive position. The timely intelligence from Mrs. Tunnel saved the regiment from running into a meeting engagement with the stronger Union force.[42]

Colonel Hill quickly positioned his 800 men and 360 attached Virginia troops around the defensive perimeter, while Major Randolph placed five of his artillery pieces to cover Hampton Road. Captain Brown mounted his howitzer on the high ground south of the stream. Lt. Col. William Stuart put part of the 3d Va. to the right of Brown's battery. Company G of the 1st N.C., commanded by Capt. C. M. Avery, guarded the breastworks on Brown's left. Brown, Stuart, and Avery occupied the most exposed and isolated part of the Confederate defenses. As a precaution, Hill advised Avery to fall back from the south side of the creek, if the Union force appeared ready to overrun the position, rather than allow his company to be overwhelmed. Company A formed a skirmish line south of the stream on the eastern (left) flank. Hill deployed the rest of the regiment and another Virginia battalion around the perimeter on the north side of the stream. The troops made the best use of the available time to improve the breastworks and camouflage their positions with freshly cut sassafras boughs.[43]

Shortly before 9:00 A.M., Pvt. Henry Lawson Wyatt and another soldier from A Company spotted the lead element of the Union column on the Hampton Road and alerted the defenders to the enemy's presence. Pierce had found nothing at Little Bethel, so he had continued the attack to Big Bethel as Butler had instructed. Instead of making a deliberate attack on Little Bethel, Pierce now had to make a hasty attack on an unknown Confederate position at Big Bethel. To make matters worse, a local lady and a free Negro informed Pierce that the Confederates had four thousand troops at Big Bethel. Capt. Judson Kilpatrick of the 5th N.Y. Zouaves took the initiative to reconnoiter the defensive position and reported seeing a Confederate force four times larger than its actual size. Lt. Col. Gouverneur K. Warren had also gone forward but returned with a different outlook. He advised Pierce that the left (west) flank of the Confederate position could be turned. Pierce accepted Warren's recommendation to attack Brown's Battery on one of the "commanding eminences," despite Kilpatrick's discouraging, though inaccurate, report.[44]

Pierce ordered his regiments to form into a "line of battle" (a linear formation with the troops standing abreast, two ranks deep, facing the enemy). As the Union regiments moved into their attack formations, the Confederate artillerymen observed their main body. "About nine o'clock the glittering bayonets of the enemy appeared on the hill opposite, and above them waived [sic] the Star Spangled Banner. The moment the head of the column advanced far enough to show one or two companies, the Parrot gun of the howitzer battery opened on them, throwing a shell right into their midst." "Who will forget that tremendous moment, ushering in the war!" While the Union infantry scampered for cover, Pierce pushed the 2d U.S. Artillery forward to within a few hundred yards of the Confederates. The Union guns, under 1st Lt. John T. Greble, returned the Confederates' fire. For more than an hour, the big guns blazed away at one another. Protected by breastworks, the Confederates sustained little damage from the Union artillery. "Within our encampment fell a perfect hail-storm of canister shot, bullets and balls. Remarkable to say, not one of our men was killed inside our encampment." Benjamin Huske overheard one of his soldiers confess, "Col. Hill knows more about good [breastworks] and ditches than I do, and I'll never grumble again about throwing dirt!"[45]

In an effort to calm his green troops and partly out of contempt for his northern opponents, Harvey Hill nonchalantly puffed on a short pipe and stood exposed to the incoming fire. "Boys, you have learned to dodge already. I am an old hand at it." Hill demonstrated his "scientific dodging" techniques as an artillery round roared past. Wagging his finger at the enemy he derided the Union gunners, "You dogs! You missed me that time."[46]

The Union infantry did not fare so well. "The enemy's fire at this time began to tell on us with great effect. My men were falling one after another," Captain Kilpatrick recalled. On the eastern flank, some of Duryea's Zouaves made an abortive attempt to cross the ford. A company of Virginians reinforced an F Company picket near the ford and fired a single howitzer round at the Zouaves. They gave up any thought of crossing after that. By 11:00 A.M. Pierce had his infantry regiments arrayed for the attack on Brown's Battery. Townsend's 3d N.Y., supported by Duryea's Zouaves, advanced to capture the battery south of the stream. Townsend sent two companies of skirmishers forward to measure the Confederates' strength on the western flank and "to draw the enemy's fire." The Confederates poured heavy fire across the field as soon as they noticed the Union skirmishers moving about the orchard. Townsend went forward to the skirmish line and verified that the Confederate western flank could be assaulted, just as Warren had stated. He then ordered the rest of his regiment to move forward to a narrow road crossing in front of the defensive position. Contrary to Gouverneur Warren's advice, Townsend maneuvered his regiment in the open rather than swing around Brown's Battery through the trees. Townsend's movement drew severe fire from Brown's Battery and G Company.[47]

Suddenly, an unfortunate incident offered Pierce's command an opportunity to seize the battery. One of Brown's gun crew mistakenly broke the priming wire on the howitzer, which spiked the gun. With the howitzer out of action, Stuart's Virginia infantry and G Company withdrew from the exposed position to the north side of the stream. Kilpatrick's Zouaves eagerly dashed across the field, just as the Confederates abandoned the position. "The charge was then sounded . . . The enemy were forced out of the first battery, all forces were

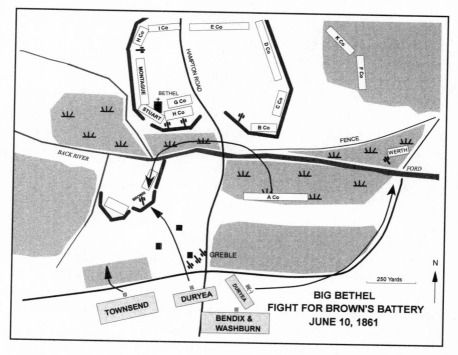

BIG BETHEL
FIGHT FOR BROWN'S BATTERY
JUNE 10, 1861

250 Yards

N

rapidly advancing and everything promised a speedy victory." The Zouaves had capitalized on the Confederates' withdrawal but the Union regiments had not acted in concert. Duryea failed to coordinate his assault with Townsend's regiment, which still maneuvered in front of the battery.[48]

Colonel Hill realized that the loss of Brown's Battery on the "commanding eminence" could doom the perimeter defense north of the stream. The colonel quickly organized a counterattack. He gathered up A Company, which had pulled back from the skirmish line, and ordered an assault across the stream with C Company in support. Captain Bridgers, commanding A Company, formed his soldiers into a line of battle, then led them in a bold charge. "They advanced calmly, coolly; when at the distance of sixty yards the Zouaves fired on them . . . not a muscle was moved, but they leaped right on at the double-quick." Kilpatrick's Zouaves had just captured the battery and were engaging A Company "when we were ordered to fall back." Colonel Duryea recalled his Zouaves when he observed Bridgers's vigorous counterattack. The New Yorkers fell back just as the Edgecombe Guards swept into the key position. Stuart's and Avery's infantry joined

Bridgers's men, and Major Randolph sent a replacement howitzer to restore the battery. The resolute response to the crisis by A Company saved the day, as Hill attested in his report. "It is impossible to overestimate this service. It decided the action in our favor."[49]

Colonel Townsend squandered his chance to support the Zouaves at the decisive moment because he wasted time moving his regiment around near the orchard. "By the time the regiment had arrived at its position it became evident that the right portion of the battery had been strongly re-enforced by men from the enemy's left, and that an effort to take the battery then was useless." His regiment still could have turned the Confederates' western (right) flank, but Townsend became alarmed when he noticed troops moving through the brush to his left. "Upon seeing among the breaks in the hedge the glistening of bayonets in the adjoining field, I immediately concluded that the enemy were outflanking us, and conceived it to be my duty immediately to retire and repel that advance." To his chagrin, he learned that the troops who caused him to retreat were some of his own men who had gotten separated from his main body.[50]

Once A Company repelled the Zouaves, Colonel Hill came over to the battery. Hill noticed that some of the Zouaves had taken refuge in a blacksmith shop in front of the breastworks and were sniping at the Confederate position. "Captain Bridgers, can't you have that house burned?" Hill suggested as he walked by. Bridgers immediately acted on the suggestion and called for a squad of volunteers. Pvt. Henry Wyatt, the scout who first sighted the Union column, and four other A Company soldiers stepped forward. The five soldiers leaped over the breastworks and dashed thirty yards across the open field toward the structure. One of the volunteers, Pvt. John H. Thorp, recalled, "A volley was fired at us as if by a company, not from the house, but from the road to our left. As we were well drilled in skirmishing, all of us instantly dropped to the ground, Wyatt mortally wounded. He never uttered a word or a groan, but lay limp on his back, his arms extended, one knee up and a clot of blood on his forehead as large as a man's fist." The others eventually crawled back to the safety of the breastworks. Wyatt's body lay in front of the Confederate breastworks as a grim reminder of the danger of exposing oneself to enemy fire.[51]

A lull descended on the battlefield after Pierce's force stalled in front of Brown's Battery. Pierce ordered Duryea and Townsend to fall back, while two additional regiments, commanded by Colonels Allen and Carr, came forward to keep "the enemy at bay." Pierce had evidently lost control over Bendix's and Washburn's troops who were still trying to cross the stream. While Townsend and Duryea attacked Brown's Battery, troops from the New England battalion swung well to the east through the woods and swamp. They found a crossing over the stream and advanced to assault the main defensive perimeter. Colonel Bendix exercised little direct control over this part of the action, but one Union officer did emerge to lead the last serious Union effort. D. H. Hill witnessed this attempt to storm the position. "A strong column, supposed to consist of volunteers from different regiments, and under the command of [Maj. Theodore] Winthrop, aide-de-camp to General Butler, crossed over the creek and appeared at the angle on our left . . . They now began to cheer most lustily, thinking that our work was open at the gorge, and that they could get in by a sudden rush. Companies B and C, however, dispelled the illusion by a cool, deliberate, and well-directed fire. Colonel Magruder sent over portions of Companies G, C and H of my regiment to our support, and now began as cool firing on our side as was ever witnessed." Magruder had reacted

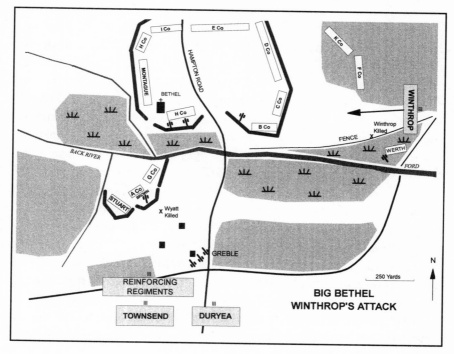

to a mistaken report that Winthrop's charge had carried the Confederate breastworks but Major Randolph put him at ease. "Colonel, the North Carolina boys are doing the prettiest kind of work." "Then sir they are whipped," Magruder replied. Benjamin Huske, who overheard the exchange between the two men, shared their confidence. "The firing was incessant, and the roar awful — but I felt perfectly secure because Col. Hill was there."[52]

Heavy firing from B, C, and D companies forced the New Englanders back to the cover of the swamp. Major Winthrop still did not give up, and he tried to rally the wavering soldiers. One southerner observed his action. "Their captain, a fine looking man, reached the fence, and leaping on a log, waved his sword, crying, 'Come on, boys; one charge, and the day is ours.' The words were his last, for a Carolina rifle ended his life the next moment, and his men fled in terror back." D. H. Hill, also, noticed Winthrop's brave act. "He was the only one of the enemy who exhibited even an approximation to courage during the whole day." In contrast to Winthrop's leadership, Colonel Bendix reported his part in the engagement. "After firing some time [we] withdrew back into the woods. When we got into the woods I found the troops retiring, and followed."[53]

General Pierce gave up any further attacks and retreated. He ordered the two reinforcing regiments from Hampton to cover the withdrawal of the three and a half regiments involved in the battle. The Union's march discipline dissolved as soon as the rearward movement began. One of the men in a relieving regiment took a dim view of Pierce's disorganized flight. "The troops from this post are certainly lacking in discipline, if not in valor, for on our return march there was not the least attempt at order among them . . . [They] presented nothing but an indiscriminate horde of stragglers." Colonel Allen, who commanded one of the rear guard regiments, imagined that the Confederates were outflanking him, abandoned his covering position, and retreated. Lt. Col. Gouverneur K. Warren appeared to be the only Union officer to keep his head during the retreat. He stayed behind to collect the wounded and the corpse of Lieutenant Greble who died toward the end of the engagement. Warren had to commandeer an artillery limber to evacuate the casualties.[54]

Once the Union force abandoned the field, the Confederates got their first shocking look at the aftereffects of war. "Around the yard were the dead bodies of the men who had been killed by our cannon, mangled in the most frightful manner by the shells . . . The gay looking uniforms of the New York Zouaves contrasted greatly with the pale, fixed faces of their dead owners." Benjamin Huske felt especially moved after he examined the watch of Major Winthrop and saw the pictures of two lovely women inside. "The death of that poor officer affected me more than anything else, for I knew there was one home whose light had gone out. Great God! avert the horrors of this civil war! That we should conquer was all for me while it lasted, a man's blood gets up and he doesn't mind danger. But when the time of action is past we feel the truth of what Wellington said, 'But one thing is more terrible than victory, and that is defeat.' "[55]

Colonel Magruder withdrew the Confederate force to Yorktown that evening, apprehending an even greater Union effort to storm the main defensive line. Once safely back at Yorktown, the officers and correspondents began filing their reports. Magruder had nothing but praise for Colonel Hill and Major Randolph. "These officers were not only prompt and daring in the execution of their duties, but most industrious and energetic in the preparations for the conflict." Magruder singled out John Bridgers of A Company for the bold counterattack to recover Brown's Battery. "Capt. Bridgers deserves the highest praise for his timely act of gallantry."[56]

Besides the capable leadership of the Confederate commanders, the troops showed commendable steadiness under fire. Stories of close calls abounded. "I had the but [sic] of my gun shot off in my hands," Warlick told his sweetheart. The youthful Captain Ross bragged, "I saw six Zouaves take deliberate aim at me and fire but fortunately they missed me." "Gracious! how the balls showered around us . . . You can form no idea how they hissed and struck just like a shower of hot stones falling into the water," Benjamin Huske exclaimed. The extra security of lying behind breastworks and the calm demeanor of Hill and Magruder helped steady the nerves of the volunteers. "There was something sublime in the spirit of the men fighting for their homes and friends." They had done very well in their first fight.[57]

Of course, northern ineptitude contributed as much to the victory as southern valor. The horrible fratricide below Little Bethel clearly unnerved the Union leaders. None of them showed any real fighting spirit, except for Major Winthrop. The failure to coordinate the assault

of Townsend's and Duryea's regiments, followed by Duryea's withdrawal and Townsend's retreat at the sight of his own troops, surrendered the victory, needlessly, to the Confederates. General Butler tried
to put the engagement in a favorable light by poor-mouthing the
importance of the fight at Bethel. "We have gained much more than
we have lost by the skirmish at Big Bethel, and while the advance
upon the battery and the capture of it might have added *éclat* to the
occasion, it would not have added to its substantial results." Butler
could not deny the casualties suffered at Bethel. Besides Winthrop and
Greble, the Union lost sixteen enlisted men. Five more were missing
and fifty-three had been wounded. Butler endured seventy-six casualties; yet, he had nothing to show for it beyond the burning of Little Bethel Church.[58] The setback at Bethel served as a harbinger of an
even bigger humiliation awaiting the Union army at Manassas one
month later.

The news that twelve hundred Confederates had defeated a force
of over four thousand Union soldiers quickly flashed to Richmond.
The southern press reacted to the victory with feelings of euphoria.
As the first battle between the armies, the Battle of Bethel assumed an
exaggerated significance and justified the most optimistic appraisals of
southern prowess. "It is one of the most extraordinary victories in the
annals of war," proclaimed the *Richmond Dispatch* in a fit of hyperbole.
"Does not the hand of God seem manifest in this thing!" Governor
Ellis read Colonel Hill's dispatch to the North Carolina Convention,
which received it "with every demonstration of joy." The convention
proceeded to vote its thanks to the governor for reading the dispatch
and offered testimonials to the brave Tar Heel soldiers. The pro-union-
ist newspaper, *North Carolina Standard,* joined the chorus of praise for
the 1st N.C. Volunteers, "Honor to them now and hereafter! The old
state is proud of them all."[59]

Only the death of poor Private Wyatt dampened the rejoicing. In
his official report, Magruder lamented, "Too much praise cannot be
bestowed upon the heroic soldier whom we lost." The entire South
mourned the loss of its first soldier killed in battle, a brave nineteen-
year-old from Tarboro. Wyatt's solitary sacrifice seemed to magnify his
stature in the southern consciousness. No one could have known how
many Confederate sons would soon follow him to the grave.[60]

YORKTOWN

Summer 1861, York Peninsula, Virginia

Magruder got his reward a week after the battle; the Confederates elevated him to the rank of brigadier general. D. H. Hill must have gritted his teeth at the news. Although Magruder held the overall command at Bethel, "Col. Hill did nearly all the commanding," Pvt. John T. Jones confided to his family. An episode the next week further undermined confidence in Magruder and fueled Hill's growing contempt for his superior. General Magruder reacted to a report of a heavy Union force advancing up the peninsula by evacuating Bethel and pulling those troops back to join the North Carolina regiment at Yorktown. The hasty abandonment of Bethel offended the Tar Heels. "Col. Hill was mortified by their retreating without a fight." The report proved to be another false alarm, which made the sudden withdrawal look that much worse.[61]

Magruder was not the only man unnerved by the alarm and the closeness of the Union army. A newly arrived recruit with the Enfield Blues suddenly panicked at the sound of the morning drum roll and fired away at the nearest person he saw, killing Pvt. B. F. Britt and wounding another. The commanders mercifully sent the terrified young man home with a medical discharge. The frightened soldier belonged to a group of reinforcements recently sent to the regiment from North Carolina. The home communities continued to build up their volunteer companies in the 1st N.C. even as new regiments formed in the state. Besides the recruits, two new companies from the eastern part of the state augmented the regiment after the battle of Bethel, although they did not arrive until August. Company L, commanded by Capt. Jesse Jacocks, haled from Bertie County near the coast. 2d Lt. Francis W. Bird, one of the company's officers, would play a memorable part in the regiment's subsequent history. Capt. James K. Marshall commanded the other unit, M Company, which came from Chowan County.[62]

A strange period of quiet followed the regiment's hurried entry into combat. After the abortive attempt to advance up the peninsula, the Union army shifted its attention to northern Virginia. The Union main army under Brig. Gen. Irvin McDowell clashed with the Confederates commanded by Gen. P. G. T. Beauregard at Manassas on July 21, 1861. The battle (remembered by the name Bull Run in the North), though much larger than Bethel, ended in an equally gratifying victory for the South. After the disaster at Bull Run, the Union army concentrated on training its swelling ranks of volunteers. The defensive line around Yorktown remained tranquil throughout the summer and fall of 1861, despite the Union's advantage in strength.

The 1st N.C. did not remain idle, however. The officers and men kept busy fortifying the Yorktown defenses. The troops' spirit was sustained while working on the entrenchments. One soldier admitted, "Since the battle of Bethel we don't mind a little dirt digging." The quiet time did not fulfill the soldier's thirst for action, though. They had enlisted to fight, not sit. Soon boredom settled over the camp. Colonel Hill kept the troops busy with regular drills and entrenching, but that did not satisfy them for long. After a couple of weeks, the Yorktown fortifications were finished, and the drills became routine. Clever troops quickly devised a way to keep the stern drillmaster from bothering them. Whenever someone spotted Harvey Hill walking through the camp, the troops would pull out a copy of the *Presbyterian* and start reading it in front of their tents. The deeply pious Hill would nod his approval and leave them alone. By mid-July, one of the correspondents complained, "Things are very quiet here just now. Besides the arrival of the 'Logan', the only thing around here that seems to have had any life, . . . there is nothing to disturb the dull routines of work and drill." A month later, his complaints took on a note of desperation. "Oh! that something would turn up to relieve the everlasting monotony of this place."[63]

Several other factors played heavily on the regiment's morale. Their poor diet proved to be inadequate and unappetizing. Pvt. Lewis Warlick remarked, "Often we have hard ship biscuits and they are so hard I have to soften them in coffee." "All we get from [the government] is meat, flour, meal, rice, soap, sugar, coffee and candles," he complained. Louis Leon and the other Jewish soldiers from Charlotte had a different problem with their mess. To sustain the men, southern rations relied heavily on pork, which conflicted with a kosher diet.

The paltry rations soon overcame Leon's religious inhibitions over pork. "We took a good long walk away from the camp, and saw several shoats. We ran one down, held it so it could not squeal, then killed it, cut it in small pieces, put it in our knapsacks, returned to the creek, and from there to camp, where we shared it with the boys. It tasted good." Most members of the regiment seldom got a chance to supplement their meals the way Leon did. Caring families often sent baked goods from home to help feed their loved ones at the front. Still, for the soldiers accustomed to life on the farm or in school, the provisions seemed very slim. The youthful Captain Ross pleaded with his family, "Why in the world don't you send me something to eat? I am nearly starving." The men tried to purchase food locally, but lack of money kept most from getting fresh fruit and vegetables.[64]

A vexing administrative problem kept the men of the 1st N.C. Volunteers from getting their pay. The state and Confederate governments continued to argue over the transfer of volunteer units into Confederate service. The volunteers had enlisted for twelve months at the first call for recruits, but the Confederate War Department later imposed a rule not to accept any volunteer regiments unless the men signed three-year enlistments. Of course, while the bureaucrats haggled, the 1st N.C. had answered the call, deployed to the front, and fought the enemy. That minor fact did not persuade the bureaucrats to accept the regiment into the Confederate army. The soldiers might not have cared about formal acceptance, except for its effect on their pay. The central government refused to pay the salaries of volunteers until the army accepted them, and the state had not authorized pay for the volunteers, as it assumed they would be paid by Richmond. While the stalemate lasted, the troops received nothing except a small enlistment bonus. Finally, in late July, the Confederate Congress settled the issue by authorizing six-months' pay for the regiment from the date they officially mustered in North Carolina, May 15, 1861.[65]

The troops faced more serious problems than poor provisions and poor pay. The low-country Virginia climate and the confined living space within the Yorktown camp bred disease. By late June Egbert Ross noted, "It is very hot and mosquitoes by the millions. Cannot sleep for them at night." Before long, cases of ague (fevers and chills now identified as malaria) began to appear. "I tell you they pulled me down in a hurry. I do hope I will have no more for they make a person feel awfully mean and very sick at times," confessed Lewis War-lick. At the time, no one made the connection between "the chills" and mosquitoes. Other maladies ran through the camp. A measles out-break struck in June, adding to the misery and taking the lives of sev-eral soldiers. Such health problems were common, but the officers could have done more to prevent the contagion with better hygiene and discipline. The Reverend William H. Wills visited Yorktown to help care for his ailing son and was appalled by the living conditions. "Much of the sickness might be avoided with proper sanitary regula-tions. First, there is great want of attention in Camp, and second, the men themselves are very imprudent." The officers commiserated with the sufferers but the heat, mosquitoes, and crowded conditions con-tinued to sap their strength.[66]

By the beginning of August, measles, malaria, typhoid, and dysen-tery wrought havoc within the regiment. "There is a great number of our regiment sick. We report about three hundred and seventy sick, including officers, nearly one third of our number," Private Warlick reported. Captain Ross wrote home from his own sick bed, "Our men here are dying every day, average I suppose five or six per day. Such mortality I never knew before in any regiment." J. M. Cutchins, an A Company soldier, believed that the youthful recruits from the col-leges could not hold up to the rigors of army life. "These boys, used to luxury and ease, a life very different from the hard life of the Con-federate soldier, soon fell prey to typhoid fever and other ills." The troops from urban backgrounds did suffer greatly, but large numbers from the rural areas of North Carolina succumbed, also. City dwellers, who had previous contacts with contagious diseases, had acquired some immunities, but the soldiers from remote farms and the back-woods had little resistance to these diseases and quickly contracted them. Nearly every man in the regiment suffered from some type of illness over the summer months. Even D. H. Hill succumbed to over-work and the heat. Disease proved to be a far deadlier adversary than the Union army. Fifty-two soldiers perished from the ravages of dis-ease within six months. Bored to death, eating substandard rations, serving without pay, and wracked by disease, it is a wonder the troops did not get up and leave. Amazingly, only four men deserted during the regiment's six-month term of service.[67]

D. H. Hill may not have done all he could to enforce camp sanitation, but he did attempt to relieve the suffering of his troops. In early August, while struggling with his own poor health, he went to Richmond to request the transfer of the regiment to a "more healthy place." Egbert Ross prayed for Hill's mission, "I hope that he will succeed, if he does not I believe that our regiment will all die. We have near five-hundred sick. Oh 'tis awful to visit the hospitals and see the sick and dying all around you." Relief did not come until August 22, when the regiment moved to Ship Point, Virginia, near the mouth of the Poquoson River. "This place is said to be a healthy location and some think it is for that that we were moved here in order to recruit our health," Lewis Warlick hopefully wrote. The change of sites disappointed the men once they settled into the new camp. One soldier complained, "Its the sickliest place on top of earth . . . the water here is perfectly awful." At last, cooler weather and the supplement of fish to the diet helped restore the health of the regiment. The dismal, boring, and morbid summer had consumed much of the regiment's morale but had not broken its spirit.[68]

Events back home aroused that fighting spirit to a fever pitch. News reached Ship Point at the end of August of General Butler's assault on Fort Hatteras, North Carolina, and the surrender of its Confederate garrison. The capture of the fort on the Outer Banks opened the Pamlico Sound to the Union navy and threatened half of the state's coastal region. "Our camp has been thrown into great consternation by hearing that troops had landed in North Carolina," Henry Huske observed. Lewis Warlick boasted about the regiment's reaction. "When we heard it every man was anxious to strike tents and go at once and whip them out. Our officers say we can whip ten thousand for we whipped five thousand on Va. soil and they know we can whip twice that number on our own." The threat at home stirred the regiment's officers to petition the Confederate War Department for an assignment in North Carolina. "Maj Lane is going to start to Richmond today [September 1, 1861] to see if our Regt. will be allowed to go there," remarked Henry Huske. "I hope it will, nothing would give me more pleasure. They [Butler's forces] are some of the same that we whipped at Bethel." The North Carolina troops soon learned that Union activity on the coast of their home state did not excite the Confederate high command so long as a Union army threatened Virginia. Request denied.[69]

The Union blow at Fort Hatteras helped drive the first wedge between the defensive interests of North Carolina and the military strategy of the Confederate government. Initially, the state felt pleased by Richmond's assurances that it would defend the entire South and that individual states would not have to implement separate defensive measures. North Carolina willingly turned its regiments over to the Confederate army and stopped working on its coastal fortifications. Unfortunately, the Union struck before Richmond could continue the suspended defensive preparations. Gov. Henry T. Clark, who replaced the recently deceased John Ellis, immediately requested the Confederate army to come to the state's rescue, but Richmond treated the invasion as a local concern, instead of a strategic threat to the Confederacy. Richmond refused to return any of the Carolina regiments in Virginia. Governor Clark's exasperated complaint expressed a growing distrust of the Confederate government. "We are out of arms, and our soil is invaded, and you refuse our request to send us back some of our own armed regiments to defend us . . . we have disarmed ourselves to arm you."[70] While the two capitals bickered, the 1st N.C. Volunteers sat at Yorktown, itching for action.

The regiment's men had to satisfy their appetite for fighting with a simple raid. A small party set out on a mission to destroy the lighthouse on the very eastern tip of the peninsula six miles north of Fort Monroe. Lewis Warlick volunteered for the expedition, although he had not fully recovered from a bout of ague. "We started about three hours before sundown (twenty-three in all) in small boats and was gone the whole night, did not return until daylight. [I] was traveling all the time, had no way of lying down to rest, being exposed all the while to the night air . . . After all our trouble and danger to which we were exposed we succeeded only in part . . . We arrested the lighthouse keeper and brought him prisoner to Ship Point. The lighthouse we could not burn nor could we blow it up as it is solid masonry from the base for forty feet. Therefore, we had to leave that fine piece of property to benefit only the Yankees."[71]

D. H. Hill, who had just been promoted to brigadier general, visited the men at Ship Point on September 2. His arrival put the camp in a jubilant mood. "Last evening was a joyful one to the First North Carolina Regiment. Near night I heard loud shouting throughout the entire camp, and on inquiring the cause, found it was because of the arrival of our much-loved General Hill, who has been absent from us some five or six weeks, trying to regain his health, which had been much impaired by his constant and arduous duties at Yorktown." That night, several hundred troops surrounded Hill's tent and paid their respects with "three loud, long and lasting cheers." Hill playfully acknowledged their boisterous welcome. "You have out flanked me and surrounded me — I must submit to the surrender." He then addressed the throng with heartfelt emotion. "It is with inexpressible gratitude that I am allowed to be again among you. Since I have seen you last I have suffered more than I ever suffered before, more than in all my life together. Yet the suffering of my body did not surpass the anguish of my soul in remembering your afflictions here. While I was on my back burning with fever, I thought of you suffering in like manner, while others were dying. And another thought occurred to me, that you might be fighting while I could not be with you to show you how to dodge, and to tell you, 'Give it to them boys!' "[72]

Hill turned to the recent news of the debacle at Fort Hatteras. "Well, we have met with reverses in North Carolina. It is no more than I expected. Our proud and boastful spirit, especially of our press, has taken to ourselves our victories. We have been saying, 'I did this with my own might and power.' We have accredited our successes to our own prowess instead of to God. We have been disparaging the bravery of our enemies. I know some of them; I know the commander at Newport News [Union Maj. Gen. John E. Wool]. A braver man never lived. The difference between them and us as soldiers is the cause. They come among us as marauders; it is that, that makes them cowards. Apply the same to yourselves. Suppose you were to invade their country, driving their women and children before you with the torch and dagger. You could not meet their men boldly, but would feel like running. They are not natural cowards. Let us learn from this a lesson; let us learn to cultivate a strict moral discipline. With a consciousness of a strictly moral purpose what need we to fear!"[73]

General Hill assumed his new duties as a brigade commander shortly after his visit, so the regiment assembled to vote for his replacement. As expected, Charles C. Lee and James Lane each moved up one rank. Lt. R. F. Hoke from Lincoln County surprised several people by leapfrogging all the captains in the regiment to win the election to the major's position. No sooner had the regiment elected its field grade officers, than Lt. Col. James Lane left the regiment to assume command of the 28th Regiment. Capt. Joseph B. Starr took Lane's place as second in command after another election.[74]

Magruder again shifted the regiment around the peninsula in early September. The regiment moved to Camp Fayetteville between Bethel and Yorktown where they celebrated a special event. To commemorate the regiment's victory at Bethel, the legislature enacted a bill to award the regiment a unique flag that followed the design of the new state flag. The pattern had a white star centered on a red field with the dates "May 20th 1775" above and "May 20th 1861" below. Two broad horizontal stripes, one blue, one white, covered the rest of the flag. The name "BETHEL" was stitched onto the white stripe. On September 9, the regiment formed on the parade ground to receive its new colors, the specific gift of the ladies of Fayetteville who had sewn the flag and its inscription. Colonel Lee called the regiment to dress parade for the presentation by John W. Baker, Jr., of Fayetteville. Mr. Baker, although impaired by some "Virginny Tangle-leg," spoke "in behalf of the ladies of Fayetteville" and presented the "beautiful regimental flag" with the word "Bethel" inscribed. The standard bearer grasped the colors, while Charles Lee expressed the gratitude of the regiment for "the kind remembrance in which the ladies of Fayetteville have held them." From that day forward the 1st N.C. Volunteers, and later the 11th N.C., carried the colors bearing the name "Bethel." The soldiers of the regiment developed a particularly strong bond to their colors, perhaps because it represented the exceptional honor given to them by the people of North Carolina. The regiment would bear the flag through numerous battles and engagements over the next three and a half years. Eventually, the specially inscribed colors gave the name "Bethel" to the regiment itself.[75]

With D. H. Hill gone and the Union army showing no initiative on the peninsula, the war seemed to pass by the Bethel Regiment. That fall the adjutant general called for the services of the men but not as part of the Bethel Regiment. On November 8, 1861, the regiment pulled out of the line at Yorktown in order to "stand down." The state's first adjutant general, J. F. Hoke, had limited their term of service to six months when the regiment formed in April. Since then the Confederate Government had changed its enlistment policy. Only volunteers who joined for three years would be accepted into the Confederate army. The new adjutant general, J. G. Martin, held firm to the expiration date of the enlistments, so the regiment was forced to disband.

Undoubtedly, the adjutant general needed the experience of the 1st N.C. to build the commissioned and noncommissioned officer structure of many new regiments. The 1st N.C. mustered out at Richmond on November 12. Naturally, the soldiers regretted the closing of their proud regiment, but they could look forward to some time at home. Lewis Warlick planned to propose a second time to his sweetheart; she had put him off once before the war. Romance may have engrossed Warlick's thoughts, but his writing reveals a touch of regret about ending his army career. "Port [his brother] and I will have to stay at home after this as father is getting old . . . If Port goes into the army next spring I will be necessarily compelled to remain at home unless my country should make a call for all to aid in the defence of her rights and institutions, then it will become every man's duty to adhere at once and march against the enemy of our beloved country." Even as he prepared to go home Warlick's thoughts returned to the Bethel Regiment. "There is some talk of reorganizing the 1st regiment in a month or two after it is disbanded, which I hope will be done, for it is considered to be one of the best in the field and I would like to see it keep up and retain its reputation throughout the entire war."[76]

Regardless of how sentimental the men must have felt about the 1st N.C. Volunteers, the judgment of the adjutant general proved to be wise. The original Bethel Regiment became the school for North Carolina's officer corps. By the end of the war the regiment had contributed one lieutenant general, one major general, two brigadier generals, fourteen colonels, ten lieutenant colonels, eight majors, and fifty-seven captains to the Confederacy, many of whom gave their lives. Even more than providing the South with its first battlefield victory, the wealth of experienced officers, sergeants, and enlisted men became the Bethel Regiment's greatest legacy.[77]

Daniel Harvey Hill. The Mexican War veteran hated two things with a passion: Yankees and volunteers. Yet, he led a regiment of volunteers to victory on the Civil War's first battlefield. (Collections of the Library of Congress)

Egbert A. Ross. "I am in the War!" boasted the youthful commander of the "Boy Company" in 1861. He died an untimely death while leading the assault on the first day of Gettysburg. (Southern Historical Collection of the University of North Carolina at Chapel Hill)

Lieutenant Charles B. Cook wearing the ceremonial uniform of the Fayetteville Independent Light Infantry. (North Carolina Department of Archives and History)

"It must not be. I was born to accomplish more good than I have done," John T. Jones moaned from his deathbed at the Wilderness. Private Jones posed for this photograph while serving in the Orange Light Infantry in 1861. He later rose to the rank of Lieutenant Colonel in the 26th NCT and commanded Pettigrew's Brigade as it withdrew from Cemetery Ridge. (Society for Historical Preservation of the 26th Regiment NC Troops, Inc.)

"Then, sir, they are whipped." The Union army assaults, then retreats from the position defended by the 1st North Carolina Volunteers at Big Bethel, Virginia. (North Carolina Department of Archives and History)

Four of the Edgecombe Guards who rushed forward from their breastworks at the Battle of Bethel: 1) Corporal George Williams; 2) Private Henry Lawson Wyatt; 3) Private R. H. Bradley; 4) Private John H. Thorpe. Wyatt was the sole Confederate fatality in the first battle of the war. (North Carolina Department of Archives and History)

A North Carolina regiment enjoying a quiet day in a bivouac. (North Carolina Department of Archives and History)

2

In Defense of My Home and My Country

WILMINGTON

Spring–Summer 1862, Eastern North Carolina

As soon as the Bethel Regiment disbanded, a large number of its officers and men joined other units from the state to continue fighting for the Confederacy. Two field grade officers, Charles C. Lee and R. F. Hoke, went on to command their own regiments. Colonel Lee died while leading a charge on June 30, 1862. He was shouting to his men, "On, my brave boys!" when a cannon ball cut him down. The Burke County secessionist, Clark M. Avery, commanded the 33d N.C. and served in the same brigade as C. C. Lee and James H. Lane. James K. Marshall, M Company Commander, rose to command the 52d N.C. First Lt. Benjamin Huske accepted a promotion to major in the 48th N.C. The staunch unionist officer gave his life for the Confederacy in July 1862 following a minor engagement in Virginia. A few of the enlisted men took commissions in other units, including John T. Jones. Jones joined the 26th N.C., organized under Col. Zebulon B. Vance, the former Whig congressman from the western mountains. Still, many members of the Bethel Regiment remained at home and spent the winter of 1861–1862 relaxing. Lewis Warlick proposed to his sweetheart, but the young lady demurred once again. Second Lt. Francis Bird remained busy over the winter, recruiting another infantry company in Bertie County in the hope of joining a new regiment. As events unfolded, the state would soon call for his company.[1]

A new military crisis visited North Carolina in the spring of 1862, when Maj. Gen. Ambrose Burnside led a Union invasion of the coastal region. At the time, the state had only a small force to repel an invasion, so it cried to the Confederate War Department to send reinforcements from Virginia. Richmond sent its regards but no help. President Davis did little more than offer some advice, and he appeared to show more concern for the railroads running to Virginia than for the Tar Heel citizens. "Call on every man in your State that can come with arms to rally with the utmost dispatch to defend your line of railroad." New Bern fell on March 14, 1862. Burnside then followed up his success by recapturing Fort Macon and cutting off the city of Beaufort, another deepwater port. The inadequate Confederate reaction convinced the governor that North Carolina would have to stop Burnside's army alone. Governor Clark issued a call for more volunteers from the militia.[2]

Throughout North Carolina, large numbers of young men in their late teens, twenties, or thirties answered the call to arms. In addition, many middle-aged men volunteered. Forty-two-year-old William G. Parker left his wife and three children to enlist, although Union forces threatened his Bertie County plantation. Several others in their forties and fifties joined, though most of them could not physically withstand the strain of an infantryman's life. One Lincoln County farmer, Matthew Hubbard, signed up at age sixty-four. Hubbard, who was born in the eighteenth century, later received a medical discharge that cited "the natural infirmities of age." The recruits had other noteworthy characteristics. Unlike the well-educated volunteers of 1861, the recruits of 1862 tended to come from the general population and included many poor and illiterate volunteers. One company raised in Mecklenburg County enrolled twenty-seven troops who could not write their names and had to sign the muster roll with a mark. Although most soldiers could read and write, the number of extant letters and diaries from the new companies did not compare to the numerous written accounts left by the 1st N.C. Volunteers.[3]

Many of the Bethel Regiment's veterans banded together during this crisis to form the nucleus of a new regiment. After their six-month tour of duty, the passionate war cries of 1861 may have sounded hollow, but the old Bethel soldiers still had their patriotism. When Lewis Warlick left the army in the autumn, he stated that only a desperate call to arms would cause him to reenlist. The crisis of 1862 met that condition. Warlick left his sweetheart and signed on with a Burke County company along with his brothers, Portland and Pinckney. His reenlistment stirred another argument between the troubled lovers. His girlfriend had never shown any enthusiasm for his military service, and she vented her anger at Warlick for leaving. "You very well know that it is hard for me to leave you but I consider I am doing rightly," he tried to explain. "I think my first duties are to my country and then to you."[4]

When the new regiment gathered at Camp Mangum in Raleigh, twenty-five of its officers had come from the Bethel Regiment — well over half of a regiment's normal complement. Many of the enlisted men came from the ranks of the old Bethel Regiment, as well. Because of the large number of 1st N.C. carryovers, the adjutant general designated the new regiment as the successor of the Bethel Regiment and gave them the special "Bethel" colors. On March 29, 1862, the adjutant general's office mustered the regiment into service. "The following companies having reorganized are assigned to and will be known as the 11th Regiment N.C. Troops 'Bethel'."[5]

Company	County	Commander
A	Mecklenburg	Capt. E. A. Ross
B	Burke	Capt. M. D. Armfield
C	Bertie	Capt. F. W. Bird
D	Burke	Capt. C. S. Brown
E	Mecklenburg	Capt. J. S. A. Nichols
F	Chowan	Capt. E. A. Small
G	Orange	Capt. J. R. Jennings
H	Mecklenburg	Capt. W. L. Grier
I	Lincoln	Capt. A. S. Haynes
K	Buncombe	Capt. J. M. Young

North Carolina had changed its numbering scheme for the state's regiments since the deactivation of the 1st N.C. Volunteers. The regimental numbers 1 through 10 had been set aside for "State Troops," while the volunteer regiments formed in 1861 had been forced to add ten to their original regimental numbers. Therefore, the newly formed Bethel Regiment became identified as the 11th Regiment N.C. Troops [hereafter identified as the 11th N.C.].

The regiment elected its field grade officers three days later. Col. Collett Leventhorpe, then commander of the 34th N.C., won the election for regimental commander. The reputation of the Bethel Regiment induced him to accept the assignment. Collett Leventhorpe projected a regal, dominating presence wherever he went. He stood nearly six feet six inches tall and accentuated his height with a very erect posture. Born in Exmouth, England, in 1815, he had served ten years in the British Army, attaining the rank of captain. He resigned his commission in 1842, and immigrated to Rutherfordton, North Carolina, where he married the daughter of militia general Edmund Bryan. Before proposing to the young lady, Leventhorpe acquired a trade by studying medicine and becoming a physician. The versatile Englishman dabbled in poetry in his spare time and published a few poems under the *nom de plume* Reveur before the war. Leventhorpe adopted the cause of the South and accepted a commission in November 1861, beginning his second military career at forty-six years of age. Ingrained with the discipline and polish of the British Army, Leventhorpe would mold the 11th N.C. into a sharp and efficient fighting machine. The regiment also went outside its ranks to find the second in command. The officers elected William J. Martin to the position of lieutenant colonel. Martin, a native of Virginia, had been a professor of mineralogy at the University of North Carolina, where he had been a popular and highly respected educator. One historian called him "one of the most lovable men this state ever had." Egbert A. Ross, the commander of the Charlotte Greys (the Boy Company) in the original Bethel Regiment, became the regiment's major. The regiment's field grade officers certainly had the distinctive backgrounds of American citizen-soldiers: a physician, a professor, and a boy.[6]

Colonel Leventhorpe relinquished his previous command in Goldsboro and then joined the regiment at Camp Mangum (renamed Camp Bethel) in early April. His first dress parade left a lasting impression on the troops. Standing before the formation, Leventhorpe drew his sword then shouted, "THE ELEVENTH!!!" "in the most powerful voice we had ever heard from human lips." The men, startled and amazed by their commander's thunderous roar, began to laugh. Leventhorpe cut them short and quickly taught them to take pride in the name of their regiment. "That laugh was never heard again."[7] Leventhorpe proved to be strict and demanding as a commander which, if anything, helped endear him to the soldiers. The men of the 11th N.C. knew that the English giant would turn them into a well-trained and disciplined unit.

Leventhorpe wasted no time in putting his personal stamp on the regiment by setting down detailed instructions for guard mount and dress parade. "The commanding officer is most desirous that 'The Bethel Regiment' should be distinguished by the soldierlike bearing of the sentinels." He meant business, too. One unfortunate soldier, Pvt. Reuben Yaunts, fell asleep on guard duty. Leventhorpe punished him with six months of cleanup duty wearing a ball and chain! The colonel took keen interest in the regiment's ability to move smartly on dress parade. Drill and ceremonies on the parade ground did more than present a good military image. Civil War units had to move quickly and neatly from one formation to another to execute tactical maneuvers on the battlefield. The repetitious drills infused discipline, teamwork, and maneuver proficiency within the ranks. Leventhorpe assigned permanent color guards and guides to ensure the unit performed its drills with precision. To help maintain high standards among the enlisted men, he appointed James G. McCorkle as the regiment's sergeant major.[8]

More guidance was handed down the next day. The colonel issued specific directions for sanitation within Camp Bethel. "The health of the regiment depends very much upon the strict observance of the regulations enforcing cleanliness. The Commanding Officer directs that officers commanding companies will see that their men are regular in daily ablutions. On Saturday afternoon a cleansing of the whole person should be practised . . . The police regulations already established must be rigidly observed . . . By attention to these essentials the Commanding Officer trusts that the scourge of armies—the typhoid fever—may be averted." Leventhorpe looked to the health and welfare of his men by insisting on high standards in drill, discipline, and cleanliness. In this respect, he demonstrated more vigilance than his predecessor, D. H. Hill.[9]

Military necessity called the 11th N.C. out of Raleigh in the first week of May. With the Union army and navy active along North Carolina's coast, the governor wanted the state's own regiments to defend the coast, instead of sending everyone to Virginia. Colonel Leventhorpe reported to the department commander in Goldsboro, Maj. Gen. Theophilus Holmes, while en route to the coast. "I saw General Holmes, who ordered us arms and ammunition & sent us the same evening onto General French at Wilmington." The men inspected their new English Enfield rifles, just off the blockade runner *Nashville,* as they headed to the only remaining deepwater port north of Charleston. Once the Bethel Regiment detrained at Wilmington, Brig. Gen. S. G. French placed Leventhorpe in command of the Cape Fear District, giving him operational control over the 43d and 51st N.C. regiments, as well as some cavalry. The regimental commander now had to devote much of his attention to the overall defense of the Wilmington area. Leventhorpe was not promoted, although he was considered to be "the best finished and equipped regimental field officer in the Confederate service" and had brigade-level responsibilities. In his typical gentlemanly manner, Leventhorpe overlooked the slight and set about his new tasks.[10]

Holmes, French, and Leventhorpe worried about Union ships taking soundings along the coast near the Masonboro Inlet, so they sent the 11th N.C. to Camp Holmes, seven miles from Wilmington, to prevent a Union landing at the inlet. Fortunately, nothing developed from the navy's prowling in the area. Burnside had directed his efforts to Plymouth, North Carolina, on the Roanoke River, instead. On May 14, Leventhorpe moved the three regiments to nearby Camp Davis on Hewlitt's Creek, eight miles outside town.[11]

Once in camp, the regiment resumed its training under the exacting standards set by Collett Leventhorpe. The 11th N.C. experienced "the severest drilling that any troops ever underwent in all America." William Martin and Edward Outlaw described the daily routine. "With reveille at daybreak, company drill at 6 A.M., guard-mounting at 8 A.M., squad drill at 9 A.M., battalion drill at 11 A.M., company drill again at 1 P.M., battalion drill again at 3 P.M. and dress-parade at 5 P.M., the regiment soon became so complete a machine that its evolutions were as accurate as clock-work and obtained from its Colonel the compliment (as he one day dismissed the battalion): 'Not quite as proficient as

British regulars.' " Capt. Frank Bird wrote to his sister of the regiment's progress. "Our regiment is becoming very well drilled . . . I become daily more pleased with our Col. Leventhorpe he is a very fine gentleman." The regimental commander's strict policies on matters of discipline began to produce results. By the end of June the level of performance within the regiment earned a compliment from the demanding Leventhorpe. "The commanding officer is happy to notice most marked improvement in the soldierlike bearing of the sentries of the Bethel Regiment." Because of their accomplished drills, the regiment's dress parade became one of the social highlights for local residents who enjoyed listening to the regimental band and watching the troops march to the beat of "Goober Peas" and "The Bonnie Blue Flag."[12]

While the 11th N.C. guarded the Cape Fear District, the Confederate chain of command issued its policy for granting furloughs. The promise of two or three weeks' leave to visit home naturally excited the homesick troops. The officers announced a specific rotation of furloughs within the unit that limited the number of soldiers on leave at any given time. Each soldier received a designated place on the waiting list based on marital status, rank, and seniority. The troops felt the policy was fair and accepted the furlough schedule. Although fair, the policy forced some to wait nearly a year before their turn would come. The officers also designed the policy to help discourage desertions. If a soldier failed to return from leave, the next man would not be released from duty. Most soldiers respected the rights of the others and returned to duty promptly. A few soldiers, however, overstayed their time at home or, worse yet, deserted. The men waiting their turn for leave did not appreciate the delays caused by these tardy soldiers. Some of the late arrivals had legitimate problems, despite their best efforts. During the spring campaign of 1863, W. H. Neave, a member of the regimental band, started back from Salisbury to rejoin the regiment. The regiment's sudden departure stranded him in Tarboro for weeks, until one of the regiment's officers returned to the town.[13] Still, the knowledge that every man would have time to see his family gave each soldier something to anticipate during the tedious weeks of duty.

Strangely, as the year progressed, the war once again seemed to pass by the Bethel Regiment. The Union army did not exploit its initial success along the North Carolina coast. Washington directed Burnside to hold his army in check while Maj. Gen. George McClellan concentrated the Army of the Potomac on the Virginia peninsula for a thrust against the Confederate capital. Ironically, the Bethel Regiment had defended this avenue to Richmond throughout the summer of 1861. Now the regiment sat in camp around Wilmington while the Confederate armies commanded by Gen. Robert E. Lee fought a major campaign over the very ground they once guarded. With the Union threat growing in Virginia and the North Carolina sector remaining quiet, the Confederate high command asked Governor Clark to send the state's recently organized regiments to Virginia. The governor could not refuse the urgent plea of the War Department, so he graciously sent all but a handful of regiments. The 11th N.C. got its marching orders on June 14, 1862, but not for Richmond. The regiment tramped through deep sands and sweltering heat to Camp Wyatt, near the present-day town of Kure Beach. From this position, the regiment would help defend Fort Fisher at the mouth of the Cape Fear River. As the governor considered the Bethel Regiment to be his best, he preferred to retain it in the Cape Fear district. The men did not appreciate the governor's decision. "We were very much disappointed when ordered here having expected an order to Richmond," Captain Bird admitted.[14]

The conditions at Camp Wyatt added discomfort to the disappointment the troops already felt. "We came on here with the intention of going into the barracks that the 2nd regiment had left," Lewis Warlick related. "But when we arrived we found that the whole place was covered with fleas and our colonel said we should not take quarters there atall [sic]." The sand fleas along the beach tormented the troops in the heat. Warlick gave his hesitant fiancée a graphic description of the infestation. "You might take up a bucket of sand at night and by the next morning it would be all jumped out." The men rejoiced when they got new orders for Richmond a week later. They quick stepped back through the deep sands on their way to catch the trains for Virginia. Another disappointment awaited them at the depot. "After arriving here [Wilmington] the order was countermanded, then officers as well as privates began to grumble, as they did not wish to return to Camp Wyatt . . . They all expressed a desire to go on to Richmond or join Jackson rather than go back among those fleas." Only part of their wish was fulfilled. The regiment did not return to Camp

Wyatt; instead, it remained in Wilmington to defend the Cape Fear District.[15]

The grumbling of the troops revealed a growing divergence in attitude from the rest of North Carolina's citizens. The Bethel men had enlisted to defend their homeland, yet they were soldiers at heart. They trained for combat and longed to do their duty in battle. If the fight was in Virginia, that was where they wanted to go. The politicians and citizens of North Carolina began to view the war from a far different perspective after the invasion of the coastal region. The fighting in Virginia had siphoned off the troops needed to defend the citizens' families and property. The people in the coastal counties distrusted Richmond and felt abandoned by the Confederate army. The passage of the conscription act by the Confederate Congress further alienated the state's citizens; personal liberty had been one of the rallying cries behind the state's secession. Resentment toward Richmond produced a political upheaval in North Carolina. Zebulon Vance led a conservative political coalition, supported by former unionists and former Democratic editor William Holden, to oust the Democrat–secessionist administration of Governor Clark. Vance and Holden campaigned on an anti-Richmond platform that blamed secessionists for pushing the state into a war with the North and Democrats for the military calamities in North Carolina. At the same time, Vance strongly supported the war for southern independence and promised to push vigorously the state's military effort. Vance trounced the Democrats in the July elections and ushered in an era of political tension with the Confederate government.[16]

The Bethel Regiment spent the rest of the summer in the Cape Fear District moving between outposts, guarding salt works, watching inlets, and picketing possible landing sites. W. H. Neave made the most of his time at Camp Davis. "Our Reg't is in fragments at the different salt works on the sound. I am here with the main body enjoying our beautiful country camp vastly, and sea bathing . . . We enjoy ourselves very well here. I take the band out to bathe every afternoon to a pretty little bay . . . thousands of fishes jumping about all around us." The duty may not have been difficult, but the regiment had to protect the vital port that served the blockade runners bringing arms and goods from Europe. Occasionally, the troops had to pitch in to off-load steamers that could not make it through the blockade to the

Cape Fear River and had to moor off the sounds. When the *Modern Greece* ran itself aground near Fort Fisher in early July, A and B companies helped recover the cargo. Major Ross went to check on the detail and discovered that the duty had not been entirely disagreeable. "Our boys worked hard but had quite a lively time of it drinking Champagne, wine etc., smoking cigars, eating Pine Apples, raisins and other fruits." Leventhorpe took a dim view of this undisciplined pilfering and court-martialed the officer in charge.[17]

The blockade runners brought excitement and boom times to Wilmington, though not all the changes were for the better. "Suspension of the civil law, neglect of sanitary precautions, . . . the advent of lawless and depraved characters . . . had quite changed the aspect of the whole community." The arms and munitions from England allowed the South to keep its army in the field, while the cotton taken out propped up its economy. Daring steamer captains risked everything to slip past the Union fleet on moonless nights to serve the cause and get rich from the lucrative trade. Lewis Warlick described his thrill when he saw the steamship *Kate* come into port. "I was orderly for the General Court Martial and was in the third story of the Post Office, which is near the wharf, looked out of the window and saw her coming most beautifully up the river, went down stairs immediately and proceeded to the wharf and went on board to hear the news and to have it said that I was on board a vessel that had been so fortunate as to get [past] the blockading squadron."[18]

Protecting the flow of goods helped the cause but did not suit the soldiers who anxiously awaited some action. While the regiment languished along the North Carolina coast, its sister regiments won glorious victories under Lee and Jackson in Virginia. Nevertheless, the regiment suffered its share of losses, as the summer heat and humidity produced widespread sickness among the troops. Leventhorpe's stern measures regarding sanitation could not prevent attacks of malaria, measles, dysentery, and typhoid. "Our company has suffered more from sickness than the old company [Company G 1st N.C. Volunteers] did during the whole six months last year," Warlick remarked. "Nearly all the cases of fever we have had proved fatal." The regiment suffered through a second period of high mortality. Sixty-seven soldiers succumbed to disease while they served in North Carolina. An outbreak of yellow fever in Wilmington added to the losses. The yellow fever epidemic, rumored to have been brought to the area by the blockade runner *Kate,* killed 446 civilians and numerous soldiers that fall. New cases appeared daily, along with notices of the victims who had perished.[19]

Wilmington virtually came to a standstill as citizens huddled in their homes, afraid to venture out into the pestilential air. The city's paper stopped its presses because no one was left to print it. The new Confederate district commander, Brig. Gen. Thomas Clingman, refused to reside within the city. He ordered Leventhorpe to remain in Wilmington and run his headquarters for him, while he kept safely out of danger. During the morbid season, the regiment lost three of its captains to typhoid and yellow fever. One of them, Capt. James R. Jennings, died on the train taking him home on convalescent leave. The epidemic became so severe that Leventhorpe withdrew the regiment in September to Camp Davis to isolate the troops from its ravages. As the regiment left the town, the few citizens brave enough to move about ignited smudge pots to ward off the dreaded fever. "The black pall of smoke from the burning tar barrels added solemnity to the deadly silence of the streets; designed to purify the air and mitigate the pestilence, it seemed more like fuliginous clouds of ominous portent, a somber emblem of mourning." The epidemic did not abate until later in the fall. Meanwhile, the regiment virtually quarantined itself at Camp Davis, waiting for the sickness to subside or orders to move to another theater. Warlick and others began to despair of ever fighting another battle. "When I hear of our friends doing so much in Va. and Maryland it makes me want to be with them for we are doing nothing here and I don't believe we ever will." Not until October 5 did the 11th N.C. get relief from duty near Wilmington when it was, finally, sent north.[20]

WHITE HALL

Fall 1862, Eastern Virginia and North Carolina

*U*nion forces had occupied Suffolk, Virginia, by the fall of 1862 and opened a wide avenue of advance south of the James River where they could threaten the vital rail link between Weldon, North Carolina, and Petersburg. The Confederates organized a weak defensive line along the Blackwater River, west of Suffolk, but an expedition against the Blackwater in early October forced them to call up the 11th N.C. Collett Leventhorpe took command of the forces defending the Blackwater River once the Bethel Regiment arrived at Franklin, Virginia. Again, Leventhorpe had the responsibilities of a general but the rank of a colonel. The Blackwater line extended twenty-six miles up and down the river but was punctuated by several fording sites. Two augmented infantry regiments could not secure such an extended line against the Union's superior strength. "We occupy a dangerous position and expect to fight any day," Captain Bird confided to his sister. "Our force at present is too small to resist that of the enemy." Leventhorpe made up for the lack of defenders by keeping his units alert and on the move. "The line to be guarded was so long, and the troops to guard it so few, that forced marches were of constant occurrence, and the term foot-cavalry, facetiously applied to us, aptly described our role."[21]

When they were not marching, the 11th N.C. had to construct artillery emplacements and field fortifications because Leventhorpe wanted the river fortified. He worried that Union forces in Suffolk might bring up heavy siege guns on rail cars or gunboats from the Albemarle Sound to blast away the Confederate entrenchments. The Bethel troops started building an iron battery to secure the crossing sites. B Company's 1st Sgt. Elam Bristol proudly wrote about the artillery emplacement. "We are throwing up batteries down at Franklin and we are covering them with railroad irons so it is impossible to batter them down with the heaviest siege guns so we will be better prepared for the Yankees next time." Leventhorpe used the iron battery to mount two famous siege guns, "Long Tom" and "Laughing Charlie." The big guns and some additional troops helped mend the risky situation along the Blackwater. By November, Leventhorpe commanded a force of four infantry and two cavalry regiments. The reinforcements came none too soon.[22]

On November 18, 1862, Union forces advanced against the ford guarded by the Bethel troops. Cpl. Lewis Warlick recalled, "Before day the long roll called us again into line—marched to headquarters. There the Col. assigned to each captain his place — two companies beyond the river, A & G, the remaining ones on this side . . . The Col. told us that from all he could gather from the scouts and prisoners that they [the Union] had a very large force . . . but he said 'I am determined to hold the place at all hazards and he hoped the Bethel Regiment would still retain the reputation she had for valor . . .' after he got through three hearty cheers were given for our commander." Warlick watched the fight unfold. "As soon as [the scouts] and the pickets were driven in our batteries opened fire . . . When each side opened I tell you there was a thundering for two hours almost equal to the Bethel fight — bang, crack, sing went the shells and pieces all around us; you ought to have been there to have seen me dodge . . . We had to lie and take it all and couldn't get a shot. There was no infantry firing atall [sic]. After two hours their batteries were silenced and they skedaddled for Suffolk which relieved one of a good deal of dread."[23]

The Union stabbed at another ford, but Leventhorpe had already anticipated the move. He bragged to his wife how his foresight avoided disaster. "Under Divine Providence, my management saved the Blackwater. Against the opinion of almost all, I [posted] Marshall's Regiment [52d N.C.], at Lawrence Ford — & there they tried to flank us in the last fight. Had they succeeded they had probably 6000 or 8000 men ready to rush in there." Later the departmental commander, Maj. Gen. S. G. French, complimented the forces that had defended this district. "Although I have never been able to place an adequate force on the line [Blackwater], yet by defensive works and constant vigilance it has been held since July last against a force five or six times our number." Brig. Gen. Roger A. Pryor, sent to the Blackwater from General Lee's army, superseded Leventhorpe on December 4, 1862. Pryor left Leventhorpe with operational control of the units, while he located his headquarters four miles to the rear. The fortunes of war soon spared Leventhorpe the discomfort of working for his own replacement. Another crisis in North Carolina called him and the 11th N.C. away.[24]

For some time Maj. Gen. John G. Foster, Union commander of the Department of North Carolina, had planned a joint army–navy assault on Wilmington. Foster saw two preconditions for a successful operation against Wilmington. First, his offensive had to coincide with Union offensives in other theaters to keep Confederate reserves committed in distant areas. Second, he had to sever the Wilmington rail line to slow the movement of reinforcements from Goldsboro, Raleigh, or Weldon. Foster learned that General Burnside, the new commander of the Army of the Potomac, intended to attack Lee's army at Fredericksburg in the second week of December. Foster then signed a memorandum of understanding with the Union forces in Suffolk to launch cooperative diversionary efforts beginning on December 11. With the Confederate high command preoccupied with Fredericksburg and Blackwater, Foster felt confident that he could march into the interior of North Carolina and achieve the two prerequisites for the Wilmington operation. He planned to attack Kinston, North Carolina, crush the small Confederate force guarding the town, then proceed to Goldsboro where he would destroy the rail bridge over the Neuse River.[25]

Foster advanced northwest from New Bern to Kinston on December 11, 1862, with a force of ten thousand men. The Confederates, commanded by Brig. Gen. N. G. Evans, had only two thousand troops to oppose them. On December 13, General Evans appealed to the department commander, Maj. Gen. Gustavus Smith, for reinforcements. Luckily, Lee had just quashed Burnside's attack on Fredericksburg, and General Smith correctly perceived that the Union move on the Blackwater was only a diversion. Smith figured that Foster's advance into eastern North Carolina represented the biggest remaining threat. He telegraphed Evans that he had transferred three regiments to North Carolina from Virginia, including "one from the Blackwater" [11th N.C.].[26] The Bethel Regiment and Brig. Gen. Beverly Robertson's dismounted cavalry crammed aboard railcars in Franklin on December 14 to begin the long train ride to Kinston.

Foster did not wait; he struck the Confederate defensive positions along Southwest Creek, a southern tributary of the Neuse River. After a vigorous fight, Foster's troops broke through the defense, assaulted across the Neuse River bridge, and captured Kinston on the north side. Evans's Confederates suffered heavily in the action, losing four hundred men to Foster's close pursuit. Evans fell back to Falling Creek west of the town to prepare a new defensive position and wait for help. In the predawn hours of December 15, the trainload of reinforcements from Virginia pulled into Camp Campbell, a few miles west of Kinston. The president of the railroad stopped the train short of Kinston to warn General Robertson of the town's capture. "It was not thought advisable that the train should proceed further," Leventhorpe recalled. "By General Robertson's invitation, I accompanied him 3 or 4 miles further on the tender to find General Evans." They found him just outside Kinston. General Evans briefed Robertson and Leventhorpe on the extent of the disaster and the latest intelligence of Foster's movements.[27] The Confederate officers worried that Foster would exploit his success the next day and penetrate far into eastern North Carolina.

Instead of expanding his control over more territory, the Union general looked for a way to get past the Confederates and advance on Goldsboro. Foster did not care to occupy Kinston nor destroy Evans; he wanted to demolish the railroad bridge over the Neuse River. Foster noticed that the Confederates had reinforced and fortified a naturally strong position along Falling Creek north of the Neuse River. He decided to switch his advance to the south side of the river vacated by the defenders. "The next morning, the 15th, I recrossed the river and took the river road for Goldsborough." The Confederates alertly detected Foster's movement on the opposite side of the Neuse, but Evans misread Foster's intent. Evans set his defense to prevent Foster from advancing north of the river. "Hearing early next morning that the enemy had recrossed the river and was advancing on White Hall [Seven Springs] in my rear, I immediately dispatched one regiment (the Eleventh North Carolina Troops, Col. Leventhorpe) and 600 dismounted cavalry, the whole under the command of Brig. Gen. B. H. Robertson, to proceed in haste and dispute his crossing at White Hall."[28]

Leventhorpe returned on the tender and formed the regiment to march directly for White Hall. After enduring a twenty-hour train ride the men had to move quickly to prevent a possible Union crossing over the White Hall bridge, only eighteen miles downriver from Goldsboro. The 11th N.C. moved briskly over the coastal plain and won the race to the bridge by nightfall. They had hardly started preparing it for demolition before the 3d New York Cavalry approached through the darkness. Pvt. John C. Warlick of I Company remembered, "We beat the enemy to the bridge spanning the stream, and barely had time to knock the barrels of rosin to pieces and apply the torch when we could see the Yanks coming on the opposite bank." The disappointed Union troopers scouted the White Hall site and saw something suspicious along the north bank. They set fire to a turpentine warehouse in White Hall "to cast a heavy reflection of light on the enemy." The glow from the flames illuminated the night sky for miles around White Hall. Looking into the glare, the Union cavalry discovered the incomplete hull of the CSS *Neuse* sitting on stocks and immediately tried to destroy it. A few brave troopers stripped and dove into the river to reach the gunboat, but C and I company riflemen drove them off with a shower of lead. The Union cavalry then brought up their artillery and poured solid shot into the *Neuse* as the Tar Heel infantrymen watched helplessly. The shelling turned the unfinished gunboat into a wreck. The evening fight lasted about two hours, while the blaze shed enough light to sight targets.[29]

The Confederates made plans during the night to defend the crossing site. Leventhorpe posted B and H companies along the river as pickets early on December 16. The riflemen from Burke and Mecklenburg counties expected an assault at first light and were pleasantly surprised when the enemy did not attack. Instead, the Union cavalry continued its advance toward Goldsboro south of the river. The Bethel pickets spotted the horsemen as they tried to bypass White Hall on the river road and opened fire. The Union horse artillery returned fire, until Foster's main body arrived. The Union cavalry turned over the fight to the main body and then proceeded on its original mission. Coming upon an action already in progress, Foster decided to use the unexpected engagement to his advantage. "The column having arrived at White Hall and finding the bridge burned and the enemy in some force, with infantry and artillery on the other side, and this being the direct road to Goldsborough, I determined to make a strong feint, as if to rebuild and cross. The Ninth New Jersey and Colonel Amory's brigade were sent forward and posted on the bank of the river to engage the enemy. I then ordered up several batteries and posted them on a hill overlooking the enemy's intrenchments."[30]

On the north bank of the river, Robertson moved the newly arrived 31st N.C. forward to reinforce B and H companies at the bridge site. "I then posted the artillery as well as the nature of the ground would admit . . . Owing to a range of hills on the White Hall [south] side the enemy had the advantage of position." The Bethel Regiment remained in reserve behind the 31st N.C. The Union artillery batteries and infantry brigade easily outgunned the Confederates, who had only two artillery pieces, and pounded the helpless Confederate infantry. One incident stuck in Pvt. John C. Warlick's memory: "While lying in a low depression some few hundred yards from the river bank, eighteen pieces of artillery were turned on us. A bombshell bounced over and landed just in the rear of my company, but it had no sooner landed than Sergt. William Jetton seized it and threw it into a pond of water just in our rear."[31]

Foster's feint at White Hall began to indicate the possibility of a breakthrough. The violent Union fire proved to be too much for the 31st N.C. "The fire of the guns was very effectual, driving the [31st N.C.] out of the works they occupied." General Robertson described the crisis on the Confederate side: "The cannonading from the enemy's batteries became so terrific that the Thirty-First Regiment withdrew from their position without instructions but in good order." The premature withdrawal left a hole in the Confederate defense that Robertson desperately tried to plug. "I immediately ordered Colonel Leventhorpe forward. The alacrity with which the order was obeyed by his men gave ample proof of their gallant bearing."[32]

The regiment withstood the savage Union fire from "point-blank range," as Leventhorpe quickly shoved his men forward into the action. "I took my position, & sheltering my men behind the logs with which the swamp was strewed, ordered them to fire at will. The Union troops fired by regiments & in volleys. Both the artillery and infantry overshot us, whilst the enemy's men exposed in line on the high banks, fared very badly." Colonel Amory's Union Brigade attempted to force a crossing under the protective fire of the artillery, but each time they formed into a line of battle, the Tar Heel riflemen picked them off. Robertson watched with admiration as the 11th N.C. held Foster's force at bay. "Three times did they drive the Yankee cannoneers from their guns and as often prevent their infantry regiments from forming line in their front. In spite of the four hostile regiments whose standards waved from the opposite bank did these brave men continue to hold their ground." Foster finally pulled Amory's Brigade back from the exposed river bank, as the 11th N.C. was getting the better of them. Foster advanced his artillery batteries to blast the Bethel Regiment from the river bank, but the logs still protected the Confederates.[33]

Sgt. Lewis Warlick expressed his appreciation for the cover of the fallen trees. "The only thing that saved us from all being killed was the heaps of logs on the river bank. . . . I was behind a big stump on my knees looking over and a cannon ball went into the root of it, which made the dirt and chips fly like everything and which made me get low." Pvt. Walter Duckworth was not so lucky; a rifle shot hit him in the head. Duckworth slumped over onto Pvt. Pinckney Warlick's leg and bled all over his pants. Pink Warlick (Lewis Warlick's brother) was so busy firing that he failed to notice the dead man leaning against him until the fighting subsided.[34] Despite the mounting casualties and intense fire, the Bethel Regiment held fast.

The Union artillery may not have broken the spirit of the 11th N.C., but they did succeed in shooting the two Confederate guns to pieces, giving the Union gunners a sense of accomplishment. Foster watched the battle from the southern bank and abandoned any thought of crossing at White Hall. "The enemy still maintained their admirable position with sharpshooters, but deeming my object accomplished I moved my command forward toward Goldsborough." Foster's feint at White Hall detained his command for most of a day and cost him the opportunity to reach Goldsboro on December 16. He moved on, content with having silenced a troublesome Confederate artillery section. During the battle, the Bethel Regiment's rifle fire had riddled Foster's troops, causing eighty-one casualties, eighteen of those among the artillery batteries. Despite the Union's fire superiority, the Confederates lost fewer men, ten killed and forty-two wounded. The regiment suffered twenty-seven casualties; seven of those were killed in action, including Elam Bristol of B Company. The cover provided by the logs and the skyline position of the Union regiments gave the Confederates an important tactical advantage, which Leventhorpe had observed. "The disproportion in loss was entirely owing to the difference in position." The 11th N.C. had passed through its first major combat test. Their timely commitment stopped the break in the Confederate defense at the critical moment of the engagement. William

Martin summed up the performance at White Hall: "Here the regiment had its first real baptism of fire . . . it was pounded for several hours at short range by a terrific storm of grape and canister as well as musketry, but it never flinched." General Robertson went out of his way to compliment them. "The conduct of this regiment reflects the greatest credit upon its accomplished and dauntless commander."[35]

The next day, December 17, Foster's expedition reached the Neuse River railroad bridge near Goldsboro. After a sharp encounter, Foster pushed a Confederate brigade under General Clingman to the north bank and destroyed the railroad bridge. The 11th N.C. marched to Goldsboro to help defend the city but did not participate in the action. Once he destroyed the bridge, Foster made no attempt to occupy any territory he had overrun. He simply marched back to New Bern. The Confederate commanders sighed with relief to see the Union army withdraw.

Gustavus Smith, the Confederate department commander, claimed that Foster's troops had been "driven back from their position" and complained "that this grand army of invasion did not remain in the interior long enough for us to get at them." He downplayed Foster's achievements while acknowledging the loss of the Neuse River bridges. "At present we are subjected to the temporary inconvenience of transshipment across the county bridge." Foster countered by claiming that his operation had been a great success and had achieved his objectives. He did satisfy the prerequisite for his Wilmington mission, but he had to cancel the follow-up operation, nonetheless. Burnside's failure at Fredericksburg dashed Foster's hopes for a joint army-navy attack against Wilmington, and Confederate reinforcements made a march to Wilmington impractical. Ultimately, General Smith's assessment of the outcome came closer to the truth. Foster's 591 casualties was a heavy price to pay for the slight benefit of one burned railroad bridge.[36]

Nevertheless, Foster's army had marched with impunity across eastern North Carolina, smashed local defenses, and forced the Confederates to pull reinforcements all the way from Virginia. Luckily, the Union high command did not learn the strategic lesson of this little-known campaign. The Confederacy depended on North Carolina for its survival but could not allocate the resources to defend its wide coastal plain. Even a modest Union incursion in this sensitive region would compel them to draw units from other theaters. Simultaneous pressure in North Carolina and Virginia could have forced the Confederacy into a serious strategic dilemma.

Siege of Washington, N.C.

Winter—Spring 1862–1863, Eastern North Carolina

The 11th N.C. helped reoccupy Kinston on December 22, 1862, after Foster retired to New Bern. The regiment did not remain long; the Confederates still needed them to defend the vital Weldon Railroad. That night, the department commander, Gustavus Smith, ordered the 11th N.C. and Brig. Gen. J. Johnston Pettigrew's Brigade to move by train to Weldon. The troops loaded onto the cars for another long, tiring trip. They had barely begun when they found their way blocked by an empty train. Collett Leventhorpe jumped off, ran forward to the locomotive, and ordered the empty train to precede them up the line to a turnout at Goldsboro where it could get out of the way. Before the empty train reached the turnout, it collided with another empty train that was backing down the line to Kinston without a warning light. The train carrying the regiment came roaring up the line within a couple of minutes. "Crash went our engine into her [the first empty train] lifting the rear car on top of the engine carrying away the smoke stack and running back nearly as far as the tender before we stopped." Three trains lay crumpled together on the tracks, while the Bethel troops tried to untangle the mess in the dark. Luckily, the accident did not cause any injuries, but the troops had to spend the night rolling the smashed cars off the rails. Another locomotive attached to the troop cars the next day and pulled the regiment to Camp Robinson in Weldon, North Carolina.[37]

Upon arrival, the regiment was added to Pettigrew's Brigade, which included the 26th, 44th, 47th, and 52d N.C. regiments. The Bethel's veterans greeted the new assignment with pride and pleasure. The officers and men had petitioned Leventhorpe a month earlier to "endeavor to procure admission into General Pettigrew's Brigade." The regiment hoped that an assignment to a brigade would help get them into the main theater of action. The men asked specifically for Pettigrew because he was a North Carolina native and had already won acclaim as a bold fighter. Johnston Pettigrew had graduated from the University of North Carolina with the highest marks for scholarship in the school's history. "By every account, he is one of the most brilliant men of the day," Leventhorpe remarked to his wife. He had the qualities of a superior military leader, combining an active mind with exemplary courage. Pettigrew, the scion of a wealthy plantation family and a lawyer by profession, wholeheartedly embraced the Confederacy and threw himself into the profession of arms. He felt great sympathy with the code of chivalry, captivated by its romantic ideal, and he went on to prove his worth in battle. Pettigrew was critically wounded and captured during the Peninsular Campaign. He recovered from his wounds and, subsequently, returned to the South after a prisoner exchange. Pettigrew rejoined the Confederate army but he vowed never again to be taken prisoner, a pledge that later contributed to his death.[38]

Pettigrew's Brigade had responsibility for defending the entire length of the Weldon Railroad from Wilmington to Petersburg. This railroad served as the lifeline for the Army of Northern Virginia. The presence of Union forces along the coast, backed by navy gunboats, threatened this vital supply link for much of its length. The brigade commander strung out his regiments at strategic spots to respond quickly to any threat. The 11th N.C. encamped at Weldon to cover the railroad where it crossed the Roanoke River. Cold winter weather had settled over the region when the regiment arrived without their tents. The men had to build their own crude shelters to protect themselves from the elements. Lewis Warlick tried to make the best of the modest conditions. "We have little huts made of split logs and dirt — something like a potato house . . . A man don't know what he can stand till he trys [sic] it." A smallpox outbreak in Weldon kept the men in camp in early January. After the horrible losses to disease in Wilmington, Leventhorpe acted quickly to safeguard against the pestilence by ordering vaccinations for everyone. The inoculations helped ward off the epidemic, but a few soldiers suffered from the crude procedure. Sgt. William Parker got an infection after his vaccination because the surgeon cut his arm during the treatment. Nevertheless, Parker took steps to protect his wife and family, as the disease had already spread to Bertie County. "I send you a scab I took off a man's arm. Take a lancet or knife and make the hole in the arm and put a piece of the scab in and pinch it up."[39]

As soon as the troops settled in at Weldon, the regimental commander resumed the daily routine of training. The 11th N.C. had already gained renown for its prowess at close order drill. One Confederate army inspector declared, "There is no doubt, this is the best drilled regiment in the service . . . Yesterday, I drilled them & they moved like regulars. Their manual of arms is the admiration of every one who sees it . . . They are a brave, steady sort of boys & always cheerful." A warm mutual respect had grown between the commander and men. "The Colonel was justly proud of his splendid command, & his men almost adored him." Morale remained high at Weldon. The regiment's success at White Hall gave them confidence and deaths by disease slackened.[40]

As the new year arrived, storm clouds gathered once more over North Carolina. The Union navy and General Foster still planned a joint attack against Wilmington. Before Foster would commit his army to the operation, he insisted that the navy force its way up the Cape Fear River. The navy ordered the USS *Monitor* and two other shallow draft ironclads to cross the western bar under the river's mouth, sail upstream, and shell Fort Fisher from the rear. This ambitious operation foundered when the *Monitor* sank in a gale off Cape Hatteras on December 31. Without the *Monitor,* the navy did not have sufficient ironclads capable of crossing the river's bar to make the assault. The War Department lost interest in Wilmington and transferred a large contingent of troops to South Carolina.[41]

By the time Foster abandoned the planned operation, Confederate intelligence deduced that the Union planned to attack Wilmington. The Confederacy reinforced North Carolina and, for the first time, enjoyed a favorable balance of strength against the Union. The Bethel Regiment received orders to move on January 18. "I received orders today for myself & Burgwyn's Regiment [26th N.C.] and Cumming's Battery to proceed, as soon as possible, to Magnolia." Leventhorpe explained to his wife, "Magnolia is, I think, half way between Goldsboro and Wilmington. It is a very likely point of attack, & within supporting distance of both Goldsboro and Wilmington. We are thus likely to operate against a force directed to either of these points." Two days later, Leventhorpe wrote from Magnolia, "I reached this point at about 3½ o' clock this morning . . . I cannot say what the Yankees are doing. They were advancing in force — supposed for this point. I doubt it. The last news is they have retired toward Swansboro." Unknown to the colonel, the crisis had already passed. Later Leventhorpe correctly guessed the reason. "Their plans were evidently disconcerted by the storms sinking the *Monitor,* a most clearly providential event." He went on to give an indication of the confidence and pride he had in his men and, perhaps, a touch of regret that they did not get a chance to prove their mettle. "My Regiment is in beautiful drill & fine spirits, & if they are called on, they will make their mark once more. No regiment in the whole war has behaved with greater gallantry in action in almost fabulous odds, than mine."[42]

The Bethel Regiment stayed with Pettigrew's Brigade at Magnolia until mid-February, still eagerly awaiting action. The troops had to content themselves by entertaining the local citizens at dress parade each evening and attending worship services at the local Baptist church. Lewis Warlick admitted, "Our regiment made a good turn out, if for nothing else to see the ladies." Warlick liked to tease his sweetheart with stories about young ladies he met, apparently with the idea of arousing some jealousy. However, he was not impressed with the appearance of the available females. He confided to his girl that the local ladies were "some very hard looking ones." The troops did not look that good, either. They had to burn dead pine trees for their campfires and, before long, tar soot covered their faces, hands, and uniforms. "We are the worst set of smoked men, or rather a set of the worst smoked men I ever saw." The month spent at Magnolia did have one social highlight. Lt. Col. William J. Martin married a young lady from Wilmington on February 9 and brought her up to the camp the next day. The regiment threw a gala ball to honor the couple. While the regimental band played waltzes and lively polkas, the gallant soldiers and local ladies danced until four the next morning. William Parker laughed at the revelers' appearance after he returned from guard duty. "They looked worse than our gard [sic] did. I think they must be very stiff for they worked pretty hard."[43]

Pettigrew dispersed his command when he realized that the threat to Wilmington had waned. The 11th N.C. moved by rail and foot to

Tarboro where it could guard against Union raids. After four days of rest, it resumed movement to Greenville. Sergeant Parker complained to his wife, "I have a place to stop at once more after marching as hard as I ever have marched & my feet is sore . . . both is blistered."[44] The move to Greenville put the regiment within striking distance of the Union stronghold at Washington, North Carolina, only twenty miles down the Tar River.

A new general soon took command of the Confederate Department of North Carolina. Maj. Gen. Daniel Harvey Hill, an old friend to the Bethel veterans, visited the regiment in Greenville. To welcome their past commander, the regiment entertained the general's party and local citizens with one of their splendid reviews. The precise maneuvers impressed D. H. Hill and the spectators. The regiment looked magnificent and bespoke Leventhorpe's skill as a drillmaster. The appearance of the native Carolina general evidently triggered some resentful thoughts in Leventhorpe's mind about his own overdue promotion. He complained to his wife, "I feel very keenly the injustice done me about promotion. I am always given posts of danger, & the command of brigades but the honors are reserved for others . . . but as I am not a political hack, I am quite ignored." Regaining his composure, he finished on a more patriotic note. "At any rate, if I am spared, I shall have the satisfaction to know that I have fought for the independence of the South." Leventhorpe had a legitimate complaint about the handling of general officer promotions. Many North Carolinians, especially Governor Vance, believed that Richmond slighted the state's officers in favor of Virginians. Although North Carolina provided 20 percent of the Confederate troops, less than 6 percent of the general officer slots went to state officers. Obviously, Jefferson Davis's cabinet mistrusted the loyalty of officers coming from a state so reluctant to join the Confederacy and so sympathetic to Whig politics. The climate between Raleigh and Richmond had turned decidedly colder after the election of Vance's anti-Richmond party. Being a foreigner and a North Carolinian, Collett Leventhorpe had poor prospects for promotion.[45]

Leventhorpe did not ruminate for long because Harvey Hill soon put his force in motion. Hill displayed a more aggressive spirit than previous department commanders. He realized that his limited force could not possibly protect the wide coastal plain of eastern North Carolina from Union incursions, as long as the Union navy could use the sounds and rivers to penetrate inland. He adopted a bold strategy to attack the Union forces and pin them back into their coastal strongholds. With the approach of spring, Hill proposed an offensive in eastern North Carolina. Robert E. Lee had consistently argued against offensive operations in North Carolina because the Union army could easily fall back on the support of the navy's gunboats.[46] However, Hill and Lt. Gen. James Longstreet, the commander of the southern Virginia and North Carolina department, convinced Lee to approve a limited offensive to augment a foraging expedition.

The coastal counties of the state still produced much of the provisions consumed by the Confederate army, even while the Union held key towns along the coast. Longstreet wanted to draw off as much subsistence as possible from this area to supply Lee's army for the coming spring campaign and to minimize the Union army's forage. Hill and Longstreet concocted a plan to divert attention away from Virginia and cover the Confederate supply trains venturing into the coastal counties. Hill directed Pettigrew to attack New Bern and reduce the Union fortress with an artillery bombardment. Pettigrew detached the 11th N.C. to guard the town of Greenville, while the rest of the brigade moved out on March 9. Unfortunately, Pettigrew's expedition failed owing to problems with their artillery. Shortly after Pettigrew departed for New Bern, D. H. Hill organized another expedition against Plymouth under the command of Brig. Gen. R. S. Garnett, a Virginian. Hill attached the 11th N.C. to Garnett's Brigade, partly because Collett Leventhorpe knew the terrain. Randolph Abbott Shotwell, a soldier in Garnett's Brigade and a personal friend of Leventhorpe, maintained a journal of his experiences on the Plymouth expedition. His journal entries provide entertaining insights about the campaign in the North Carolina low country.

"March 15th . . . We are off! Destined, rumor says to Plymouth . . . Our march of 18 miles today has been the wateryest I ever knew, the mud and slush being rarely shallow enough for us to see our own shoes! Our route lay through a vast wilderness — called the 'Great Swamp Country' (or if it isn't called thus it ought to be) which is one interminable stretch of low level land, thickly overgrown with tall pines, thro' which the narrow road has been chopped out." "March 16th — Worse, worser, worsest! Rain still falling, water still rising; land still

sinking!" While on the march, Shotwell overheard an amusing question from a bewildered resident. "One old granny after a long astonished look at the column of men, innocently inquired: 'Does you-uns
allus go in such droves as this yere?'" Shotwell did make an interest-
ing observation about the 11th N.C., as the Virginia troops followed
the Tar Heels. "I notice there is quite a difference in the discipline of
the North Carolinians and our own men. They march regularly
through the deepest mud-holes, while we dodge round for rods seek-
ing to escape the cold-water bath. Of course, they are right, and we
are not, for who knows at what moment we may be ambushed and
assailed while straggling for miles?"[47]

Garnett's force bottled up the Union troops inside the town of Plymouth, while Confederate wagon trains scoured the countryside for
forage. According to William Parker, the quartermasters gathered one
hundred thousand pounds of bacon and fifteen "buffaloes" within a
week's time. "We could of gotten more but . . . the roads was in a
dreadful condition." Once they filled the wagons, the soldiers headed
back to Greenville. None too soon for Shotwell! "March 21st — Boo-
oo-ooh — we are half frozen . . . We suffer beyond description. Our
clothes are soaking wet and this chill wind seems to cut off skin! Our
wagons are coming in — loaded with provisions, but how in the world
shall we retreat over the canal-like roads from here to Greenville?"
Somehow they managed to bring in the large haul of victuals through
the swampy terrain.[48]

The splendid harvest of the Plymouth expedition encouraged Hill
to continue the offensive after Pettigrew's expedition returned. On
April 1, 1863, Hill attacked the Union stronghold at Washington,
North Carolina, under the direct command of General Foster. The
Confederates drove off the Union gunboats, but they lacked the
strength to crush Foster's fortified position because a serious shortage
of artillery ammunition prevented their reducing Washington by fire.
Hill deployed Garnett's, Daniel's, and Pettigrew's brigades to invest
the town. Pettigrew defended the south side of the Pamlico River,
including the roads leading to New Bern. The 11th and 26th N.C.
regiments, under Leventhorpe's control, blocked the approaches to
the besieged town along the south shore of the Pamlico. His sector
included Hill's Point, a promontory along the south shore where the
Confederates placed an artillery battery to interdict shipping on the

river. The battery only had one twelve-pound Whitworth and one ten-pound Parrot gun, not much to guard the broad Pamlico River. To protect Hill's Point against a land approach, Leventhorpe positioned the 11th N.C. at Blount's Creek. The creek drained a large swamp into the south side of the Pamlico River, providing a natural obstacle on the only stretch of dry ground between the swamp and the river. Leventhorpe described the situation, "I have the command of the lowest point [downriver], with two regiments & 8 pieces of artillery. All the fighting on this [south] side will most probably fall on me, as seven transports & gunboats have already tried to force a passage by the Fort [Hill's Point], which is under my charge . . . I am ordered to keep Hill's Point to the last extremity. It entirely commands the Pamlico River, probably 6 miles below Washington. There must be a strong attempt to pass or take the Fort, and relieve the beleaguered town."[49]

Even as Leventhorpe composed that letter, Brig. Gen. Francis Spinola of the Union army decided to steam past Hill's Point on the night of April 4–5, using the gunboats and transports he had assembled downriver. Just as he set sail, Brig. Gen. Henry Prince, his immediate superior, arrived from New Bern and canceled his daring plan. General Prince's interference thoroughly disgusted Spinola. "I had made all the above arrangements under the belief that the favorable moment to re-enforce the garrison had arrived . . . All the officers and men of my brigade were both willing and anxious to incur any risk or to encounter any danger necessary to relieve the beleaguered city." After returning to New Bern, Spinola prepared to lead a land expedition to relieve the besieged town. General Foster, from his command post in Washington, directed his subordinates in New Bern to attack the Confederates at once. Spinola still fumed over his aborted waterborne expedition when he called on General Prince. The conversation hardly improved his spirits. "I found General Prince in a state of mind denoting that he was very much exercised in regard to the propriety of making the contemplated march, and he freely expressed his opinion to me that the expedition could not succeed, that it must be a very great failure, for he did not believe that any of those who accompanied it would return, as we would all be captured, and that it was like making the rebels a present of all the artillery." Nevertheless, Foster's orders left Prince and Spinola no latitude; Spinola set out with three brigades on April 8.[50]

Spinola's sense of daring vanished as he commanded a landward expedition, a course of action he personally rejected. The direct avenue to Washington passed over Little Swift Creek and the Swift Creek Road to Washington, but information about Confederate dispositions convinced him to try a different route. On the night of April 8, Spinola wrote his estimate of the Confederate forces opposing him. "From all the information I have received it establishes the strength of the enemy not less than 20,000, under Hill, Pettigrew, and Garnett . . . It appears to me now that the only possible successful way to relieve the garrison is to take the battery at Hill's Point, and in that way raise the blockade . . . It is my intention to start from here in the morning for Blount's Creek, and engage the enemy there, and drive them, if possible, beyond the battery on Hill's Point with a view of taking it." Whether out of natural inclination or spite, Spinola chose the same avenue that he intended to follow five days earlier, only this time he was confined to land. Spinola's pessimistic report revealed his downcast fighting spirit. "Should I not be successful, I shall retreat to Fort Anderson, as I am satisfied it is utterly impossible to march on Washington by the Swift Creek route without endangering my entire command." Spinola, like other Union generals, used wildly exaggerated estimates of Confederate strength to justify his lack of aggressiveness.[51]

Spinola's indirect route fulfilled Leventhorpe's prediction. From New Bern, the Union force would have to cross the peninsula to reach the Pamlico River, then turn west and advance up the south bank. This route hit a choke point at Blount's Creek where the 11th N.C. waited. The Confederates had selected the defensive position wisely. The men of the Bethel Regiment dug entrenchments on the west side of the creek covering the two bridges over the stream. A nearby swamp limited the exposure of the regiment to a narrow front directly over a causeway. "I had fortified the inner position & made it tremendously strong," Leventhorpe boasted. "My regiment was intrenched so as to command the road at every point." He deployed skirmishers on the east side of the creek under Major Ross to provide early warning and confuse the attackers.[52]

Spinola's column reached Blount's Creek on the afternoon of April 9. Egbert Ross with two hundred sharpshooters waited to ambush the lead element. "They kept their fire till the enemy was close, & then poured in several vollies." The Union soldiers "were completely demoralized" by the sudden fire and "not a gun was fired by the Yankees in answer." Having done their job most effectively, Ross led the skirmishers back across the creek over one of the bridges to occupy part of the main defensive position. Spinola's column recovered from the surprise volley but ran into problems as it tried to mass against the Bethel Regiment. "Owing to the condition of the ground it was impossible to develop a large force against the enemy," Spinola complained. The Union commander tried to soften up the 11th N.C. with an artillery bombardment. Once again, the regiment's men held their ground under the pounding of heavy guns. The well-prepared position kept the casualties to a minimum. Fifty-eight-year-old Pvt. Patrick Black was one of the few men wounded by the Union's fire. He earned the dubious distinction of being the oldest casualty the regiment suffered during the war. For nearly two hours, the Union and Confederate guns blazed away at each other but inflicted little damage. Spinola confessed, "We were unable to drive them from their position, as our infantry and artillery fire were without much effect upon them, owing to the nature of their earthworks and the position of our guns. It was equally impossible to enfilade their works or to cross or ford the creek at any other point."[53]

The clever defense of swampy ground thwarted Spinola's advance. The Bethel Regiment's infantry, plus their supporting artillery, covered the main approach and eagerly waited for the enemy to storm the causeway. Spinola could not maneuver around the position because of the swamps, nor could he drive the defenders off with artillery fire. Yet, he could not give up his advance without making some effort to break through. Finally, he ordered one hapless company to charge across the causeway and seize the bridges. Thankfully, a Union staff officer challenged the decision to sacrifice the company, and Spinola canceled the face-saving assault.[54]

Spinola convinced himself that his relief expedition was doomed, so he abandoned the advance and withdrew. He lamely justified his premature withdrawal. "I shall leave this place for New Berne to-morrow morning, feeling conscious that I have done all that was in my power to comply with the requests of General Foster." Collett Leventhorpe expressed a harsh judgment of Spinola's command in a letter to his wife. "They disgracefully retreated . . . the cowardly loons felled trees on the road & withdrew in the night, fully believing that

D. H. Hill, of whom they have a great horror, was after them." Characteristically, Leventhorpe closed his letter on a reverent note, "I devoutly praise God for our preservation & for our victory."[55]

Foster was disgusted with the feeble efforts to relieve Washington, when he learned of Spinola's retreat. He decided to return to New Bern to undertake personally the relief effort. The steamer *Escort* had just slipped past the guns at Hill's Point and reinforced the garrison with men and supplies. Foster hopped aboard the *Escort* and traveled downriver on the night of April 13. The *Escort*'s passage down the Pamlico River touched off a blazing artillery duel across the dark waters. The Confederate guns at Hill's Point and Rodman's Point scored forty hits on the *Escort* but failed to stop the ship.[56] Back in New Bern, the Union commander quickly organized another relief operation and advanced to the Pamlico River, by way of Blount's Creek. Foster's decision to follow Spinola's route suggests that he felt Spinola could have succeeded if he had attacked with more vigor. As it turned out, Foster did not have to fight the Confederates to reach Washington.

Harvey Hill lifted the siege of Washington on April 15 and withdrew his forces. The Confederate foraging expedition into the coastal counties had completed its mission and they no longer needed the siege to divert the Union forces from the supply trains. In all probability, Hill realized that Foster was too strongly entrenched in Washington and a continuation of the siege would produce no tangible gain. Hill's hope of starving the garrison into submission faded when Union supply ships sailed past Hill's Point and delivered provisions to the besieged town. Hill had to answer General Longstreet's call to release the troops under his command. Longstreet wanted to scale back the action in North Carolina because the spring campaign in Virginia was about to begin. Hill's departure avoided a further clash with the Union relieving columns and gave Foster an undisturbed advance into Washington.

The abrupt end of the siege left the entire command feeling that it had been cheated out of a victory. "We were all disappointed at leaving Washington in the hands of the enemy." The North Carolina press sang a chorus of complaints about the failure to recapture Washington and placed the blame on Hill. D. H. Hill, himself, felt frustrated by the outcome. That became apparent when he discovered that someone had left a spiked cannon back at Washington. He reacted furiously to the news and ordered Pettigrew's and Daniel's brigades to remain under the fire of Union gunboats while a team retrieved the lost gun. Pettigrew could not bear to see his men needlessly exposed to enemy fire and objected. Hill responded with a chilling rebuke. "General Pettigrew, if you do not like to stay under fire, turn your command [over] to Colonel Leventhorpe." Pettigrew indignantly turned and walked away without saying a word. Henry K. Burgwyn, the youthful commander of the 26th N.C., summed up D. H. Hill's shortcomings. "He [Hill] set out without any definite plan. He should either have made up his mind to storm the place at once, or he should have prepared to undertake a regular siege . . . It is an absolute fact that we were out of ammunition the very first day of the siege. Our guns & ammunition came in by dribblets . . . It seemed to me that Gen. Hill relied upon circumstances & events to suggest ideas & plans. I think he has lost the confidence of the people entirely, & to a very great extent of the army."[57]

Although the campaign fell short of a triumph, Hill issued a congratulatory letter to his men. "The Department Commander returns his heartfelt thanks to the troops, under his command, for their courage in battle, patient endurance . . . vigilance on duty and uniform good behavior." Hill, famous for his arrogant opinions, then lauded the soldiers while he lambasted those civilians who hired substitutes to serve in their stead. "How much better is it thus to deserve the thanks of the country by your courage and patience than to skulk at home as the cowardly exempts do. Some of the poor dogs have hired substitutes as though money could pay the service every man owes his country . . . When our independence is won, the most trifling soldier in the ranks, will be more respected as he is more respectable, than an army of these skulking exempts."[58]

Harvey Hill's diatribe against substitutes and exempts ran counter to the sentiments of many of the state's citizens. North Carolinians resented the Confederacy's conscription act as an encroachment on individual liberties. Governor Vance understood this and proclaimed the most liberal exemption policy among all southern states. The Bethel soldiers sided more with D. H. Hill; they had little sympathy with able-bodied men who shirked their duties. Lewis Warlick bristled when his girlfriend suggested that he hire a substitute to fight in his place.

"You say I ought to go home and hire a substitute . . . it shall never be thrown up to my relations in future years that . . . [I] was too cowardly, afraid of the Yankees etc. but hired a substitute to fight in my stead. Never, never shall it be said of me or my descendants; death before dishonor."[59]

D. H. Hill's strident polemics may have struck a sympathetic note among the volunteers, but William Parker seemed to have been motivated more by thoughts of home. The recent campaign had taken him within fifteen miles of his plantation. His wife and children remained within easy marching distance of the Union raiding parties from Washington and Plymouth. "I know your anxiety and I would be glad, glad to relieve you of all but my arm is too short. But I hope it is long enough to help some and as long as I have strength enough to raise it I shall strike in defense of my home and my country and all who do not is not worthy of a home in this beautiful land of ours. All I can do is to trust in God and fight on."[60]

Pettigrew's Brigade had to resume defensive duties after the siege, so the general dispersed his regiments to cover Greenville and Kinston. The Confederates reacted to a series of raids by Foster, who seemed to be embarking on a campaign of retribution for the recent Confederate offensive. The Union threat caused a bewildering series of movements for the regiment that they performed under very unpleasant conditions. By this time, the soldiers had learned how to travel light and carried only their blankets, canteens, haversacks, cartridge cases, and rifles. The light load, much reduced from the first march to Bethel in 1861, helped ease the burden but left the men exposed to the cold weather that chilled eastern North Carolina. Without a change of clothes and shelter, the men suffered through an uncomfortable night when a light dusting of snow swept over the area on April 20. Parker complained about the miserable circumstances to his wife, "We have not slept in a tent but one night since the 9th of March." Sergeant Warlick conveyed the weariness he felt in a letter to his sweetheart. "We came to this place [Hookerton] last Sunday [April 18] from Washington via Greenville in two days and you may guess that we were somewhat fatigued; remained here until Tuesday morning when we got marching orders, fell in and marched back the road 9 miles towards Greenville, piched [sic] camp and the next morning received marching orders for Kinston to report there that night but to our gratification the orders were countermanded when we reached here." The regiment spent a week at Hookerton, North Carolina, living on cornbread and shivering in the cold.[61]

Shortly thereafter, Union moves caused the regiment to resume its back and forth marching across the eastern counties. The 11th N.C. marched to Kinston on May 1, but the Union troops withdrew before contact could be made. While trudging back to Hookerton, Leventhorpe received new orders. The Bethel Regiment had to return to Kinston and board a train bound for Virginia. At last, the Bethel Regiment was on its way to the main theater of action.

3

For Glory or for Shame

GENERAL LEE'S ARMY

May–June 1863, Northern Virginia

*A*new campaign in Virginia caused the Confederate high command once again to call up reinforcements from North Carolina. Maj. Gen. Joseph Hooker, commander of the Army of the Potomac, launched an offensive against Lee's Army of Northern Virginia. Hooker attacked Lee at Chancellorsville while he sent a powerful cavalry force under Brig. Gen. George Stoneman toward Richmond. Lee could not afford to detach his cavalry to protect the capital, so the War Department ordered Pettigrew's and Daniel's brigades to defend Richmond. The regiment's tired troops climbed aboard rail cars in Kinston for the long ride on Friday evening, May 1. The train raced north on the Weldon line to reach the city before Stoneman. They had reached Halifax, North Carolina, when the locomotive crashed into the rear of the train carrying the 26th N.C. (the regiment never had much luck with trains). Besides killing two men and injuring several others from the 26th N.C., the crash delayed the move to Richmond. "We lay over at Halifax till late Saturday evening [May 2] and a train came down from Petersburg." The regiment boarded the new train, but it crawled from Halifax to Petersburg because of an overly cautious crew. They reached Petersburg Sunday morning and then disembarked to wait for a locomotive to take them on to Richmond. Meanwhile, a crisis developed in the capital; not a single Confederate unit remained to fend off Stoneman's troopers. Another locomotive finally arrived and hauled the 11th N.C. north. The regiment arrived at the Richmond depot by 3:30 P.M. on May 3 and then marched to the fairgrounds. It was the first unit to relieve the city.[1]

Cpl. Jacob Bartlett of K Company remembered their greeting. "As the 11th Regiment marched through Richmond the old citizens gathered on the sidewalks and asked whose brigade it was. The answer was 'It ain't anybody's brigade its the 11th North Carolina Regiment.' The old gentlemen would sigh and say 'Its a fine regiment, but boys you'll never all get back.'" The troops settled down at the fairgrounds that evening. Before they had a chance to sleep, they saw a man madly pumping a handcar down the rail line, coming to warn them of an advancing Union cavalry force. The soldiers rushed forward to occupy nearby breastworks and remained alert until morning. Strangely, Stoneman did not appear. Sgt. William Parker reported, "We got orders to go to intercept the yanks but did not get more than a mile before we got orders to come back. There has been a dispatch rec'd here that Lee has driven all the yankees across the Rappahannock and taken a good many prisoners." Lee had smashed the Union army at Chancellorsville with a brilliant counterattack, and the threat to Richmond faded. On May 5, Pettigrew's Brigade moved north to clear Stoneman's cavalry away from Hanover Junction, an important rail intersection near a crossing over the North Anna River. The brigade ran into the horsemen and then ran them off after a sharp engagement. "Our men had a brush with them and took thirty prisoners and killed and wounded fourteen. We lost one man." Once Pettigrew reached Hanover Junction, he deployed the brigade to guard several bridges and crossing sites over the North and South Anna Rivers.[2]

The regiment spent the next month on duty at Hanover Junction in comparative quiet. Lee's victory put the Union back on the defensive, although the presence of Hooker's army across the Rappahannock left the Confederates feeling uneasy. They issued instructions for the 11th N.C. to concentrate and stay on alert. "We are confined entirely to camp now as we are to be in readiness at two hours notice."

The orders did not sit well with the impatient troops who still had not seen a major battle. Capt. Frank Bird complained to his sister, "My life in camp is very dull and boring." Leventhorpe took advantage of the inactivity to go on furlough. William Parker remarked about the effect of his absence on the regiment. "The Reg.t looked like it had lost its best friend. Everything seemed to [pass off] heavily and none did their several duties with any life. But when he came back they were like a parcel of wild children. I was a mile off on picket at the time & I heard such an awful hallowing [hollering] that I could not imagine & at night the band played for half an hour. Many shouts and huzzahs. I came back [from picket duty] yesterday & found the Reg.t itself again and on dress parade." The colonel may have cut his furlough short due to an absence of William Martin, his deputy, who ended up in a hospital. In Martin's case, a sudden change in orders sent the regiment into action before he could return.[3]

Things may have seemed calm to the Bethel Regiment, but Jefferson Davis's cabinet wrestled with a weighty decision. The cabinet searched for a way to lift the siege of Vicksburg by Maj. Gen. U. S. Grant's Union army, but General Lee pushed for a conclusive action in the east where he had put together a string of remarkable victories. Lee wanted to invade the North where a military victory might lead to the capture of the national capital or force the Union to give up the fight. Either way, Lee was bidding for a military solution to the war. Still basking in the glow of Lee's latest triumph, the Confederate high command sensed that it was time to strike for final victory. Davis and his cabinet decided to ignore the pleas for help from the western theater and approved Lee's bold scheme. They were not alone in feeling that the decisive moment had arrived. Collett Leventhorpe confided his thoughts about a significant undertaking to his wife, "I somehow feel hopeful that the hour of our deliverance from so many troubles is at hand." Parker later echoed the same thoughts to his wife as the campaign got underway, "I hope this one will end the war." Optimism now fueled southern strategy.[4]

Before he could launch an invasion, Lee had to reorganize the army to replace losses and fill the leadership vacuum left by the death of "Stonewall" Jackson. Lee formed the Army of Northern Virginia into three corps under General Longstreet and two new corps commanders, Lt. Gen. Richard Ewell and Lt. Gen. Ambrose Powell Hill. A. P. Hill had been the army's most successful division commander and was the natural successor to Jackson. His brave and bold demeanor in battle earned Lee's respect. The gaunt, red-bearded West Pointer loved to attack, and that fit well with Lee's offensive tactics. Regrettably, Hill never quite mastered the duties of a high level commander. He had an unfortunate tendency toward reckless and hasty decisions that later cost the lives of several Bethel soldiers. In addition, a medical condition that stemmed from a youthful case of venereal disease would hamper his ability to lead in combat. Despite these flaws, Powell Hill would prove to be a well-schooled tactician who would lead the Tar Heels to many victories.

A. P. Hill's previous command, the huge "Light Division," had to be broken up to help create the new corps. Maj. Gen. Henry Heth would command a new division built around two brigades from the old Light Division. Heth [pronounced *Heath*] is remembered as the "unluckiest" Confederate general because misfortune kept him from the top of the Confederate officer corps. Heth may have been victimized by misfortune, but the hot-cold nature of his career may have been as much of an impediment as bad luck. He secured the bottom position in his class at West Point, then went on to an excellent career in the U.S. Army. He failed an important mission in Western Virginia early in the war but salvaged his career by serving effectively as a brigade commander. Later in the war, his best day as a division commander would be immediately followed by his worst. He performed capably in several later campaigns but was eclipsed by more energetic officers, such as John Brown Gordon and William Mahone. Robert E. Lee had a warm, personal relationship with Heth and often called him by his first name, "Harry" (the only officer Lee would address with such familiarity). Yet, Lee never quite placed complete trust in Heth's abilities. A competent, controversial leader, Harry Heth would play a large role in the regiment's future.

Heth needed two more brigades for his division. Lee asked Jefferson Davis to return two veteran brigades to the army, but Davis refused to release them. Instead, he sent Pettigrew's Brigade and a brigade of Mississippi troops commanded by his own nephew. Reluctantly, Lee agreed to take the two "untested" brigades in place of the more experienced ones he wanted. Lee's veterans viewed the newly arrived Tar Heel brigade skeptically. The victors of so many battles in Virginia tended to look contemptuously at units that had spent their time in the backwaters of North Carolina. The Tar Heels had their own reasons for skepticism; all three of their senior leaders came from Virginia. General Heth directed an inspector to check out the fresh troops before he took them into his division. The brigade staged a formal review for the inspector on June 3. The five large, well-appointed regiments put on a convincing show under the immediate direction of Collett Leventhorpe. After impressing the inspector with their drill and maneuver skills, the brigade, along with the Bethel Regiment, gained acceptance into the Army of Northern Virginia. This chain of command remained largely in effect throughout the war.[5]

Command	Commander
Army	Gen. Robert E. Lee
Corps	Lt. Gen. A. P. Hill
Division	Maj. Gen. Henry Heth
Brigade	Brig. Gen. J. Johnston Pettigrew

By this time, the new campaign began to unfold. Lee sent Ewell's Corps west to the Shenandoah Valley on June 4, 1863, while A. P. Hill's Corps guarded Fredericksburg. On June 7, Hill brought the Bethel Regiment north to cover Hamilton's Crossing east of Fredericksburg and keep a watchful eye on Hooker's troops. Powell Hill might have been distressed to learn how close the contact was between the two sides. "I have gotten low down on the river between Hamilton's Crossing and Port Royal, and nearly in front of the enemy's lines," William Parker observed. "But there is no expectations of a fight here as our pickets and the enemy exchange papers every day. I saw a yankee swim the river day before yesterday [June 9] and brought some papers with him and got some papers in return. He sat with us for some time & talked."[6]

The westward movement of Lee's army soon produced a reaction from Hooker. The Army of the Potomac pulled away from the Rappahannock on June 14 to shadow the movement of Ewell's Corps. The departure of the Union army released A. P. Hill's Corps from its mission to defend Fredericksburg, and it began concentrating for its march that same day. Parker told his wife about the move, "Orders came for the troops to move immediately and we were on the road at

10 o'clock and marched till night. We have just got in the rear of Fredericksburg." The 11th N.C. rested until 11:00 A.M. on June 15 before marching toward Chancellorsville with the rest of Heth's Division. The division started its march at 3:30 A.M. on June 16 and covered eighteen more miles on its way west. Heth's troops reached Culpeper Court House by ten the next morning after another predawn movement. At Culpeper, the troops spent the remainder of the day resting and preparing for an extended march. Heth ordered all baggage stripped to the bare essentials and the excess shipped home. That meant the soldiers could only carry a blanket, canteen, haversack, cartridge box, and a rifle. "I have to throw away my clothes," Parker wrote to his wife. "I only have one change now of underclothes and the socks you sent me. But I have two blankets and I shall have to throw one away or give it away." Like Parker, many of the troops used this day to send their last letters home as Culpeper marked the farthest extent of the Confederates' supply lines. The army could not depend on any logistical support, including mail service, once it moved beyond that point. The men would need food on the march, so word came down to cook three days' rations for each man to carry in his haversack. They put three more days of meals in the regimental wagon train. That many rations portended a long march north.[7]

When the regiment moved out the next day, the veteran troops proceeded according to the army's familiar march routine. The division typically began moving in the predawn hours to avoid the heat of late afternoon and prevent Union scouts from trailing them from their campsite. The men walked for periods of up to ten hours, resting for twenty minutes each hour. The rest stops gave the troops time to tend their feet and forage for fruit. The commander of the 26th N.C., H. K. Burgwyn, expressed the general feelings of the brigade. "The men are all in good spirits & the Whole army expects to go into Pennsylvania. We have had little or no rain which makes the roads exceedingly dusty & a hot sun makes a long march the most disagreeable thing conceivable. We lie down at night upon a single blanket & have a biscuit or two & piece of ham for each meal."[8] The long days of marching wore on the weaker soldiers. Straggling plagued the army, and the long march to Pennsylvania caused several men to fall out. Officers worked hard to keep their units together and often spent the rest periods encouraging the stragglers to catch up.

A serious problem with desertion arose on the march to Pennsylvania. Whenever units moved farther from their homes, the men became uneasy about the increased separation from their loved ones. A march into enemy territory necessarily suspended all furloughs and increased homesickness. Carrying the campaign into the North also may have given the men a sense of misgiving. The regiment had always fought to defend against the "northern invaders." A few of the troops may have become disturbed by the prospect of becoming invaders themselves. As the 11th N.C. headed north, men from the two Burke County companies slipped away at night and went home. Only twenty-five soldiers had deserted the regiment since the 1862 reorganization, but ten bolted in the two nights preceding the crossing of the Potomac.[9] Many of these deserters eventually returned to duty, but they would be sorely missed in the upcoming battles.

After Culpeper, the regiment marched through Sperryville and then crossed over the Blue Ridge at Chester Gap into the lovely Shenandoah Valley on June 20. That same day, the Army of Northern Virginia issued Colonel Leventhorpe the regiment's new Confederate battle flag. Lee's army had a regulation that prohibited units from carrying into battle anything other than the square battle flag. Henceforth, whenever the regiment advanced against the enemy, the color guard would have to leave the Bethel flag in camp and carry the prescribed battle flag. The regulation did not apply on the march, so the familiar Bethel flag still waved overhead as the 11th N.C. perambulated the Virginia countryside. Following a one-day layover at Berryville on June 22, Heth's Division traveled north to Shepherdstown, Maryland, where it crossed the Potomac River on the 24th. Two more days of marching brought the regiment to Chambersburg, Pennsylvania, where the Tar Heels got their first glimpse of the North. The farm boys from North Carolina surely admired the scenery as they hiked through the fertile farmland of the Cumberland Valley.[10]

With his army advancing through the enemy's land, General Lee enjoined his troops to show the utmost respect for personal property. Lee disapproved of wanton behavior by soldiers out of principle. In this case, he had other reasons for restraining the troops from despoiling the farms and fields. Lee sought a military victory on northern soil to convince the Union to give up its effort to subdue the Confederacy. A total war policy could backfire and stir the North's war passions. The invasion of Pennsylvania reversed the usual roles of the Union and Confederate armies; now the Confederates were the invader. The psychological factor of defending their homes from the invading enemy had always helped motivate the Confederate soldiers. Would it motivate the Union troops to fight harder? Worse yet, would it undermine the Confederates' morale? D. H. Hill had cautioned the Bethel Regiment about this back in 1861. *"Suppose you were to invade their country . . ."* If the troops began marauding the northern soldiers' homeland, could the Confederates still meet their men boldly? Lee decided to enforce a strict moral discipline on the Confederate troops during their march across Union territory.

Johnston Pettigrew had his own reasons for enforcing strict discipline within the brigade. The Tar Heel soldiers had witnessed, firsthand, the depredations of Union soldiers in the eastern part of their state, including the general's ancestral property in Hyde County. Pettigrew dreaded the consequences if the men lapsed into retribution. He had cause to fear. Lt. Billy Taylor of A Company expressed a commonly held attitude, "I hope the officers will devastate the territory and give the enemy a taste of the horrors of war."[11] Fortunately, the men behaved well as they passed through the Pennsylvania towns. However, Lee's orders against seizing property applied to the troops, not to the army itself. The Confederate commissaries roamed the countryside and "requisitioned" supplies in great quantities from local farms, shops, and factories. The Pennsylvania citizens had to accept payment in Confederate currency for the goods taken by Lee's army. From their perspective, they had been robbed by gentlemen, but robbed nonetheless.

Once Heth's Division reached Chambersburg on June 26, it split off from the route taken by Ewell's Corps and headed east. The new direction of march took them toward Fayetteville, Pennsylvania, where they rested. The men still did not know the purpose of the mission, their destination, or what was expected of them. Most assumed they would keep marching until they found the enemy and then fight. Leventhorpe shared their disquiet and sought out General Pettigrew to voice his concern. "I remember conversing with him about the movement, the exact object of which was, of course, known only to Gen. Lee; and upon my remarking that I thought our rear was exposed and that the trains bringing supplies of ammunition might be endangered, he replied in the quick manner which was peculiar to him. 'We have no rear.'" Leventhorpe would have been more concerned had he known that Lee remained in the dark about the movements of the Union army. The Confederate cavalry under General Stuart lost contact with Lee's main army and stopped providing updates on the Army of the Potomac. Lee worried about the uncertain situation, especially after a spy reported that the Union army was on the move. He decided to concentrate the Army of Northern Virginia before he stumbled blindly into the Union army. Lee chose to pull Ewell's Corps, which was the farthest north, back south, while he moved Hill's and Longstreet's Corps east. The three corps would rendezvous on the east side of South Mountain. Heth's Division assumed the lead of Hill's Corps, as it left the protected Cumberland Valley, crossed South Mountain, and entered Cashtown on June 29.[12]

The easy march through the countryside was deceiving; danger lurked behind the low, peaceful ridges. The men of the Bethel Regiment were about to face their most terrible trial.

McPherson's Ridge

June 30–July 1, 1863, Gettysburg, Pennsylvania

The men of the 11th N.C. advanced down the Chambersburg Pike from Cashtown on June 30, 1863. A sporadic rain fell on the troops throughout the morning making the march uncomfortable but, at least, it kept the dust down. The move seemed completely routine to the troops. They had no idea that they were initiating a monumental clash of arms. After all, their division commander, Maj. Gen. Harry Heth, had sent them and the rest of Pettigrew's Brigade on a simple mission to procure shoes from a manufacturer in the nearby town of Gettysburg. Many soldiers had worn out their shoes over the previous sixteen days and had to march barefoot down the dirt roads. Heth wanted shoes to avoid losing soldiers to foot injuries; hence, the trip to Gettysburg.

The Bethel Regiment led Pettigrew's Brigade on the approach to

Seminary Ridge. Two miles west of town, the skirmishers arrested a local physician who was riding in the area and brought him back to the regimental commander. Colonel Leventhorpe interrogated the doctor (one physician probing another) to get a picture of the situation in Gettysburg, quizzing him with the usual questions: What is happening in Gettysburg? How are the citizens reacting to the presence of Lee's army? Have you seen any Union soldiers? The doctor's response that several thousand Union soldiers were nearby caught Leventhorpe off-guard; he had been given no indication of Union forces nearby. This intelligence caused the colonel to halt the column and confer with Pettigrew. The two officers discussed the implications of the physician's statement. Lee had given strict orders not to engage any enemy force until he had time to concentrate the army. Pettigrew and Leventhorpe considered Lee's order versus the need to collect shoes. They decided to advance cautiously with skirmishers forward to locate the suspected Union troops. On the way, the brigade ran across a Confederate spy who verified the information passed by the doctor.[13]

Pettigrew himself rode ahead to Seminary Ridge, northwest of Gettysburg, where he could survey the scene. He soon observed a Union cavalry brigade belonging to Brig. Gen. John Buford's Division trotting into Gettysburg. The physician had told the truth; Union cavalry had come to Gettysburg, too. If the Union cavalry had arrived, how far away could their infantry be? To avoid contact, Pettigrew canceled the mission to gather shoes. Leaving two mounted men to keep an eye on the cavalry, Pettigrew hurried back to Cashtown and reported to General Heth. The 11th N.C. withdrew toward Cashtown in accordance with Lee's guidance. As they fell back, the Union cavalry became increasingly aggressive. Four times during the movement, the regiment formed line of battle to the rear to ward off the enemy's mounted maneuvers.[14]

Back at Cashtown, Pettigrew briefed a skeptical Harry Heth about the sighting. Pettigrew tried to persuade his superior by clearly describing that he had seen Union troops and not local militia. Heth still discounted Pettigrew's personal observations. Heth's skepticism indicated that he had doubts about Pettigrew's dependability, apparently because Pettigrew had not previously fought beside him. While the two generals debated, the corps commander, A. P. Hill, arrived at Heth's headquarters and joined the discussion. Hill also treated the report of Union cavalry lightly. Pettigrew tried in vain to convince the two generals that a part of the Union army was at hand and not back in Maryland, as the latest intelligence report concluded. Finally, Heth grew impatient. He cut Pettigrew short and directed a question to Hill, "If there is no objection, I will march my division tomorrow, go to Gettysburg and secure those shoes." Hill answered, "None in the world."[15]

The next morning, July 1, Hill's Corps began its advance down the Chambersburg Pike without its commander because Powell Hill felt poorly that morning and remained at Cashtown. Ground fog hung along the creek bottoms and clouds blocked the sun as the Confederates formed along the pike; it would be a hot, steamy day. Before the movement began, Hill reiterated Lee's instructions to Heth not to start a general engagement. Heth duly noted the guidance and then put Archer's Brigade in motion for Gettysburg. Davis's Brigade came next with Brockenbrough's and Pettigrew's following in support. Archer's skirmishers had hardly started their movement over the Marsh Creek bridge before Buford's cavalry vedettes brought them under fire. General Archer pushed ahead and forced the annoying cavalry pickets to retire, but they sniped at him for over two hours.[16] Once they cleared the bridge, Davis's Brigade shifted to the north side of the pike and marched quickly to come abreast of Archer. Pettigrew's Brigade, including the 11th N.C., followed Archer on the south side of the road. Archer pressed forward, as the cavalry pickets could do nothing more than harass the Confederate infantry. As the lead brigades approached the western edge of Gettysburg, they reached a stream, Willoughby Run, where they ran into more serious opposition. General Buford's dismounted cavalry division defended positions on McPherson's Ridge, a small rise between the stream and Seminary Ridge.

Buford's defensive line proved beyond a doubt that Heth faced a part of the Army of the Potomac. Pettigrew had been correct. Until then, Heth had not encountered any infantry, only cavalry, and he felt confident that he could shove them aside. Still, the unexpected resistance changed his estimate of the situation. Heth faced an unclear picture of the battlefield, so he decided to test the Union's strength. The division commander brought up his artillery to soften up Buford's defense and gauge the response from the Union guns. Once the guns opened fire across the creek, he ordered Archer and Davis to drive off the Union cavalry. The two brigades plowed into Buford's troopers, who responded with a stiff fight. The pressure of Heth's determined infantry attack eventually forced the cavalry to give way, but only after Buford had delayed them for a couple of critical hours. Archer and Davis finally forced their way over Willoughby Run.

Suddenly, disaster struck Heth's lead brigades. Union infantry from Maj. Gen. John Reynolds's I Corps came up to relieve the cavalry and braced the defense. Elements of Brig. Gen. James Wadsworth's Division arrived first and crashed headlong into Archer. Worse yet, an infantry brigade emerged from a concealed position and enveloped Archer's exposed southern flank. This was no ordinary Union brigade; it was Brig. Gen. Solomon Meredith's "Iron Brigade," the most renowned unit in the Army of the Potomac. The tough brigade of western regiments wore distinctive black bell-crowned hats instead of the normal forage caps, which made them easily recognizable. "There are those damned black-hatted fellows, again!" Archer's men groaned. "T'aint no militia; it's the Army of the Potomac!"[17] The Union infantry slammed into the two Confederate brigades, threw them back across Willoughby Run, and captured General Archer in the process. A large number of Davis's troops took cover in a railroad cut but were trapped by Wadsworth's infantry. Hundreds had to surrender. The Union I Corps mauled Heth's lead brigades. Except for the killing of General Reynolds by a Confederate sharpshooter, the I Corps troops enjoyed complete success against Heth's Division.

This was not supposed to happen! Heth had expected to roll over some stray militia, but now he had stumbled into a full-scale meeting engagement with part of the Union army. Once the infantry locked into combat, he could not bring himself to abandon the field. Doggedly, Heth stood his ground, although he took care to prepare for a deliberate battle. Heth deployed all four of his brigades to face the Union infantry across Willoughby Run, while he waited for Pender's Division to reinforce him. Heth arrayed his division in the woods west of the run on Herr Ridge. He put the remnants of Archer's Brigade in the south, somewhat back from the division line. Just north of Archer, Pettigrew's Brigade formed in the woods. Pettigrew posted the 11th N.C. in the left center among the brigade's four regiments, with the 26th N.C. on their left. Brockenbrough's Brigade extended the line north from Pettigrew's flank to the Chambersburg Pike.

Davis's Brigade formed a short line north of the pike, although they were in poor condition to fight.

Back in the rear, the booming of Heth's and Buford's artillery alerted General Lee that his troops had made contact with the enemy. He rode forward to Cashtown where he found the ailing A. P. Hill. The corps commander could shed no light on the situation, other than to reassure Lee that Heth knew that he should not become embroiled in a battle. Without waiting for Hill, Lee headed for Gettysburg to find out what Heth was doing. Lee arrived on the scene by the time Pender's Division came up to provide support for Heth (about 2:00 P.M.). The division commander reported to the army commander to explain how he had become entangled with the Union army. He finished his report by saying that he was ready to drive through the Union resistance. Lee rejected Heth's suggestion.[18] Although ready to advance, Heth had to hold tight in the face of the enemy. While the generals sorted out the situation, Union artillery fired on Pettigrew's Brigade. The men of the 11th N.C. could do nothing except suffer and wait.

Meanwhile, Maj. Gen. Abner Doubleday, who succeeded the fallen Reynolds, fed the rest of the Union I Corps into the defensive line facing Hill's Corps. The Iron Brigade set up a defensive position east of Willoughby Run in McPherson's Woods. Doubleday remarked, "These woods possessed all the advantages of a redoubt, strengthening the center of our line, and enfilading the enemy's columns should they advance in the open spaces on either side." Doubleday admonished the Iron Brigade to hold McPherson's Woods "to the last extremity."[19] The Iron Brigade's southern flank faced the 11th and 26th N.C. of Pettigrew's Brigade. Just to the south of McPherson's Woods, Brig. Gen. Chapman Biddle's Brigade extended the defensive line, *en echelon,* into a wheat field farther along the rise. Biddle's troops formed into two lines of battle and crouched down, using the wheat for concealment. The 151st Pa. served as a reserve farther back on Seminary Ridge. Cooper's Battery of Union artillery covered the I Corps' southern flank. Biddle and Meredith threw a skirmish line forward along the overgrown banks of the run.

Heth and Doubleday lined up their forces, while both armies rushed to Gettysburg from all directions. Hill's Corps approached from the west, Ewell's Corps from the north and east, and Union divisions from the south. As the Tar Heel soldiers took cover under the timber on Herr

Ridge, they could see the Union I Corps reinforcing on McPherson's Ridge. Grimly, Pettigrew's men waited, watched, and worried as the enemy used the time to strengthen their defense. The Confederates knew that the longer they waited, the tougher the fight would be. Johnston Pettigrew grew restless at the protracted delay. He paced fretfully in front of his men, ignoring the Union sharpshooters who took potshots at him. Pettigrew must have been silently fuming inside. His superiors had ignored his warning about the presence of the Union army and then fumbled the morning's battle. Now, the senior commanders were giving the enemy time to prepare their defense. Soon his own men would pay the price for Heth's, Hill's, and Lee's indecision.[20]

Shortly after 2:00 P.M., a new attack against Doubleday developed. Maj. Gen. R. E. Rodes's Division of Ewell's Corps, marching south from Carlisle, bore down on the Union northern flank. Doubleday shifted some of his corps to meet this new threat. Parts of the Union XI Corps joined the battle at the same time and shored up the Union line north of Gettysburg. Heth saw Rodes launch his attack just north of his position and then rode over to Lee. "Rodes is very heavily engaged, had I not better attack?" he inquired. "No," Lee responded. "I am not prepared to bring on a general engagement today. Longstreet is not up."[21] The two generals watched as the Union I and XI Corps realigned their defense and chewed up Rodes's initial thrust. Poor synchronization had allowed the defenders to rebuff the separate assaults by Heth and Rodes. Ewell's Corps continued the pressure. Rodes threw more brigades into the attack, and Maj. Gen. Jubal Early's Division entered the battle from the northeast. Early's fresh attack caught the XI Corps on the flank as the Union commanders tried to adjust their defense. Lee and A. P. Hill (who had just arrived on the scene) observed the shift. Lee sensed an opportunity. He quickly changed his mind and ordered Hill to storm Doubleday's position with his corps. At 3:00 P.M. Heth's Division resumed its attack across Willoughby Run with Pettigrew and Brockenbrough providing the main punch.

For more than a year, the regiment had longed for the chance to fight in a major battle; now, they were going to get it. The Bethel Regiment prepared to launch its first full-scale attack. Down the line, company commanders barked, "Attention!" The soldiers jumped to their feet and formed into a line of battle. The regiment prepared to march, just like the countless drills they had performed so many times before.

The troops pressed together into two compact ranks. Elbow to elbow, they drew comfort from their comrades' touch. Once the signal was given, the officers roared, "Forward!" The 11th N.C. stepped off in its neat line. Leventhorpe, tall and erect, marched at the front of the regiment as the ranks advanced down Herr Ridge.

As his brigade moved forward in grand style, Pettigrew observed a weakness in the Union defensive line; Biddle's left (southern) flank could be turned. Pettigrew decided to envelop the exposed flank, using his two right regiments, the 47th and 52d N.C. Pettigrew's remaining regiments, the 11th and 26th N.C., had no tactical options except a frontal attack straight into the heart of the Union defense. Emerging from the woods into a wheat field, the 11th and 26th N.C. started taking fire from Cooper's Battery on McPherson's Ridge and the Union skirmishers in the low ground. The well-drilled regiments maintained excellent marching order, while the rear rank plugged the holes made by the Union's fire. The interlocking fire from Biddle, Meredith, and the Union artillery intensified as the 11th and 26th N.C. advanced. Shaking off the fire, the brigade marched into the thick underbrush along the sides of the creek and routed the Union skirmishers.

By the time Pettigrew's Brigade reached Willoughby Run, the Confederates had returned fire, but the Union artillery still wrought havoc with oblique fire against the 11th and 26th N.C. Undaunted, the Bethel Regiment assaulted across the run against the northern flank of Biddle's Brigade and the southern flank of the Iron Brigade. One Union colonel remembered, "They came on with rapid strides, yelling like demons." Despite fearful losses and the Union fire, Pettigrew's infantrymen pushed the assault east of Willoughby Run and threw the first Union line of battle back on the second. The Confederate leaders stayed forward with the troops to set an example of courage for the men, though Leventhorpe became concerned about the reckless behavior of Pettigrew. "When the battle was at its height General Pettigrew rode up to me under a tempest of bullets, unconcerned and cheerful, as he always was in action, and ordered the line forward. Whilst performing the enjoined duty I could not refrain from looking at the general, fearing every moment that he might be struck from his horse. I never saw him again."[22]

Pettigrew's assault produced a head-on collision between two dis-

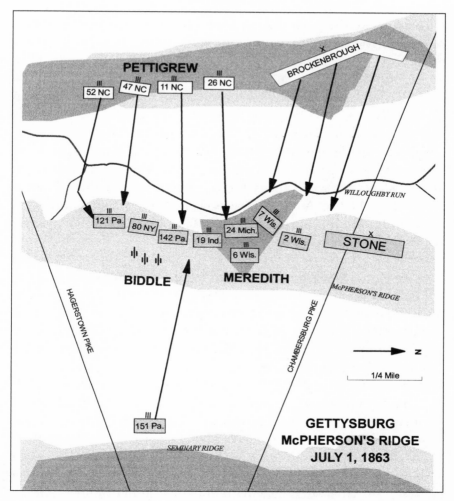

PETTIGREW

BROCKENBROUGH

52 NC   47 NC   11 NC   26 NC

WILLOUGHBY RUN

121 Pa.   80 NY   142 Pa.   19 Ind.   24 Mich.   7 Wis.   2 Wis.   STONE

6 Wis.

BIDDLE   MEREDITH

HAGERSTOWN PIKE

McPHERSON'S RIDGE

CHAMBERSBURG PIKE

N

1/4 Mile

151 Pa.

SEMINARY RIDGE

GETTYSBURG
McPHERSON'S RIDGE
JULY 1, 1863

ciplined and determined opponents. Although Pettigrew's Brigade
had broken the Union's forward line, Biddle's and Meredith's troops
continued fighting from their second line of battle. Maj. John T. Jones
from the 26th N.C. described the action. "On this second line, the
fighting was terrible — our men advancing, the enemy stubbornly
resisting, until the two lines were pouring volleys into each other at a
distance not greater than 20 paces." At such close range, the rifle fire
cut down the soldiers and shattered the lines of battle. Leventhorpe,
"who towered over his fellow soldiers like Saul," made a conspicuous
target as he marched at the front of the regiment's battle line. A minié
ball splintered his arm and another smashed into his hip. The colonel

fell prostrate to the ground as the Bethel Regiment's front rank passed over him. The regiment, numbering six hundred infantrymen at the start of the battle, melted away under the withering fusillade. "The Federal forces fought desperately, inflicting so heavy a loss, that too few were left for a successful bayonet charge. But our men pressed on persistently."[23]

Meanwhile, the 47th and 52d N.C. on the southern (right) flank enveloped Biddle's left and helped collapse the Union defensive line on McPherson's Ridge. The Union artillery battery and Biddle's left began falling back to Seminary Ridge where they could fire from the cover of a rail fence. As the two sides clashed along Willoughby Run, a spent Union round struck General Heth in the head. Fortunately for Heth, he had stuffed a wad of paper into his new hat to help it fit better. The wading saved his life, although the spent round knocked him senseless. Heth relinquished command of the division to General Pettigrew, who urged the division forward with his own brigade leading the charge. However, Brockenbrough's Brigade on the left (north) could not dislodge Stone's Brigade nor Meredith's Iron Brigade, which was living up to its name. Brockenbrough's inability to break the Union line left it up to Pettigrew's Brigade to penetrate the stubborn Union defense. The 26th N.C., on the 11th N.C.'s immediate left, locked into mortal combat with the southern flank of the Iron Brigade. That regiment lost fourteen color bearers in its assault, including the colonel and lieutenant colonel who fell holding their flag. Their opponents, the 24th Mich., suffered brutally under the Tar Heel onslaught and lost several color bearers, as well. At one point, the commander of the 24th Mich. grabbed his regiment's colors only to have it snatched away by a Michigan private. The private exclaimed, "The colonel of the 24th shall never carry the colors while I am alive." The next instant he fell dead, slain by a Tar Heel marksman.[24]

The Bethel Regiment kept attacking and blazing away at the 80th N.Y., 142d Pa., and 19th Ind. Third Lt. Billy Taylor fought with A Company toe-to-toe against the northern line. "We stood within 20 yards of each other for about 15 moments." The regiment's discipline and spirit held firm against the storm of fire. Their relentless pressure forced Biddle's Brigade back in the center. "They had to give way and when they [did] we just mowed them down." Major Ross, the regiment's second in command, led A, D, F, and I companies as they plunged into the Union line. Cooper's Battery turned their guns on the advancing Confederates and fired into the assaulting line. A chunk of lead "about the size of an egg" hit the boy major as he led the charge. "He was shot with a grape shot in the right side and it went nearly through him." Leaderless, the regiment struggled forward, fighting by instinct. Moving and shooting, the men surged ahead and tore apart the Union second line of battle.[25]

As the 11th N.C. threw back Biddle's line and the 19th Ind., the 26th N.C. bent back the 24th Mich.'s southern flank. The Confederates pressed hard, but the Iron Brigade held McPherson's Woods tenaciously. The attack of the Bethel Regiment had widened the gap between Biddle and the Iron Brigade, which the 26th N.C. exploited with a vigorous thrust. The Iron Brigade pulled back slightly and then received help from the 151st Pa., Biddle's reserve regiment, that had been ordered forward to cover the dangerous interval between the Union brigades. The 151st Pa. confronted the 11th and 26th N.C. head-on. The commander of the Union regiment wrote, "The enemy greeted me with a volley which brought several of my men down, ere I had halted in position. My gallant officers and men fell thick and fast." The two Confederate regiments traded volleys in close combat with five smaller Union regiments. The persistent assault by the two Confederate regiments drove through the Union line. Meredith's Brigade finally withdrew to an alternate defensive line on Seminary Ridge, ending the thirty-minute death struggle for McPherson's Ridge. General Heth later acknowledged that the 11th and 26th N.C. "displayed conspicuous gallantry" while driving back Biddle's Brigade and the Iron Brigade. Union prisoners admitted, "There was no withstanding such an attack."[26]

At this crucial moment, A. P. Hill committed his supporting division. Pender's Division passed through Heth's exhausted troops and continued the attack up Seminary Ridge. Pender's soldiers made a final push against the Union I Corps that desperately tried to hold the line along the crest of the ridge. Ewell struck the XI Corps, simultaneously, from the north and northeast. Finally, the Confederates arranged a coordinated attack. This time the dam burst. Pender's men broke the Union defensive position on Seminary Ridge and sent the Union soldiers into flight. The Union force fled through Gettysburg and reorganized on Cemetery Hill to the south. With his men utterly exhausted and Heth's Division badly cut up, Powell Hill halted the assault.

The battlefield around McPherson's Ridge gave cruel testimony to the savagery of the brief but violent struggle. Bodies of the wounded and the dead littered the ground. In places corpses lay in neat rows marking the spot where an entire line of battle had been cut down, as if by a giant scythe. Pettigrew's adjutant, 1st Lt. Louis Young, became unsettled by an eerie, gruesome encounter immediately after the assault. "When we occupied the wood recently held by the enemy my attention was attracted by the dreadful — not moans but — howls of some of the wounded. It was so distressing that I approached several with the purpose of calming them if possible, and to my surprise I found them foaming at the mouth as if mad, and evidently unconscious of the sound of their voices. This was the only occurrence of the kind which came under my observation during the war, and I attribute it to the effect upon the nerves of the quick, frightful conflict following several hours of suspense."[27]

The commander of the 24th Mich. admitted to the terrible losses in the battle. "The field over which we fought, from our first line of battle in McPherson's Woods to the barricade near the seminary, was strewn with the killed and wounded. Our losses were very large." Indeed, the Tar Heel regiments inflicted tremendous casualties on their opponents. The five Union regiments engaged by the 11th and 26th N.C. (19th Ind., 24th Mich., 80th N.Y., 142d, and 151st Pa.) suffered nearly 1,300 casualties at Gettysburg; the vast majority of those fell before the Tar Heels' fire. That savage attack across the creek helped collapse the Union's defense west of Gettysburg. "No troops could have fought better than did Pettigrew's Brigade on this day," Louis Young proudly stated. "Its conduct was the admiration of all who witnessed the engagement."[28]

The day's victory came at a dreadful cost to the Bethel Regiment. Colonel Leventhorpe, the regimental commander, lay in a hospital seriously wounded. He never returned to the regiment. Nor would Maj. Egbert Ross. The young man who organized the Boy Company of the original Bethel Regiment lingered for four hours with his devastating wound before he died. Billy Taylor helped bury his young comrade nearby. He grabbed a plank and scratched Ross's name and rank on it, then used it as a grave marker. It seemed like such a humble resting place for such a promising and earnest young man. The loss of these key leaders left the regiment with no field grade officers present for duty since Lt. Col. William Martin remained on sick leave. The ranks suffered heavily, as well. In the thirty minutes it took to overrun McPherson's Ridge, the regiment endured well over two hundred casualties; more than forty had been killed. Several more lay mortally wounded. Pvt. Reuben Yaunts, the sleepy sentry sentenced to wear a ball and chain, was among the slain. Company C was severely battered and had only four men and its commander, Capt. Francis Bird, remaining of an initial force of forty-one. One of the C Company sergeants, William G. Parker, suffered a grazing head wound and was evacuated to a makeshift hospital in Winchester, Virginia. Sadly, he received little medical attention and died three weeks later of fever. His devoted wife and three children never recovered his body from the mass grave at the hospital. Pettigrew's Brigade lost more than one thousand men while driving back the Union forces on McPherson's Ridge. Once the fighting subsided, the brigade retired to the woods near Willoughby Run where they tried to recover from their staggering losses.[29]

The heavy casualties did not dampen the mood in the Confederate camp. Hill and Ewell had won an impressive victory. They had dislodged Union forces from a naturally strong defensive position and gained control of Gettysburg's road network. The converging attacks of their corps smashed two enemy corps during the unexpected battle. Furthermore, Lee now had his army concentrated around Gettysburg and anxiously prepared to deliver a crushing blow to the Union army. He would get his chance. Maj. Gen. George Meade, the newly appointed commander of the Army of the Potomac, spent the night gathering his army around the natural defenses of Culp's Hill, Cemetery Hill, Cemetery Ridge, and Little Round Top. Throughout the night of July 1, both armies squared off for a larger engagement.

CEMETERY RIDGE

July 2–3, 1863, Gettysburg, Pennsylvania

The Bethel Regiment's survivors took a day of rest on July 2, while noncombatants performed the somber duties of helping the wounded, clearing the battlefield, and burying the dead.[30] The surgeons spent much of the night in the field hospitals treating the injured and trying to save the lives of the seriously wounded. How could they replace such terrible losses? The Army of Northern Virginia would need the services of the regiment again, so the remaining captains and lieutenants worked to reorganize their companies. As the day progressed, the commanders resorted to extreme measures to reconstitute the force. All duty personnel had to take up arms as infantrymen and the walking wounded returned to duty. These steps made only a marginal difference in the effective strength of the regiment and did little to raise the downcast mood of the troops. The survivors, naturally, felt depressed with so many of their leaders, compatriots, and friends among the dead and wounded. Col. James K. Marshall, the acting brigade commander, decided the men needed a lift, so he excused members of the band from the burial details. During the afternoon, the 11th and 26th regimental bands entertained the troops with patriotic tunes. The melodies of "God Save the South" and "When This Cruel War Is Over" soothed the men and cheered them a bit. Bewildered Union soldiers across the battlefield heard the music between shellings and wondered "what the Rebels were doing with a band playing in the middle of a fight."

For the rest of Lee's army, July 2 was supposed to be the decisive day they would shatter the Union army. Lee delivered massive blows to both flanks of the Union's defense. Ewell's Corps struck the Union right at Culp's Hill, defended by the XII Corps. After a desperate struggle, Ewell's men gained a foothold, but the northerners still clung to the high ground. To the south, Longstreet's Corps pummeled Sickles's III Corps in a peach orchard and folded them back. A quick stab by Longstreet's men barely missed capturing Little Round Top and turning the Union's left flank. The Army of Northern Virginia failed to win the battle, but it had come very close. The nearness of victory intensified Lee's resolve to try one more strike against the Army of the Potomac. Lee believed that the battle on the flanks had consumed the Union army's strength and that another powerful blow would break their resistance. He decided to crush Meade's army with a continuation of Longstreet's attack against Cemetery Ridge. After so many victories, Lee had complete faith in the fighting spirit of his soldiers, and that faith lulled him into a battle plan that relied on brute force to shatter the Union left-center.

A problem arose over finding the force to make the assault. The first two days of fierce fighting had battered most of the Confederate army. Only Maj. Gen. George Pickett's Division from Longstreet's Corps was still fresh but one division clearly could not take Cemetery Ridge by itself. Lee figured that the mission would require three divisions. Even then, Longstreet expressed his doubts that any fifteen thousand troops could capture Cemetery Ridge, but Lee had already made up his mind. He initially planned to throw Longstreet's other two divisions, McLaws's and Hood's, into the attack, but Longstreet overturned this idea by pointing out that these two divisions protected the army's right (southern) flank and could not be used without inviting a counterattack. The disagreement with his senior corps commander caused Lee to reconsider, so he turned to A. P. Hill's Corps to provide the rest of the attacking force.[31] Inattentive staff work caused a serious mistake in the assignment of the attack divisions. Lee decided to commit Heth's Division (commanded by Brig. Gen. Johnston Pettigrew) and Pender's Division (commanded by Maj. Gen. Isaac Trimble) to the attack. This decision overlooked the fact that both divisions lost heavily on the first day of the battle. A cursory examination of the casualty lists would have revealed that Anderson's Division was in much better shape to make the attack than either of the two Lee selected.

Lee called Longstreet and A. P. Hill to a morning meeting behind the woods on Seminary Ridge to deliver his attack order. The three generals sat together on the trunk of a fallen tree while Lee sketched out his ideas on a map.[32] Pickett's, Pettigrew's, and Trimble's divisions would strike the Union's overstretched center on Cemetery Ridge, oriented on a "copse of trees" situated in the center of the Ridge. Two brigades from Anderson's Division would be available to cover the right flank of the attack, if needed. The terrain did not favor the attacker. A mile-wide valley separated the Confederates on Seminary Ridge from the Union army on Cemetery Ridge, and open fields covered the distance between the two gently sloping ridges. Any moving force would have very little cover as it crossed the valley. A stone wall ran along the western slope of the ridge just in front of the trees, providing a convenient breastwork for defending infantry. The wall stayed straight except for an eighty-yard jog to the east a little north of the grove, which created a salient in the stone fortification north of the copse of trees. Emmitsburg Road cut through the valley separating the two armies. The road angled slightly to the northeast, which brought it close to the stone wall a little north of the salient. A post fence ran the length of Emmitsburg Road and presented another obstacle to the attacking force.

To support the main attack, Lee ordered the largest concentration of artillery fire the army had ever seen. The Confederates would focus the fire of 140 cannon, all of Longstreet's and Hill's guns, to pulverize the objective and prepare the way for the infantry. Lee hoped to blast the Union soldiers off Cemetery Ridge and silence their guns. The Confederates planned a powerful artillery preparation, but they missed a chance to make it even stronger. Lee's artillery chief, Brig. Gen. William Pendleton, neglected to include the artillery from Ewell's Corps in the bombardment. Ewell's guns had the unique advantage of being able to enfilade the Union center on Cemetery Ridge. Their angle of fire was parallel to the lines of assaulting infantry and would have allowed them to maintain fire on Cemetery Ridge as the infantry advanced.[33] This oversight would cost Pettigrew, Trimble, and Pickett the benefit of suppressive fire during the final phase of the assault.

Lee then announced that Longstreet would command the attacking divisions, even though the majority of the force would come from Hill's Corps. Obviously, Lee felt more comfortable with Longstreet as commander than with A. P. Hill. Hill had plenty of fighting spirit, but this was his first battle as a corps commander. Lee wanted an experienced leader for this crucial attack, so Hill had to swallow his pride as Lee gave away two of his divisions to another corps commander. Curiously, Longstreet felt extremely uncomfortable with this mission and would resort to acts that bordered on insubordination in an effort to abort it. He did not share Lee's confidence that the Union soldiers on Cemetery Ridge would give way to the Confederates.

Lee might have shared Longstreet's misgivings had he known that Meade's army held Cemetery Ridge with a considerably stronger force than he anticipated. Hancock's II Corps dug in behind the stone wall. Dependable fighters with a dependable leader, the II Corps would not crack easily. Maj. Gen. Winfield Scott Hancock had already earned a reputation as the Union's best corps commander. Hancock had served in the U.S. Army during the Mexican War during which he became friends with many of the Confederate senior officers, including Harry Heth. Heth fondly remembered their days in Mexico and admired how the handsome Hancock had seduced so many Mexican señoritas. At the start of the war, Hancock served as the quartermaster in Los Angeles. The southern press derided him when it reviewed a list of the Union's "California generals." "He is vain and empty, more of a politician than a general."[34] Hancock proved them wrong. His performance in the 1862 campaigns earned promotions and the sobriquet "Hancock the Superb."

Hancock had two divisions on Cemetery Ridge. Gibbon's Division defended the wall near the copse of trees, with Webb's Brigade occupying the forward angle of the stone wall immediately south of the salient. General Webb posted only two regiments along the wall while he held his other two regiments in reserve several hundred feet back on high ground. Remarkably, the distribution of Webb's regiments left a relatively weak force to defend the stone wall at the very point of attack designated by Lee. Just north of Webb's Brigade lay the salient. Brig. Gen. Alexander Hays, commanding a division, placed two brigades with roughly 2,100 infantrymen behind the stone wall in the rear of the salient. Col. Thomas Smyth's Brigade held the left (southern) part of the stone wall and Col. Eliakim Sherrill's Brigade defended the right (northern) side. Both brigade commanders had all of their regiments, a total of eight, defending immediately behind the wall where they could fire into the salient. The II Corps put a skirmish line in front of the salient, close to the road. From their fortified positions on Cemetery Ridge, the Union soldiers looked across the open valley toward the Confederates.

The Union Chief of Artillery, Maj. Gen. Henry Hunt, had developed a highly effective fire plan to cover the Union center with massed artillery fire. A battery of six rifled cannons, commanded by Capt. W. A. Arnold, covered the salient. Another battery of twelve-pound smoothbore Napoleons from the 1st U.S. Artillery, commanded by 1st Lt. George Woodruff, could fire into the salient from a position a little to the north. Arnold and Woodruff covered Hays's front with close range interlocking artillery fire. Three more batteries directly supported Gibbon's Division. Besides the II Corps artillery, Hunt planned to cover the center with the heavy guns of all the other corps that could reach. From Cemetery Hill in the north to Little Round Top in the south, the Union artillery could bring 135 guns to bear on the center of their line, almost as many as Lee planned to fire against Hancock.[35] The big difference came in the types of targets each side could engage; General Hunt's guns would be firing on troops in the open.

The Confederate army spent the morning staging units for the attack. Pickett's Division arrived on the scene mid-morning. The dashing Virginian formed the right flank of the attacking force. He put Kemper's Brigade on the southern flank with Garnett's Brigade to their left. Armistead's Brigade followed behind Garnett as the supporting brigade. Pettigrew's Division (Heth's) constituted the left half of the first echelon. The initial order designated Pettigrew's Division as the follow-on force for Pickett, but the senior officers quickly changed the order to put Pettigrew abreast of Pickett. Misunderstanding over Pettigrew's mission would lead to some ugly accusations after the battle. Pettigrew put Archer's Brigade (Colonel Fry commanding) on the south flank next to Pickett. Next to them he placed his own brigade (Colonel Marshall commanding). The Bethel Regiment would attack on the left (northern) end of the brigade front. The depleted brigade could only muster fifteen hundred infantrymen for the attack. Davis's Brigade formed to the left of the 11th N.C. and Brockenbrough's Brigade (Colonel Mayo commanding) held the northern flank of the division. Each brigade formed into two ranks. Longstreet put two brigades from Pender's Division (Maj. Gen. Isaac Trimble commanding) behind the right (southern) half of Pettigrew's Division. Scales's Brigade (Colonel Lowrance commanding) would follow Archer, while Lane's Brigade would support Marshall. This deployment of Pender's second echelon division suffered from one major oversight; it left the northern flank (Davis's and Brockenbrough's brigades) without a follow-on force or flank support. Once all the instructions had been issued, the commanders organized their units for the attack. Pettigrew moved his four brigades forward from Herr

Ridge to the woods within the staging area. The regiments lay down behind the artillery batteries on Seminary Ridge as the time for the artillery preparation neared. Not all of the regiments found shelter under the trees. The 11th N.C. halted in the open without the benefit of shade.[36]

The assignment of General Trimble to succeed the mortally wounded Dorsey Pender raised a few eyebrows. Apparently, Lee did not trust Brig. Gen. James H. Lane, the former major of the Bethel Regiment, with the command of Pender's Division. He tapped Isaac Trimble, instead, to fill the vacant division command. Trimble, who outranked Lane, had no permanent assignment and was available to occupy the major general's slot. Lee came to inspect Pender's Division along with the new division commander shortly before the attack. Noticing some bandaged troops, he commented, "Many of these boys should go to the rear; they are not able for duty." Looking more closely, he observed that familiar faces were missing from the formation. Lee must have realized belatedly that he had made a mistake in tasking Heth's and Pender's divisions to make the attack. The two divisions from Hill's Corps were worn down from the first day's battle and not close to full strength. The majority of the attacking force consisted of brigades that had to use walking wounded to fill their infantry ranks. In fact, the three divisions in the attack would number only 12,500 infantrymen, not the 15,000 that Longstreet assumed.[37]

At 1:15 P.M. the Confederate artillery opened fire on Cemetery Ridge. One hundred forty guns fired the biggest cannonade ever witnessed in America to that time. The smoke from the cannon filled the valley and enshrouded the battlefield. The blasts shook the earth and gave confidence to the waiting infantry. "Not as a figure of rhetoric, but as a perceptible fact, the earth quivered under the incessant concussion." One of the soldiers in Smyth's Brigade shuddered as the shells roared over the heads of the Union infantry. "It seemed as if all the Demons in Hell were let loose, and were Howling through the air." The effect of the guns did not match their booming. Most of the rounds overshot the defending infantry and landed in the Union rear. The Union guns replied to the bombardment and inflicted damage, more to the Confederate infantry than to the artillery batteries. A shell fragment hit one of the acting brigade commanders, Colonel Fry, while he waited for the attack to begin. The Confederate gunners kept firing, hoping to destroy more Union targets, but failed to see that their shots were missing the primary target. For well over an hour, the big guns thundered across the valley with marginal results.[38]

While enduring the Confederate bombardment, the Union artillery commander, Henry Hunt, decided to curtail the artillery duel. Hunt wanted to save ammunition for the real threat, the coming advance of infantry. Ceasefire instructions passed down the line to all the guns on Cemetery Ridge. The lack of response by the Union batteries irked General Hancock. He ordered more of his corps' artillery to return fire, primarily to help boost the morale of his infantry. He worried needlessly. Despite the massive noise and shaking ground, the tough Union veterans understood that the fire was passing harmlessly over their heads. Across the valley, the Confederate gunners noticed the waning Union fire, mistakenly assumed that the Union artillery had been suppressed, and soon stopped their own fire. Longstreet's artillery chief sent word that the time for the infantry attack had arrived. The Confederate gunners probably could not have sustained the artillery duel much longer anyway because their own stock of ammunition had nearly run out. The Confederate guns put some Union artillery out of action but not a significant number. Worse yet, the Confederates had neither worn down nor demoralized the Union infantry. Once the artillery battle ended, they prepared to fight. A captain from New York wrote, "Not a man flinched, but every brow was knit and lip compressed with stern determination to win or die." Another element of Lee's battle plan had failed.[39]

The end of the artillery fire signaled the time to form up the regiments. The infantrymen glanced nervously at one another, trying to derive some degree of confidence from their buddies. Everyone knew that a terrible ordeal awaited them on Cemetery Ridge. At a gesture from Pettigrew, the Bethel Regiment stood and lined up in two ranks. Even with so many men missing from the formation, the regiment displayed its characteristic precision at drill. The companies, regiments, and brigades fell into line, and Pettigrew called out to James Marshall, the acting commander of his own brigade, "Now, colonel, for the honor of the good old North State, forward." The long ranks of gray soldiers pressed forward, dressing their line as Leventhorpe had taught them so often at dress parade. The 11th N.C. advanced over Seminary Ridge into the open. Even as they began moving, some of the men fainted from the oppressive heat. The regiment's exposure to the sun during the artillery duel had drained many of their energy, just when they needed it most. The regiment marched into its position on the left of the brigade and near the center of the division, while company sergeants revived those who had passed out. Captain Bird and C Company's four remaining enlisted men strode alongside the regimental colors and the eight-man color guard. Bird would play a dramatic role in the historic charge.[40]

The Confederate divisions marched in grand style into the mile-wide valley. Pettigrew and Pickett had started from different positions on Seminary Ridge, so they had to link up their lines of battle after emerging from the woods. Officers barked out commands to dress on Pickett's line. The infantry ranks gradually pulled together, forming an imposing line of battle nearly a mile wide. Randolph Shotwell, one of Pickett's men, vividly recalled the scene. "The whole column is now within sight, coming down the slope with steady step and superb alignment. The rustle of thousands of feet amid the stubble stirs a cloud of dust, like the spray at the prow of a vessel. The flags flutter and snap — the sunlight flashes from the officers' swords — low words of command are heard — and thus in perfect order, this gallant array of gallant men marches straight down into the valley of Death!" The vision of the Confederate infantry greatly impressed one Union soldier. "Beautiful, gloriously beautiful, did that vast array appear in the lovely little valley."[41]

The Union artillery gunners were equally impressed but reacted more vigorously. They poured long-range fire into the advancing formation by the time it reached half way across the valley. The Union artillery quickly proved the value of General Hunt's centralized fire plan. The guns from the I, III, and XI corps hurled long-range fire on the advancing lines of battle, although the Confederate attack aimed only at the II Corps. Without a supporting attack against their position on Cemetery Hill, the XI Corps' fifty-two guns could direct their fire against the lucrative targets in the valley. The long-range solid projectiles punched holes in the Bethel Regiment's line with terrifying shrieks. Troops from the second rank immediately stepped in to fill the gaps. *Esprit de corps* and discipline kept the battle line in order. Pettigrew's and Pickett's divisions held their formations but gradually compressed as they focused on the objective.

The Union artillery switched to canister shot as the attacking line came within a few hundred yards. Canister rounds were simply tin cans filled with lead shot that turned a cannon into a gigantic shotgun. These munitions had a deadly effect on exposed infantry. Woodruff's and Arnold's batteries tore into the 11th N.C. and the rest of the division as they neared Emmitsburg Road. One blast shot Pettigrew's horse from underneath him and compelled the general to advance on foot. Before his division reached the fence along the road, the artillery had blown large gaps in the neat infantry formations, but the men remained steady. "They opened upon us a tremendous shower of grape and canister; but on we dashed, our brigades and Pickett's men." On the right flank, Pickett's Division had already crossed the road, as it angled farther to the west across his route of advance. The lead divisions kept crowding their lines in toward the copse of trees. As they compressed, Pickett's three brigades and Pettigrew's right-flank brigade (Archer's) marched toward the trees and the forward angle of the stone wall. Pettigrew's other three brigades moved toward the eastward salient in the stone wall defended by Hays's Division.[42]

An aggressive Union regimental commander noticed Brockenbrough's Brigade, on the left flank, angling south of his regiment. The

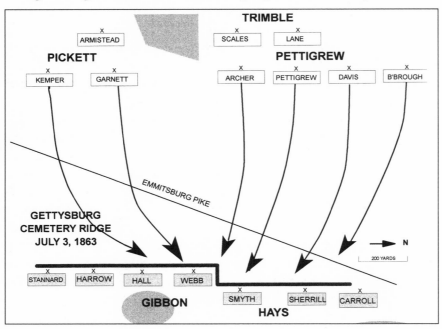

commander of the 8th Ohio moved his regiment forward from the Union skirmish line, swung around Brockenbrough's left flank, and poured deadly enfilade fire down the Confederate line. This proved to be too much for Brockenbrough's men; they withdrew in haste from the attack. Pettigrew watched in horror as his northern flank crumbled. "Rally them on the left," he cried.[43] With the collapse of his left flank brigade, and his right flank brigade hitting the forward angle of the stone wall, Pettigrew had to attack Hays's two brigades behind the salient with only Davis's and Marshall's brigades. The troublesome Ohio riflemen soon turned on Davis's exposed flank and chewed up more of the assaulting line.

The 11th N.C. pressed its attack through the horrific canister fire. Pettigrew's forces routed the Union skirmishers along Emmitsburg Road, capturing several of them. The troops did their best to maintain a solid line of battle, but the orderly advance ran into trouble at the road. The post fence blocked the way and forced the attackers to climb over the rails, while Woodruff's and Arnold's batteries fired a "storm of lead" at them. Once over the fence, the regiment tried to reform its thinning line of battle, but the defenders struck a mighty blow as the Confederates strained to reform their line. Smyth's and Sherrill's brigades rose as one mass and leveled their weapons at the line of gray. With a single thunderous volley, the Union troops opened fire from behind the rear wall of the salient. More than 2,000 rifles, added to the artillery fire, produced a terrible slaughter among Pettigrew's men. The neat infantry formations disintegrated, blown apart in a whirlwind of smoke, minié balls, and canister shot. One Union officer noted, "Arms, heads, blankets, guns and knapsacks were blown and tossed into the clear air."[44] The shock of the rifle volley caused some of the fainthearted to break ranks and flee. Others hit the dirt to seek shelter from the devastating fusillade. Most of them returned fire, but the 3,000 men in the open fared poorly against the 2,100 men firing from behind a stone wall, supported by artillery.

Still, the Bethel Regiment and their comrades carried on. The regimental adjutant, 1st Lt. Henderson Lucas, fell with a grievous wound. Lying helpless on the battlefield, the adjutant exhorted the passing infantrymen to "press on to victory." In small groups and in clusters around the flags, moving and shooting, the attackers kept coming. Whenever a color-bearer fell, another color guard grabbed the regiment's colors and kept the attack moving. One by one, the regiment's color guard dropped from the deadly rifle fire. The rebel yells were gone. Instead, the cries and groans of the wounded and those still fighting produced "a vast mournful roar" that could be heard above the din of battle.[45]

Despite the determined efforts of the 11th N.C. and the other regiments, Pettigrew's Division lost its momentum. Smyth's and Sherrill's fire had staggered the first echelon, but help was on the way. Trimble with Lowrance's and Lane's brigades closed up behind Pettigrew's remaining force. A major from Lane's Brigade recalled, "As we overtook the first line (Pettigrew's), and the two lines became one, the advance was continued." Shouting out, "Three cheers for the Old North State!" the two North Carolina brigades pushed forward into the salient amid the furious fire. James Lane swung his men around to the left flank to shore up Davis's attack that was collapsing under the merciless enfilade fire. Lowrance joined Marshall's and some of Fry's troops in the salient. The attackers struggled forward, shooting as they advanced. By this time, all eight of the Bethel Regiment's color guards had been hit, so Frank Bird seized the colors himself.[46]

Attackers and defenders poured unrelenting volleys into one another. Smoke from the blazing guns billowed up and blanketed the salient, offering the exposed infantry some concealment. Union riflemen armed with breech-loading rifles doused their weapons with water to keep the barrels from melting and continued blazing away at the diminishing ranks of attackers. The Confederates scored their own hits on the enemy crouched behind the stone wall. One round slammed into Col. Eliakim Sherrill's abdomen, mortally wounding him. The battle in the salient raged as leaders and troops fell. Colonel Smyth later said that the Confederates had "fought with a fiery determination that he had never seen equaled." For one tantalizing moment, victory seemed to be within the Confederates' grasp. The leading attackers pushed into the salient and closed the distance to the stone wall. The Confederates finally silenced Arnold's battery in the salient after it blasted a desperate rush by the 26th N.C. Pickett's men, with Fry's help, had already pushed across the stone wall by the angle. Defending troops began to fall back from their positions under the pressure. Then the Union forces abruptly snatched victory from the attackers.[47]

The Union commanders rallied their troops along the crest of the ridge, and reserves came up to reinforce them. A counterattack from the front and southern flank by Gibbon's Division ejected Pickett's men from the angle in the stone wall. In the north, General Hays sent the 126th N.Y. to join the 8th Ohio that had flanked the Confederates' left. These troops and Woodruff's artillery battery sent devastating enfilade fire against the scattered bands of Confederates in the salient. The artillery and rifle fire from the northern flank crushed Pettigrew's and Trimble's left. Union rifle fire shattered General Trimble's leg, and grape shot hit General Pettigrew in the hand. General Lane tumbled to the ground from his dead horse. Colonel Fry was shot through the thigh. The acting brigade commander, Colonel Marshall, fell dead from his horse after a round pierced his body. Marshall, a former company commander in the old 1st N.C. Volunteers, died with the reborn Bethel Regiment under his command.[48]

The Bethel Regiment fought valiantly against the storm of fire. One of the company commanders, Capt. A. S. Haynes of I Company, fell within fifty yards of the stone wall. He got up but was shot down again. Captain Haynes later wrote, "I had no one in my company to fall back. . . . We were all cut down—no one but wounded left in my company, save two." Frank Bird still carried the regimental colors, but twice Union fire shattered the flag staff in his hands and grazed his thigh with a minié ball. The new acting brigade commander, Maj. John T. Jones, described the mêlée. "On we pushed, and were now right upon the enemy's works, when we received a murderous fire upon our left flank. I looked to see where it came from, and, lo! we were completely flanked upon our left, not only by infantry, but artillery." The enfilade fire rolled up the Confederate force from the north. With Gibbon counterattacking Pickett's men on the right and the left flank rapidly collapsing, the attackers' situation became hopeless. Trimble looked to the right to check Pickett's progress but saw "nothing but a few men in squads moving to the rear." One of Pickett's survivors, Randolph Shotwell, tried to join Pettigrew's attack in the salient. "I started back but halted in the road to see the result of Pettigrew's assault upon the left. . . . Judging by a momentary glance, about one thousand or twelve hundred North Carolinians and Tennesseeans swept over the road and up to the enemy's works. . . . I picked up a musket and started to move towards the left . . . [but] the enemy was pouring a terrible volley into the retreating Confederates and all was over."[49]

The Bethel Regiment fell back from the salient. Turning back from the failed assault left the Confederates in an extremely vulnerable position because they could no longer suppress the Union defenders. Smyth's and Sherrill's troops shot round after round into the smoke-filled salient as Trimble's and Pettigrew's force withdrew. Unfortunately, the men who advanced the farthest were in the worst predicament. They could not push forward across the stone wall, but they had advanced too far to pull back through the field of fire. Scores of men had no choice except surrender, once the attack receded. The regiments of Pettigrew's and Trimble's divisions lost nearly all their colors because they had advanced as far as the bravest men could carry them. Captain Bird stared at the stone wall as he faced a brave man's dilemma — surrender or carry the colors back through the fire-swept salient. Bird turned back through the salient holding onto the broken staff. The smoke, dust, confusion, and sporadic return fire helped cover his withdrawal.

The survivors drifted back in small groups to friendly lines; there were no formations left. Frank Bird returned to Seminary Ridge with the precious flag draped over his shoulder. Captain Haynes of I Company, left for dead on the field, managed to crawl back on his own after dark. The adjutant, Henderson Lucas, made it back to friendly lines only to die from his wounds a month later. Sadly, many did not return. Sgt. William Jetton of I Company, the brave man who tossed the bombshell into a pond at the battle of White Hall, was among the dead. Dozens of others lay dead or mortally wounded. Some of Smyth's force jumped over the stone wall and captured a large number of the Confederates pinned down in the salient. The Union defenders rounded up captains Hand, Armfield, and Small, as well as many of their men. The victorious northerners even captured the regiment's sergeant-major, James McCorkle.[50]

The attack on Cemetery Ridge wrecked the Bethel Regiment. Loss estimates for the regiment at Cemetery Ridge are difficult to calculate because of the extensive casualties, the confusion during the retreat, and the fact that the regiment fought battles on two separate days. The regiment's muster rolls identified at least twenty killed in action, forty wounded, and eighty-four missing during the attack on July 3. Many of the missing were actually wounded and left on the field to be captured. Combined with the slaughter of July 1, the attack on Cemetery Ridge further decimated the infantry ranks. Company A had one lieutenant, Billy Taylor, and eight enlisted men remaining. The combined C and I companies numbered no more than a handful. During the three-day battle, the regiment suffered 108 battle deaths among 366 total casualties! The loss rate reached 61 percent of the soldiers present for duty on July 1. Of the entire Army of Northern Virginia, only the 26th N.C. exceeded the Bethel Regiment's huge losses. Making matters worse, the command structure lay in ruins. The regiment had no field grade officers and averaged only one officer for each company. Years later, Leventhorpe remarked, "I took 28 officers into the battle. 14 were killed and most of the remainder wounded." Only one field grade officer, Maj. John T. Jones, remained within the entire brigade, and he had been wounded! The two generals, Heth and Pettigrew, had been wounded, although both continued to serve.[51]

General Lee greeted the men as they returned to Seminary Ridge. The burden of defeat lay heavily on his shoulders. One retreating officer overheard him mutter, "It's all my fault! I thought my men were invincible." Lee tried his best to raise the spirits of the retreating Confederates and encouraged them to reform their regiments. As he spoke to the men, he heard loud cheering coming from the Union lines. Lee ordered a junior officer to scout Cemetery Ridge and determine the cause of the yelling. The lieutenant scanned the enemy lines and observed a single Union officer riding about in front of the stone wall to the huzzahs of the northern troops. Across the valley, Brig. Gen. Alexander Hays reveled in his division's victory. He had gathered the fallen colors of fifteen Confederate regiments, seized by his men, and strung them behind his horse. Like Achilles dragging the body of Hector around the walls of Troy, Hays dashed about the salient trailing the Confederate battle flags over the bodies left on the field.[52]

The attack against Cemetery Ridge failed to achieve its purpose. Far from cracking Meade's army, the attack left the Army of Northern Virginia severely weakened. General Longstreet proved to be correct; no fifteen thousand soldiers could possibly have taken that objective. The attack verified what had already become obvious to military observers. Soldiers attacking across open terrain could not defeat a determined enemy defending fortified positions. The desperate charge to end the war on favorable terms fell short. Like the Charge of the Light Brigade at Balaclava and the final attack of Napoleon's

Old Guard at Waterloo, the attack on July 3, 1863, became famous as a heroic, but futile, effort by valiant soldiers. Southerners remember fondly the glorious moment at Gettysburg when the Confederacy reached its high-water mark . . . the stuff of legends.

FALLING WATERS

July 1863, Potomac River

The heavy losses of July 3 forced Lee to admit defeat and order a retreat from Gettysburg. With the Union army so close, the Confederates had to exercise caution in getting a head start toward the Potomac River. To avoid slowing down the army, Lee reluctantly abandoned the most seriously wounded soldiers who could not move with the march columns. The ambulance train moved back on its own without protection. The seriously wounded commander of the 11th N.C., Collett Leventhorpe, rode in one of the defenseless ambulances. He sadly recorded, "The Union cavalry dashed at the wounded train when near the Maryland line and captured the ambulance in which I was lying." For the proud colonel, capture added humiliation to the pain of his wounds. Conveyed to a prison hospital, Leventhorpe was advised by a Union surgeon that his arm had to be amputated because of the onset of gangrene. Leventhorpe refused to bear the added indignity of amputation. The surgeon then offered to treat the gangrene with nitric acid. Leventhorpe agreed to this but disdained the use of anesthesia. He suffered through the excruciating treatment without making a sound. Leventhorpe later told a friend that he preferred to die "rather than let an enemy see that a Confederate officer could not endure anything without a complaint." Scores of the Bethel Regiment's wounded shared Leventhorpe's fate, including Sergeant Lewis Warlick. He had been shot in the leg during the battle and later captured.[53]

Destiny required Captain Bird, acting regimental commander, and the men of the Bethel Regiment to play another significant role in the history of the Gettysburg campaign. Just as they had opened the great battle near Willoughby Run, so too did they close the campaign by the Potomac River. To save his army, Lee withdrew south to the crossing sites over the Potomac. Meade's army did not pursue vigorously, and the Confederates enjoyed an unimpeded move to the river. Their relief turned to frustration when they discovered that the bridges over the Potomac had been destroyed and the river was flooding. Several days passed before a new pontoon bridge could be built at Falling Waters. The army finally began crossing to the Virginia side on July 13.

Heth's Division had been serving as the rear guard for the army in the breastworks near Hagerstown, Pennsylvania, while the army waited for the completion of the bridge. On the night of July 13, Heth withdrew his division toward Falling Waters. The troops marched throughout the night in utterly wretched conditions. Heth recalled, "It rained incessantly; the roads were eight or ten inches deep in mud and water. My command brought up the rear of the army; we were compelled to halt every half mile; the road was blocked by wagons, artillery, etc." Mile after mile, hour after hour, the weary soldiers slogged their way toward Falling Waters. With each step, their feet sank into the mire, adding to the fatigue of the march. The frequent stops caused by stuck wagons merely prolonged the ordeal and provided little opportunity for the soaked troops to relax. At approximately 8:00 A.M., the division finally reached the last row of high ground above the crossing site, a mile short of the pontoon bridge. Heth received orders to form a line and face his men to the rear. Once the cavalry retired, his troops would provide security for the artillery, wagon trains, and other divisions of Hill's Corps as they crossed. Pettigrew received "instructions to let the men lie down and take all the sleep possible." At last, they could get some rest. An exhausted Maj. John T. Jones welcomed the orders. "We stacked arms and lay down on the ground and were soon all asleep feeling secure as there was a force of cavalry between us and the enemy." The men rested, but Pettigrew still felt uneasy about the situation, particularly because he had no supporting artillery. He turned to his adjutant and asked rhetorically, "Did you ever hear of the rear guard of a retreating army without artillery?" Pettigrew took additional time to scout the area and post a few pickets before he lay down.[54]

Near midday of July 14, the division commander rode up to Pettigrew to pass on instructions for the final withdrawal. Pettigrew acknowledged the orders and then complained to Heth about the lack of artillery support. While the generals conversed, some cavalry appeared outside the perimeter. Heth and Pettigrew saw them but assumed they were a contingent of Confederates they had seen on the road the previous night. Suddenly, a small troop of cavalry emerged from nearby woods and galloped straight for their position. The troopers rode to within a couple of hundred yards of the Confederates when the generals realized that the horsemen carried the "Stars and Stripes." Some alert infantrymen grabbed their rifles to halt the cavalry rush, but Heth shouted to hold fire. The division commander thought the riders were Confederates returning with a captured Union banner. Heth did not discover his error until the troopers from the 6th Michigan Cavalry burst upon Pettigrew's Brigade with sabers and pistols drawn. The cavalrymen rashly charged into the rear guard, apparently assuming that they were a group of stragglers. The sudden attack shook the rest of the men from their sleep. "I was aroused . . . and jumping up I saw the Yankee cavalry all among us cutting and sabering," wrote a startled Major Jones. "The men jumped for their guns and then commenced a hand to hand fight as is seldom seen in this war. The men clubbed their guns and knocked the Yankees off their horses. One man knocked one off with a fence rail and another killed a Yankee with an ax." Pettigrew's men quickly destroyed the cavalry troop, but not before the enemy had dealt a cruel blow to the brigade.[55]

The sudden charge carried the cavalry into the midst of Pettigrew's and Heth's conference. Heth witnessed the brief action. "A sergeant passed within a few feet of General Pettigrew and myself. In the melee which occurred, Pettigrew's horse reared and fell." The Union horseman found a position behind the Confederate infantry near a barn and began firing into the defenders. Pettigrew saw the sergeant firing unnoticed into his men and decided to kill the soldier himself. The general drew a small pistol from his coat; he could not handle his service revolver because wounds had disabled both of his hands. Pettigrew came within eight feet of the Union soldier on foot to get a clear shot, but his derringer misfired. "The sergeant shot him in the groin." Jones and the Confederate infantry reacted immediately when they saw Pettigrew get shot. "When the general fell the Yankee was riddled by our men."[56]

The Confederates had very little time to tend their critically wounded general. About an hour later, a larger Union cavalry force, under the command of Brig. Gen. Judson Kilpatrick, converged on Heth's Division. Major Jones, commanding the brigade once again, took charge of deploying the brigade's men. "I then received orders to fall back gradually to the river which I did. After going about 3 hundred yards the Yankees again charged us but we turned and gave them a volley which sent them back." Having fended off two cavalry thrusts, Heth observed more Union cavalry threatening the division's front and left flank. Heth sent word across the river to General Hill requesting artillery and more infantry, but Hill rebuffed his plea. Hill told Heth to pull back over the pontoon bridge, instead. The 11th N.C. and the rest of the division had to withdraw without support and under intense pressure from the Union horsemen. Heth fanned the brigades out in a wide skirmish line to prevent the cavalry from flanking his division and cutting them off from the bridge. Using alternating bounds by brigade, the division worked its way back toward the bridge as the Union cavalry advanced. One of the brigade's soldiers described the fighting withdrawal, "We would run, then fight then run again [then] fight until we got to the river." Twice the division routed charges from the aggressive troopers. Although the division fought stubbornly, command and control started to fall apart. The acting brigade commander, John T. Jones, soon discovered how grave the threat had become. "I fell back slowly in order to protect the troops on my left but after a while I found they were gone and left me entirely unsupported."[57]

The extended skirmish line and rough terrain made it impossible to maintain unit integrity, especially with Kilpatrick's cavalry snapping at their heels. The long, woeful march from Hagerstown had sapped the men's strength, and now the brigade had to hurry to the river as the enemy cavalry moved in to finish them off. Jones tried desperately to save the brigade. "I fell back as fast as I could but not before I was flanked on the left and several of my men taken." Frank Bird worked to keep the Bethel Regiment together, but the cavalry broke up the retreating southerners. Many soldiers collapsed from sheer exhaustion and fell into enemy hands before they reached the bridge. The Confederates managed to hold off the enemy long enough to get most of the survivors back to the bridge. Pettigrew's Brigade crossed the Potomac just before the Confederates cut the pontoon bridge loose. "Lee was willing to sacrifice our brigade to save the army but I tell you we had no notion of being taken." Once again, Bird had saved the Bethel Flag from capture. Unfortunately, ninety-four soldiers did not escape. The losses at Falling Waters compounded the casualties from the battle of Gettysburg.[58]

Once across the Potomac, the men of the 11th N.C. finally "drew a free breath." They had suffered terribly at Gettysburg and then lost more men during the night march and withdrawal to the crossing. Of the 650 soldiers who marched into Pennsylvania, more than 450 were killed, wounded, or missing, an astounding 70 percent casualty rate! The regiment may have been wrecked, but the survivors could take pride in their brave endeavor. The widows, orphans, and bereaved parents of those who fell would be comforted with the knowledge that their beloved soldiers had died valiantly in the great Gettysburg campaign. General Pettigrew's plight further saddened the Tar Heels. Although badly wounded, Pettigrew refused to be left on the field to be tended by Union surgeons. He knew that he probably would not survive the move to the nearest Virginia hospital, but he had previously vowed never to become a captive again. Frank Bird mourned Pettigrew's condition. "Since the fight [Gettysburg] I have in some way made a very warm friend of him. I understand he thinks I acted well on the field. Every flag in his brigade except mine was lost on the battlefield and I had to bring that off with my own hands, that may be the reason." Pettigrew held on for three days before dying at Bunker Hill, Virginia.[59]

Louis Young found some verses written down by Pettigrew in a pocket book, while he attended to the general's personal effects. Pettigrew must have kept them close as a source of inspiration and spiritual comfort. The poem provides a clue to the motivations of this brilliant and complex commander; a man driven by great ambition, yet tempered with a sense of humility.

> *Alone I walked the ocean strand,*
> *A pretty shell was in my hand,*
> *I stooped and wrote upon the sand,*
> *My name, the year, the day.*
> *As onward from the spot I passed,*
> *One lingering look I fondly cast,*
> *A wave came rolling high and fast,*
> *And washed my lines away.*

And as I thought, "twill shortly be
With every mark on Earth from me."
A wave of dark oblivion's sea
Will sweep across the place.
Where I have trod the sandy shore
Of time, and been — to be no more.
Of me — my day — the name I bore
To leave no track or trace.

And yet with Him who counts the sands,
And holds the waters in his hands,
I know a lasting record stands,
Inscribed against my name,
Of all this mortal part has wrought,
Of all this thinking soul has thought,
And from these fleeting moments caught,
For glory or for shame. [60]

Regrettably, the battle of Gettysburg left another bitter legacy for the regiment and the other North Carolina soldiers who attacked Cemetery Ridge. A war correspondent for a Richmond newspaper broke the story of Gettysburg to the southern press on July 22, 1863. His report dramatized the role of Pickett's Division of Virginia troops (Pickett was a Richmond native). He lavishly praised their heroic assault against Cemetery Ridge and penetration of the Union line. The virtuous soldiers of Virginia had sacrificed themselves in a great chivalrous charge. The story played perfectly to southern sympathies. The correspondent went on to explain how the flower of southern manhood, under the leadership of Virginia's own Robert E. Lee, could be beaten in battle. He attributed Pickett's repulse to lack of support from Pettigrew's command. The story contrasted the bravery of the Virginians with the timidity of Pettigrew's troops who were reported to have rushed "pell mell to the rear" without making an assault.[61] As Pettigrew and his brigade came from North Carolina and Trimble's two brigades were composed entirely of North Carolina regiments, the blame for the defeat landed squarely on the Tar Heel soldiers.

The slanted press report gave a one-sided view of what happened on Cemetery Ridge and added the dramatic effect to promote Virginia's self-image at North Carolina's expense. The correspondent may have heard of the resentment Pickett felt over not getting enough support to maintain his penetration. Pickett's official report contained such virulent criticism of the supporting columns that Lee forced him to withdraw the report for the sake of harmony within the army. Pickett may have been under the impression that Pettigrew would follow and support his attack as had been originally planned. Certainly, Pickett's soldiers deserved the praise heaped on them by the press for breaching the stone wall, a feat that Pettigrew and Trimble did not accomplish. Nonetheless, Pickett and the correspondent did not need a scapegoat to explain the defeat at Cemetery Ridge. They need not have looked further than Lee's defective operational plan to find the reason for the failure, but no one thought of criticizing Lee.

Pickett and the Virginia journalist expressed a theme that would become increasingly familiar during the latter stages of the war. Confederate commanders frequently excused their inability to seize an objective on the failure of other units to properly support their attack. Sometimes there was an element of truth in this excuse, as there was at Gettysburg where Longstreet held back two divisions that could have joined the attack. However, this excuse overlooked the two obvious explanations: first, the defender fought well; second, the attack lacked the strength to succeed. In some instances, Confederate commanders blamed a failed attack on "the supporting columns" when none had existed. These commanders apparently found it easier to blame their failures on lack of support than to confess that their units could not overwhelm a defender. Southern honor could not admit to any limits in the ardor of its attacking infantry.

Did Pettigrew and Trimble abandon Pickett and allow the II Corps to overwhelm his division? Only southern sources claimed so. None of the testimony of the Union soldiers suggested that the II Corps massed solely against Pickett's men. Lt. Frank Haskell, a Union staff officer who helped rally the II Corps defense, recalled the critical moment when Armistead punched into the Union line. Haskell immediately tried to organize a counterattack. "I thought of Hays upon the right; but from the smoke and war along his front, it was evident that he had enough upon his hands, if he staid [sic] the in rolling tide of the Rebels there."[62] Haskell did help mount a counterattack against Pickett's front and southern flank by Gibbon's Division, with help from some I Corps troops. The deadly enfilade fires that swept the northern flank struck Pettigrew's and Trimble's Divisions, not Pickett's. Though the attack in the salient failed to achieve a penetration, the regiments under Pettigrew and Trimble kept Hays completely occupied on the northern half of the objective. These troops could not be blamed for Pickett's repulse.

The Virginians' censure particularly rankled the North Carolina troops because the Virginia soldiers of Brockenbrough's Brigade were the only ones who truly failed to perform their duty in the attack. John T. Jones, who commanded the brigade's withdrawal from Cemetery Ridge, recalled a conversation with Pettigrew that expressed the general's feelings. "With tears in his eyes he [Pettigrew] spoke of the loss in his brigade, and then remarked, 'My noble brigade had gained the enemy's works, and would have held them had not Brockenbrough's brigade given way. Oh! had they have known the consequences that hung upon their action at that moment, they would have pressed on.'" Of course, the officers under Pettigrew and Trimble insisted that their attack advanced as far and as long as Pickett's. Third Lt. Billy Taylor denounced the news article. "It said that Pettigrew's brigade run on the 3rd day at Gettesburg [sic] but it is false." Captain Bird tried to explain the newspaper's mistake to his sister: "When I saw the article in the Richmond paper to which you allude I feared it might be taken for Pettigrew's Brigade. The article said Pettigrew's Command — meaning Heth's Division. . . . The left of our line [Brockenbrough's Brigade] is the part charged with backing and they did before the right." Major Jones seethed at the paper's insinuations even more than Bird. "On the 3rd day we were not in support of Pickett but were to his left and on the same line. That we never came up is all a lie. Tell a man in this army that North Carolinians failed to go where Virginians went and he would think you a fool." For years afterward, North Carolina veterans vehemently denied the allegation that they had abandoned Pickett in the attack. The debate led to the meaningless claim by some North Carolinians that their troops had advanced "farthest at Gettysburg" because they had reached the stone wall at the rear of the salient, which was a few yards farther east than the limit of Pickett's advance.[63]

Ultimately, the two thousand casualties suffered by Pettigrew's and Trimble's commands testify to the intensity of their attack on Cemetery Ridge far more than all the arguments and claims. The Bethel Regiment had 108 soldiers killed or mortally wounded at Gettysburg; thirty-five to forty of these fell on July 3. The death toll confirms that the Bethel Regiment left as many dead on Cemetery Ridge as Pickett's regiments.[64] The reporter's story did a grave injustice to these North Carolina troops who had sacrificed themselves so bravely.

Nevertheless, the romantic image of Pickett's gallant men, charging by themselves against Cemetery Ridge, rooted itself into the southern consciousness. The facts could not reverse the public's perception. Noted historians with access to the official records and contemporary testimony continued to focus on Pickett's Division and slighted the contribution of Pettigrew's and Trimble's commands. Lee's adjutant general, Col. W. H. Taylor, wrote in 1878 that Pettigrew's Division had wavered then retired, leaving Pickett to attack on his own. In his book *Memoirs of Robert E. Lee,* A. L. Long wrote, "Heth's division . . . faltered and fell back in disorder . . . leaving Pickett's men to continue the charge alone." He exonerated Lee from fault by commenting, "His plan had gone astray through the failure of the supporting columns."[65] Despite the many years that have passed, the deeds of Virginia's regiments still overshadow those of North Carolina, Alabama, Tennessee, and Mississippi. The very name "Pickett's Charge" tends to dismiss the valiant effort of the North Carolina troops in the attack against Cemetery Ridge. In a cruel ironic twist, the Battle of Gettysburg, which cost the Bethel Regiment so many of its leaders and men, even robbed the regiment of its dignity.

BRISTOE STATION

Fall 1863, Northern Virginia

*L*t. Col. William J. Martin rejoined the regiment on July 20, 1863, after the unit returned to Virginia. The sight of the diminished ranks saddened the professor. So many brave boys gone. Although he wanted to tend to the needs of the regiment, Martin had to devote himself to other duties. He took command of the brigade from Major Jones temporarily, as none of the colonels and lieutenant colonels remained with the four depleted regiments. When the 44th N.C. linked up with the brigade at the end of July, Martin relinquished command to Colonel Singletary and resumed command of the Bethel Regiment. Army regulations prevented Martin's promotion, as the 11th N.C. still carried Colonel Leventhorpe on the rolls. Leventhorpe officially commanded the regiment, despite being held prisoner. The Englishman was later exchanged and offered a general officer position but he declined for health reasons. His wounds forced him to resign from active service.[66] Only then was Martin promoted to colonel.

William J. Martin was born in Richmond in 1830. He grew up in the Old Dominion and graduated from Washington College. Martin stayed there to teach chemistry until he transferred to the University of North Carolina in 1857. When the war began, Professor Martin briefly taught tactics at the university, but he left his faculty position in September 1861 to enter the army. Throughout his career as an educator and a soldier, Martin always earned the admiration of his charges. "He was so noble, dignified, and withal unassuming—he was so true, sincere and frank, who could help trusting and reverencing him?" Like his two predecessors, Harvey Hill and Collett Leventhorpe, Martin was a devout Christian and rigid disciplinarian. Years later one of his students would write, "To Col. Martin there was no small infraction of the law. No 'little sin' . . . with him, education was for the purpose of disciplining and training the soul to think and act aright at all times, and especially under trying circumstances." The campaigns ahead would certainly test Martin's disciplined soul.[67]

The heavy casualties at Gettysburg and Falling Waters fractured the regiment's leadership, so Martin had to rebuild the weakened command structure. Naturally, he wanted to fill Major Ross's slot immediately, but he found his hands tied by regulations. Capt. M. D. Armfield had seniority over Captain Bird and, therefore, was entitled to the major's position. Although a prisoner and unable to serve, Armfield held down the position at the expense of Bird who was present for duty. For the time being, Martin served as the only field grade officer on duty with the regiment. Years later, he complained, "This defective organization continued to mar the efficiency of the regiment to the end of the war." The frustrating promotion bottleneck may have discouraged Frank Bird about his career prospects. In September his family and friends began a letter writing campaign to the secretary of war. They petitioned the Confederate authorities to appoint Bird to a military judgeship. Before the war, he had served as the state's attorney in Bertie County. The family justified the transfer by pointing to the poor state of his health. Bird had barely survived grave illnesses in 1862 and 1863; he suffered from chronic dysentery. Despite the merits of his case, nothing came from the petition, and events soon forced him to remain with the regiment.[68]

Martin also had to fill numerous lieutenant vacancies. Over the next six weeks, nearly every company in the regiment held elections to replace their fallen officers. The companies elected nine lieutenants from the enlisted ranks. The Bethel soldiers wanted men of merit to lead them and usually voted for the strongest candidates. Frank Bird expressed confidence in the officers selected by C Company: "They are all the men I wanted, best qualified to fill the positions." The men rewarded bravery by voting for proven fighters. Duncan Waddell of G Company jumped from the rank of private to first lieutenant by virtue of his heroic conduct on Cemetery Ridge. Waddell could not assume his new duties, however, as he had been wounded and captured. Six more enlisted men won promotions to lieutenant after the fall campaign and would serve with honor in the grueling battles of 1864. Despite the promotions, many officer positions remained unmanned. Company I could not elect any new officers as their commander, Capt. A. S. Haynes, and two of his lieutenants had been wounded and had fallen into enemy hands at Gettysburg.[69]

The regiment gradually reconstituted its strength, as the wounded and sick returned to duty, and new recruits came into camp. Cpl. Jacob S. Bartlett had missed the Gettysburg ordeal after falling ill at Hamilton's Crossing. When he and some of the other 'hospital rats' heard of the battle, they decided to leave the hospital at Harrisonburg, Virginia, and rejoin the regiment. "The doctor refused to discharge [the other enlisted men] unless they could get a non-commissioned officer to go with them. They asked me to get a discharge from the hospital and go with them, which I did, the doctor telling me at the same time that I ought to remain at the hospital longer." They saw a disheartening sight when they came upon their comrades. "The ranks had been thinned until it seemed that only a skeleton of an army had returned. Company K . . . lost three lieutenants, and almost all of the non-commissioned officers and a great many privates. The other companies suffered equally as much." The state continued to enlist men into the 11th N.C. to help replace the fallen veterans. D. Logan Warlick, Lewis Warlick's oldest brother, volunteered to serve in B Company. Logan may have joined to take Lewis's place in the ranks after the latter's capture at Gettysburg. These steps helped rebuild the regiment. By late July, Lieutenant Billy Taylor could write that A Company's strength had increased to fifty men. A few months later, the Union army exchanged a number of the soldiers captured at Gettysburg and Falling Waters. The fortunate survivors gladly left the wretched prisons and returned to the South. Some of these returning prisoners helped refill the ranks. Duncan Waddell came back to accept his commission in G Company. Others remained in southern hospitals or at home. Sgt. Lewis Warlick came home to Burke County to recover from his wounds. This time his hesitant sweetheart consented to his proposal, and they married while he was home recuperating.[70]

The army had to backfill critical leadership positions, too. The deaths of several generals, including Johnston Pettigrew, obliged Lee to name a new batch of brigade commanders. In September, he selected a North Carolinian, Brig. Gen. William W. Kirkland, to lead the five regiments of Pettigrew's Brigade. William Whedbee Kirkland had earned an appointment to West Point in 1852, but the young cadet was expelled for numerous disciplinary infractions. He stuck with a military career by obtaining a commission in the Marine Corps, where he served until the war started. Kirkland gained a lasting reputation as a fearless warrior and an inspiring combat leader. His courage won the respect of the Bethel Regiment and helped restore its fighting spirit. Yet, Kirkland's leadership did not quite measure up to the standards set by Pettigrew. He tended to ignore matters of discipline and he did not rigorously enforce regulations. Although postwar histories often praised Kirkland as a battlefield commander, they never cited resolute leadership as one of his characteristics, an omission with a clear meaning.

The regiment worked hard to reconstitute its fighting strength, but health problems still dogged the 11th N.C. throughout the summer. The late summer months of 1861 and 1862 had been times of great mortality within the Bethel Regiment, but that trend did not continue in 1863. Relatively few men died from illness, although fevers, ague, and measles reappeared. The veteran soldiers had endured two years of army life by that time and may have become inured to some of the diseases. More likely, the active campaigning kept the soldiers in the open, which reduced their exposure to contagion. The regiment's stay in the piedmont region certainly provided a better climate than the Carolina and Virginia low country where so many had expired in previous years.

Desertions suddenly increased dramatically among the western soldiers in late July. More than a dozen members of K Company headed for home. Six more from D Company took to the hills. The regiment had lost some strength to desertion during the march into Pennsylvania, but it had not previously witnessed such a large-scale exodus. A growing threat from the Union army and a declaration of martial law in the mountain counties of eastern Tennessee may have impelled the desertions. Other regiments also had problems with desertions. The 44th N.C. lost forty men in one night.[71]

Political developments in North Carolina may have undercut morale. During the summer of 1863, editor William W. Holden unleashed an editorial campaign against the Confederate government and began calling for a peace convention. The North Carolina troops in the Army of Northern Virginia reacted furiously to Holden's movement. The soldiers held firmly to the cause they defended on the battlefield. The regiments from the Old North State held their own meetings to denounce the peace movement and to affirm their support for Davis and General Lee. John T. Jones expressed his disgust with Holden's faction by stating, "I am ashamed of the course the Old North State is taking. If we ever are subdued it will be the fault of the citizens and not the armie's [sic]."[72]

Fortunately, these political developments took place during a period of relative calm. After Falling Waters, the Army of Northern Virginia retired to the defensive line of the Rappahannock and Rapidan rivers. The Army of the Potomac, under General Meade, pursued but did not disturb the Confederate position. The two sides spent the rest of the summer staring uneasily at each other across the river. The strategic situation changed in September when Longstreet's Corps transferred to General Bragg's army for an offensive in Tennessee. Lee maintained an anxious watch for moves by Meade while the Confederates were reduced in strength. On September 13, the Union army crossed the Rappahannock and occupied the area between the Rappahannock and Rapidan rivers near Culpeper Court House. The 11th N.C. answered an early reveille the next morning. "At the grey dawn our corps was on the march, crossing the Rapidan & taking the road towards Culpeper." Kirkland's Brigade stopped at the river to cover the crossing site at Rapidan Station. From their position, the Bethel infantrymen could look across the Rapidan and see the smoke of hundreds of Union campfires billow toward the sky. The Union cavalry soon probed the upper fords of the Rapidan. Meade's army appeared ready to strike, but the attack never came. Instead, Meade withdrew two corps on September 24 and sent them west to reinforce the Union Army of Tennessee. The strategic situation had reversed itself. Now Lee had a chance to take the offensive against a depleted Army of the Potomac.[73]

On the night of October 8, word came down to the Bethel Regiment to draw three days' rations from the commissary and prepare for movement. As the companies formed, the questions quietly passed down the line. "What's up?" "Dunno — Guess Marse Bob is after Meade's scalp." The officers confirmed that assessment when they addressed the troops. The Army of Northern Virginia was about to embark on a long turning movement around the Union army's western flank. Lee hoped to strike Meade in the flank or force him to battle on terrain of Lee's choosing. The regiment's officers went on to excuse any soldiers lacking shoes from the upcoming mission. They did not want to force shoeless soldiers to endure the long march. There would be no reproach for the barefooted troops, as Lee did not expect men with torn and bleeding feet to be able to keep up. Lack of shoes plagued many of the regiment's troops. They had worn out their footgear during the march into Pennsylvania and had been barefooted ever since. Most ignored the compassionate warning and remained in line with their feet wrapped in blanket fragments or strips of cloth. Obviously, motivation remained high. Around midnight, the bugle sounded the command to march, "the line wheeled into column and stepped off at quick time."[74]

The march started during the hours of darkness to help conceal the move from Union scouts. Lee wanted to get a head start before the Union army could react. He sent A. P. Hill's and Ewell's corps well to the west to get around Meade's flank, so they had to move rapidly.

Heth's Division spent a long day marching from Rapidan Station. The Confederates walked forty minutes and rested twenty minutes of each hour and reached Madison Court House by 9:00 P.M. on October 9. Over the next two days, the column turned north, hiking along the narrow roads between the Blue Ridge and its foothills. Hill's Corps skirted around the west side of Thoroughfare and Turkeyhole mountains and then moved toward Sperryville, using the foothills to screen themselves from the eyes of the Union cavalry. Up and down the ridges and valleys the troops marched, carefully avoiding dry spots on the road to prevent kicking up a tell-tale dust cloud. The troops foraged apples and chestnuts from local orchards as they headed north. At night they "tumbled down and slept" along the trail. "No bugles now, everything on the quiet — no fire — no talking."[75]

Although they failed to conceal their movement from the Union pickets, the stealthy measures served their purpose: General Meade had difficulty discerning Lee's intent from the intelligence reports. Initially, he could not decide whether the Confederates were withdrawing to Richmond or moving against the Union right flank. On October 10, General Kilpatrick's cavalry determined that Lee was heading around the western flank, so Meade shifted his forces in anticipation of an attack near Culpeper. By evening, the Union cavalry reported that the Confederate column had passed farther west and north of Culpeper. Meade had an opportunity to strike west and pin the Confederate army against the Blue Ridge, but he still had three of his corps back on the Rapidan River. He chose, instead, to fall back and catch Lee's army while it attempted to cross the north fork of the Rappahannock River near Warrenton.

A minor action on October 11 further confused Meade, so he kept the bulk of his army around Culpeper. Not until the evening of October 12 did Meade realize that A. P. Hill's Corps had reached the fords of the upper Rappahannock River west of Warrenton. Meade had allowed the Confederates to get around his western (right) flank and threaten to cut him off from Washington. On October 13, the Union army hurried northeast along the Orange and Alexandria Railroad, as Meade decided to move back to a blocking position at Centreville behind Bull Run. From this position, Meade hoped to force Lee's army into a general engagement.[76]

On the other side, the Confederates continued their forced march on October 13. By dawn the Bethel Regiment turned east and headed down the ridges toward the rising sun. The troops crossed the Rappahannock at noon, after building a makeshift bridge from rails to help the guns cross. As the men waded across the ford, they saw Harry Heth and Powell Hill sitting on their mounts by the riverbank. The two generals discussed the situation as the Tar Heels saluted and marched silently past. Hill's turn to the east meant that his corps was closing on the Union army. If they were going to hit Meade while in motion, they would have to move quickly. That would not be easy, as Meade had a direct line of retreat along the Orange and Alexandria Railroad. Hill urged Heth to keep his troops moving east after dark. They passed through Warrenton, "a village without a fence & with more bare chimneys than houses" in the twilight. As the evening wore on, the Tar Heels received word that they had to push on without the usual breaks until midnight. By the time they tumbled to the ground for the night, a cold drizzle fell on the weary troops.[77]

Heth's Division started its march early on the morning of October 14. The men were in for a cold, raw day; the drizzling rain had turned into a wet snowfall overnight. At New Baltimore, Heth turned off the Warrenton Pike and headed southeast to Greenwich; beyond Greenwich, the column would head toward the Orange and Alexandria Railroad at Bristoe Station. Heth now led the advance for Hill's Corps, with Kirkland following Brig. Gen. John Cooke's Brigade to Bristoe Station. Just before reaching Greenwich, Cooke's Brigade picked up stragglers from the Union III Corps. The division pressed forward eagerly, hoping to intercept the retreating Union corps. Adrenaline was pumping as both generals and privates realized that they had the Union army on the run. If they moved quickly enough, they might catch Meade and destroy his rear guard. The men prepared for a fight while they hustled along. "First one then another would swing his gun to the front examine the lock, see that the vent was open in the tube, wipe off any moisture that was seen, loosen his cartridge box & see that they were all safe and dry."[78]

Anxiously, Powell Hill rode forward to Bristoe Station to see the enemy for himself. The road from Greenwich approached the rail terminal from the west over a small rise. The railroad ran through the station on a southwest to northeast orientation. Northeast of the station the rail bed ran over an embankment before crossing the Broad Run.

As Hill rode up to the high ground overlooking Bristoe Station, he observed Union troops on the near side of the run waiting their turn to cross over the fords. Hill immediately concluded that he had come upon the rear of the Union III Corps. His quick survey proved that the Union troops in the valley had no idea that a Confederate corps was bearing down on them from the west. Hill reacted with excitement. Here was a fine opportunity to smash an unprepared Union force if he could strike quickly. Hill sent urgent orders for Harry Heth to hurry forward and attack Bristoe Station directly from the march column.[79]

Heth formed Cooke's and Kirkland's brigades into lines of battle a mile and a half short of the station, Cooke on the right side of the Greenwich road and Kirkland on the left (north). The 11th N.C. held the far left (northern) flank position of Kirkland's Brigade. "Silence on pain of death. Slowly and silently we executed the order taking care not to break a twig or speak a word as we went forward. When the line was formed we moved forward to the front with the brigade in line of battle." At Hill's insistence, Brig. Gen. Henry Walker's Brigade followed Kirkland's movement rather than attack on line; there was insufficient time to bring him abreast of Kirkland. Heth designated Davis's Brigade as the division reserve. With only two brigades on line, Heth's Division marched over the high ground, then stopped in a pine thicket overlooking Broad Run. Kirkland's path headed east from the high ground, toward the objective on the far side of Broad Run. The men held their breath as Hill's artillery battalion pulled forward to a firing position that could cover the valley. "A motion from Hill, the bugler raises his bugle & ye Gods what a crash! 40 guns at once belch forth fire, hail and death."[80]

Across the valley, Union soldiers scurried for cover as artillery shells pelted their position. They appeared totally confused as some raced across the bridge. The Confederates laughed at their startled reaction, except for A. P. Hill. He noticed something that immediately bothered him — a line of Union troops approached Bristoe Station from the southwest along the railroad. From that angle, these forces could hit Cooke's Brigade in the right rear flank as they advanced across the valley. As a precaution, Hill ordered Heth to delay his advance until another division could be brought up on his right. As soon as the van of the other division appeared — about ten minutes later — Hill ordered Heth to resume his attack. Heth and Cooke still had misgivings and expressed their apprehensions to Hill about the enemy force threatening Cooke's flank. Hill would not listen. He directed the attack to proceed without delay. They had to attack immediately or the opportunity would be lost. Hill cut short normal operational procedures in his haste to strike the confused Union rearguard. "The skirmishers were not allowed to feel the enemy."[81]

Cooke's and Kirkland's lines of battle marched out of the pines and down the slopes to Broad Run, preceded a short distance by the skirmishers. Cooke's Brigade veered to the right to keep the Union troops in the south from firing into their flank. This movement caused the whole line to shift to the right as it advanced toward the railroad embankment. Heth's attack changed from a straight thrust to the east into a right wheel, pivoting on Cooke's Brigade while swinging Kirkland's Brigade to face southeast. Soon the infantrymen detected a disturbing enemy reaction. Across the valley, a Union artillery battery dashed up a hill to get into a firing position. Kirkland's and Cooke's surged forward in a race against the Union guns. They had to get within rifle range to kill the horses before the Union gunners could swing into position and blast away at them. Kirkland's line of battle

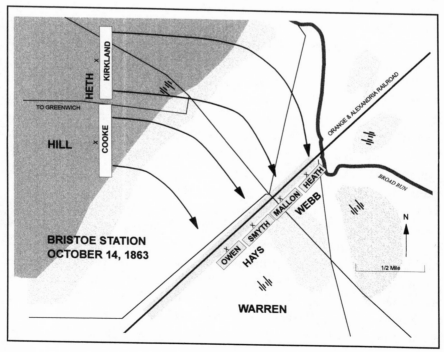

BRISTOE STATION
OCTOBER 14, 1863

charged ahead toward the railroad embankment in a mad dash to get at the Union guns. Suddenly, the embankment came alive with motion. Thousands of blue-coated soldiers rose from the earthwork, as if by magic, and leveled their rifle barrels toward the advancing Confederate line. The charging Tar Heel infantry barely had time to comprehend the meaning of the sudden apparition before the embankment exploded with "a roar as from the portals of Hell."[82] The massed rifle volley clobbered the Confederate line.

General Hill had misread the situation. What he thought was the rear of the Union III Corps turned out to be the lead of the II Corps under Maj. Gen. Gouverneur K. Warren. Warren's Corps had been moving northeast along the railroad through Bristoe Station on its way to Manassas. Warren chose to defend along the railroad with Webb's and Hays's divisions, using the embankment to provide cover and concealment. General Webb put his right flank brigade, Col. Francis E. Heath commanding, within 150 yards of Broad Run and extended his line to the southwest. Col. James E. Mallon's Brigade formed to the left of Heath and connected to Hays's Division. Warren had been able to move his brigades into position behind the embankment and out of the Confederates' sight. Hill's overriding desire to hit the Union rear caused him to forsake a reconnaissance of the enemy and throw two of his brigades against four Union brigades defending a well-protected position.

The volume of fire coming from the concealed position alerted the Confederate commanders that they had encountered a much larger force than expected. Cooke's Brigade and the right flank regiments of Kirkland's Brigade took a terrible beating from the II Corps fire. Luckily, the 11th and 52d N.C. had maneuver room on the left flank, beyond the direct fire of the embankment. As the extreme left flank regiment, the 11th N.C. had to march the farthest and brush against Broad Run as they wheeled to face southeast. Martin pushed the troops forward rapidly. The wide swing extended the regiment beyond the right flank of the 82d New York, the extreme right flank regiment of Webb's Division. Wheeling around to face the enemy, the Bethel Regiment and 52d N.C. dashed at the Union line with their voices raised in a rebel yell. They drove through the Union skirmish line and then dislodged the New Yorkers from the northeast end of the embankment. The rest of the Confederate attackers were not so fortunate.

Corporal Bartlett of K Company wrote, "As we swept down the slope
the enemy opened fire with their artillery and before we reached the
enemy's position; the center of the Division was so badly shattered
that they could not go through."[83] Cooke's Brigade and the right half
Kirkland's absorbed massive fire from Heath's, Mallon's, Owen's,
Smyth's brigades. Their attack only approached to within one
hundred yards of the embankment before the intense fire swept them
. Union minié balls cut down both brigade commanders and
d the attackers to pull back.

e failure of the attack left Martin in a precarious spot. He had
ol over his regiment and the 52d N.C. They held an advanta-
position on the northeast end of the railroad embankment and
punishing the 82d N.Y. with fire down the embankment. Mar-
uld press the attack down the enemy's defensive line, but with
her regiments falling back, such an attack was doomed. He could
onto his position at the end of the embankment and hope for
Walker's Brigade was moving up to reinforce the left flank, but
. not yet joined the battle. Already, Union troops were putting
ire on the 11th and 52d N.C., and a Union battery on the far
f Broad Run pounded the Confederate foothold. The last alter-
: was to withdraw, under fire, across the open ground. Withdrawal
e face of a defending enemy placed them at extreme risk because
could not suppress the defenders' fire once they turned their backs
e enemy. The defending riflemen could deliberately aim at their
ts without the fear of getting hit by return fire. Martin under-
l the hazards, but he knew that withdrawal offered the only chance
aving his command. Reluctantly, he ordered both regiments to
at to the high ground overlooking the valley.

he troops hastily fell back "under a galling fire from behind." While
ing back, rifle shots struck William Martin in the head and left
. The commander crumpled to the ground. Some of the men
ped him to his feet and carried him back to the cover of the woods.
hough badly wounded, Martin directed his soldiers to assist the
er injured troops before he retired to the ambulances. Many did
. escape. The prospect of crossing the open ground looked too risky
some. "A number of men shrank from crossing the field and were
ptured at the railroad." The timely withdrawal saved the two regi-
nts, but it had been painful.[84]

From the II Corps' view, the rifle volleys easily destroyed the Confederate attack. "They fell thick as leaves, stricken by our rain of bullets, — they broke and fled, — again they rallied behind the high ground, — and advanced, — again the rail road blazed, — the Rebels utterly broken haplessly fled, — our Infantry shouted, and rushed after them firing and shouting as they advanced." As daylight waned, Heth reformed his broken division on the high ground as Ewell's Corps came up to support the southern flank. General Warren knew he could not risk crossing Broad Run with Ewell's and Hill's corps at hand, so he patiently held his ground until darkness concealed his withdrawal. While a cold misty rain shrouded the battlefield, the II Corps troops noiselessly left their positions and filed across the bridge to the safety of the north side. One of Warren's staff officers recalled the one noise heard by everyone present. "The only sound we heard as we left the field was the groans of the Rebel wounded. Of this class we took away only such as could walk, — in accordance with our plans, we could not care for the rest, and so hundreds of poor fellows, on the field where they had lain since three o' clock, or in ditches whither they had crawled for shelter from the bullets, were making their piteous complaints to the unfriendly darkness alone, with none to help them. It was sad. I hope their own people found them and cared for them before morning." The Confederates did exactly that. One of Kirkland's officers related, "We groped out into the dark as far as we dared and brought out a number of poor torn & limp fellows."[85]

Despite the enemy fire, the 11th and 52d N.C. escaped with moderate casualties. The Bethel Regiment suffered four men killed and eleven wounded, including William Martin. The regiment lost forty-seven men who refused to withdraw with the regiment and surrendered at the railroad embankment. Captain Bird again assumed command, as there were no field grade officers left in the regiment. The application for a military judgeship did not matter now; the Bethel Regiment needed him. Although the battle turned out poorly for the Confederates, Bird felt pleased by the regiment's performance. "Our Regt. behaved very bravely." The Confederate losses for the battle generated great concern. General Heth's Division lost 143 men killed and 773 wounded. Another 445 men had been captured. The Confederates only inflicted 335 casualties on the Union forces engaged. Thirty-seven Union troops were killed in action; seven of those came from the 82d N.Y. The battle hardly inconvenienced the Union command, and Warren was able to establish his defense as he had been originally instructed.[86]

A. P. Hill reaped a harvest of criticism for the defeat. Hill himself realized that he had failed to develop the situation properly, failed to examine the terrain, committed Heth's Division too impulsively, and wrongly dismissed the apprehensions of Heth and Cooke about their vulnerability. Heth inserted an ill-disguised indictment of General Hill in his official report. "No military man who has examined the ground, or who understands the position and the disproportionate number of the contending forces, would attach any blame to these two brigades for meeting with a repulse." Powell Hill manfully acknowledged his mistake in his official report. The next day General Lee examined the ground while Hill explained the course of the fight. Lee offered no consoling words after the corps commander finished his explanation. He simply responded, "Well, well, general, bury these poor men and let us say no more about it." One of Kirkland's officers said plenty in an angry letter he sent home. "I am fully convinced that somebody, high in command, is greatly to be blamed, and if justice were done, would be cashiered. I wish North Carolina brigades could be placed in North Carolina Divisions." The bitter setback added to the growing friction between North Carolinians, who provided the most regiments, and Virginians, who provided the most generals. The Cemetery Ridge controversy, the anger over general officer appointments, and now the Battle of Bristoe Station poisoned relations between the Carolina and Virginia soldiers. This antagonism did not bode well for the Confederate cause.[87]

The bloody reversal at Bristoe Station gave William W. Holden a good excuse to launch an editorial campaign against the secessionists who had pushed the state into war. "One after another the pins erected by fanatical enthusiasts are being knocked from under us, and the naked reality is opening to the view. . . . The North is in earnest, terribly in earnest in this war, and her people are united almost to a man in their determination to prosecute the sanguinary struggle." Holden played on the sympathies of North Carolina's conservative voters at the expense of the government in Richmond and the old Democrats at home. He even called for a peace convention to negotiate an end to the war. On this point, Holden broke from the policies of Zeb Vance.

The governor shared many of Holden's political views, but he still hoped for southern independence. The strain between the two political partners moved closer to an open confrontation.[88]

The débâcle at Bristoe Station caused another reversal in the strategic military situation, and Lee retired to the Rappahannock River. The Army of the Potomac trailed the Confederate army back south, dislodging a Confederate position on the river in early November. Lee pulled his army behind the Rapidan River and fortified a new defensive line. Both armies found themselves in nearly the same positions from which they had started in October. In late November, Meade decided to take the offensive against Lee before the winter set in. He did not have much time for a campaign as the weather had already turned raw. The troops described the conditions with an expressive mixed metaphor, "Cold as Hell, clear as a bell and blowing like damnation."[89] The northern army crossed the Rapidan over the Germanna and Ely fords east of Lee's positions. The Union crossing put Meade between Lee's army, clustered around Orange Court House, and Fredericksburg. With the enemy across the river on his right flank, Lee shifted his army into a new defensive line facing east along Mine Run, a small southern tributary of the Rapidan. Hill's Corps moved east from Orange Court House on the Orange Plank Road with Heth's Division leading. They moved to the southern (right) flank of the Mine Run defensive line and entrenched. Meade advanced westward and pushed back Lee's forward elements on November 27.

Upon examination of the Confederate defenses, Meade decided against a frontal attack across Mine Run. He preferred to move Warren's II Corps and part of the III Corps around to the south and attack the Confederate right flank. At the same time, Meade ordered the V and VI corps to make a supporting attack against the Confederate northern flank. Meade scheduled the attack for 8:00 A.M. on November 30, but it was never launched. Gouverneur Warren, who had the responsibility for the Union's main attack, carefully reconnoitered the Confederate breastworks with the practiced eye of a military engineer. As he scanned the ground his men would have to attack, he noticed Heth's well-prepared fortifications. Warren concluded that the Confederate breastworks were too strong to assault. The junior corps commander canceled the attack on his own authority. That decision caused Meade to call off the entire operation. If Meade resented his subordinate's presumptuous decision, he did not publicly criticize Warren, which may have reinforced Warren's unhealthy tendency to question his commander's orders. Warren had an intelligent mind but an imperious personality that annoyed his superiors. The brash general would later suffer a personal humiliation owing, in large part, to his irritating manners.

Regardless of the odd way the attack was canceled, the decision appeared to be correct. Harry Heth felt disappointed that the Union army did not strike his entrenched line. "Had Warren attacked, his left and left center would have met my division. I was hoping he would attack; in order that I might square accounts with him for his treatment of me at Bristoe Station."[90] An uneasy stalemate followed the canceled attack. The two armies stood facing each other across Mine Run, neither side willing to attack the other. General Meade could have resumed his movement south. However, the winter season approached, and Meade worried that his wagon trains would bog down on the sodden roads. He terminated offensive operations and assumed a defensive posture for the winter. Meade preferred to fall back to Fredericksburg, south of the Rappahannock River, but Washington overrode his desire and directed him to position his army north of the Rapidan-Rappahannock line. This timid decision would force the Union army to fight its way across the river when it resumed offensive operations in 1864. Both armies returned to their previous positions and settled in for the winter. The 1863 campaign had come to a close.

The 11th N.C. remained near Orange Court House for the rest of the long, dreary winter. The cattle herd taken during the Gettysburg campaign had been exhausted by this time, and the commissary had to reduce the rations. The reduced subsistence did not satisfy the men, and morale suffered accordingly. Pvt. Bellfield King wrote in a January letter, "I reckon if they don't give the soldiers more to eat there is a heap of them will come home and I would not be surprised if I wasn't one of them." By early spring the regimental quartermaster, John Tate, reported, "I am now hauling forage from near the NC line — about 130 miles! Officers of every grade draw the same ration as the men." Even Tate suffered the effects of the poor diet. "I am hungry all the time. . . . [I] make it a point to say in the presence of the troops that the ¼ lb. bacon & ⅛ lb. meal is just as much and as good living as I want. (But I don't mean it.)"[91]

The shortage of shoes had not improved after the Bristoe Station and Mine Run campaigns. L. A. Bristol wrote to his brother to complain about the harsh life in the army. "Nothing to eat, nothing to drink and out of soap. I am bare footed, I haven't had rest and shoes since I came back from Gettysburg. I have been doing duty all the time, but if they don't soon give me a pair, I will resist doing duty, for I am not going to stand guard bare footed any longer." Bristol may have threatened to avoid duty, but his letter went on to acknowledge the impracticality of exempting shoeless soldiers from duty. "There is a heap in the same fix I am, but we have duty to do, and if they let all the bare footed escape duty there wouldn't be anybody left for nearly all are bare footed." Finally, Bristol decided to fix the problem on his own. He sent a request to his brother for leather to make some shoes for himself and his buddies.[92]

During the dismal winter months Capt. Calvin Brown of D Company received a pathetic letter from 1st Lt. W. J. Kincaid. Kincaid had been captured at Gettysburg and wrote from the Federal prison at Johnson's Island, Ohio. Kincaid complained about his own crippling injuries and the miserable prison conditions. "I am dreadful tired of prison life." He did pass on one piece of intelligence. Capt. M. D. Armfield had died of dysentery on December 3, 1863. Armfield had enlisted as a corporal in the Burke Rifles at the age of fifty-four. When the Bethel Regiment reorganized in 1862, the Burke County soldiers elected him captain. The old man served with the regiment until his capture at Gettysburg, but his health could not withstand the harsh conditions of prison life. The winter of 1863–4 saw many of the regiment's soldiers perish from disease. The winter deaths afflicted both the ones imprisoned in the north and those still serving with the regiment. The cold weather, poor living conditions, and improper diet left the troops vulnerable to more illness beyond the usual dysentery and fevers. Pneumonia became one of the dread killers during the cold season. It took the life of Lewis Warlick's brother, 2d Lt. Portland Warlick, in December. Earlier in the war, the humid summer months caused the most deaths; now, the winter months became the deadly season. The unfortunate captives in northern prisons suffered the most. In the nine months following Gettysburg, nearly half of the regiment's deaths by disease occurred among its prisoners.[93]

Armfield's death produced some movement within the regiment's command structure. The loss of the senior captain allowed the regiment to promote Francis W. Bird to the rank of major. In March 1864, Colonel Leventhorpe returned to the South in a prisoner exchange. The high command offered Leventhorpe a promotion to the rank of brigadier general, but he eventually had to refuse the promotion owing to poor health. Leventhorpe resigned on April 27, 1864. His departure allowed William J. Martin, who had returned from the hospital, to assume the rank of colonel and F. W. Bird to rise to lieutenant colonel. The regiment still could not fill the major's slot, as the Union held the senior captain, A. S. Haynes, a prisoner.

Back home in the Old North State, politics heated up the winter months as William W. Holden, the editor of the *North Carolina Standard,* formed a political opposition party and declared his candidacy for the governorship in the upcoming July elections. Holden made the issue clear in a March editorial. "He [Holden] was for peace, Vance for war." Governor Vance crafted his platform to denounce the "Destructives" who had pushed the South into secession while he pledged his full support for southern independence. He reasoned that the old Democrats could not mount their own candidate and would side with him as a lesser evil than Holden. On March 26, 1864, Vance paid a visit to the North Carolina brigades in Lee's army to drum up support for his reelection. The governor's visit delighted General Lee who worried about the motivation of the numerous Tar Heel regiments in his army. Lee went out of his way to give Vance royal treatment. The army commander formed the North Carolina regiments into two ranks on a parade field near Orange Court House. Lee and Vance mounted their horses to review the state's veteran soldiers. As cannon boomed in salute and troops cheered, the governor and commanding general rode between the lines. Lee rode abreast of the visiting politician, which was a demonstration of support that impressed the soldiers. After the inspection, Governor Vance moved to a platform where he delivered a patriotic address to the regiments. The governor's remarks stirred the enthusiasm of the troops and General Lee who stated, "Vance's visit to the army was equivalent to a reinforcement of 50,000 men."[94]

Vance addressed individual North Carolina brigades over the next few days, including Kirkland's on March 30. His message had a special appeal for the Bethel troops. "Patriotism, fidelity to their living companions and reverence for the memory of those who had died,

scorn for those who would betray a trust, the assurance of the gratitude of their countrymen and, especially, the affectionate appreciation of their services by the womanhood of the South, and the horrors
of subjugation were his theme." The regiment's quartermaster, John
Tate, listened carefully to Vance's address. Tate, an old Burke County
Democrat, had advocated secession and did not appreciate Vance's con-
demnation of the "Destructives" and his anti–Davis message. He criticized Vance's address in a letter to a business associate. "I don't think
it was calculated to make him much reputation among strangers."
Nevertheless, Tate reacted in exactly the fashion Vance had expected
of the old secessionists. "I shall support him, as a better man than his
opponent, tho' not as my choice of all men in N. C." Vance went back
to Raleigh feeling much better about the political support he could
expect from the soldiers in his upcoming campaign.[95]

The Warlick family also held steadfast to the cause as the new year
unfolded. Lewis Warlick's youngest brother, William Julius, enlisted in
B Company to fill the void left by Port Warlick's death. All four
remaining Warlick brothers (Lewis, Pink, Logan, and William Julius)
now served in B Company. The B Company soldiers had elected Lewis
to take his late brother's place as an officer, which convinced him to
rejoin the regiment and accept a commission as a 2d Lieutenant. The
company had changed since Lewis fell at Gettysburg. "When I
returned I found the old 'Bethel' looking quite different. . . . Upon
the whole it is not the regiment it once was." Warlick then turned his
thoughts to his wife back in western North Carolina. She had protested
in 1861 and 1862 when he had signed up with the Bethel Regiment.
Undoubtedly, she fought with him about serving again. He tried to
console her about his return. "I hated very much to leave but otherwise I could not do." His bride's entreaties failed to keep him home
in Burke County.[96]

4

A Butchery Pure and Simple

WILDERNESS

May 1864, Rapidan River

D uring the first days of May 1864, the Army of Northern Virginia looked across the Rapidan River at Meade's Army of the Potomac and Burnside's IX Corps. The two armies held positions similar to the ones they had held the previous autumn. The Army of the Potomac occupied the area around Culpeper, while Burnside's Corps guarded the Orange and Alexandria Railroad. Lee put Ewell's Corps south of the Union army to defend several fords over the Rapidan River. A. P. Hill's Corps bivouacked around Orange Court House, ready to reinforce Ewell. Longstreet's Corps remained further south and west to protect Lee's left flank, yet close enough to support Ewell and Hill.

Although the positions of the armies appeared similar to those of the previous year, a major strategic change had occurred; the Union armies had a new supreme commander, Lt. Gen. Ulysses S. Grant. U. S. Grant would prove to be a more formidable opponent than any previous Union commanding general. When he assumed command of the Union's armies, he adopted a military strategy that called for a full-scale, simultaneous offensive by Union forces in all theaters to overwhelm the South. The Virginia theater had always occupied center stage in the Union's military plans because Lee and his army posed the principal threat. Lee's army stood between Washington and Richmond, from which position it protected the Confederate capital and threatened the national capital. For three years, the Army of Northern Virginia had frustrated every Union attempt to capture Richmond. Before the South could be vanquished, Grant would have to deal with Lee and his army. Grant chose to play a direct role in the movements against Lee, although he commanded all Union armies in the field. Grant had to destroy Lee's army in Virginia or, at least, pin it down while Maj. Gen. William T. Sherman's western army subdued Georgia.

Grant faced a tough challenge. First, he had to cross the Rapidan River, then attack Lee on terms favorable to the larger Union army. He chose to turn Lee's eastern flank by crossing the Rapidan River between Mine Run and Fredericksburg. The area south of the Rapidan, known as the Wilderness, did not offer Grant good terrain for fighting the Confederates. Dense woods, thick underbrush, and numerous streams would force extremely short-range engagements and negate Grant's numerical advantage. Grant preferred to swing south of the Wilderness to force a decisive battle with Lee in an area where he could mass the Union's four corps and long-range artillery fire against Lee's three corps. From its present position, the army would have to march the better part of three days to cross the fords and traverse the Wilderness before reaching open country. Grant and Meade wanted to pass through the Wilderness before Lee could pin them down in the dense forest. To accomplish this, Meade and his staff ordered the move to Germanna and Ely's fords to begin at midnight on May 3–4. The Union columns would continue marching over the fords and well into the Wilderness before halting on May 4. Another hard day of marching on May 5 would allow them to reach the farmland to the south before Lee could bring them to battle. On May 6, Grant planned to turn west and crush Lee in the open terrain.

The Germanna Plank Road would serve as the main avenue for Grant's right (western) column on its advance through the Wilderness. The left (eastern) column of the army could use Ely's Road on a parallel route. The Germanna Plank Road crossed the Orange Turnpike at the site of the Wilderness Tavern, five miles southeast of the ford. The road extended three miles farther southeast before ending at the

Orange Plank Road intersection. The Orange Plank Road ran west-southwest along a narrow plateau that separated the watersheds of the Wilderness Run and the Ny River. The plank road ran past Parker's Store three and a half miles southwest of the Germanna Plank intersection. Another plateau rose above the surrounding lowlands just north of Parker's Store where the Chewning farm was located. A forest road wound its way northeast from Parker's Store over this plateau to the Orange Turnpike near Wilderness Tavern. The upcoming battle would swirl around the rough triangle described by these three roads.

Lee saw the same situation as he conferred with his generals atop Clark Mountain on May 2. Looking down on the Union camps across the Rapidan, Lee confidently predicted that Grant would attempt to turn his right (eastern) flank. Obviously, the Confederates preferred to fight in the Wilderness where the dense vegetation would permit their infantry to fight on more equal terms. Could they hit Grant's army in the Wilderness? The Orange Turnpike and the Orange Plank Road headed east into the Wilderness from the army's current position. If Grant tried to turn the right flank, these roads provided Ewell and Hill quick routes along interior lines into Grant's flank. The problem for Lee was the amount of time it would take Longstreet's Corps to reach the battle. Longstreet would need two full days to reach the Wilderness, but Lee wanted his full strength to fight Grant. Assuming the Union army would spend one day moving to the fords and one day crossing the Rapidan, Lee figured that he could strike on the third day while Grant's troops marched through the Wilderness. The army commander closed the conference by ordering his subordinates to prepare for a sudden march to strike Grant's force in the Wilderness.[1]

As Grant had planned, the Army of the Potomac started for the fords at midnight on May 3–4. Gouverneur K. Warren, now commanding the V Corps, led the way to Germanna ford on the western route, followed by Sedgwick's VI Corps. Hancock's II Corps (the hero of Gettysburg had returned to his command) marched on a parallel road to Ely's ford. All three corps sustained their movement through the morning of May 4, until they had crossed the river and entered the Wilderness. By the end of May 4, Grant had reason to be satisfied with the Union's progress. With similar progress on May 5, they would reach the open country and then turn west against Lee.

The Confederates did not remain idle. Observers on Clark Mountain and pickets at the fords reported the Union movement on the morning of May 4. Lee issued orders to move according to the contingency plan. The Bethel Regiment's soldiers hurriedly prepared for the march around the Orange Court House campground. Tents came down and the quartermasters collected excess personal property. The infantrymen stuffed hastily cooked rations into their haversacks, rolled up their blankets, rechecked their cartridge boxes, and fell into company formations. The company commanders reported to Colonel Martin that their companies were ready to move. "In less than an hour . . . all [were] gone, marching eastwardly." A. P. Hill's Corps marched out from Orange Court House by noon. Heth's Division, including the 11th N.C., led the advance on the Orange Plank Road. Heth kept the troops moving at a blistering pace all afternoon, and they reached New Verdiersville by the end of the day. The small town lay about twelve miles from Parker's Store and fifteen miles from the critical Orange Plank-Brock Road intersection. Heth's men bedded down behind the Mine Run fortifications erected the past November. To the north, Ewell's Corps rested on the parallel Orange Turnpike, on the way to the Germanna Plank intersection.[2]

The enemy situation remained unclear as the Bethel troops unrolled their blankets and lay down that night. Lee still did not know which way Grant's forces would turn on May 5. Would he turn west to attack Lee near Mine Run or south to force Lee to retire from the Rapidan River? Lee wanted to disrupt whatever Grant intended. He decided to test Grant with a reconnaissance in force the next day. Hill's Corps would push against the Union western flank along the Orange Plank Road, while Ewell's Corps probed on the Orange Turnpike. He cautioned the corps commanders against starting a major fight until the entire army could concentrate. Lee wanted to avoid a general engagement, though he hoped to interfere with the Union advance. He would hit with full force once Longstreet arrived. For the men of the 11th N.C., this meant an early start the next morning. While Colonel Martin and his men slept, the Union forces organized their security outposts. The Union's dispositions did little to help their intelligence gathering. Along the critical western flank the 5th N.Y. Cavalry stood watch at Parker's Store but did not send any scouts farther west to locate the Confederates. Consequently, Grant and Meade knew nothing of the force approaching from Orange Court House.

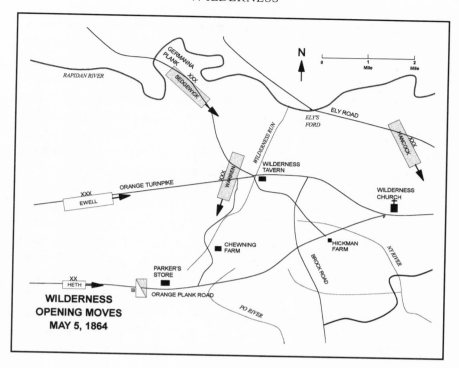

**WILDERNESS
OPENING MOVES
MAY 5, 1864**

General Warren planned to continue his advance across the Chewn-ing Plateau over the small forest path that ran between Wilderness Tav-ern and Parker's Store. Before dawn on May 5, he posted a division on the Orange Turnpike to detect any threat coming from the west-ern flank as the corps moved southwest. By 6:00 A.M. that division discovered Ewell's Corps advancing east. This initial report of Con-federate movement against the western flank prompted Meade to order Warren to concentrate against the Confederates on the turnpike. Until a clearer picture emerged, Meade decided to halt the southward move-ment of Hancock's II Corps, which marched on the eastern parallel route. Lee's strategy for slowing the Union advance by probing the western flank worked very well. Too well. Like two powerful mag-nets, the Army of Northern Virginia and the Army of the Potomac drew toward each other in a premature clash on the Orange Turnpike. Intelligence soon confirmed that a large Confederate force approached on the turnpike. Meade decided, with Grant's concurrence, to face Warren's entire corps to the west and attack. The decisions by Meade and Lee led to a major battle in the Wilderness on May 5. Neither

Grant nor Lee fought the battle he desired. From Grant's perspective the battle was in the wrong place, the Wilderness; for Lee, it started too soon — one day before Longstreet had arrived.

At the time, the Union commanders had no idea of the situation developing on the Orange Plank Road where events also were moving rapidly. Kirkland had awakened his men before dawn to start their march. A cheer sounded as they scrambled over the Mine Run breastworks and left the position behind; the Bethel men realized that Lee was taking the offensive. Ever confident in the attack, the Tar Heels geared up for a hot day of action. Kirkland's Brigade, followed by the rest of Heth's Division, had covered ten miles by early morning and bore down on the Union pickets. The 47th N.C., Kirkland's lead regiment, struck two troops of the 5th N.Y. Cavalry two miles west of Parker's Store. The rest of the cavalry regiment quickly joined the fight. The New York troopers put up such a heavy volume of fire with their Spencer carbines that Kirkland thought he faced an infantry brigade. He deployed his entire brigade into a line of battle to push back the cavalry. Aiming, shooting, and reloading, the 11th N.C. moved steadily forward. The infantrymen pressed the Union horsemen in the front while trying to turn their flanks. The New Yorkers could not hold off the Carolina infantry and fell back. The scrub oak helped to conceal the cavalrymen, but the infantrymen got enough clear shots to punish the troopers. The cavalry left a trail of dead and dying men on the road to mark their running battle with Kirkland's infantry. Although the brigade deployed on line, their steady advance allowed the rest of Heth's Division to keep moving in a march column behind them. General Lee rode right behind Heth's men and watched approvingly as Kirkland drove the cavalry east. By mid-morning Kirkland's regiments had pushed the delaying cavalry force east of Parker's Store.[3]

U. S. Grant heard two disturbing reports when he arrived at Meade's headquarters that morning. Warren still had not attacked owing to difficulties in aligning units in the thick underbrush. Grant slowly fumed when he heard of the delay. Then he received the distressing news that a second Confederate infantry force had already passed Warren's left (southern) flank while the Union forces had frittered away precious time. That did it! Grant reacted immediately and forcefully. He ordered Warren to attack with whatever troops he had available to charge. Grant directed Hancock's II Corps to turn back from its route, march to the Orange Plank Road by way of the Brock Road, and counter-attack the Confederates on the Plank Road (A. P. Hill's Corps). Because Hancock would need time to reach the Plank Road, Grant sent Brig. Gen. George Getty's Division of Sedgwick's VI Corps to secure the vital Orange Plank-Brock Road intersection.

Kirkland's troops had driven back the Union cavalry for several miles, but the constant advancing, dodging, and firing had exhausted them. When the fatigued infantrymen pushed past the forest trail on the Chewning Plateau, part of Warren's V Corps fired into their flank. Heth pulled Kirkland to the left to secure this flank and then ordered Cooke's Brigade to lead the attack down the Plank Road. Kirkland's Brigade followed later as the reserve brigade as soon as the next division (Maj. Gen. Cadmus Wilcox's) relieved them. As Cooke's skirmishers came within sight of the Brock Road, they spotted more mounted Union soldiers holding the intersection. The skirmishers fired at them but could not drive them off. Cooke's men maneuvered through the thickets to get better shots at the defenders. The skirmishers did not realize that the only soldiers defending the Brock Road intersection were General Getty and his staff. No infantry! The officers stood their ground while rifle shots whizzed past their heads; George Getty was not about to run for cover with so much at stake. Getty's act of raw courage paid off. His lead infantry element arrived on the scene just before Cooke's men closed around the intersection. The Union infantry threw back Cooke's skirmishers, killing some of them within thirty yards of the Brock Road. The Union army won the race to the intersection by the barest of margins.[4]

Getty deployed his men along the Brock Road oriented to the west, while Cooke sent word back to Heth that the Union army held the crucial intersection in force. Harry Heth halted the advance and deployed his division astride the Plank Road until he could develop the situation. Cooke's Brigade straddled the road, supported by Kirkland's Brigade to their rear. Davis's Brigade formed alongside Cooke's left (northern) flank, and Walker's Brigade deployed south of the road somewhat away from the front. Kirkland deployed (from north to south) the 47th, 44th, 26th, and 11th N.C. directly behind Cooke. He kept the 52d N.C. in reserve. This deployment put the Bethel Regiment south of the Orange Plank Road. Heth had to hold the Plank Road by himself because Lee and Hill had diverted Wilcox's Division to the Chewning Plateau to cover the yawning gap between Ewell's Corps on the turnpike and Hill's Corps on the Plank Road.[5]

For the next several hours, Getty and Heth faced each other in the dense forest, both certain that the other side was massed in greater strength. Colonel Martin and his men scratched out temporary fighting positions in the woods behind Cooke, although the infantrymen had trouble finding clear fields of fire through the brush. The Bethel men were grateful for the chance to rest their feet after the long march, but they knew the reprieve would not last. They could hear the steady roll of musketry coming from the turnpike and figured their turn was coming. A few miles away, an impatient George Meade had already decided to start the action on the Plank Road.

Hancock's Corps began arriving at the intersection around mid-afternoon. Before Hancock could assemble his corps, orders arrived from General Meade to attack immediately. General Getty launched his attack at 3:30 P.M. with all three brigades abreast. Col. Lewis A. Grant's Vermont Brigade attacked south of the Orange Plank Road, as Wheaton's and Eustis's brigades advanced on the north side. Getty's Division slightly outnumbered Heth's but was compressed into a denser

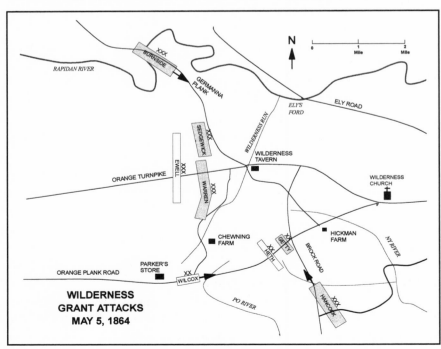

line of battle that allowed Heth's line to extend beyond Getty's flanks. South of the Plank Road, Colonel Grant organized his Vermont Brigade into two lines of battle. The 3d and 4th Vt. led the attack while the 5th, 6th, and 2d Vt. followed. L. A. Grant's advance led him straight into the right flank of Cooke's Brigade, which the Bethel Regiment supported. The Vermont Brigade's attack got off to a poor start. The 3d Vt. drifted too far left (south), passed by their skirmish line, and was ambushed by Cooke's defensive line. The commander of the 3d Vt. remarked, "We met the enemy, who gave the first indication of his presence by delivering a full volley in our front, in consequence of which I lost many valuable lives. . . . After receiving the enemy's fire I ordered a charge, but the nature of the ground and the heavy fire of the enemy rendered it impossible." The 4th Vt. fared no better against Cooke's rifles. "Their line melted like wax." L. A. Grant observed, "As soon as the first volleys were over, our men hugged the ground as closely as possible, and kept up a rapid fire; the enemy did the same." Separated by only ninety yards, the opposing lines of battle blazed away at each other through the underbrush.[6]

Wheaton's and Eustis's brigades, like L. A. Grant's, advanced only about 300 yards when they ran into a "terribly destructive fire." The denser Union formations pressed Cooke's Brigade in the center, requiring support from Kirkland's men. Heth had to commit his reserve brigade (Kirkland's) piecemeal into the action to plug gaps and shore up the weak spots. The 11th N.C. helped the troops of the 15th N.C. absorb the shock of the Union assault. The stubborn Confederates refused to break, despite intense pressure from Getty. "Though forced back some distance in the center, they held in the main their ground and repulsed every attack," Getty admitted. South of the Plank Road L. A. Grant brought forward the 2d and 6th Vt. from his second line to fill the gap between his lead regiments and bring more firepower into the fight. The intense Confederate fire compelled the 2d Vt. to crawl forward to reach the front line while minié balls whistled through the thickets and ricocheted off tree trunks. Colonel Grant finally got his regiments on line, but the whole Vermont Brigade was pinned down by the Tar Heels.[7]

Getty called for immediate help from Maj. Gen. David Birney, the nearest division commander from Hancock's II Corps, to regain the initiative. Birney answered Getty's plea by splitting his division, sending Alexander Hays's Brigade to the north flank and Brig. Gen. J. H. Hobart Ward's Brigade to the south. General Ward brought three regiments forward to support L. A. Grant's attack. Colonel Grant coordinated directly with the 20th Ind., 40th N.Y., and his own 5th Vt. to make a fresh assault around the southern flank. "The order for the charge was given, and all advanced in good style, and the enemy partially gave way." Just as Grant and Ward surged forward, Heth brought up Brig. Gen. Henry H. Walker's Brigade to form on line with the right (southern) flank of Cooke's Brigade. L. A. Grant's and Ward's fresh assault crashed into Walker's Brigade as they came abreast of the forward defensive line. Although L. A. Grant had swung the attack around his own left (southern) flank, he had not enveloped General Walker's. The Confederates turned on the exposed Union flank and chewed up the 5th Vt. Their commander complained, "We suddenly found ourselves 40 or 50 yards in advance of the remainder of the line, wholly unsupported and exposed, not only to a front fire of unprecedented severity, but also to a raking fire on both flanks of the most galling description."[8]

This menacing attack on the southern part of Heth's line drew the 11th N.C. into the swirling fire fight to reinforce the sagging forward line. Colonel Martin stated, "[Kirkland's Brigade] was actively engaged . . . in repelling assault after assault . . . and in counter charges." The combined attack by Grant and Ward still could not break Heth's line and bogged down. The senior officers lost control of the battle, as small units locked into close combat and the thick vegetation disoriented leaders. L. A. Grant stated, "It was so dense that it was impossible for an officer at any point of the line to see any other point several yards distant." The fighting grew extremely intense as the battle lines surged back and forth through the oak scrub. Although the Union had launched a general attack, the two sides changed roles from offense to defense as the tide of battle ebbed and flowed, usually favoring the defenders. Colonel Grant noted, "The moment our men rose to advance the rapid and constant fire of musketry cut them down with such slaughter that it was found impracticable to do more than maintain our present position. The enemy could not advance on us for the same reason."[9]

At one point, Getty noticed a concerted effort by Heth's force. "The enemy charged and forced back our lines some 50 yards, when they were checked and repulsed." Colonel Martin recalled a peculiar incident involving the Bethel Regiment at this stage of the battle. "In one of these charges our brigade formed part of a second line of battle, Cook's [Cooke's] Brigade, commanded by Colonel [William] MacRae, afterwards our Brigadier-General, being on the first line. In advancing we came upon MacRae's line lying down, and as we charged over him with a yell, he sneered sardonically, 'Go ahead, you'll soon come back.' And sure enough we did. We struck, as he had done, the Federal line behind entrenchments, from which in vain we tried to dislodge it, and recoiled, lying down in turn behind MacRae's line. I fancy he smiled sardonically then."[10]

With Getty's and Birney's divisions halted, General Hancock committed Brig. Gen. Gershom Mott's Division to extend the southern flank of L. A. Grant's and Ward's battle line. General Mott put his two brigades on line and advanced toward the sound of rifle fire. Mott failed to envelop Heth's flank; he merely fed his troops into the battle. His division was soon entangled in the forest, its own formations, and the southern flank of Grant's Brigade. Col. Robert McAllister, commander of Mott's right flank brigade, discovered that his line of

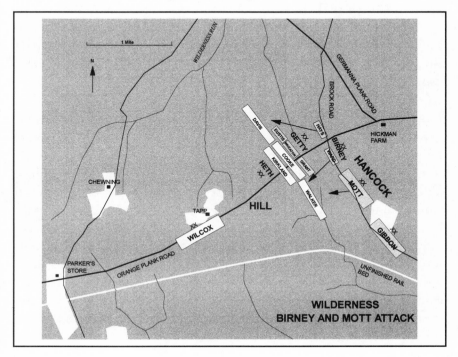

WILDERNESS
BIRNEY AND MOTT ATTACK

advance crossed the path of Mott's other brigade and ran into the rear of the 5th Vt. One of McAllister's officers wrote, "It became necessary to halt and reform the line. This was found to be almost impossible." Just then the Confederates assaulted Mott's exposed left flank and collapsed his line as Union officers watched helplessly. "A few volleys of musketry were heard to the extreme left and rear, and immediately the line on the left, as far as I could see, commenced falling back in confusion. This was rapidly carried on to the right . . . my regiment followed and all efforts to rally the men were fruitless. The troops seemed panic-stricken."[11]

Back at the Brock Road intersection, General Hancock received word that Getty's Division was running low on ammunition, just as another staff officer rode up and reported the disaster on the southern flank. "General Mott's division has broken, sir, and is coming back." One witness recounted Hancock's reaction. " 'Tell him to stop them, sir!' roared Hancock in a voice like a trumpet. As he spoke, a crowd of troops came from the woods and fell back into the Brock Road. Hancock dashed among them 'Halt here! Halt here. Form behind this rifle pit.' "[12] Through forceful leadership, Hancock restored order to Mott's shaken troops. At this critical moment, Brig. Gen. John Gibbon's Division came marching up the Brock Road. Hancock immediately ordered them to face left and attack to relieve Getty's exhausted division in the center. Col. Samuel Carroll's and Brig. Gen. Joshua Owen's brigades turned into the Wilderness.

Owen's Brigade of Gibbon's Division passed over L. A. Grant's troops and hit the center of Heth's Division with a vigorous assault. Owen arrived in time to relieve the Vermont troops who had expended their ammunition. This attack by fresh soldiers covered the same ground that had been hotly contested by Getty's and Heth's men. William Martin recalled the grisly scene: "Our regiment lay down behind a line of dead Federals so thick as to form a partial breastworks, showing how stubbornly they had fought and how severely they had suffered." The Bethel soldiers fought with a fiery spirit. Above the roar of battle the infantrymen shouted, "Pour it to 'em boys! Pour it to 'em." Gibbon's infantry could not break the stalwart Confederate defense, either. Heth's soldiers had just enough strength to stymie the latest assault. Owen and Carroll stalled in the dense vegetation just like all the previous attacks that afternoon.[13]

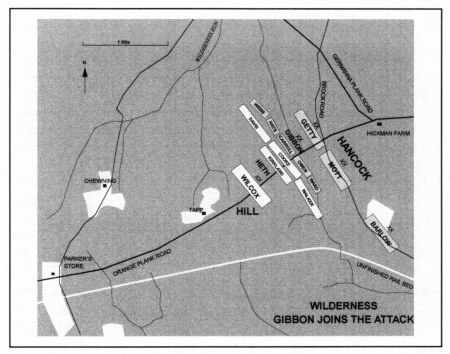

WILDERNESS
GIBBON JOINS THE ATTACK

Heth's men held valiantly against the swelling Union attack, but they had exhausted themselves and their ammunition. The renewed pressure from Gibbon's fresh troops would soon crack Heth's depleted defensive line if they kept up the pressure. A. P. Hill and Lee realized that Heth could not hold indefinitely against such odds. Lee ordered Hill to commit his second division, Wilcox's, to relieve the pressure. Lee preferred to leave Wilcox on the Chewning Plateau to close the gap between the two corps, but the fury of Hancock's attack gave him no choice. Reluctantly, Lee sent Wilcox down the road at the expense of leaving Hill's northern flank unprotected. Wilcox's counterattack passed through Heth's line in the same dense woodland that had enclosed the afternoon's fierce combat. Wilcox's troops ran headlong into Carroll's, Webb's, and Owen's brigades of Gibbon's Division. Neither side could gain a significant advantage in the whirling action. The two opposing lines of infantry fought to an impasse against each others' determined resistance. After Wilcox passed through his command, Heth redeployed his brigades about 500 yards behind the front, as daylight ebbed away.[14]

The troops took a terrible pounding from the back and forth struggle, fought at extremely close range. Poor command and control, owing in large part to the thick vegetation, reduced tactics and maneuver to a simple piling on of regiments. One officer from Cooke's Brigade assessed the tactics of the battle: "A butchery pure and simple it was, unrelieved by any of the arts of war in which the exercise of military skill and tact robs the hour of some of its horrors. It was a mere slugging match in a dense thicket of small growth, where men but a few yards apart fired through the brushwood for hours, ceasing only when exhaustion and night commanded a rest."[15]

General Hancock had been denied a victory by the poor terrain, the stubborn resistance of the Confederate soldiers, and the aggressive leadership of their junior officers. Heth's and Wilcox's troops drove back every Union attack, despite an unfavorable balance of strength. By day's end, Hancock and his subordinate commanders drew solace from the fact that they had at least held Hill's two divisions at bay. U. S. Grant did not feel satisfied with such a trifling accomplishment. He ordered one last attack, sending a division south from Warren's V Corps to exploit the gap and crush the exposed northern flank of Hill's Corps. Brig. Gen. James Wadsworth's Division advanced through the thick underbrush in the twilight, but an alert line of Confederate skirmishers ambushed Wadsworth's men and threw them into confusion. Before the Union officers regained control, darkness descended on the forest, which ended the constant musketry.

Grant's army lost an opportunity to deal a crushing blow to the Army of Northern Virginia on May 5. The II Corps and Getty's Division should have gained a decisive advantage on the Orange Plank Road. Had Hancock overwhelmed Heth's Division, he could have forced Lee to withdraw, but he failed to push through a solitary Confederate division. Harry Heth felt justly proud of the way his division had fought. For three hours they single-handedly "repulsed ten successive and determined attacks of the enemy. . . . They nevertheless had not yielded up an inch of ground." That evening Powell Hill congratulated Heth for his unit's performance. "Your division has done splendidly today; its magnificent fighting is the theme of the entire army." Harry Heth would remember the first day of the Wilderness as his best day of the war. Hill had reason to be proud of his entire corps. His two divisions had stopped the advance of the Union's II Corps and Getty's Division of the VI Corps — a remarkable performance. Sadly, the corps commander could not savor his success. Hill's prostate condition had worsened, and the hard day of riding had severely inflamed his groin. He was so wracked with pain that he could do nothing more than ease himself into a camp stool and stare into a small campfire.[16]

General Lee did not feel as pleased as his subordinates. He had wanted to avoid a fight on May 5 to give time for Longstreet's Corps to arrive. With all three corps available, Lee wanted to wallop the Union army with a powerful stroke. Despite his intent, Ewell and Hill had gotten embroiled in a desperate struggle because Lee had not anticipated the Union general's aggressiveness. How long had it been since the Union army had spontaneously attacked his army? Grant's impetuosity robbed Lee of strategic initiative. As he analyzed the prospects of combat on May 6, he realized that he had lost freedom of action. The wide gap between his two engaged corps had to be closed and Hill's depleted force relieved before he could gather a force to attack Grant. Longstreet's Corps, the only force not pinned down by Union troops, would have to strengthen the southern flank, then Hill's Corps could shift over to plug the gap. Lee had to forsake any bold counterstroke until he could gain more latitude.

That night word came down to the 11th N.C. that Longstreet's Corps would relieve them in place before morning. The officers instructed the men not to dig in but to "rest on their arms as night found them." Lee and Hill wanted to give the men a full night's rest after the grueling day of combat. They had marched ten miles, fought a running battle for several more miles, and then battled savagely for three hours. The exhausted soldiers fell asleep without the benefit of entrenchments, reassured by the promise of relief in the middle of the night. The regiment ended the day on the left flank of the second defensive line, about 500 yards behind Wilcox. Heth pulled Cooke's Brigade farther back as the reserve force to secure the artillery. Contrary to instructions, General Cooke ordered his men to dig in behind a clearing on Widow Tapp's farm.[17]

Confusion and misunderstanding during the hours of darkness brought Hill's Corps near to destruction. Longstreet's Corps did not arrive during the night; the men stopped to rest several miles short of the battlefield. In the middle of the night, a worried Harry Heth rode over to Hill's camp. He urged A. P. Hill to arouse the troops and adjust the defense in light of Longstreet's delayed arrival. "Let me take one side of the road and form line of battle, and Wilcox the other side and do the same; we are so mixed, and lying at every conceivable angle, that we cannot fire a shot without firing into each other. A skirmish line could drive both my division and Wilcox's, situated as we now are. We shall certainly be attacked early in the morning." Hill listened to Heth's argument but decided against shuffling the troops. He felt concerned for his soldiers' welfare and chose to let the men sleep instead. This decision may have reflected Hill's own exhaustion and ill health rather than a reasoned military choice. Heth left in a quandary over Hill's unwise decision. He returned later to get it reversed. "A second and third time I saw Hill and begged him to order Wilcox to get his men out of the way. . . . The last time I saw Hill he got vexed and said, 'Damn it, Heth, I don't want to hear any more about it; the men shall not be disturbed.' "[18] Frustrated and piqued by the corps commander's rebuke, Heth squandered the predawn hours searching in vain for General Lee in the hope of having the order counter-manded. Heth could have better used the precious time by discreetly ignoring Hill's instructions and organizing his troops into some kind of defensive line. As it turned out, word of Longstreet's delay did not reach the brigades, and they remained in place without preparing for the next day's struggle. Although Hill's Corps had fought off the Union forces on May 5, the day had ended with Wadsworth's Division poised to strike their northern flank and Hancock's Corps ready to make an overwhelming attack on their front.

When the troops of the 11th N.C. awoke, they realized that the relief in place had not occurred. The men began forming a line of bat-tle in the predawn twilight, grimly awaiting another day of intense combat. "We had just formed in time to make some little obstructions . . . when a courier rode up and informed Gen. Kirkland (our brigadier) the enemy was close by." Kirkland became nonplussed as he realized how poorly prepared the Confederates were to repel an attack. "Kirkland showed himself quite restless and uneasy walking backward and forwards casting his eyes towards his men and toward the advancing enemy." Before the brigade could organize, Wadsworth's force struck the northern flank. At the same time, Hancock's divisions charged into the front of Wilcox's Division. The disaster that Hill's troops had so narrowly avoided the previous evening overwhelmed

them the morning of May 6. The command had done nothing to prepare for the heavy blow. A. P. Hill's misguided attempt to "take care
of the troops" cost the lives of hundreds of those troops. Colonel Martin described the impact of Wadsworth's attack on the unprepared
Confederates. "A furious attack was made on our left flank and the
unformed line was rolled up as a sheet of paper would be rolled, without the power of effective resistance." He acknowledged ruefully the
neglect of the Confederate command. "If even a single brigade had
changed from front to left before the enemy struck their flank they
might have stemmed the tide and have stopped the rout. But no
Brigadier seems to have thought of it."[19]

Hancock's attack against the front of Hill's Corps enjoyed similar
success. The Confederates' disordered line of battle did not provide a
cohesive front against Hancock. The II Corps attack poured through
gaps in the line, overrunning Wilcox's Division and hitting parts of
Kirkland's Brigade. The 52d N.C., which held a position behind
Wilcox, was surprised by a volley fired into its rear. Col. Clark M.
Avery, one of the commanders from the old 1st N.C. Volunteers, tried
to rally the 33d N.C. in Wilcox's Division when Union rifle fire cut
him down. Another Bethel veteran, Lt. Col. John T. Jones, fell while
leading the 26th N.C. against the rolling tide of the Union assault. The
stalwart soldiers who had fought the larger Union force to a standstill
on May 5 broke and ran. Heth's and Wilcox's divisions fell back in disorganized flight, streaming to the rear under the horrified gaze of
Robert E. Lee. In a matter of minutes, Wadsworth and Hancock
routed, though not destroyed, the Confederate forces that had frustrated them the day before.[20]

Cooke's Brigade alone held its place during the rout, benefiting
from the emplacements dug during the night. Some of Heth's disorganized troops ran across Cooke's entrenched troops as they fled. Seeing a defensible position, the retreating soldiers rallied and joined
Cooke's tentative defense.[21] The men from the Bethel Regiment and
Kirkland's Brigade quickly recovered their discipline and fighting spirit,
despite the unnerving rout. Even as men poured past them, the troops
of Cooke's, Kirkland's, and other fragmented units braced for the surg-
ing Union forces. Getty's Division soon smashed into their position.
The defenders and a supporting artillery battery fired across the open
field staggering the onrushing attackers. The effect was only tempo-

rary; other Union brigades appeared and swarmed around the flanks of the Tapp farm. The Confederates had to fall farther back to avoid being overrun.

Suddenly, elements of Longstreet's Corps dashed eastward past the retreating Confederates and into the head of the Union attack. Longstreet's long-awaited troops attacked out of their march column straight into the advancing Union line. General Lee, sensing the urgency of the moment, dashed to the front of the Texas Brigade to personally lead Longstreet's counterattack. The Texans refused to advance with the army commander so dangerously exposed and shouted for him to fall back. Lee acknowledged their determination not only to drive back the enemy, but also to remove him from the front. He quietly turned to the rear as the Texans threw themselves forward into the charge. To Hancock's dismay, just as his successful attack was losing momentum, he absorbed the shock of Longstreet's fresh corps. The timely counterattack retrieved the day for the Confederates and sent Hancock's divisions reeling backward. In a series of savage, yet skillful, attacks, they pushed back Hancock's force. Longstreet hammered against the Union divisions over the same battle-scarred ground where Hill's soldiers had fought the day before. Unlike the Union attacks of May 5, Longstreet executed a bold envelopment of Hancock's Corps that folded their battle line and pushed them back to the Brock Road. Hancock reformed his weary corps along the Brock Road entrenchments. Despite a valiant effort, Longstreet could not break through Hancock's entrenchments and was severely wounded while leading the counterattack.

Meanwhile, Heth's Division reorganized and formed a defensive line on the Chewning Plateau that finally connected Ewell's, Hill's, and Longstreet's corps into a continuous front. After the humiliating panic of the morning, Heth must have felt relieved to shift to a quiet sector away from Lee's disapproving stare. In his memoirs he admitted, "I think General Lee never forgave Wilcox or me for this awful blunder." Glory is fleeting! This time, Heth's officers had the men dig into their positions.

The fighting in the Wilderness took the lives of many North Carolina leaders. The Confederates evacuated Lt. Col. John T. Jones of the 26th N.C. to a field hospital. As a surgeon attended him, Jones asked whether his wound was mortal, which the surgeon sadly confirmed. "It must not be. I was born to accomplish more good than I have done," he lamented. The veteran of the 1st N.C. Volunteers died a short time later.[22]

At the end of the second day of fierce fighting, Grant's army had been forced into a defensive position along the Germanna Plank and Brock roads. The Confederates felt upbeat about the battle. They had taken a lot of punishment, especially in Hill's Corps, but they had stopped Grant cold and thrashed him in the Wilderness. Lee had faced the new Union commander and had beaten him. Everyone could see that the Confederate infantrymen still had superior fighting spirit. They admitted that Grant and his men had shown more aggressiveness than usual, but the Confederate soldiers still prevailed. Around their campfires, Powell Hill's staff talked about the prospects for the next day. "Tis generally thought that Grant will recross the river tonight."[23] They misread the Union commander's will. Grant had no thought of giving up. He recognized that further attacks in the close quarters of the Wilderness would be fruitless, so he decided to move in a different direction where he could strike Lee's army on advantageous terms. The next day, Grant issued orders to move south toward Spotsylvania Court House.

SPOTSYLVANIA

May 7–21, 1864, Northern Virginia

The campaign suddenly shifted from the Wilderness to Spotsylvania in the evening of May 7, 1864. U. S. Grant moved his army south on the Brock Road in an attempt to interpose the Union army between Lee and Richmond. Unlike McClellan, Burnside, and Hooker, Grant remained determined to pressure Lee's army, despite the bloodletting in the Wilderness. He maneuvered Warren's V Corps from the northern flank, behind the other corps, and then south to Spotsylvania. The Union commanding general, as a precaution, kept Hancock's Corps in place on the southern flank. Lee's surprise attack on May 5 taught Grant the importance of guarding against a sudden assault. Lee, who anticipated a move by Grant, reacted swiftly and sent Longstreet's Corps, commanded by Maj. Gen. Richard Anderson, to Spotsylvania. Anderson's troops reached the crucial road junction just before Warren, which frustrated Grant's plan. Unable to "steal a march" on the Confederates, Grant chose to take Spotsylvania by force. Severe fighting erupted on May 8, as the Army of the Potomac assaulted Anderson's (formerly Longstreet's) and Ewell's corps. The Confederates quickly entrenched around Spotsylvania and held off the Union attacks.

A. P. Hill's Corps did not march with Anderson and Ewell to Spotsylvania. Lee could not be certain that Grant had moved his entire force to Spotsylvania, and he had to protect his rear from attack. Lee left Hill's Corps on the Orange Plank Road until the enemy situation became clear, so the Bethel Regiment sent scouts forward to locate any enemy still in the area. Lewis Warlick wrote, "We remained on the field till Sunday evening of the 8th and not an enemy could be found in front by our scouts." What the scouts did find provided shocking evidence of the horrible punishment suffered by the northerners. Sgt. Jacob Bartlett, one of the scouts, made a mortifying discovery. "I went to the front and in rear of General Grant's battle line and found that he had moved away without burying his dead, many of whom had been killed the first day and carried a short distance to the rear; they laid in rows and one could have walked over acres of ground and stepped on a dead Yankee every step."[24]

When Hill's Corps marched from the Wilderness it did so without its commander. Following the battle of the Wilderness, A. P. Hill became so ill from prostatitis that he could not mount his horse. Lee had to make a temporary command change, so he placed Hill's Corps under the irascible Maj. Gen. Jubal Early. After verifying that the Union army had vacated the Wilderness, Heth's Division marched with the rest of Hill's (now Early's) Corps toward Spotsylvania late on May 8. The men had the good fortune to miss the fighting that they could hear raging near Spotsylvania. On May 9 the 11th N.C. continued traveling to Spotsylvania Court House, the far right of Lee's defensive line, and deployed around the village just as Burnside's IX Corps approached from the east. Burnside saw Early digging in across the Spotsylvania-Fredericksburg road and realized that the opportunity to seize the courthouse had passed. He deployed his soldiers opposite the

Confederate breastworks. Early's arrival at the courthouse marked the consolidation of Lee's army at Spotsylvania and the failure of Grant's effort to turn Lee's flank.

The Tar Heel soldiers got no time to settle in. The next day, May 10, Lee sent Heth back to the opposite (western) flank to help eliminate a new threat. Birney's and Brig. Gen. Francis Barlow's Divisions of the II Corps had crossed the Po River and menaced Lee's left flank. These two divisions had thrown pontoon bridges across the river and secured the wooden bridge on the Shady Grove Church Road. The Po River, which generally flowed to the southeast, meandered south in this area across the path of the Shady Grove Church Road. The river separated Barlow and Birney from the rest of the II Corps, which remained on the north and east side of the Po. General Early ordered Heth to drive the isolated Union force from the south side of the Po and secure the Confederate left. Heth and his men welcomed the chance to fight the II Corps again, in an attempt to atone for the embarrassing collapse on May 6.[25] By noon the division had hustled six miles from the courthouse to Talley's Mill on Gladys Run.

General Birney sent four regiments from his division south of the Shady Grove Church Road as far as Gladys Run to establish the II Corps skirmish line.[26] The skirmishers had hardly gotten set before the Union commanders changed the corps' mission. General Meade had misgivings about deploying the two divisions south of the Po River. Around mid-morning, he ordered Hancock to withdraw Birney and Barlow before their troops became engaged. In addition to worrying about their isolated position, Meade wanted the divisions to join in a major assault against a different part of the Confederate defense. Birney's Division began withdrawing, while General Barlow shifted his four brigades to cover the rearward move. Col. Paul Frank's Brigade, in the west, and Col. John Brooke's Brigade, farther east, initially entrenched along the south side of the Shady Grove Church Road. They defended a clearing that went from the road north to the Po. This clearing was bounded on the west and east by two wooded areas that offered concealed routes of withdrawal to the pontoon bridges. Miles's and Smyth's brigades occupied positions farther east.

Kirkland's and Davis's skirmishers made contact at midday with the Union skirmish line along Gladys Run. Kirkland put his regiments into a line of battle and advanced. "We came up with and immediately commenced driving the enemy's skirmishers. . . . We drove them from a fine position on Glady Run." Birney's four regiments of skirmishers pulled away from the run and headed to the pontoon bridges. Heth's Division pushed forward into an open field and began shelling the positions of Barlow's covering force. The infantry caught their breath while Richardson's artillery battalion softened up the Union entrenchments next to the Shady Grove Church Road. The Confederates hastened the Union withdrawal. Barlow pulled Miles and Smyth back to the Po River and shifted Frank's and Brooke's brigades into a delay position in the open ground north of the road.[27]

Around 2:30 P.M. Heth resumed the attack. Kirkland's Brigade charged forward through the open ground near Wait's Shop, halted to realign its formation, and then pressed forward again. They ran into some of Frank's skirmishers who held a line of fortifications just south of the road. "[We] charged upon them in thare [sic] breastworks and drove them out of thare [sic] breastworks and got in them ourselves." The Tar Heel infantry threw the second Union skirmish line across the road into Frank's main defensive line. The Confederate skirmishers soon crept into the woods on the south side of the road and opened fire on Barlow's two dug-in brigades. The two sides amused themselves by trading shots across the road. General Heth could see that Frank's and Brooke's brigades would require a full-force attack to dislodge. He brought up his other brigades and formed his division for the assault. Cooke's Brigade moved into line on Kirkland's right. The 11th N.C. tried to rest during the interlude, but the II Corps artillery shelled them "very heavy all the time." Once the division formed, orders to attack passed down the line, and the Confederates charged, "pressing forward with loud yells." The 11th N.C. and the other regiments charged across the road, "delivering a terrible musketry fire as they advanced." Heth's Division threw its full weight against Frank and Brooke, but the fire from Barlow's two brigades proved to be too heavy. The assaulting infantry fell back to reform their line of battle in the roadway and returned more fire against the Union breastworks. As the battle turned into a brief stalemate, General Early rode to the front to keep the attack moving. He approached some Mississippi men in time to hear them complain that they had run out of ammunition. The crusty general replied, "What of that? Damn it, can't you halloo? You can drive them by hallooing. Forward!" Early's encouragement did the trick. Heth's line leapt to their feet and charged again with a loud chorus of rebel yells.[28]

Across the battlefield, another crisis assaulted the defenders just as the Confederates launched their attack. The woods behind Frank's Brigade caught fire and threatened their route of withdrawal. Barlow, worried that his brigades would be cut off by the fire, ordered them to retreat. The Union move to the rear heartened Heth's forces. The Confederate infantry "charged to thare [sic] second breastworks and drove them out." The Bethel soldiers plunged into the flaming woods and poured rifle fire into the retreating Union regiments. Still, Frank's men gave ground grudgingly in a brisk exchange of rifle fire. Before long, the intense pressure from the pursuing Confederates, and the confusion caused by the burning woods, placed Frank's and Brooke's brigades in a critical situation. Command and control fell apart when the forest fire prevented staff officers from reaching some of the retreating units to pass instructions. Regiments were separated from their brigades and cohesion dissolved. Heth's soldiers riddled the Union troops once they started driving them. The retreating soldiers could not stop the Confederate assault nor could they evacuate their wounded. A number of Frank's soldiers were hit and fell helplessly to the ground, while their comrades scurried back to the Po River bridges.[29]

To the Bethel soldiers, the scene must have looked like a vision of Hell — whistling bullets, scorching flames, and choking smoke. Above the roar of the battle, they heard the piteous cries of the Union wounded perishing in the flames. No time for humanitarian acts. The regiment had the enemy on the run and had to press the assault while it had the advantage. Frank's and Brooke's brigades fell back to the position of the other two brigades where they finally gained relief from the Confederate pursuit. Barlow's strong position and the heavy fire from the artillery across the river brought Heth's attack to a halt. The Union brigades slipped across the pontoon bridges under the covering fire of the II Corps artillery. General Early ended the action since Heth had driven Barlow to the north side of the river and cleared the objective. The 44th N.C. even had a prize from the final assault. During the hasty withdrawal, the Union II Corps lost a rifled cannon that had gotten wedged between two trees and had to be abandoned. In his official report, General Hancock acknowledged, "This was the first gun ever lost by the Second Army Corps and was deeply lamented by us all."[30]

Early and Lee felt delighted by the outcome. Heth's Division had eliminated a threat to the army's left flank in handsome style and with only a modest loss. Colonel Martin suffered a slight wound but remained on duty with the regiment. General Heth published a letter of congratulation, endorsed by Lee, to the division. Besides expressing confidence in the men, the official letter may have been the generals' way of apologizing for allowing the disaster in the Wilderness to occur. The troops of the Bethel Regiment felt redeemed for the humiliating retreat on May 6, and spirits rose within the ranks. On the other side of the fence, the Union army resented Heth's self-congratulation. When Hancock heard about the letter, he groused that Heth "would have had no cause for congratulation" had Barlow been allowed to fight with his full force. As the Union intended to withdraw from the south bank, Hancock did not feel that Barlow had suffered a defeat. In fact, he was pleased by Barlow's ability to withdraw under such pressure. Still, the Union commanders could not overlook the heavy casualties in Frank's and Brooke's brigades nor the loss of the "gallant wounded who perished in the flames." Although the Confederates only won ground the Union had decided to relinquish, Barlow had suffered heavily. As with many Civil War battles, the long casualty list was the most notable result of the conflict.[31]

Elsewhere along the front, Grant had ordered attacks by all four Union corps against various points of the Confederate fortifications. Most of these assaults failed to produce any positive results, except a VI Corps charge that penetrated Ewell's breastworks. Fortunately for the Confederates, the VI Corps did not follow up their success — lack of support, again. The stalemate around Spotsylvania continued.

That evening Heth marched his division back to reoccupy the ground on the far right in front of the Spotsylvania Court House. Their breastworks still faced Burnside's IX Corps. However, the piecemeal fashion in which the brigades shuffled in and out of the entrenchments mixed up the units from their standard organization. Division commanders had responsibility for sections of the breastworks that were defended by brigades from other divisions. Kirkland's Brigade dispersed on several missions. Kirkland sent one of his regiments to guard a wagon train delivering corn for the artillery's horses, while the others protected artillery batteries scattered along the breastworks on the north side of the Spotsylvania-Fredericksburg Road.[32] The 11th and 44th N.C. took up positions near an eastern bulge in the defensive line known as "Heth's Salient."

Both sides had witnessed the advantages of defending behind breastworks, so the infantry routinely dug in as soon as they occupied a new position. The soldiers tried to get accustomed to their life behind entrenchments, but the duty was not pleasant. The weather had turned nasty and made life miserable in the trenches. "Staid thare all night— in the rain, mud and water, very disagreeable." Things did not improve after daybreak; the IX Corps probed the defensive line in front of Spotsylvania Court House. Harry Heth recalled several distinct thrusts by Burnside's men that the Confederate pickets had to drive back. "The skirmishers fighting all the time in front." Discomfort at night, danger in the day, the men of the Bethel Regiment were becoming familiar with the rigors of trench warfare.[33]

That night Lee, A. P. Hill, and several other generals congregated at Heth's headquarters in the Massaponax Church. A discussion arose among the generals about Grant's tactics. Unlike any other Union general they had fought, Grant had launched sudden assaults against them on May 5, 6, 8, and 10. These attacks failed to overpower the Confederates and cost thousands of Union lives. Grant's aggressiveness not only amazed the senior officers, it also appalled them. The Confederate generals severely criticized Grant's bludgeoning tactics. To their astonishment, General Lee voiced a different opinion. "Gentlemen, I think that General Grant has managed his affairs remarkably well up to the present time."[34] More than any other Confederate general, Lee understood that Grant's pugnacity had smothered their ability to strike a powerful counterblow. Heth, Hill, and the others saw the body count and thought they were winning. Lee saw an opponent who kept attacking and worried.

As the conversation turned to the current situation, Lee predicted that Grant would withdraw in preparation for another move toward Richmond or Fredericksburg. He then expressed his desire to attack Grant's forces as they moved. Lee turned to Heth and said, "I wish you to have everything in readiness to pull out at a moment's notice, but do not disturb your artillery, until you commence movement. We must attack these people if they retreat." Powell Hill responded to Lee's directive to Heth. "General Lee let them continue to attack our breast-works; we can stand that very well." Harry Heth and others concurred by pointing out the favorable results of their defensive engagements behind breastworks. Lee rebutted their arguments with a remarkable insight: "This army cannot stand a siege; we must end this business on the battlefield, not in a fortified place."[35] Lee held a greater apprecia-tion for the strategic situation than did his subordinates. They had to achieve more than a stalemate to survive; they needed a victory.

Lee's warning order to "pull out at a moment's notice" had unex-pected consequences. To prepare for the expected movement, Ewell's Corps jumped the gun by withdrawing its artillery from a salient called the Mule Shoe. The Confederates attempted to reposition the artillery in the predawn hours of May 12, but they did not make it back. Before dawn, Grant launched yet another massive assault against the Confed-erate defenses. This time, he threw Hancock's II Corps against the Mule Shoe, with a supporting attack by Burnside's IX Corps against the eastern face of the Mule Shoe near Heth's Salient. Burnside struck at 4:30 A.M. with Potter's Division on the right (north) flank and Crit-tenden's Division on the left. Brig. Gen. Robert B. Potter reported on the poor outcome of Burnside's morning assault. "By 5 o'clock the engagement had become very hot. We had taken two lines of detached rifle-pits and some prisoners and assaulted their main line. . . . The enemy's works were charged repeatedly with heavy loss, but without our being able to carry them." Burnside's attack pressed against pock-ets of the 11th N.C. Lt. Col. Frank Bird described the savage fighting as "the hardest fought battle probably of the war. The enemy made repeated charges on our works but was repulsed with most terrible slaughter. . . . I am unhurt, how I am unable to say. I have been in the hottest battles."[36]

Hancock's troops had more success than Burnside's. They pene-trated the Mule Shoe, partly owing to the absence of the Confeder-ate artillery. Once inside the breastworks, the II Corps overwhelmed the defenders, captured hundreds of Confederates, and collapsed the Mule Shoe. A bold counterattack by the Confederates sealed the breach and held Hancock's forces at bay until more breastworks could be thrown up at the rear of the Mule Shoe. Lee threw whatever units he could spare to shore up the center of the line where Hancock had punched through. The 11th N.C. was "hurried in hot haste" to the

Mule Shoe but arrived after the situation had stabilized.[37] At the end of the battle, the regiment remained near the courthouse facing Burnside's men who threw up their own breastworks within a half mile of the Confederate trenches.

Despite the intense combat and persistent Union assaults, the regiment suffered only light casualties. Obviously, the breastworks spared the regiment heavy losses, while the attackers absorbed tremendous punishment in the open. Frank Bird explained the disproportionate loss rate to his sister: "The accounts which you see in the papers of our having killed and wounded so many more of them [Union troops] than they of us, are not I think exaggerated. The difference is truly wonderful and I only account for it in one way. They advanced on us in so many lines of battle, and were therefore so thick that we could not miss them." The Bethel Regiment had seen heavy action on May 5, 6, 10, and 12, but still had not suffered severe losses. The unit's fighting spirit remained undiminished. A letter to the *Hillsborough Recorder* from one of Kirkland's soldiers illustrated the general attitude. "This brigade was never in better spirits or more anxious to engage the enemy. It has and will, under the leadership of the fearless Kirkland, prove itself worthy [of] the name and fame acquired under the lamented Pettigrew." Although the regiment suffered little, personal tragedy struck Lewis Warlick. Pvt. Logan Warlick, his brother, was one of the few men killed on May 12. Warlick wrote home to his sister-in-law to break the sad news to the family. A second Warlick son had died while serving in the Bethel Regiment.[38]

A lull followed for the next several days as U. S. Grant waited for replacements to replenish the Union's depleted ranks. Grant interrupted the quiet on May 18 with a renewed attack on the center, supported by Burnside on the eastern flank. "The enemy assailed . . . our line near the Court-House. Having gotten a number of guns into position to enfilade part of our line, he attempted under cover of their fire to advance his front batteries. . . . A furious cannonade ensued," Lee's artillery chief recalled. The men of the Bethel Regiment held their positions under the artillery's pounding. "There was a terrific shelling . . . for two hours with very little damage," Warlick wrote to his wife. Fortunately, Burnside made no effort to advance his infantry and the artillery battle died down. The Bethel men felt grateful for their sturdy fortifications.[39]

The Confederate soldiers began having their first doubts about the course of the campaign as the battle of Spotsylvania persisted. On one hand, the soldiers took satisfaction from the enormous casualties they had caused the Union army. "There has no doubt been an awful slaughter in their ranks," Lewis Warlick remarked. "Men who fought over many bloody fields in Va. say they never saw dead Yankees lie so thick on the ground." Yet, Grant did not retire from the field like so many other Union commanders. The Tar Heels sensed, as Lee had a few days earlier, that the Union commanding general intended to continue relentless pressure on them. "Grant is twice as badly whipped as was Burnside and Hooker but he is so determined he will not acknowledge it," Warlick wrote. Frank Bird shared that assessment. "Grant seems to be untiring." Actually, Grant was not dismayed by the questionable results of the campaign to that point. The heavy fighting at Spotsylvania merely convinced him that the Confederate positions were too strong to break through. He concluded that he could accomplish nothing at Spotsylvania. Grant did not abandon the offensive. Instead, he resumed maneuver warfare.[40]

TOTOPOTOMOY

Late May 1864, Northern Virginia

Once again, Grant tried to slip around Lee's right to get between him and Richmond. On May 21, Hancock's II Corps headed east and south to Milford's Station where they crossed the Mattaponi River, hoping to outpace the Confederates to Richmond. Lee's army joined the race by midday of May 21 on a parallel route. Hill's Corps (Powell Hill had resumed his duties) pulled out of their positions at Spotsylvania that night and followed the rest of the Army of Northern Virginia to a new defensive line along the North Anna River. The sudden Union movement did not allow the troops enough time to draw and prepare rations. Kirkland's Tar Heels trudged over the Virginia roads "the hole [sic] day without anything to eat."[41] The 11th N.C. completed the thirty-mile march to the new defensive line by the afternoon of May 22. After a brief rest, the men began fortifying a position on the North Anna River that protected Hanover Junction where the Fredericksburg and Virginia Central railroads intersected twenty-five miles north of Richmond. Hill's Corps held the left (western) flank of the army, defending the stretch of land between the North Anna River and Little River near Anderson's Station. Lee had confounded Grant's strategy, again, by moving rapidly along interior routes to stay between Grant and Richmond.

The Confederate defense looked secure, but the Union army caught the defenders napping. Warren's V Corps carefully reconnoitered the banks of the North Anna west of Hill's Corps and located a fording site at Jericho Mills that the Confederates left undefended. Warren's soldiers crossed the ford in four feet of water and established a defensive perimeter. By 4:10 P.M., engineers had completed a pontoon bridge and the artillery started over the river. Warren sighed with relief once he had his corps massed on the south bank. He was none too soon. Confederate scouts spotted Warren's river crossing in the early afternoon. A. P. Hill saw an opportunity to crush an isolated Union force south of the river and, without waiting for an estimate of the Union's strength, ordered Maj. Gen. Cadmus Wilcox to attack the Union bridgehead. Wilcox quickly got his division underway because daylight was slipping away and the Union crossing would be firmly established by morning. Sometime after Wilcox moved out, Hill became uneasy about the size of the counterattack, so he decided to reinforce Wilcox with Heth's Division. The men of the 11th N.C. formed up with the rest of the division around 5:00 P.M. Heth's men hustled forward to catch up with Wilcox, but their late start proved fatal to the mission.

By this time Union troops moved to occupy the last gap in their perimeter. Some V Corps men, convinced that the Confederates were not going to show, began cooking their rations. Confederate cavalry scouts saw the V Corps soldiers rummaging in their haversacks and reported this promising information to General Wilcox. The scouts gave Wilcox the impression that he was attacking an isolated, unsuspecting Union force but neglected to give him an accurate estimate of Warren's strength.[42] Wilcox struck the V Corps perimeter at six in the evening. The Confederates penetrated the east side of the Union lodgment and slashed through the unclosed gap in the perimeter. For a few moments, Wilcox's assault threatened to drive Warren's entire corps into the river, but the Confederates lacked the combat power to carry through on their initial success. The tide of battle turned to the V Corps' favor when the Union artillery opened fire on the attackers and blasted their advance. Wilcox bravely tried to press his initial advantage, but the superior Union strength and confusion among the attackers caused his attack to falter.

Heth's Division, including the 11th N.C., arrived on the scene near dusk. Harry Heth put his brigades in line of battle behind Wilcox's front to serve as a supporting force. The Bethel Regiment had just formed on line when General Wilcox galloped up and spoke directly to Heth's brigade commanders. Kirkland and the other brigadiers responded to the urgency of Wilcox's voice and his description of the situation. Acting under Wilcox's orders, the brigades shifted to the right to restore order to his crumbling flank. Heth dashed forward to find out why his men were moving and discovered that they were following Wilcox's instructions. Heth rode over to Wilcox to demand an explanation but graciously approved Wilcox's disposition of his troops. Unfortunately, darkness forced the Confederates to cancel the mission before they could renew the attack; they had lost their chance to smash the isolated Union corps. The 11th N.C. marched back in the darkness to its position near Anderson's Station. The terribly uncoordinated fight at Jericho Mill had not pleased the troops. Wilcox came close to routing an entire Union corps from a defensive position on May 23. Feeling cheated, he issued the standard complaint about the failure of the supporting units (Heth's Division), though he misdirected his anger. A. P. Hill bore responsibility for the failure at Jericho Mill. Hill repeated his mistake at Bristoe Station when he ordered a spontaneous attack without properly developing the situation. Apparently, General Lee held Hill accountable for the missed opportunity. He chastised Hill the next day with uncharacteristic harshness. "Why did you not do as Jackson would have done — thrown your whole force upon those people and driven them back?"[43]

The Army of Northern Virginia reverted to the defense after the débâcle at Jericho Mill. Grant forced other crossings over the North Anna River closer to the Fredericksburg Railroad but then learned that the Confederates had fortified positions behind a swamp just north of Hanover Junction. The entrenchments proved too formidable to risk an assault. Indeed, Lewis Warlick figured that the Union army would not attack the regiment's fine defensive position. "We have good earthworks here and I very much fear the enemy will not attack us." Grant still wanted to fight a decisive battle with Lee, if he could fight in favorable terrain and circumstances. Lee's careful movements and constant fortifying denied Grant this chance. Grant grumbled in a letter to Washington, "A battle with them outside of intrenchments cannot be had."[44]

Robert E. Lee suffered the same frustration felt by Grant. Lee desperately wanted to attack the Union army because of his fear of getting pinned into a siege. He wrote a letter to President Jefferson Davis on May 18 describing the situation at Spotsylvania and his own plan of action. "His [Grant's] position is strongly intrenched, and we cannot attack it with any great prospect of success, without great loss of men, which I wish to avoid if possible. . . . My object has been to engage him when in motion. . . . I shall continue to strike him whenever opportunity presents itself."[45] Ironically, both Lee and Grant yearned to fight a decisive battle, but they denied each other the opportunity by their caution. Both commanders would be frustrated by this campaign.

Unwilling to give up, Grant decided to continue the offensive with another maneuver. "I have determined, therefore, to turn the enemy's right by crossing at or near Hanovertown."[46] This town, twenty miles downriver from Hanover Junction, gave the Union army space to secure a lodgment on the south bank before Lee swooped down to counterattack. Maj. Gen. Horatio Wright's VI Corps quietly pulled out of the Union's line from the western flank and marched east behind the rest of the army on May 26. Carefully, Grant shifted his army toward Hanovertown without giving Lee a chance to strike. By 11:00 A.M. on May 27, Wright's VI Corps secured a bridgehead over the Pamunkey River. One day later, Grant's army crossed the river in force.

Once Lee confirmed the Union withdrawal, he moved quickly to get in front of Grant. The Bethel Regiment marched with the rest of Hill's Corps on the westernmost routes to the vicinity of Ashland on May 27. A heavy rain soaked the roads and forced the Bethel troops to slog fifteen miles through knee-deep mud. They marched over muddy roads all the next day to a blocking position near Totopotomoy Creek. Hill's Corps spent the night of May 28 one mile north of

Shady Grove Church where they served as the Confederate reserve force.[47]

Because of poor intelligence the Union army wasted May 29 cautiously groping for the Confederates with three corps, instead of assaulting in force. Warren's V Corps crossed the Totopotomoy Creek near Via's Farm and moved south toward Bethesda Church where he ran into Ewell's Corps, now commanded by Maj. Gen. Jubal Early. Hancock's II Corps moved west to Polly Hundley's Corner. The II Corps located skirmishers of Maj. Gen. J. C. Breckinridge's Division that had recently joined Lee's army and pushed them south of the Totopotomoy Creek. Wright's VI Corps moved directly west from the bridgehead to Hanover Court House. The VI Corps passed north of the Confederate army and reached the courthouse without finding any defending infantry, although they traded shots with the Confederate cavalry. This move put Wright's Corps directly north of General Breckinridge's left flank. Lee ordered Hill's Corps to protect this exposed flank by entrenching a defensive line on the south side of the Totopotomoy. Late that evening, Kirkland's Brigade moved north from Atlee's Station to the Totopotomoy where they dug in.[48] Lee's commitment of Hill's Corps protected his left flank from Wright's Corps, but it sacrificed the reserve he needed to strike the Union army while it moved into position.

Grant still did not have a clear picture of the Confederate defense on the night of May 29. Only Hancock's Corps had definitely located the main defensive line southwest of Polly Hundley's Corner. The Union army continued a cautious advance on May 30. Hancock's II Corps pressed back Breckinridge's skirmishers and seized the Confederates' forward breastworks. Farther west, Wright's VI Corps moved south to locate and attack the left flank of Lee's defensive line. The VI Corps troops made poor progress, taking the entire day to establish itself on the Union's west flank. Only Brig. Gen. Frank Wheaton's Division made contact with Hill's skirmish line along Totopotomoy Creek. Meanwhile, Grant committed Burnside's IX Corps to fill the gap between Hancock's Corps and Warren's V Corps, which had already advanced toward Bethesda Church.

Except when briefly probed by Wheaton's Division, the men of the 11th N.C. spent May 30 fortifying their positions on the far western (left) flank of the Confederate army near the Virginia Central Rail-

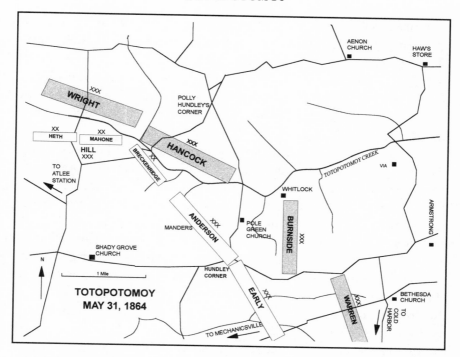

AENON
CHURCH

HAW'S
STORE

WRIGHT

POLLY
HUNDLEY'S
CORNER

XX
HETH

XX
MAHONE

HILL
XXX

HANCOCK

BRECKENRIDGE

TOTOPOTOMOY CREEK

VIA

TO
ATLEE
STATION

WHITLOCK

ANDERSON

ARMSTRONG

MANDERS

POLE
GREEN
CHURCH

BURNSIDE

N

SHADY GROVE
CHURCH

1 Mile

HUNDLEY
CORNER

BETHESDA
CHURCH

TOTOPOTOMOY
MAY 31, 1864

EARLY

WARREN

WARREN

TO
COLD
HARBOR

TO MECHANICSVILLE

road. The Bethel men made good use of the time digging breastworks and throwing obstacles. Their defensive preparation pleased A. P. Hill. "I have a good line and would like to fight it," he reported to Lee. He nearly got his wish. On May 31 General Meade ordered an advance for the purpose of confirming the Confederates' dispositions. General Wright moved forward to inspect Hill's defenses but sent back a very discouraging report. The VI Corps soldiers would have to cross a swamp 300 yards wide before reaching the Confederate positions that Hill's troops had reinforced with slashings of timber. Meade relented and instructed Wright to find another way to approach Hill's defense. The best he could do was link up with Hancock's Corps. The only action from the VI Corps advance was a brisk exchange of fire with Hill's skirmishers. Wright's difficulties proved that there was no prospect of breaking Lee's left (western) flank.[49]

Although the Union army did not strike, the steady pace of Grant's campaign abraded the Tar Heels' endurance. From their standpoint, the campaign seemed to be an endless series of marches, entrenchments, and battles that numbed the senses. Colonel Martin would later admit, "In the course of these movements . . . many engagements . . .

took place on the line of the North Anna, Pamunkey and Totopota-
moie [sic] Rivers and around Cold Harbor and the Chickahominy.
Our brigade took part in a number of them, marching and counter-
marching and doing some very hard fighting, but the details I find
myself unable to record in their order satisfactorily." One soldier in the
brigade expressed his weariness. "I have been marching, fighting and
throwing up breastworks nearly all this month."[50]

Because he could not find a weak point to strike, Grant resumed
his sideways movement around Lee's flank. His attention had shifted
from Totopotomoy Creek to Cold Harbor, which Sheridan's cavalry
had just captured. Grant decided to follow up the success with a major
push to turn Lee's right (southern) flank. Grant knew that Cold Harbor offered the shortest route to Richmond's defenses. On the night
of May 31, the VI Corps received orders to move from the right (western) flank of the Army of Potomac to the left (eastern) flank near Cold
Harbor. The VI Corps began withdrawing at 9:45 P.M. Sometime after
they departed, Hancock pulled his right flank division, which now
held the army's western flank, back to the north side of the Totopotomoy to prevent the Confederates from quickly enveloping it (a tac-
tic known as refusing the flank). At the same time, Grant moved the
XVIII Corps, commanded by Maj. Gen. William F. Smith, from the
James River front up to Cold Harbor. Wright and Smith intended to
relieve Sheridan's cavalry, which held onto Cold Harbor under increasing Confederate pressure.

Grant was not alone in recognizing the importance of Cold Harbor. General Lee brought Maj. Gen. Robert F. Hoke's Division from
the James River to Cold Harbor. Hoke had been a major in the 1st
N.C. Volunteers and had since risen to command a division. Simultaneously, Lee shifted Hill's and Early's corps to relieve Anderson's Corps
from the Totopotomoy front so he could send Anderson to Cold Harbor. On May 31, Heth's Division vacated their breastworks and moved
over to occupy a position near Pole Green Church.[51] The simultaneous moves by Grant and Lee were not coincidental. Once the two
armies had fully developed their opponent's line and deployed all their
corps along the Totopotomoy, the opposing commanders realized that
there was no vulnerable point to penetrate. Naturally, they searched
for the best place to turn their opponent's line, and they both selected
Cold Harbor.

As the battle of Cold Harbor unfolded, the action at Totopotomoy Creek continued. Lee had shuffled his frontline on June 1 to fill the gaps left by Anderson's troops. He put Heth's Division to the right (east) of Breckinridge's Division facing Pole Green Church. By midday on June 1, Heth occupied a line from Hundley's Corner on the right, to the vicinity of the Mander's house on the left where he placed Kirkland's Brigade. Although the Union army focused on the Cold Harbor sector, Meade ordered Burnside and Hancock to attack the Confederate lines to their front to support the attacks by Warren, Wright, and Smith at Cold Harbor. The II Corps division commanders expressed reservations about attacking the Confederate lines, but Meade wanted to keep the Confederates from reinforcing Cold Harbor. Around mid-afternoon, Gibbon's Division pushed south of the Totopotomoy Creek to fix the Confederate line near the Mander's House.

The men of the 11th N.C. were cleaning up after a sudden rain shower when they observed the Union troops emerge from the woods. The Tar Heel soldiers quickly crouched in the red mud of their breastworks and primed their rifles as Gibbon's line of battle drove in the skirmishers. The Confederate officers watched the approaching Union assault force and confidently calculated that it lacked the strength to break their defensive line. Kirkland decided to smash Gibbon's attack with a decisive volley delivered at close range. "As the enemy started across an open field the order was given us not to fire until a certain cannon fired, and company commanders were to order the fire by file. The Federal officers threw themselves in front of their men and most gallantly led them, but when the cannon sounded the signal, our deadly fire opened on them within fifty yards and it was so steady and accurate, for our men were perfectly cool, that before the companies had fired a round, the enemy was completely broken and routed, a large number of them killed and wounded." One of Kirkland's officers, 1st Lt. William S. Long, remembered that he "could see the officers making frantic efforts to urge their men to move forward again but they could not and they ran back into the woods." Lieutenant Long watched as one small group of Union soldiers retreated to the Mander's House where they halted in plain view of the Confederate batteries. One shot from an artillery gun crashed into their midst. "When the smoke cleared away I could see a half a man lying on the top of the house and three or four others lying on the ground." The Confederates enjoyed a lopsided victory over the brave but futile attack by the II Corps troops. "Our loss was almost nothing as the enemy, depending on giving us the bayonet, withheld their fire, until they were repulsed."[52]

This action marked the end of the Totopotomoy phase of the campaign. The constant maneuvering and entrenching since Spotsylvania had taxed the Bethel men almost as much as active combat. The men had spent the entire time, since leaving Orange Court House, exposed to the elements and exhausted by their exertions. Still, the Bethel soldiers could be grateful that they had been spared serious casualties since Spotsylvania. This respite was about to end. Another sideways shift by Grant and Meade would set the stage for more heavy fighting.

COLD HARBOR

June 1864, Eastern Virginia

Both Lee and Grant were determined to control Cold Harbor. Lee sent Hoke's Division up from the James River and Anderson's Corps south from the Totopotomoy to drive back Sheridan's cavalry. Although Lee's forces arrived sooner, the Confederate commanders displayed uncharacteristic lassitude. Only Hoke attacked on June 1, but his two brigades could not recapture the town. Lee's absence owing to ill health undoubtedly played a part in the inadequate Confederate attack. Sheridan hung on until the Union infantry relieved him. Wright's VI Corps marched all the way to Cold Harbor from the opposite flank during the night and arrived mid-morning on June 1. Smith's XVIII Corps joined Wright by 3:00 P.M. The two Union corps combined their efforts to regain the initiative and stabilize their front before evening. Both sides were caught in a stalemate. Grant still hoped that a more vigorous push could rupture the new Confederate line around Cold Harbor and give him a straight shot to Richmond, so he issued orders to shift Hancock's II Corps from the far right (northern) flank to reinforce a general attack at Cold Harbor on June 2. Lee's scouts and infantry skirmishers detected Hancock's withdrawal in time for Lee to match the move. He pulled Breckinridge's Division and Hill's Corps (less Heth's Division) from the Totopotomoy and sent them to the southern flank. This shift left Kirkland's Brigade, including the Bethel Regiment, holding the extreme northern flank.

Grant assumed that Hancock's, Wright's, and Smith's corps would overwhelm Hoke and Anderson with a full-scale assault on the morning of June 2. Unfortunately, he had not given proper allowance for the difficulties and inevitable confusion of night moves. The II Corps could not complete the march in time. Hancock confessed, "The head of my column reached Cold Harbor at 6:30 A. M., June 2, but in such an exhausted condition that a little time was required to allow the men to collect and to cook their rations."[53] Meade postponed the attack to late afternoon, but meanwhile Hill's Corps and Breckinridge's Division reinforced the Confederate line at Cold Harbor. Meade eventually delayed the attack until the next morning.

The lack of a reserve corps contributed to the Union army's failure to attack on June 2. If Grant had been able to maintain a corps in reserve, the shifts to the south could have been quick, powerful, enveloping attacks by the corps coming from the Union rear, not the opposite flank. Grant and Meade fully understood the importance of a powerful reserve and sought to establish one. On June 2 Meade issued instructions to Maj. Gen. Ambrose Burnside, who now held the Union right (northern) flank. "The major-general commanding directs that you withdraw as soon as you can do so securely, and mass in rear of the right of General Warren, and be prepared to resist an attempt of the enemy to attack or turn his right flank."[54] Meade cautioned Burnside to coordinate his movements with Warren to ensure that the Union army had a secure northern flank. Creating a reserve corps accomplished a useful purpose. By bending back his line (refusing his flank), Burnside would be much better positioned to counter a Confederate envelopment. As events unfolded, Grant and Meade made a wise decision to pull back Burnside's Corps.

The failure of the Union army to attack Lee in force on June 2 allowed Lee to seize the initiative from Grant. In the south, A. P. Hill and J. C. Breckinridge gained control of Turkey Hill and set up artillery positions that covered the low ground on the southern flank. In the north, Lee instructed Early, with Heth's assistance, to "endeavor to get upon the enemy's right flank and drive [him] down in front of our line."[55] Early planned an enveloping attack against the northern end of the Union line, pivoting on Gordon's Division. The wheeling movement required Heth's Division to attack on the outside of the maneuver.

The action started in mid-morning of June 2 when Heth sent a brigade size force across the Totopotomoy Creek to the north bank. This brigade threatened the right flank of Burnside's Corps, as it prepared to reposition. Burnside's right flank division commander, Robert Potter, reported the flanking movement and sent skirmishers across to delay the Confederates. Burnside telegraphed a report to Meade's headquarters that indicated his concern. "A force of the enemy, probably only a brigade, has crossed to the north side of the Totopotomoy and are pressing back our skirmishers on that side of the river, evidently with a view to ascertaining our position. We are preparing to withdraw to the rear of Warren's right, but may have to move carefully in case they should attempt to follow." The IX Corps formed a large skirmish line of six hundred men to cover its withdrawal. At approximately 1:00 P.M. the center and right flank divisions, Willcox's and Potter's, pulled back from the front and marched toward Bethesda Church where the corps would reassemble. Maj. Gen. Thomas Crittenden's Division formed the rearguard. Crittenden did not redeploy to cover the entire corps front; he merely remained in position. Evidently, Burnside counted on the skirmish line to hold back the Confederates.[56]

Early and Heth observed Burnside's withdrawal and immediately conferred. Harry Heth recalled, "As the enemy were withdrawing from my front, preparatory to the grand attack he was to make on June 3d at Cold Harbor, General Early commanding Ewell's Corps, (Ewell being sick) came to me and said that the enemy were retiring from our front, and that he proposed to attack, and asked me for a brigade to assist him. I told the General I was aware that the enemy was withdrawing from my front, and that I had already given orders to attack; that I would not give, or lend him one of my brigades, but would assist him with the entire division." Heth had promised to attack with his full division, but only Kirkland's and Davis's brigades were in a position to advance. The Tar Heels, sensing an approaching battle, quietly prepared for the ordeal ahead. Shaking off rain from a recent shower, they quickly checked and cleaned their rifles for the expected charge.

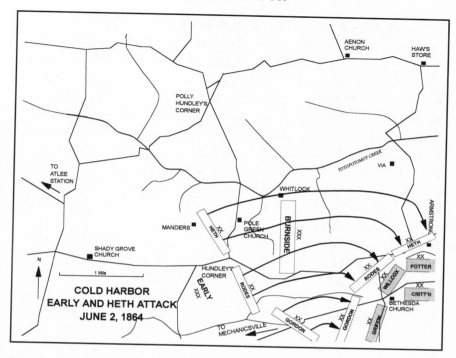

COLD HARBOR
EARLY AND HETH ATTACK
JUNE 2, 1864

"Each man looked into the eyes of his comrade with a long steady gaze which was returned . . . as tho' each said 'I'm with you old man.' Then a quiver ran thru the line as each man touched elbows & shoulders and they were as one man, a unit in feeling & determination." At the sound of the bugle, the Bethel soldiers and the rest of Kirkland's men leapt over their breastworks and raised the rebel yell.[57]

The Confederates pounced on the IX Corps skirmish line and sent the Union pickets scurrying to the rear. "Fury seized us and with redoubled cheers & accelerated speed we rushed forward and the enemy turned in terror & fled." A colonel in Crittenden's Division described the rout of the Union skirmishers. "Before our troops could be put into position, the enemy advanced rapidly upon our old pickets, taking many prisoners, and they as quickly followed up our march." The skirmish line could not hold back Early and Heth's assault, and the Confederates soon threatened Crittenden's Division. The Union troops gained the cover of some breastworks erected earlier by Warren's Corps and prepared to fend off the attack with the help of an artillery battery.[58]

The Tar Heel troops charged across open ground in the face of the

Union guns. One of Kirkland's soldiers vividly recalled the terrifying experience of attacking the artillery battery over open ground. "As soon as they got behind their guns they [the artillery] began to belch forth shell, grape & canister. You see the fire as the flash leaves the muzzle of the gun—you hear the swish of the shrapnel—the hum of the minie, the plunge of grape, the groan of the wounded, the agonizing shriek of terror & pain from the mortally wounded." Crittenden's entrenched force kept back the storming Confederate line for a while but could not hold. The bold assault by Kirkland and an enveloping move by Gordon on the right forced Crittenden to fall back closer to Bethesda Church. The Tar Heels enjoyed a brief moment of victory after breaking Crittenden's line. "The boys lined up and gave one big cheer for the 'Old North State', as we always did after a successful charge." The celebration did not last long. Early and Heth had thrown back Burnside's forward line, but the Confederate generals wanted to continue the advance. Kirkland and Davis reformed their lines of battle and resumed the attack against Crittenden's second line farther east. The 11th N.C. pressed forward across another open space against the Union men who stood their ground with determination. The two sides unleashed volley after volley as the Confederates bore down on the defenders. Finally, the Union soldiers broke as Kirkland's men came within fifty yards of their breastworks. The Bethel Regiment rushed forward in hot pursuit.[59]

Neither the skirmish line nor Crittenden's Division could stop the Confederate advance, but the delaying action served its purpose. Willcox's Division formed a defensive line beside Bethesda Church, while Potter's Division established a position on the right near the Armstrong Farm. The wide enveloping attack by Kirkland swung the line of battle to the east with the hope of turning the Union's northeastern flank. The exhausted Tar Heels caught their breath as they reached the Shady Grove Church Road. The men quickly dismantled the rail fence along the east-west road and scraped out a hasty breastwork. They had hardly had a chance to take a drink from their canteens when General Kirkland rode up and ordered them to attack. At the sound of the bugle, the 11th N.C. stepped over the rails and advanced. "As we pressed forward we found a stubborn skirmish line that disputed every foot & we knew from experience of past fights that a stubborn skirmish line meant a heavy line behind." Once again, Heth's advance ground up the Union skirmishers as the Confederates pressed against Burnside's Corps.[60]

The skirmish line fought fiercely to give Potter's Division time to fortify a new defensive line near the Armstrong Farm. One of Potter's officers wrote, "We were none too soon. The rear guard had hardly got in before the heavy columns of Ewell's corps [Heth's Division] suddenly and in mass were hurled on our flank; but the echo of the first gun of the pickets had hardly died away before three lines of battle were confronting the foe, and our batteries were adding their roar to the din of battle." The Confederates made some headway and shoved Potter's first line of battle back on the second. Kirkland urged the men onward, and the bugle sounded again to renew the charge. "What's that? Another bugle for another charge. Great God! are we never going to stop." Kirkland's and Davis's exhausted brigades assaulted their fourth entrenched position in as many hours. They finally ran out of steam against Potter's Division. Heth noticed trouble with Rodes's Division on his right flank as his own assault reached its limits. "These troops did not attempt to advance. The consequence was that after Davis had driven the enemy a quarter of a mile his right [western] flank was assaulted and his brigade driven back some 200 yards." Kirkland had problems on the left flank. Potter's second line of battle held its ground obstinately. A Union officer wrote, "The enemy advanced on our lines only to be mown down and driven back. Every attempt was foiled, and at dark, having lost heavily, they were glad to give up the contest." Potter could not be dislodged.[61]

The approach of darkness came as a welcome relief to the Bethel Regiment. Their attack from the Mander's House to the Armstrong Farm had consumed most of the afternoon. The 11th N.C. and its sister regiments had driven the IX Corps back three and a half miles in a sustained four-hour attack. During the grueling advance, the Confederates had overrun two skirmish lines and three entrenched positions before stalling in front of Potter's Division. Even then, Harry Heth believed the attack could have driven through if Rodes's Division had kept up the pressure on the right flank. Following the norm, Heth blamed the attack's check on the supporting attack. "As Rhodes [Rodes], of Ewell's Corps, Early's division, failed to advance, my right flank became fearfully exposed and I gave the order to my brigade commanders to fall back."[62]

Luckily, the regiment suffered comparatively light casualties because they had kept the defenders on the run most of the way. The brigade did suffer one important casualty. During the course of the assaults on Potter's position, a Union minié ball tore through General Kirkland's thigh. He bravely stayed with his command until the battle ended and then retired. Kirkland's wound would keep him out of the rest of the campaign. Although he eventually returned to duty, Kirkland never rejoined his old brigade. General Lee would later appoint him to the command of a different unit, after he gave the command of his brigade to another officer. Lee's action suggests that some of the North Carolina regimental officers had complained about Kirkland and requested a new commander.[63] Everyone admired Kirkland's courage, but some had reservations about his leadership. Kirkland did not earn a reputation as a strict disciplinarian, which tended to undermine the morale of his brigade. Still, the troops of the 11th N.C. and the other regiments in the brigade upheld their fighting qualities under his command. Col. George Faribault of the 47th N.C. assumed command of the brigade until a new general could be named.

The attack had carried Kirkland's soldiers across Shady Grove Church Road near the Armstrong house. Only a swamp separated them from Potter's troops, as the two sides dug in dangerously close to each other. After dark, pickets from both sides sneaked forward into the swamp to provide some security. With the skirmish line in place, Heth pulled Kirkland's men out of the line to rest them after their long attack. The tired troops plodded back in the dark to the vicinity of the Mander's House where the attack had started. The Tar Heels appreciated the chance to rest in the relative safety of the rear, while somebody else guarded the forward line. Heth replaced them with Cooke's Brigade, which drew the unenviable task of covering the front facing Burnside. One of Cooke's officers recalled, "The lines were so close that they could hear each other whisper." With two armies holding ground so close to each other, a battle the next day became inevitable. The attack by Early and Heth fell short of knocking out Burnside's Corps or driving in the Union flank; they only developed Burnside's "refused" defensive line. Yet, the attack did gain an important strategic advantage; it robbed General Grant of his reserve corps. By the end of June 2, the Confederates had fixed Burnside's Corps in position.[64]

The prospects for a Union attack at Cold Harbor looked worse on June 3 than on the previous day. Lee now had secure flanks, anchored on Turkey Hill in the south and Totopotomoy Creek in the north. Grant's only option for an attack was a frontal assault on the Confederate defensive line, which did not look particularly inviting. If Grant did not attack, he would have to shift to a new area and lose the chance to destroy Lee's army outside the Richmond entrenchments. Grant could not bring himself to abandon his strategy without testing Lee's defense. Wishfully, he reasoned that Lee had been forced to overstretch his forces to cover the front between the Totopotomoy and Chickahominy. Although no one had identified a weak spot in the Confederate defense, Grant felt that a massive attack would achieve a breakthrough. He decided to go ahead with the grand assault at 4:30 the next morning using Hancock's, Wright's, and Smith's corps. Warren and Burnside would launch a supporting attack to penetrate the Confederate line farther north and prevent Lee from reinforcing the Cold Harbor front. The supporting attack by Warren and Burnside only partially assisted the main effort. Burnside's Corps ended June 2 oriented north, facing Heth's Division and part of Early's Corps. Burnside intended to push back Heth, which would direct his attack north and away from Cold Harbor. Warren decided to use only one division to support Burnside's Corps and leave the rest of his corps on defense. In effect, Burnside's and Warren's attack became an independent action that did not support Grant's main assault.

Opposite Burnside, Heth's men prepared for the expected attack. Heth formed his defense behind a swamp south of the Shady Grove Church Road. The forward defensive line lay just inside a wood with the fields of the Armstrong farm to the rear. Before dawn, Heth brought Kirkland's Brigade (commanded by Faribault) back to the front, but he put them on the right (west) of Cooke's Brigade. Cooke had to cover the far left (eastern) flank where Kirkland had stopped the previous day. Cooke's troops had reason to regret the switch. Kirkland's Brigade had not dug in before departing, a breakdown in discipline reminiscent of the night at the Wilderness. Colonel Martin marched the regiment up to the road and began aligning the Bethel Regiment's defense. They had very little time to prepare. Shortly before 7:00 A.M., the skirmish line sounded the alarm of a Union attack. The wooded creek bottom provided concealment for Potter's Division as it approached the Confederate pickets. One of Kirkland's officers recalled, "They were in the woods, we on the edge of it with a small field behind us. This enabled them to get very near us, perhaps forty to sixty yards, and we learned by sound rather than by sight, when they arose to charge, and kept them in check by shooting in the direction of their noise, as they would attempt to encourage their men." Robert Potter described his assault: "I attacked the enemy vigorously with my First Brigade, Colonel Curtin; drove their skirmish line across the creek, taking a few prisoners; crossed the creek, drove the enemy from a house and outbuildings and some breastworks within a few yards of the road running to Shady Grove and Cold Harbor, on which was their main line."[65]

On the far left (east) flank, Cooke's Brigade tried to dig in while Potter's troops pressed them. "Before the brigade [Cooke's] formed its line the enemy drove in our pickets, advanced his line of battle and the firing became general. The front rank of the regiment was advanced a few feet, while the rear went to work with bayonets, plates, tin cups, or anything they could use to move dirt, and in a short time had a bank sufficient to afford some protection." Cooke's and Kirkland's soldiers poured steady fire at the line of blue infantry to their front. The Union attack had stalled but managed to shoot a huge volume of rifle fire back at the Confederate defenders. By 7:35 A.M., Burnside reported his progress to Meade's Headquarters: "We have carried the first line of the enemy's works, and are now reforming the line. The resistance is very determined."[66]

The two Carolina brigades held firm against Burnside's troops along the Shady Grove Church Road. On the flank, two Confederate artillery batteries blasted enfilade fire down the Union lines, using canister rounds with deadly effect. The artillery battalion commander had attempted to remove the batteries to safer ground, but General Heth refused to displace them; he needed all the firepower possible to stop the Union advance. The guns fired effectively, but Union infantry riddled the batteries from only 250 yards. Heth may have regretted the artillery losses, but he figured the sacrifice was worthwhile in helping to stop Burnside's attack. Potter's attack ground to a halt a mere sixty yards short of Cooke's main defensive line. Farther west, the heavy fires from the 11th N.C. and the rest of Kirkland's Brigade stopped the Union charge well short of their position.[67] The IX Corps troops did not seriously challenge Kirkland's defensive line and began digging for cover once they were pinned down by Heth's men.

Potter and Burnside spent the rest of the morning planning actions to get the attack moving again. Potter's message of 12:30 P.M. did not sound encouraging. "I regret to say that the losses in my First Brigade [Curtin's] are reported as heavier than at the Wilderness, including some 20 officers. . . . My nearest point to the enemy is just to the right of my left, where I am less than 50 yards from the enemy's work, who hold higher ground."[68] Potter planned to bring Brig. Gen. Simon Griffin's Brigade forward to attack the Confederate northeastern (left) flank, but he wanted to coordinate his effort with a renewed attack by Brig. Gen. Orlando Willcox's Division. Burnside had trouble reforming the attack columns with units in such close contact with the Confederates. The coordinated attack was postponed until the afternoon. By the time Willcox and Potter were ready to attack, instructions came down from Meade to cancel any further attacks.

Grant and Meade may have called off the attacks, but with the two sides so close to each other the fighting continued anyway. One officer in Potter's Division wrote, "All day, like the swelling and ebbing of the voice of the winds, the noise of battle now rose to a hurricane and now sank to a whisper." A soldier in the 15th N.C. (Cooke's Brigade) recalled, "This was perhaps the hardest day the Fifteenth Regiment had during the war, being actively engaged for fourteen hours with three times their number without one mouthful to eat, but little water to drink and several times but one round of ammunition. They used an average of one hundred and sixty rounds of ammunition to the man that day." A spontaneous firefight erupted during the afternoon between the two lines, apparently touched off by a Confederate attempt to recover an artillery section. General Potter claimed that Heth attacked him. "The enemy opened quite a furious fusillade upon the whole line early in the afternoon, and attempted under its cover to haul off their battery by means of prolongs but were prevented by our fire." On the opposite side, Jubal Early reported that Potter's Division attacked Heth. Obviously, any slight movement by either side sparked a violent reaction between soldiers in such tight proximity. Heth summed up the situation in his report, "The skirmishing along the entire line, during the day, amounted almost to a battle."[69]

Although the attack halted just short of the Shady Grove Church

Road, the Union army made one more effort to overwhelm Heth's Division. Earlier, Burnside had tried to coordinate an attack with the Union cavalry. Burnside reported, "A messenger was sent to General Wilson, of the cavalry division . . . suggesting that it would be well for him to move a portion of his command down from the opposite [north] side of the Totopotomoy, crossing it above the Via house, and attacking the enemy in the rear." Although Burnside's infantry attack had been canceled, General Wilson conducted the cavalry assault by sending part of Col. George Chapman's Cavalry Brigade against Heth's rear by the Via house. "On arriving at the creek a section of Ransom's battery was placed in position, and a force of about 400 men dismounted and crossed. The rebel infantry were found posted along the brow of the acclivity rising from the creek bottom in a line of rifle-pits near Mrs. Via's house. The Third Indiana Cavalry, Major Patton, and the Second New York, Colonel Harhaus commanding, charged at the double-quick. The section of artillery opened at the same time. The rebels after firing a few shots broke and fled, leaving 10 or 15 prisoners in our hands."[70]

This unexpected attack, late in the day, threatened to collapse Heth's defense. Fortunately, Harry Heth kept his wits about him during the crisis. An officer in Kirkland's Brigade recalled the division commander's reaction: "When the enemy's cannon sent a shell from our rear and our men craned their necks, General Heth coolly commanded an aid [sic] 'to go stop that battery — tell them they are firing into my men.' Fortune was propitious, and they did stop." Heth's subterfuge worked, and the Confederate infantry held steady against the greater menace to their front. Heth realized that the cavalry raid in his rear would not achieve decisive results so long as his infantry did not panic. Colonel Chapman, the Union cavalry commander, eventually gave up the attack. "Position was held on the south side of the creek until sundown, when, owing to the movement of the enemy, it was deemed prudent to retire across the creek." Darkness brought an end to the day's savage fighting, to the immense relief of the men of the 11th N.C. The long trying hours of close combat and the threat of being surrounded had taken a toll on the men's nerves. Heth quietly withdrew from the exposed position during the night. "At dark a detail collected every canteen and bayonet and took them out, and as soon as it was dark good, we silently stole away by the only outlet left us."[71]

Elsewhere along the front the Union army had suffered disastrously. Hancock's, Wright's, and Smith's corps attacked valiantly but accomplished nothing. The Confederate defense easily stopped the Union advance and slaughtered the hapless attackers in front of their breastworks. One regiment of dead Union soldiers gave mute testimony to their brave charge. Their bodies lay in a neat wedge formation in front of the Confederate position where they had been cut down by a fatal volley. The regiment's colonel lay at the forward point of the wedge, his head toward the enemy, face down. The three corps' main attack lost five thousand men in less than an hour. In his memoirs, Grant readily admitted to the folly of attacking Lee's prepared positions. "I have always regretted that the last assault at Cold Harbor was ever made."[72]

Collett Leventhorpe. A foreigner, soldier, poet, and physician, the versatile Leventhorpe drilled the reborn Bethel Regiment to perfection and stamped his enduring discipline into their hearts. The English giant was lost to the regiment after the disastrous battle of Gettysburg. (Collections of the Library of Congress)

William J. Martin. Martin was considered to be "the most lovable man this state ever had." The popular chemistry professor became the Bethel Regiment's commander in 1863. His quick actions saved the regiment at Bristoe Station and Jones Farm. (North Carolina Collection at the University of North Carolina at Chapel Hill)

J. Johnston Pettigrew. The son of a wealthy, aristocratic family, Pettigrew commanded a North Carolina brigade that included the Bethel Regiment. The general was mortally wounded in a meaningless skirmish just before his brigade retreated across the Potomac River. (Southern Historical Collection at the University of North Carolina at Chapel Hill)

Henry Heth. The Virginia native suffered the reputation of being the unluckiest general in the Confederate service. Despite a warm personal relationship with General Lee, Heth could not rise above division command. (Collections of the Library of Congress)

William B. Taylor. From Bethel to Appomattox the youthful native of Mecklenburg County served with the Bethel Regiment. He started the war as a private in the "Boy Company" then rose to fight as a lieutenant during the grisly campaigns of 1863 and 1864. (Gettysburg National Military Park)

William MacRae. The fiery general from Wilmington breathed new life into the North Carolina brigade in 1864. With renewed discipline and fighting spirit the Tar Heels performed brilliantly under his command, even as the Union army squeezed the life out of the Confederates around Petersburg. (Collections of the Library of Congress)

The charge of the 6th Michigan Cavalry at Falling Waters. The Confederates wiped out the Union horsemen during the misguided attack but not before the esteemed General Pettigrew fell to a cavalryman's pistol shot. (Collections of the Library of Congress)

"The prettiest fight we were ever in." The Bethel Regiment and its sister regiments attack across an open field against the Union position at Reams Station. The spirited bayonet charge broke the Union defense and routed the venerable II Corps. (Joseph Becker, Harper's Weekly)

Gouverneur K. Warren. After Bethel, the regiment never had any success against the cautious Union general. His contentious personality led to a humiliating dismissal as the Union army verged on triumph in 1865. (Collections of the Library of Congress)

Frequent Opponents. The commanding generals of the Union II Corps led their troops against the Bethel Regiment eight times from Gettysburg to Burgess Mill. Seated: Maj. Gen. Winfield Scott Hancock. Standing from left to right: Brig. Gen. Francis C. Barlow; Maj. Gen. David B. Birney; and Brig. Gen. John Gibbon. (Collections of the Library of Congress)

The grim aftermath of Petersburg. A Confederate soldier lies dead inside the Petersburg trenches following the assault on April 2, 1865. (Collections of the Library of Congress)

5

Men Determined to Win

PETERSBURG

June 1864, Eastern Virginia

T he Cold Harbor assault left the Union and Confederate armies nose to nose along the front between the Chicka-hominy and Totopotomoy. The Union troops could not withdraw because rifle fire swept the ground, so they dug in where their advance stopped. Following the instincts of infantrymen, they simply clawed out fox holes. Before long, their lines were as well entrenched as the Confederates'. After beating back Grant's assault, General Lee decided to pull Heth's Division away from Bethesda Church and abandon the northern end of the front. Heth had nearly been flanked and could be better used to reinforce Cold Harbor. Besides, A. P. Hill wanted all of his corps back together. On June 4, the Bethel Regiment marched south to occupy a reserve position near Gaines Mill. The regiment had one day of rest away from direct con-tact and then moved forward to the front line, the scene of terrible slaughter on June 3.[1]

The succeeding several days in the trenches at Gaines Mill tested the fortitude of the most hardened veterans. A tense stalemate had set-tled over the battlefield, as each side continued harassing fire against the other. "The fighting is continually going on, either in heavy skirmishing or fighting on some part of the line," Lt. Col. Frank Bird noted. Movement with the enemy so near would result in instant death from the fire of alert sharpshooters. Thousands of corpses putrefied in the hot sun between the lines while the cries of the few remaining wounded grew weaker and weaker. Confined to the trenches, the troops had no choice except to dig in and wait. "[We] lay with our heads hid in breastworks." The wretched conditions placed additional stress on their health. Frank Bird complained of a new bout with dysentery. The constant exposure to the elements troubled his delicate constitution. Without a chance to clean themselves, many in the regiment became infested with vermin. Lewis Warlick had already admitted to his wife, "We are getting lousy." John Gibbon of Hancock's Corps described the appalling conditions endured by his troops, conditions that applied equally to the Confederates. "During these twelve days the labor and military duty of the division were of the hardest kind and performed under the most disadvantageous circumstances — confined for ten days in narrow trenches with no water to wash with and none to drink except that obtained at the risk of losing life. Unable to obey a call of nature or to stand erect without forming targets for hostile bullets, and subjected to the heat and dust of midsummer, which soon produced sickness and vermin, the position was indeed a trying one."[2]

Trench warfare dominated the activities of both armies during the first two weeks of June. The Army of the Potomac and the Army of Northern Virginia began digging elaborate trenches to secure their positions. Once the troops completed strong frontal parapets, they started digging communications trenches to permit some movement within their own lines. In many cases, they dug protected routes to reach fresh water. Eventually, these trenches interconnected into a complex system of fortifications and covered passages to provide overhead cover from enemy artillery and mortar fire. "By day the troops fought or lay behind their works, by night they threw up additional defenses." These trenches were not entirely defensive in nature. The Union army dug trenches by parallels to reach closer to the Confederate line in the hopes of forcing the defenders to abandon their forward breastworks. The Union soldiers even began digging a mine to extend underneath the Confederate trenches.[3]

Deadlock at Cold Harbor presented General Grant with an agonizing strategic situation. The Virginia campaign had produced forty thousand Union casualties but little visible progress. His army stood in nearly the exact spot reached by McClellan in 1862 and only sixty miles closer to Richmond than Big Bethel. Another move around Lee's right flank would carry the Union army south of the Chickahominy River into a narrower mobility corridor and actually increase the distance to Richmond. Lee could easily counter by occupying the entrenchments between the Chickahominy and James rivers. Grant had to reconsider his options but he also had to reckon with a weakened force. The brutal assaults of the campaign had taken the lives of the Union's ablest soldiers. The North could not replace the experience, much less the fighting spirit, of these veterans. Over the next several months, the Union army would fight with far less enthusiasm and aggressiveness than it had shown at the Wilderness and Spotsylvania. Among Union generals, the virtue of caution would slide into the vice of timidity.

The horrendous losses and apparent stalemate spelled trouble for the Lincoln administration. The president had to issue another draft to replace the men Grant had sacrificed, even though expanding conscription would erode political support for the war and encourage his political enemies. Already, the Democrats eagerly prepared for the November election. Without an improvement in the military situation, Lincoln's reelection looked doubtful. Lincoln's woes brightened the South's outlook and raised the Confederacy to a new "high-water mark." Lee's army had absorbed the Union's most formidable offensive and seemed to have forced Grant into a dead end at Cold Harbor. The savage fighting had battered the southern ranks, too, but the losses had not been overwhelming. Lewis Warlick noted, "We have 42 arms bearing men in the company [B Company], more than we had at the Wilderness." The South could endure its casualties with the knowledge that the North had suffered disproportionately more. The men in the regiment retained their fighting spirit, aided by their appreciation for Grant's difficulties. "I think we will have some hard fighting yet but not as hard as Grant has done for I don't think he can, this summer, bring his men up to the scratch as well as he has on former fields," Warlick wrote. "[I] think they begin to see the folly of charging works protected by Rebs . . . already we have saved thousands of lives by sticking to the works and letting the enemy do the charging."[4]

The setback at Cold Harbor convinced Grant that he could not continue attacking Lee's entrenchments. Yet, the president's vulnerable political situation required some decisive military gains before the fall election. Never one to retrace his footsteps nor give up, Grant chose an entirely new course of action. "I have therefore resolved upon the following plan: I will . . . move the army to the south side of the James River. . . . Once on the south side of the James River, I can cut off all sources of supply to the enemy."[5] Grant set his sights on choking the life out of the Confederate capital and, with it, Lee's army. The movement of the Union army would no longer be directed toward Richmond but, rather, the crucial rail center farther south at Petersburg.

From June 8 to 12, the Union army prepared to disengage by fortifying positions behind the front line to cover the withdrawal. Warren's V Corps started the movement by pulling back on June 11 and marching ten miles to the rear. During the following night, Warren crossed the Chickahominy River at Long Bridge. That same evening, the rest of the Union army quietly withdrew from Cold Harbor and marched southeast toward the James River crossing sites. Not until then did General Lee realize that something was afoot. Lee reacted by sending Anderson's and later Hill's corps south of the Chickahominy River. Lee expected Grant to shift around the right flank again. Grant reinforced that notion by advancing Warren's Corps to within a mile of Riddell's Shop. The feint by Warren not only deceived the Confederates, but also served to cover the movement of Grant's army to the James River.

A few days earlier, on the night of June 9, A. P. Hill had moved Kirkland's Brigade (Faribault commanding) across the Chickahominy to guard the York River railroad bridge. The Bethel Regiment advanced three miles farther downstream on picket duty. The men welcomed the move away from Cold Harbor. "We are most pleased with the change of base as here there is not a continual buzing of minis from yankee sharpshooters, the continual noise of the rifle is not to be heard, nor the occasional shot from some Parrot or Napoleon." The soldiers really appreciated an increase in rations that the commissary authorized the Army of Northern Virginia. The relaxing picket duty along the Chickahominy came to an end on the evening of June 12 when Grant's new initiative forced Hill's Corps to move. The 11th N.C. joined the movement to check a possible Union advance south of the river. The next morning they marched around the White Oak Swamp where they ran into troops from Warren's V Corps on the Charles City Road. After pushing the enemy back from Riddell's Shop, Hill's men dug in to cover the eastern approaches to Richmond. The men felt relieved that they had beaten the Union troops to the punch once again. Strangely, the Union army remained inactive along its front the next morning, June 14. A. P. Hill moved forward with skirmishers to search for the Union army. His men confronted Union skirmishers and dueled with them much of the day, but they failed to find the enemy's main force. Hill advanced again on June 15, using Cooke's Brigade to execute a reconnaissance in force. Cooke's men battled with some Union cavalry but no infantry. Even against such light resistance, Powell Hill moved forward very deliberately. There were three Union corps somewhere to his front, and he did not want to stumble into such a large force. By the end of the day, Hill settled his corps into a strong defensive line between the Chickahominy and James rivers. Hill's report to Lee must have seemed reassuring at the time, but it left a troubling question. Where was Grant's army?[6]

A partial answer came from Gen. P. G. T. Beauregard at Petersburg. Smith's XVIII Corps arrived outside the Petersburg defenses and, after wasting most of June 15, captured part of the breastworks. Beauregard felt certain that Grant would attack Petersburg with his full force, so he asked Lee for reinforcements. The appearance of Smith's Corps did not convince Lee that the Union army had changed its objective to Petersburg. Lee still worried that Grant would turn toward Richmond, a possibility that dissuaded him from sending large reinforcements to Beauregard. The Union pressure south of the James River grew rapidly on June 16, and the Confederates narrowly averted disastrous ruptures at both Petersburg and Bermuda Hundred. Again, Lee hedged his bet. Despite the appearance of Hancock's Corps at Petersburg, the lack of intelligence about the V, VI, and IX corps forced Lee to keep A. P. Hill's Corps guarding the direct route to Richmond. Lee's dilemma demonstrated the flexibility Grant acquired by his new strategy. Once he disengaged from Cold Harbor, Grant could strike on any of three avenues — the direct corridor between the Chickahominy and James rivers, the wedge-shaped space between the James and Appomattox rivers, or the land approach to Petersburg south of the rivers. Grant had the initiative, the greater force, and multiple avenues to strike. Lee had to spread his forces to protect each avenue. Beauregard, with roughly three divisions, clung to an inner circle of breastworks around Petersburg. Anderson's Corps covered Bermuda Hundred. That left Hill's Corps to hold the Richmond front north of the James River (Lee's Second Corps, commanded by Jubal Early, had already departed for the Shenandoah Valley). The Bethel Regiment occupied a position north of the James River around Fraser's Farm, one of the famous battlefields of 1862. Lewis Warlick wrote home, "We are in the suburbs of the bloody field of '62 — we are in line of battle but no enemy nigh. . . . The impression in camp is Grant is going to try Richmond from [the south] side." Frank Bird echoed the same suspicion: "Grant has disappeared in our front once more and gone to the James river, probably with the intention of crossing."[7]

Union assaults against Petersburg on June 17 strained Beauregard's defense to the limit. With well-planned fire and desperate counterattacks, the Petersburg defenders held the Union army at bay. Yet, the swelling Union force could not be denied for long. That night Beauregard warned Lee that he would have to abandon Petersburg unless Lee sent more reinforcements. This letter finally persuaded Lee that Grant was directing his offensive against Petersburg, not Richmond. Once he made up his mind, Lee moved quickly to mass his forces south of the James River.

At 3:00 A.M. on June 18, the Bethel Regiment's sergeants roused the men. They had to move, along with the rest of Hill's Corps, from White Oak Swamp to the James River. The regiment got underway quickly and reached the pontoon bridge at Chaffin's Bluff by early morning. After resting briefly, the troops crossed the James and headed south on the Petersburg road. They marched at a grueling pace under a scorching sun, covering fifteen miles by mid-afternoon. Five miles outside of Petersburg they "took the cars and rode 3 or 4 miles" into town. Tired, thirsty, and foot sore, the Tar Heels marched through the city and occupied the right (southern) flank of the Petersburg defensive line. "This was the hardest day's marching we have had."[8] Their arrival in the city caused immense relief since everyone knew that the defenders now had enough strength to repel any Union attack. The Union commanders reached the same conclusion and suspended their attacks on June 19. The Confederates had foiled Grant's strategy again, although poor execution by the Union senior commanders played an equal role in the failure to seize Petersburg.

The shift to Petersburg ended the South's brief high-water mark. The North had turned a crucial corner in the campaign. Grant had maneuvered Lee out of secure entrenchments at Cold Harbor and renewed the military pressure on Richmond. Although the offensive bogged down on the outskirts of Petersburg, the Union army had gained important operational advantages. They now had secure lines of communication along the waterways of eastern Virginia. Grant could threaten both Richmond and Petersburg, which would give him tactical flexibility over the coming months. Finally, the northern army had maneuver space south of Petersburg to turn the Confederate fortifications instead of assaulting them directly. Besides the operational advantages gained by the Union army, Grant's crossing of the James gave attentive Confederates more reasons to feel uneasy. The Union commander had out-generaled the venerable Lee and had come terribly close to forcing him out of Richmond. U. S. Grant had proven to be not only the most relentless Union general, but also the most dangerous.

Once their attempts to storm Petersburg failed, the Union army besieged the city. U. S. Grant embarked on a new strategy designed to cut off the flow of supplies going through the strategic rail center. "I have determined to try to envelop Petersburg so as to have the Army of the Potomac rest on the Appomattox [River] above [west of] the city."[9] The lifeblood of Richmond flowed through Petersburg's three rail arteries, and he wanted to choke it off. The Union army had already severed the Norfolk & Petersburg line, the easternmost railroad running out of the city. The Weldon Railroad, the next line to the west, ran straight south from Petersburg to North Carolina. The Old North State shipped critical supplies over this rail line to the Confederate capital. The final rail link, the Southside Railroad, headed west along the Appomattox River to western Virginia. Petersburg served as the hub of an extensive road network, as well. The principal north-south avenue was the Jerusalem Plank Road that ran east of the Weldon Railroad but on a parallel course. Farther west, the Halifax Road stretched alongside the Weldon Railroad. Three important roads, the Vaughan Road, Squirrel Level Road, and Boydton Plank Road, fanned out southwest from Petersburg between the Weldon and the Southside railroads. This area southwest of the city became the scene of numerous battles during the next several months, as Grant applied unrelenting pressure to strangle Petersburg.

After its arrival on June 18, 1864, the Bethel Regiment occupied the western end of the Petersburg trenches facing south. The regiment pushed a thin line of pickets out front to dig individual rifle pits. The picket line provided an extra measure of security for the fortifications and helped keep the Union army at a safer distance. The men lived with the imminent danger of a sudden assault, artillery bombardment, or sniper fire hanging over their heads. Colonel Martin described the hidden dangers. "In some places these lines ultimately came so close together that no pickets could be thrown out, and picket duty was performed by sharp-shooters in the trenches, who made it hazardous for any one on either side to expose any part of his person." The two armies made ready use of sharpshooters to fire across no man's land to kill careless soldiers on the other side. "There are on both sides, keen sighted marksmen, selected for their skill with the deadly rifle, armed with the best long range guns, provided with telescopic sights, who climb trees or select some commanding position from which they pick off a man at the distance of nearly a mile. Their aim is most deadly. Sometimes a man is struck down dead without himself or any one near hearing the report of the gun that sent the fatal bullet. Such is war as now conducted."[10]

The troops soon learned about the strange and terrible weapons of siege warfare. The high trajectory heavy mortars became a common and unnerving menace to the soldiers who were better acquainted with direct-fire weapons. "Mortar shelling was also added to the ordinary artillery fire, rendering bomb-proofs a necessity, and they were accordingly built all along our lines." Nevertheless, the men adapted to the desultory duties of a siege, as Colonel Martin noted. "In spite of this dangerous proximity and the well-nigh ceaseless firing kept up during the night, our men learned to sleep as soundly and as peacefully in these trenches as they were accustomed to do in camp. One can get used to anything."[11]

The Army of the Potomac did not wait long before starting its campaign to throttle Petersburg. A Union effort against Chaffin's Bluff forced Lee to pull reinforcements out of Petersburg, which was still under General Beauregard's command. Lee ordered Heth to send Cooke's and Davis's brigades to strengthen the Chaffin's Bluff front. Kirkland's Brigade remained behind in Petersburg and attached to Maj. Gen. William Mahone's Division. Grant and Meade quickly followed up this move with a campaign to cut the supply routes coming into Petersburg. Meade sent the II Corps (temporarily commanded by Maj. Gen. David Birney) south on the Jerusalem Plank Road on June 20–21 to construct breastworks along the north-south road. Wright's VI Corps joined the II Corps late on June 21 and occupied breastworks on the far left (south) flank. Meade planned to swing the two Union corps to the right on June 22, pivoting on the II Corps' connection with the Jerusalem Plank breastworks. He wanted to build a new defensive line west to the Weldon Railroad once the II and VI corps completed the maneuver. The II Corps would halt its advance when it pinned the Confederates into the Petersburg entrenchments. The VI Corps had the outside position in the wheeling movement and had to swing through thick woods to reach the Weldon Railroad. On the morning of June 22, Birney's II Corps jumped off cleanly, wheeled to the right, and confronted the south side of the Petersburg fortifications. Because Wright's Corp had difficulty advancing through the dense vegetation, the left of the II Corps separated from the right flank of the VI Corps, leaving the II Corps' western (left) flank completely exposed and unsupported.

Powell Hill had taken note of the Union's movements south of Petersburg and organized a counterstroke to protect the Weldon Railroad. Late in the afternoon, he sent Mahone's and Wilcox's divisions from Petersburg down the Halifax Road. Hill decided to counterattack from the west — not from the north as the Union expected. Mahone split the seam between the two Union corps and crushed the exposed flank of Birney's Corps. The Confederate infantry charged aggressively down the Union line and rolled up the entire II Corps from west to east. Mahone's troops captured part of the Jerusalem Plank breastworks and nineteen hundred prisoners before Birney could stabilize his shaken men on the plank road. Wilcox only demonstrated against the VI Corps, but he distracted Wright and prevented the VI Corps from turning against Mahone. The Confederates pulled back to Petersburg before dark, in time to avoid a Union counterattack that evening. Kirkland's Brigade (commanded by Colonel Faribault) did not play an active part in the battle of June 22. The Tar Heels spent their time building abatis for the Confederate artillery and defending the entrenchments facing the II Corps.[12]

A. P. Hill's counterattack achieved remarkable results. Two Confederate divisions had repelled the advance of two Union corps. Meade, embarrassed by the setback, decided to resume the operation on June 23. The two corps advanced the next morning and swung to the right once again. This time the II and VI corps maintained a firm connection as they wheeled forward between the Weldon Railroad and Jerusalem Plank Road. The Union forces oriented their hasty defensive positions north against Petersburg, although the VI Corps pickets and one division faced west to cover the far left flank. In their effort to maintain a tight connection with Birney, the VI Corps line did not extend sufficiently far west to reach the Weldon Railroad. Because General Wright still wanted to dismantle the rail line, he pushed skirmishers and a party of pioneers farther to his left to tear up the railroad. Until this point, the Union advance had encountered very little opposition from the Confederates, but everyone knew that would change.

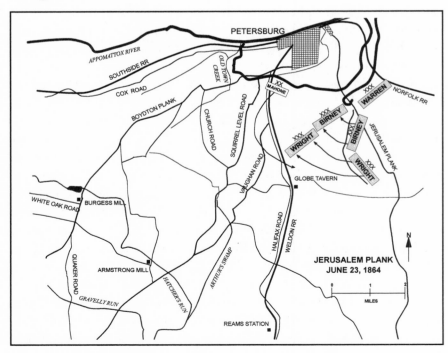

Once again, William Mahone sortied from Petersburg down the Halifax Road to throw back the Union force. This time Kirkland's Brigade marched with Mahone's Division. The Bethel soldiers pulled out of the trenches, formed into a column, and marched west to the Halifax Road. As the Tar Heels moved behind the Petersburg fortifications, the Union artillery lobbed a few rounds at them, but the men shrugged it off. They gave more thought to the upcoming fight with the Union infantry. Shortly after 3:00 P.M., Mahone deployed his brigades west of the VI Corps skirmishers on the Weldon Railroad and then burst upon the unwary Union troops, catching some as they distributed rations. The VI Corps pickets fell back and formed a hasty defense oriented to the west. Wright grew alarmed at the sudden attack on his detached picket force but failed to reinforce them. The Confederates sensed that they faced an isolated Union force and quickly enveloped both flanks of the skirmishers. Mahone's infantrymen surrounded the confused and dispirited enemy. The brigade commander of the Union skirmishers reported, "The enemy broke through at the threatened point and occupied an open field in the rear . . . when [the Union pickets] attempted to fall back . . . the [Confederate] forces on the right and left closed up and formed a line in the rear, and but a few escaped." Caught unprepared, the VI Corps lost three hundred men from their picket line. General Mahone correctly read the VI Corps' dispositions. Rather than press due east against the Union line, as he had the previous day, Mahone continued moving around and behind the VI Corps. With a boldness that bordered on brazenness, the Confederates maneuvered around the Union's left in an attempt to storm the VI Corps from the rear. This maneuver placed the II and VI corps between them and Petersburg. Obviously, Mahone disregarded the danger in his determination to strike a blow against a weak point.[13]

In contrast, General Wright became nonplussed. By 4:00 P.M. he halted his advance, asked for reinforcements, and shifted troops to his southern flank. The Army of the Potomac yearned for weeks to come to grips with the Confederates in the open and away from their entrenchments. Now, a solitary Confederate division maneuvered within easy reach of a Union corps, but the corps commander would not strike. Wright chose to shore up his left and rear to keep Mahone from turning his position. At approximately six in the evening, he gave Meade an update. "The attack by the enemy is on my left flank. He

[Mahone] is feeling all along the line, but has not yet developed his line." Wright wavered while Mahone continued to develop the VI Corps left and rear. Meade suggested, encouraged, urged, argued, everything but ordered, Wright to attack, but to no avail. By 7:05 P.M. Wright's fighting spirit vanished. "I imagine that all the disposable rebel force is moving round our left for a general flank attack. . . . I think I should withdraw after dark." Finally, Meade consented and ordered the II and VI corps to withdraw to the Jerusalem Plank breastworks. Meade closed his message to Wright with an ominous note, "You will report in person to these headquarters as soon as your line is established."[14]

Meade's decision ended the Union's first abortive effort to close down the Weldon Railroad. Mahone's Division, augmented by Kirkland's Brigade, frustrated Meade's plan to extend the Union entrenchments west to the rail line. The Confederates aggressively executed tactically sound counterattacks against the powerful but timid Union force. That proved to be enough to stop the first action in Grant's new offensive strategy. The Army of the Potomac clearly indicated evidence of its depleted *esprit de corps* during this mission. The weak fight by the Union troops inflicted few, if any, casualties on the Bethel Regiment during the attack.

The regiment returned to Petersburg and resumed defensive duties in the trenches. By June 27, General Heth notified Lee that Chaffin's Bluff was sufficiently secure to permit moving Cooke's and Davis's brigades back to Petersburg where they rejoined the Tar Heel brigade. This day also marked the beginning of a new era for the brigade. Lee named a new commander to replace Brig. Gen. W. W. Kirkland, who was still recuperating. Colonel William MacRae, the former commander of the 15th N.C., was appointed to the command and promoted to brevet brigadier general. Henceforth, the brigade was known as MacRae's Brigade. The appointment pleasantly surprised MacRae, although Harry Heth previously had promised MacRae that he had recommended him for brigade command. MacRae had confided to his brother, "If the War Department did not think anymore of General Heth than he did [then] his chance for promotion was rather slim."[15]

A man of short stature and a high-pitched, almost feminine, voice, MacRae did not present the image of a fighting man, but he soon proved his soldierly qualities to his men. William MacRae carried the tradition and soul of the Scottish tribes in his blood. The Clan MacRae had fought with Bonnie Prince Charlie at Culloden before immigrating to North Carolina. The general's own father served in the War of 1812 and went on to command a battalion in the Civil War at the age of seventy. Five of MacRae's brothers fought in the war, including one in the Union army. A strict disciplinarian, MacRae sharpened the edges of the brigade and exacted a high standard from the troops. The morale of the brigade rose as the men realized that they had a tough leader in command. His bold performance in battle would later endear him to his veteran regiments. William MacRae exhibited the finest qualities of a Celtic warrior. One of his subordinate officers later spoke admiringly of his battlefield leadership. "Nature had endowed him with a type of personal courage which made him absolutely indifferent to danger. . . . He made all around him brave. . . . His presence always steadied the men, who seemed to imbibe his spirit. I know not how to characterize this quality unless it be termed the *mesmerism of bravery.*"[16]

MacRae wasted no time applying his high standards for discipline to his new command. On June 29, the brigade drew an easy mission to guard a wagon train bringing a supply of corn from Stoney Creek. As the wagon train pulled out for a leisurely three-day expedition in hot, sultry weather, the new brigade commander appeared to take charge. "By the indulgence of the Colonel commanding [Faribault], the men were permitted to ride in the wagons. The quick manner in which General MacRae had them out, and his stringent regulations for the march furnished on the first day of his coming into command of the brigade, the opportunity of establishing his control."[17] Discipline was back!

Soon after taking command, MacRae took a step to uplift the brigade's *esprit de corps* by organizing an elite unit of sharpshooters to act as the brigade's skirmishers. Previously, the regiments culled out companies or tasked a single unit to form a skirmish line for the brigade. MacRae wanted his skirmishers to be highly motivated and aggressive soldiers, skilled in marksmanship. He pulled together a select group of soldiers from the best in the five regiments and used them to raise the fighting spirit of the entire brigade. Years later, one of the brigade's field grade officers described, with obvious pride, the formation of MacRae's Sharpshooters.

The brigade of sharp-shooters organized by Gen. MacRae afforded the strongest evidence of his extraordinary power in infusing into the minds of his soldiers morale of the highest order. This body consisted of eighty men. No one could become a member unless he had especially distinguished himself by personal courage and coolness under fire. They were allowed unusual privileges, which none begrudged them, for they were the pride of the entire brigade. They wore a gold cross upon the left arm, and upon the sleeve of each was worked in cloth, the names of the different battles in which they had taken part. The corps was armed with repeating rifles, and so thoroughly trained were they by constant practice in marksmanship that their aim was almost unerring. They always preceded the brigade into action, commencing the fight, and repeatedly drove before them the entire Federal line of battle in their front.[18]

MacRae handpicked 1st Lt. Duncan Waddell from G Company to serve as one of the five officers in the sharpshooters. Waddell's heroism at Gettysburg earned the prized assignment for the junior officer from Orange County. Another G Company soldier, Pvt. Woodston Garrett, was selected. Garrett distinguished himself at Gettysburg as well, but he suffered personal tragedy when his beloved brother died on Cemetery Ridge. Despondent over his brother's death, Garrett devoted himself to the one thing that relieved the anguish of his brother's death . . . killing Yankees.[19] Garrett, Waddell, and the other sharpshooters would get plenty of chances to fight it out with the enemy on the front line during the Petersburg campaign.

GLOBE TAVERN

July–August 1864, Petersburg

Heth's Division occupied the right (western) flank of the defensive line near the intersection of the Boydton Plank and Halifax roads, near a Confederate lead works. Heth designated MacRae's Brigade as his rapid reaction force. The mission kept the Bethel soldiers out of the forward trench line, but they remained occupied responding to each alarm along the Petersburg front. Lt. Col. Frank Bird described one such assault on July 8. "About 5 o'clock the enemy charged our lines on the left and center . . . twice and were repulsed each time." Besides the daily skirmishing and cannonading, fears of an imminent Union stroke against the Weldon Railroad kept tensions high within the ranks. In July, General MacRae heard rumors of movement within the Union lines and ordered a reconnaissance of the enemy trenches to check their dispositions. "Scouts were sent out from our Brigade, two from each regiment, with a promise of a long furlough to the man who would return with accurate & reliable information as to what troops had gone from our front their destination, & the position, numbers, etc. of those remaining." The scouts came back with news that Wright's VI Corps had left the front and boarded transports. Grant had sent the VI Corps to Washington to repel an attack against the capital by Early's Corps. The troops kept an uneasy watch over the breastworks until they could account for the VI Corps. On July 11, the whole division dashed out to answer a threat to Reams Station, seven miles south. Nothing came of it, so the troops trudged back in steamy weather the next day. Active skirmishing along the front kept many of them alert that night. The imminent threat made it hard to rest.[20]

Morale within the regiment began to slip under the strain of the siege. Lewis Warlick's hopeful feelings after Cold Harbor turned to grief when he got word that his brother, Pink, died from measles while in a Richmond hospital. He bared his soul to his wife. "Again, with a sad heart I have to inform you of the death of another dear brother, my much loved brother Pink. . . . Tis hard, tis hard, to part with those we love. Within six months to a day we have had to mourn the loss of three brothers [all members of the 11th N.C.]. O cruel war. When shall we be relieved of its dreadful consequences." Warlick had joined the army at the very beginning of the war and remained steadfast in his support of the South. Yet, he suffered intense personal loss over the years of fighting. More and more, his support of the war became tempered by his desire to see the end of it. By 1864, Warlick sensed that the war was drawing to some kind of conclusion. "I still believe, as I have for months past, this year will end the fighting." Was he predicting the future or simply wishing for peace? "It will not last longer and I pray God it may not."[21]

While Warlick grieved for his brother, he was embroiled in another argument with his wife over exposing himself to enemy fire. She held no illusions nor romantic thoughts about war and often scolded him about reckless behavior on the battlefield. Warlick calmed her down each time with reassuring letters about his desire to save himself and his promise never to run risks. Of course, these reassurances would have sounded better without the caveat, "Except when duty requires." Her anxiety flared again that summer after another soldier's wife complimented her about the brave conduct of her officer-husband. She sent off a stinging letter, lecturing Warlick to protect himself. The lieutenant patiently replied that he would be careful, as he reminded her of the importance of a soldier's honor. "I know . . . you would not have me act as the coward for anything. Now I promise you as I have before that I will not go into danger unless duty requires it."[22]

Warlick and the others may have felt the effects of siege warfare, but their loyalty held firm. They verified their stance in the state's gubernatorial election. The regiment's officers and men stood behind the governor, Zebulon Vance, against William W. Holden who promoted a peace platform aimed at reconciliation with the Lincoln administration. Vance won a 140-vote majority of the regiment's eligible voters. The vote proved that the regiment wanted to continue fighting for southern independence, although that sentiment was not unanimous. Two soldiers deserted to the Union, complaining that their officers prevented their voting for Holden. Such heavy-handed political tactics were unnecessary. Governor Vance out-polled Holden by a margin of four to one. The state's war-weary citizens and soldiers were still willing to fight.[23]

In July, the Union army hatched a novel scheme to take Petersburg. Throughout the month, they dug a mine under the Confederate trenches with the intent of blasting a hole in the defensive line. According to the plan developed by General Burnside, the IX Corps would pour troops through the gap created by the exploding mine and seize Petersburg. Grant lent his support to the unorthodox plan and added his own touch to the operation. Before detonating the mine, he sent a force to demonstrate against Richmond to divert Lee's attention away from the critical point. Grant's feint worked nicely; Lee reacted by sending Heth's Division, including the 11th N.C., north to Deep Bottom to protect the Confederate capital. On July 30, a brave Pennsylvania soldier crept into the mine and charged the explosives. The blast carried away a section of the Confederate breastworks, precisely as Burnside had planned. The IX Corps rushed into the gap that had been blown open, but they bungled the assault. The attackers got off to a slow start, then became confused when they reached the huge blast hole. Mahone's Division responded aggressively to the surprise and repelled the muddled attack. The Union regiments suffered frightful casualties when they became trapped in the blast crater. Colonel Martin accurately summed up the failed Union operation: "As it was, the mine proved a slaughter-pen for the assailants."[24]

News of the explosion reached the Bethel Regiment early in the day, and the troops quickly formed to march back. They hustled through the night and reached the site of the explosion by daybreak on July 31. General Mahone positioned the brigade to plug the gaping hole in the line. Sergeant Bartlett of K Company recalled the arduous duty. "MacRae's Brigade was placed at or near the crater and remained there for 14 days, during which was the most uncomfortable 14 days I spent during the 4 years of war. One third of the boys being required to be at the embankment—all the time keeping up a continual firing of small arms in order to keep the enemy from advancing, while they were doing the same thing in order to keep us from advancing and every morning at three o'clock the artillery of both sides would open fire and keep it up until daylight, and almost, at all times of the day the enemy was dropping bombs from their [mortar] guns into our trenches, and the boys who were not on duty in the ditch would scuttle into the bombproofs which were made by digging holes into the earth covering them with timber and then keeping dirt on the timber like a potato pit." General Mahone kept the brigade on the front line the whole time rather than rotate duty with his own brigades. MacRae's officers resented this inhospitable treatment by their temporary division commander. Meanwhile, the annoying Union snipers made life miserable for the Tar Heels. "Every time we would kindle a fire in order to make some growley [a mixture of grease, crackers, and water] the Yankees would begin shooting at the smoke and knock our growley full of dirt."[25]

The Battle of the Mine gained no ground for the Union, but Grant did unearth some valuable intelligence. The fact that Lee sent a large force to cover the feint toward Richmond indicated that his army was over-stretched. Pressure at one point could compel Lee to concentrate against the threat by thinning the lines elsewhere. Soon, Grant conceived a plan that put simultaneous pressure at widely separated points. He sent Hancock's II Corps north of the James River on August 13 to engage the Richmond front. Four days later, he ordered Warren's V Corps to move west and destroy the Weldon Railroad near Globe Tavern to interdict the Confederate supply channel. The Union V Corps marched across the Jerusalem Plank Road toward Globe Tavern on August 18. Warren's four divisions straggled through the muggy August heat to the tavern by 11:00 A.M. and then began deploying. After rousting a small Confederate detachment, Brig. Gen. Charles Griffin's Division occupied the ground around Globe Tavern and started to demolish the tracks. Ayres's Division pushed north to establish a defensive line oriented toward Petersburg. Ayres's skirmishers set up a picket line in thick woods south of the Davis Farm.

General Beauregard, Confederate commanding general south of the Appomattox River, reacted quickly, though he misread the enemy

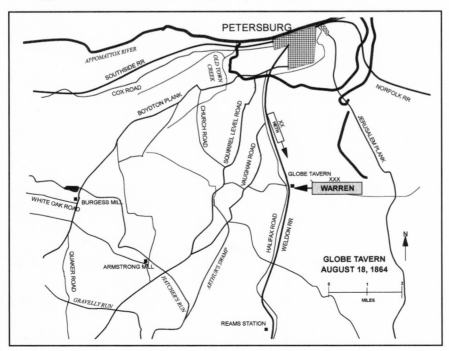

situation. Beauregard thought the Union had sent only a raiding party to Globe Tavern, so he dispatched Davis's and Walker's brigades to chase them out. He would soon regret leaving the Bethel Regiment and the rest of Heth's Division back in the trenches. Davis and Walker struck before Ayres had prepared his defense and drove the Union troops back through the woods north of Globe Tavern. The V Corps reinforced the northern sector with Crawford's and Cutler's divisions and repelled the Confederate penetration. Heth wisely broke off the attack and withdrew after dark. His report alerted the Confederate high command that the Union initiative at Globe Tavern would require a more powerful response.

While the Confederates reconsidered their actions, Grant and Meade decided to stretch the Union trenches west to the Weldon Railroad to solidify their grip on the supply line. Meade ordered the Union IX Corps under Maj. Gen. John Parke, who replaced the discredited Burnside, to extend west until they connected with Warren. Meade told Warren to establish a permanent defensive line across the Weldon Railroad, so the V Corps spent the evening of August 18–19 forming a secure defense. Things did not go well for them. Confusion over orders and a driving rain shower caused Bragg's Brigade of Cutler's Division to end up in the wrong place and left Warren's right flank exposed. Meanwhile, the II Corps relieved Parke's IX Corps from their portion of the Jerusalem Plank line, allowing Parke to send reinforcements to Globe Tavern.

While the Union V Corps dug in and the IX Corps reached out, Beauregard ordered A. P. Hill to destroy the Union lodgment with a two-division attack. Hill sent Heth's same two brigades to fix the V Corps defenses in the north and then ordered Mahone to launch the main attack with three brigades against the eastern flank of Warren's defense. The Confederates figured that the V Corps could not have tied their line back to the Jerusalem Plank, so Mahone's main attack would hit the Union position from an unexpected direction and cut it off from the rest of the army. Mahone felt confident that he could surprise the V Corps, but he worried that his force lacked the strength to overwhelm Warren. Mahone asked for more brigades to make the main attack, but Beauregard turned him down. He had taken all the troops from Petersburg that he dared.

After carefully reconnoitering the terrain, Mahone approached the

V Corps eastern flank using the cover of a ravine to avoid detection. Once his advance had turned the corner of the defending line, Mahone swung his three brigades to the west and attacked. The Confederates blew through the Union picket line and sheared off two-thirds of Bragg's Brigade. Mahone pushed forward into the right rear flank of Crawford's Division as Heth attacked from the north. Caught between Heth and Mahone, Ayres withdrew his unit to Globe Tavern, while Crawford's Division disintegrated into confusion inside the woods. Mahone's leading brigades, likewise, became entangled in the brush as they rounded up numerous parties of Union soldiers. Soon, the attacking brigades lost their momentum in the confused jumble, and Mahone had to reorganize before pressing the assault to Globe Tavern. Before Heth and Mahone could coordinate the final thrust, the IX Corps reinforcements arrived on the scene and counterattacked Mahone from the south. This time the Union troops hit the Confederates in the flank. Mahone threw his reserve against the sudden counterattack and held it off long enough to withdraw his force. The Confederates extricated most of their men as well as nearly two thousand Union prisoners from Globe Tavern.

Mahone withdrew to Petersburg where he rallied his disorganized force, content that he had severely punished the force at Globe Tavern. Heth had a different view. "Had the officer in command of this force [Mahone] obeyed his orders and attacked, the entire Federal force on the Weldon road would have been captured," he grumbled.[26] Heth's complaint struck the familiar theme of blaming someone else for a failed attack. Under the circumstances, Mahone's attack achieved all that could be expected and had dealt the V Corps a tremendous blow. The Confederates reasoned that the Union would have to withdraw after the heavy losses of August 19, but Warren disappointed them when he did not retreat during the night. Despite the impressive tactical performance by Mahone's force, the Union still held a defensive line across the Weldon Railroad. For strategic reasons, the Confederates had to organize another attack.

Beauregard started to assemble an even larger attack force, one sufficiently strong to dislodge Warren's V Corps. He replaced the five brigades used on August 19 to give them a chance to rest and refit. Lee sent units from the north side of the Appomattox River to help form the strike force, but coordination problems had the unfortunate effect of delaying the attack until August 21. The battle plan used MacRae's, Cooke's, and Ransom's North Carolina brigades, under Heth, in another supporting attack against the north side of the Union defenses. Mahone, using six fresh brigades, would make the main attack against Warren's untested western flank. Beauregard, Hill, and Mahone chose to attack Warren's left after receiving an encouraging reconnaissance report from a local soldier. The scout observed Ayres's exposed left (western) flank but failed to notice Griffin's Division guarding the western approach to Globe Tavern.[27]

Hill issued directives to pull the attacking brigades from their defensive duties on the night of August 20. Under the cover of darkness, the officers of the Bethel Regiment passed the word around to the companies to pull back from the rifle pits surrounding the crater. Once safely assembled behind the breastworks, the 11th N.C. headed south to the Davis Farm. Sergeant Bartlett felt grateful for the chance to get away from the Petersburg crater, even if it meant spending a rainy night on a tiring march. "After remaining in that place of torment for 14 days we were relieved . . . and started on the march, to we knew not where, it being night time and very dark." The weary Tar Heels had a hard time on the march down the Halifax Road. "None of us had slept much in the 14 nights and I went to sleep several times while on the march that night." The regiment halted in woods next to the Davis Farm cornfield and rested until morning.[28]

The Union defenders made good use of the extra day. Three divisions from the IX Corps took the place of Crawford's Division and tied the front line back to the Jerusalem Plank line. With his right flank secure, Warren revised his defensive position to better withstand a determined attack. The V Corps engineers laid out a tighter perimeter around the tavern that gave the corps artillery clear fields of fire to the east, north, and west. Warren pulled Ayres back from the woods into a defensive position in the open ground. The new position forced any attack to cross open terrain before it could assault the breastworks. Ayres kept his skirmishers forward on the old defensive line to contest the northern approach to Globe Tavern. Griffin's Division fortified a defensive line oriented to the west and connected with Ayres at the northwest corner. The remnant of Bragg's Brigade slid into place at the junction of the two divisions. Once the troops occupied the new line, they dug new breastworks and were thoroughly fortified by morning.

A heavy downpour at dawn soaked the Tar Heels as they stirred from their sleep, followed by an early morning fog that blanketed the area. The dense fog delayed the assault for several hours because Powell Hill needed a clear view to make a last minute check of the Globe Tavern defenses.[29] While they waited for the corps commander, the men went through the familiar routine of preparing for battle. Each soldier carefully checked his rifle and ammunition, taking precautions to keep his powder dry in the damp weather. Nine Confederate brigades moved into position and waited for the weather to clear. MacRae's Brigade formed on the right (west) side of the railroad. MacRae intended to guide his attack along the Halifax Road. The brigade had to cross the Davis Farm before striking Ayres's troops whom they thought were entrenched in the woods. Ransom's Brigade moved abreast of MacRae on the left (east) side of the railroad, and Cooke followed Ransom *en echelon*. MacRae and Ransom would attack over the same ground used by Davis and Walker on August 18 and 19. The supporting attack did not offer any tactical advantage for Heth's men; the Union troops would certainly be ready for another attack coming from that direction. Still, hitting the enemy from a direction they expected was a good method for keeping them focused against the supporting attack and away from Mahone's main attack.

As the fog lifted, MacRae adjusted his starting position by advancing his troops "about half way across the cornfield." The picked force of eighty sharpshooters led the way and cleared the Union skirmishers from the Davis Farm. MacRae's line of battle followed part way into the field and then crouched down to await the artillery bombardment. The sunshine finally cleared the ground fog at 9:00 A.M., and the Confederate artillery commenced firing. Eight guns fired over the heads of the Bethel Regiment from a position by the Davis farmhouse. Twelve more guns from the Vaughan Road added their fire against Globe Tavern. The well-posted Union artillery survived the pounding and returned fire. The men of the 11th N.C. sat uncomfortably in front of the Confederate guns and "came in for some pretty severe shelling." The solid shot crashing through the tops of the pine trees reminded the veterans of the terrible artillery duel preceding the assault on Cemetery Ridge. They shuddered at the memory of charging into the path of canister fire.[30]

The opening of the battle revealed the fact that the Union defen-

sive line had pulled back closer to Globe Tavern. This meant that
Mahone's attack had to cross more open ground before hitting the V
Corps line. Hill and Mahone consulted quickly and decided to make
the main attack with five brigades.[31] They redirected one brigade, Brig.
Gen. Johnson Hagood's, farther south to sweep into Globe Tavern
from the southwest. Mahone launched the five-brigade attack from
the Vaughan Road and then galloped over to Hagood's Brigade to
control their maneuver. To the Confederates' dismay, the main attack
ran into Griffin's Division, already positioned to repel an attack from
the west. Griffin's men and the V Corps artillery opened on the
advancing Confederates with devastating volleys of rifle fire and canister shot. As each brigade closed within range, the intense fire mowed
them down and stopped the main attack cold.

The attack of Mahone's Division alerted Harry Heth that the time
had come to attack. The lines of battle tensed in anticipation. The
Bethel Regiment dreaded charging into the fire of the Union guns,
but the steady veterans put their fears aside as they concentrated on
the attack. Heth walked forward to the skirmish line and found Duncan Waddell. He asked the lieutenant to send one of the sharpshoot-

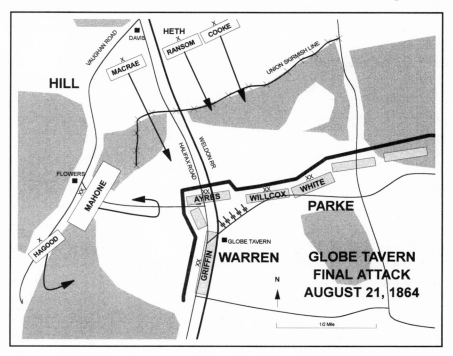

ers back for a regimental flag that he could use to signal the advance to all three brigades. Presently, the color-bearer of the 26th N.C. reported to the general. Heth ordered the soldier to hand him the flag, but the soldier refused. "General, tell me where you want the flag to go and I will take it," he replied. Heth repeated his demand, but the stubborn color-bearer refused to surrender his colors, even to a general. Finally, Heth grabbed him by the arm and said, "Come on then, we will carry the colors together." Heth and the soldier waved the regimental flag to signal the attack.[32]

When members of the Bethel Regiment saw the signal, they sprang to their feet and gave the rebel yell. With MacRae and Ransom leading, the division surged forward to strike the Purnell Legion and 146th N.Y. on the Union picket line. "We then charged, driving in their pickets and advanced line," Colonel Martin observed. Duncan Waddell described the action of the regiment's skirmishers. "The Confederate sharpshooters . . . charged through the cornfield and drove the Yankee sharpshooters back into the woods and occupied their line of battle." The quick success deceived the Tar Heels. MacRae's attack overran Warren's abandoned defensive line along the north edge of the woods but remained short of the new breastworks. The 11th N.C. and the rest of the brigade charged south through the woods overrunning a second line of breastworks and pushing the Union skirmishers out the southern edge of the woods. The Union pickets raced across the cornfield to get to the cover of the main defensive line. In their haste, they stumbled over telegraph wire they had strung across the ground to trip up the attackers. Their comrades in the main defensive line enjoyed a hearty laugh at their tumbling flight.[33]

MacRae's sharpshooters emerged from the cover of the woods and pursued the Union pickets across the open expanse, followed by the line of battle. The Tar Heels lunged forward expecting to follow up the apparent rout of the Union defense. To the east, Ransom's Brigade still struggled through the dense woods and had not appeared in front of the main entrenchments. To the west, the Confederate main attack had already receded. This left MacRae's soldiers as the immediate target for the V Corps gunners. The Union artillery swung around to the north and concentrated on MacRae's charging line. The defenders raked the open ground so effectively that "the corn-stalks were cut off by the bullets as if by a knife." The 11th N.C. and the other regiments still had plenty of fighting spirit as they took the full brunt of the V Corps artillery and rifle fire. "This seemed to make no impression on the men, who rushed for the works and would have gone there, probably to their destruction, had they not been checked." Fortunately, Billy MacRae assessed the situation, halted the brigade's advance, and shifted the troops to the cover of a ravine. Sgt. Jacob Bartlett recalled taking refuge from the enemy fire. "Captain Young [K Company Commander] was ordered to take command of the left wing of the regiment and moved to the left in order not to be so much exposed to the artillery fire." Sheltered from minié balls and canister shot, the brigade lay low and awaited word of Mahone's attack before assaulting the main breastworks. Ransom's Brigade soon struggled into the clearing only to absorb the same massed fire of the V Corps artillery. The canister shot drove most of Ransom's and Cooke's troops back into the woods where they stopped.[34]

While Heth's supporting attack ground to a halt, Mahone ordered his reserve, Hagood's Brigade, to renew the assault against Griffin's Division. Hagood's men charged bravely into the southwestern end of the V Corps position. Warren's artillery swung around once again, blasted the Confederates, and pinned them down in front of the breastworks. As the V Corps troops ceased fire, a Union captain gallantly rode forward, seized a regimental flag, and demanded that the Confederates surrender. General Hagood, in no mood to quit, confronted the Union captain and demanded that he hand back the colors. The captain refused, and Hagood shot him. The general then hopped on the dead captain's horse and led his men away under severe Union fire.[35]

Hagood's retreat left the three brigades from Heth's attack entirely unsupported, especially MacRae's. MacRae's men, unaware of Mahone's repulse, spent a very anxious day lying just in front of the V Corps' breastworks. Colonel Martin worried about the situation: "If Warren had known how few we were in his front, and had sent out an adequate force, he might have captured the most of two brigades, isolated as we were." Jacob Bartlett had a chance encounter with the enemy during this tense lull in the fighting. "Captain Young had myself and one other boy to take [an] advanced position on a road in the woods. After being in our advanced position a short time we heard men talking in front of us and heard a low rattle of canteens, we thought the Yankees were coming in force, but when they came there was only two of them; each one loaded with canteens of fresh water. We took our yanks to the rear, divided the canteens among the boys, delivered the prisoners to the rear guard and went back to our position."[36]

Luckily, the Union made only feeble counterattacks while MacRae's soldiers lay isolated in their front. Brig. Gen. Frederick Winthrop, a Union brigade commander, tried to dislodge MacRae. "I ordered the Fifth New York Volunteers and the One Hundred and Fortieth New York Volunteers to maintain a scattering fire upon the enemy's skirmishers and sharpshooters, located in the edge of the woods to my immediate front, and who were annoying our artillery by their fire." Waddell and the sharpshooters fought off the Union probes against the Bethel Regiment. "The Yankee sharpshooters, during the day, made several desperate efforts to recover the position from which they had been dislodged and in fact their regular line of battle during the evening, charged the Confederate sharpshooters but did not succeed in driving them back." Once darkness shrouded the battlefield, MacRae withdrew the brigade across the Davis cornfield.[37]

One of the regiment's sharpshooters, Pvt. Woodston Garrett, carelessly fell asleep on the skirmish line and was left in the woods when Lieutenant Waddell withdrew the sharpshooters. Garrett awoke the next morning to find himself in the middle of a Union force that had occupied the woods up to the southern edge of the Davis cornfield. Fortunately, no one had seen him. Thinking quickly, Garrett remembered that he had stashed a blue uniform from a dead Union soldier in his knapsack. Quietly, he donned the uniform and walked forward to the cornfield. Concerned Union soldiers stopped him. Duncan Waddell related, "He was warned not to [walk into the cornfield] as he would be certainly killed if he exposed himself, but he told them he wanted to get some roasting ears." Garrett noticed a Union soldier in the cornfield and explained that he wanted to join him. "They told him the man was drunk and they expected to see him get killed any moment. However, Garrett went straight to the man and found that he was drunk sure enough and he persuaded him to go a little further with him and when the man refused to go any further, Garrett suddenly drew his gun on him and told him he was a Confederate soldier and that if he did not move right in front of him, he would kill him. [Garrett] never saw a man get sober as quick in his life, and so he brought the man in the lines."[38]

The amusing incident involving Woodston Garrett could not over-shadow the regiment's close call on August 21. Once again the 11th N.C. had to pull itself out of an exposed position after a failed attack. Heth's and Mahone's soldiers demonstrated their usual fighting spirit in the attack but could not overcome Gouverneur Warren's skillful defense. The well-prepared perimeter allowed the V Corps artillery to concentrate overwhelming fire on each of the disjointed Confederate assaults. The Union artillery commander commented on the deadly effect of the fire. "Our lines being formed entirely in the open ground . . . afforded the very best opportunity possible for an effective artillery fire, which was so well employed that the infantry had comparably lit-tle opportunity to take part in the fight."[39] This time Union tactical skill beat Confederate fighting prowess. Showing more spirit than sense, Mahone complained to Lee that his attack could have succeeded had there been two more brigades to support his assault; once more, lack of support. Mahone failed to notice that Lee and Beauregard had scraped the trenches to field the nine brigades in the attack. There were none left.

The failure on August 21 convinced Lee and Beauregard to forgo any further attacks on Globe Tavern. The Union solidified its defense and made the extended front a permanent part of their trenches. Tac-tically, the Confederates had dealt disproportionate losses to the Union army and displayed excellent skill against larger Union forces. Heth and Mahone had severely punished Warren's Corps during the battles on August 18 and 19. Strategically, their failure to recapture Globe Tavern can be attributed to the inadequate force sent each day to do the job. Throughout the operation, the Confederates had been a day late and a dollar short. Over a fruitless four-day period Beauregard attacked with two brigades, then five, and finally nine. This battle had a woeful effect on the Confederates. To retain the use of the Weldon Railroad, they had to off-load the rail cars south of Globe Tavern and haul in supplies by wagon trains. The Confederates also were stretched thinner to cover the extended front. Ultimately, the attenuation of the Petersburg defensive line would have catastrophic consequences for the Army of Northern Virginia.

REAMS STATION

August 1864, Weldon Railroad

G eneral Grant wasted no time capitalizing on the Globe Tavern success. Hancock's II Corps had just returned from an exhausting expedition north of the James River and was available for a new foray to the west. Grant and Meade sent Barlow's Division, now commanded by Brig. Gen. Nelson A. Miles, to Reams Station to tear up more of the Weldon Railroad. Miles reached the station on August 23. Gibbon's Division joined them the next day, and both set about destroying the rail line while they refortified breastworks constructed weeks earlier by a cavalry unit.

Confederate scouts discovered the presence of the II Corps, and Maj. Gen. Wade Hampton, the cavalry commander, reported their activity to General Lee. Hampton thought the isolated Union force could be attacked if Lee sent a large infantry force. An attack on a Union corps five miles south of Globe Tavern looked like a risky venture. Even if a sufficient force could be gathered, the infantry would have to march past Warren's Corps before they could strike at Hancock's. Assuming they succeeded, the force would have to return to Petersburg without getting fixed by a counterattack. Still, the detached Union corps looked like an inviting target and Lee always itched for offensive action — Lee made up his mind to strike. He tasked Powell Hill to coordinate an attack using eight infantry brigades and Hampton's two cavalry divisions. Lee wished to avoid the mistake of Globe Tavern by sending an adequate force from the outset.

Hill selected MacRae's Brigade to be one of the units in the attack. The Tar Heel infantrymen had hardly gotten a chance to rest after Globe Tavern before they had to fall in for the march. As the men scurried about, Lt. Col. Frank Bird bent down on his knee to scribble a hasty letter to his sister. His family always worried about his safety and poor health, so he made a point of writing after each action. Bird feverishly penciled a few reassuring lines while the regiment formed up for another fight. Bird let his sister know that he had not been hurt in the Globe Tavern engagements but avoided any mention of an upcoming battle. He closed the hurried note with "Love to all." The regiment's second in command handed the letter to one of the soldiers collecting mail and hastened off with the unit. Hill's force moved out of the Petersburg trenches late in the afternoon of August 24 and headed south. MacRae's Brigade crossed Hatcher's Run well west of Reams Station on the Vaughan Road before stopping at Armstrong's Mill. The Bethel troops bedded down in an area that had been overlooked by previous foraging parties and were delighted to find an unmolested cornfield. The hungry soldiers gorged themselves on ears of corn and denuded the cornfield. "Such is war, crushing and blighting all in its path."[40]

The Confederate movement caught the eye of Union officers manning signal towers around Globe Tavern. That evening, Meade's headquarters warned Hancock, "Signal officers report large bodies of enemy infantry passing south from their intrenchments by the Halifax and Vaughan roads. They are probably destined to operate against General Warren or yourself. . . . The commanding general cautions you to look out for them."[41] Despite firm intelligence of a moving enemy force, Meade took no further action beyond telegraphing the warning. Hancock heeded the warning and kept Miles's Division near the station

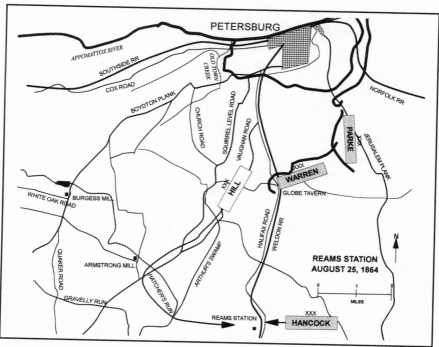

the next morning. Gibbon's Division went out to tear up more of the rail line, but before they could get any work done, Hampton's cavalry started to push in the Union cavalry screen. Hancock sensed an oncoming attack, so he put Miles's troops to work reinforcing and extending the fortifications. The Union position enclosed a half-mile stretch of the Weldon Railroad within a horseshoe perimeter. The position suffered from a major defect caused by the rail bed. At the south end of the tracks, an embankment raised the rail line above the breastworks and blocked the rear of the Union entrenchment. Near the center of the position, the railroad bed changed from an embankment to a cut. The Union cavalry, which originally fortified Reams Station weeks before, failed to use the rail bed properly in its defensive plan and laid the breastworks forward of the embankment and cut.

Initially, Hancock had shown great concern about a Confederate intrusion between his corps and Warren's Corps at Globe Tavern, but events on the Stage Road turned his attention west. Union skirmishers had engaged Confederate infantry, a sure sign of an imminent attack. Hancock recalled Gibbon's Division and readied for an assault. Gibbon positioned Murphy's and Smyth's brigades along the south side of the entrenchments. Gibbon linked with Miles at the southwest corner where Miles put the 4th N.Y. Artillery, fighting as infantrymen. To their right, he placed four regiments of Broady's Fourth Brigade behind breastworks but in front of the railroad embankment. Crandell's Consolidated Brigade, consisting of ten small regiments, stretched from the south side of the Stage Road to the rail line at the northwest corner. Most of this brigade lay in front of the railroad cut. A small gap separated the two brigades. Along the breastworks north of the Stage Road, the Consolidated Brigade slashed timber to clear fields of fire and impede infantry movement. Lynch's Brigade defended the north side of the entrenchments. Miles formed a reserve behind the Consolidated Brigade with two regiments from Broady's Brigade. Hancock provided his own reserve by placing Rugg's Brigade from Gibbon's Division behind Miles.

Shortly after noon, A. P. Hill's infantry drove in the Union pickets west of Reams Station. Hill attacked the west side of the breastworks, using a brigade from Wilcox's Division and another from Field's. Broady's Brigade and the Consolidated Brigade quickly repelled the spirited Confederate attack. At this point, Hill succumbed to another attack of prostatitis and had to relinquish command of the operation to Maj. Gen. Cadmus Wilcox. Wilcox reformed the two brigades and launched a second attack against the breastworks south of the Stage Road around 3:00 P.M. This attack pressed the defenders more heavily, but the interlocking fire of Miles's brigades stopped Wilcox within a few yards of the Union breastworks. Following his successful defense, Miles pulled four regiments from the breastworks to reestablish his picket line.[42]

While Hill's Corps menaced Reams Station, General Meade worried that the Confederates would block the Halifax Road and isolate Hancock's two divisions, so he sent Mott's Division from Globe Tavern to reinforce the rest of Hancock's Corps at Reams Station. Mott moved out sometime after 1:00 P.M., but Meade directed him to go by way of the Jerusalem Plank Road instead of down the Halifax Road. The longer route added several hours to Mott's marching time. Around 2:45 P.M., Meade notified Hancock that he was attaching Orlando Willcox's Division of the IX Corps to Hancock to help give the Confederates "a good thrashing." Again, Meade directed the reinforcements away from the direct route to Reams Station. Apparently, Meade did not want the reinforcements to make contact with Hill's Corps while en route to Reams Station. The two Union divisions could have dealt a heavy blow to the Confederates, who were preoccupied with their own attack, but the long route of march would delay them until dark.[43]

The attack, until now, had gone poorly for the Confederates. Two brigades had been battered while attempting to overrun an entrenched enemy force of equal size and had dealt only minor losses to the defenders. Harry Heth arrived on the scene with MacRae's and Cooke's brigades just as Wilcox's force fell back from its latest assault. Hill turned to Heth, who was senior to Wilcox, and gave him operational control of the corps. Heth organized a three-brigade attack using Lane's, Cooke's, and MacRae's North Carolina brigades. He brought Lt. Col. Willie Pegram's Artillery Battalion forward to add firepower to the assault. Brig. Gen. James Conner, temporarily commanding Lane's Brigade, formed his troops on the left (northern) flank. His avenue of attack went through woods before hitting the slashing in front of the Consolidated Brigade. Cooke's Brigade would advance down the Stage Road, half in the woods north of the road and half south of the road. MacRae's Brigade had to assault across an open field to hit Broady's Brigade and the left flank of the Consolidated Brigade.

General MacRae lined up his troops in a pine forest west of the clearing and then went forward to reconnoiter. He must have grimaced when he saw his path to the objective. The open ground to the breastworks offered no cover and was littered with the corpses from the previous attacks. The feisty brigade commander did not shrink from the task; instead, he ordered a full speed rush to close with the enemy before they could fire many volleys into his line of battle. MacRae warned the regiments not to return fire as it would merely slow the advance without scoring much damage against the entrenched enemy. His bold plan demanded the utmost in discipline and *esprit de corps* from the men. Capt. Louis Young, MacRae's adjutant, carefully judged the mood of the troops as he briefed the Bethel Regiment on the brigade commander's plan of attack. "As I looked into the eyes of the men . . . it was easy to see that the works would be taken." MacRae's "mesmerism of bravery" had infused the men with vigor and resolve.[44]

The brigade commander arrayed his five regiments with the 44th N.C. in the center and the 11th N.C. on the left flank next to Cooke. Meanwhile, he sent his elite sharpshooters forward to harass the defenders. The sharpshooters continued the sniping begun by Wilcox's skirmishers who picked off the horses of the Union artillery. The sharpshooters fired so accurately that the artillery teams soon had no draft animals left to maneuver their guns. At 5:00 P.M., Pegram's artillery wheeled into the field on the right of MacRae's Brigade and pounded away at the II Corps position. Broady's troops suffered little against the fire, but Pegram's artillery enfiladed Gibbon's position farther east and greatly demoralized his men. Heth watched with satisfaction for twenty minutes as Pegram pummeled the Union defenders before he initiated the assault.[45]

Lane's Brigade and the left half of Cooke's started moving through the woods toward the Union picket line. MacRae's Brigade and the other half of Cooke's held their position to allow the attack to get through the difficult terrain north of the road. Lane's men advanced quietly and surprised three Union regiments that had deployed forward on a picket line. "The enemy [Confederates] advanced with the utmost silence, refusing to answer the fire of the skirmishers till it suddenly broke with full force on the skirmish line. . . . The brigade reserving their fire for a time to allow the skirmish line to retire, poured heavy volleys upon the charging force."[46] The defenders' fire had a telling effect on the Confederates as they advanced through the slashing. MacRae watched the progress of Lane and Cooke closely. He had to time the start of his assault carefully. If he moved too soon, the brigade would reach the breastworks before Lane and Cooke and then bear the brunt of Union fire. If he moved too late, the attack through the woods might be driven back before the brigade could reach the defenders. If that happened, the entire attack would become disjointed

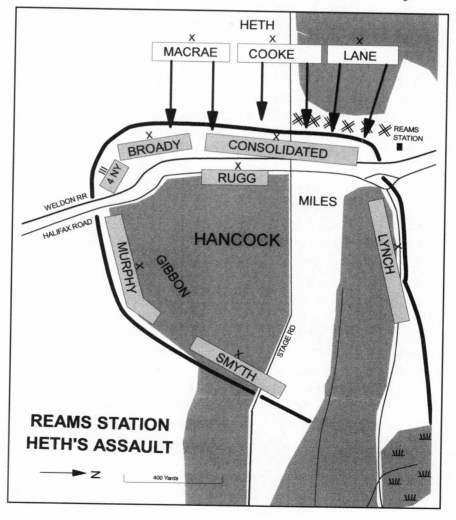

and be destroyed in piecemeal fashion. As MacRae watched, the left half of the attack force emerged from the woods and charged into the slashing.

From a position behind the breastworks, General Miles watched as Lane's and Cooke's attack developed against his front. The Confederate force "debouched from the woods in front of [the Consolidated] and the Fourth Brigade, advancing through the slashing, which was thirty yards wide. At first he was met by a sharp fire from these brigades, part of the First Brigade, which fired to the left oblique, and the Fourth New York Artillery to the right oblique. Although he pushed forward with determination, he was repulsed at several points and his organization greatly broken up by the severity of the fire and the obstacles in his front." The Union artillery poured fire into the lead regiments of the attack while Miles observed the action. Despite the punishing fire, Lane's and Cooke's troops kept pushing forward through the obstacle. MacRae, who also watched Lane's and Cooke's progress, felt that the crucial moment had come. Turning to his adjutant he said, "I shall wait no longer for orders. Lane is drawing the entire fire of the enemy; give the orders to advance at once." Shouting loudly, MacRae's soldiers "threw themselves forward at a double-quick." The Bethel Regiment surged forward with William Martin, Frank Bird, and the company officers leading the way. Once again the 11th N.C. launched a spirited charge against an entrenched enemy. "The brigade absolutely dashed along, running into Cooke's command and carrying it straight along to the enemy's works."[47]

The battle reached its crisis. Lane's and Cooke's men advanced doggedly through the slashing while MacRae's troops charged impetuously to the breastworks. They faced Miles's soldiers who poured deadly fire into the attackers. Forty yards from the breastworks a minié ball struck Frank Bird in the temple. The commander of K Company, Capt. James M. Young, dropped with a wound to his head. Lt. Duncan Waddell took a round in his chest. Another rifle shot grazed Colonel Martin, but he remained at the front of the regiment's battle line. The men kept coming with their bayonets pointed at the objective. From his vantage point, Nelson Miles felt that with a few more volleys he could finish off the assailants. "Just as his [Confederate] entire repulse seemed certain, a portion of the Consolidated Brigade . . . broke and fell into confusion. At the same time a break occurred in the right of the same brigade. I stood at the time on the bank of the railroad cut and saw a rebel color-bearer [most likely the Bethel Regiment's] spring over our works and down into the cut almost at my feet." On this day the Confederates prevailed.[48]

The bayonet charge of MacRae's Brigade reached the Union breastworks first, followed shortly by Lane and Cooke. MacRae struck the right of Broady's Brigade and the left of the Consolidated Brigade. The 44th N.C., in the center, hit the gap between the two Union brigades. The 11th N.C. mounted the breastworks on the extreme left of the Consolidated Brigade, then "precipitated themselves among the enemy's infantry." On the northern flank, Lane's soldiers pushed over the entrenchments where the regiments from the Union picket line had been defending. Some of Lane's men rushed through a hole in the breastworks where the rail line entered. As the Tar Heel brigades swarmed over the breastworks, the Union resistance crumbled. The Consolidated Brigade's official report described the collapse. "On the left of the brigade also the enemy charged with great fury through the gap in the works between the Third and Fourth Brigades, capturing a large number of men who were fighting in the pits with great desperation. . . . The thin line in the works, flanked on both the right and left, was obliged to fall back, not, however, before the colors of the One Hundred and Eleventh New York Volunteers were wrested from the color sergeant in the very rifle pits." One of Miles's reserve regiments reported, "The enemy advanced . . . up to the works, and mounting the intrenchments were met by the command. The men in many instances knocked their assailants down with the butts of their guns, and only retired when the right and left flanks were completely overpowered."[49]

General Miles watched in horror as, first, the flanks and then the entire Consolidated Brigade retreated in disorder and the Confederates poured over the breastworks. Miles immediately sought help from Rugg's Brigade, which had four regiments manning a position behind the Consolidated Brigade, but they failed to respond. Horace Rugg tried to explain what happened. "The reserves could do nothing, as [Miles's] Division apparently panic-stricken, were passing to the rear over our men, which made it impossible for them to fire on the enemy, and shortly after the panic spread to them, and they also left the field, except a majority of the Twentieth Massachusetts and Thirty-Sixth

Wisconsin Regiments, which being on the left of the line, and at the point where the enemy first crossed over our works, were compelled to surrender." One Union officer had a less charitable description of Rugg's Brigade. "These regiments remained like a covey of partridges until flushed and captured almost en masse." Three soldiers in the Bethel regiment— John Michaux, B Company first sergeant, Robert Johnston of D Company, and Alvis Pendigrant of G Company — dashed among the disorganized Union troops and wrested the regimental flags from three Union color-bearers.[50]

Frustrated by the failure of the reserves, Miles tried to rally his men to staunch the break in his division. "I then rode down the line of the Fourth [Broady's] Brigade, ordering it to move toward the right and hold the rifle pit. These troops were then fighting gallantly." Miles raced to the other flank to shore up the defense in the north, which also faltered. "The panic had become somewhat general, and it was with the greatest difficulty that any line could be formed." With the help of Colonel Lynch and an active artillery battery, the north flank stabilized.[51]

Meanwhile, MacRae's Brigade crushed Broady's attempt to hold the southern flank. MacRae turned the center and right of his brigade and began sweeping Broady's men from the breastworks. Broady's regiments were "compelled to fall back or be captured." The 4th N.Y. Artillery (fighting as infantry) jumped over to the outside of the breastworks to avoid MacRae's onrush. One of MacRae's officers saw the defense fold: "Their works stormed in front, their lines carried in flank and rear, the [Union's] infantry gave way at all points and abandoned the field in confusion and without appearance of order." Although Miles's infantry had collapsed, his artillery fought fiercely. The 1st R.I. and 10th Mass. artillery fired double-shotted canister rounds in an attempt to break up MacRae's assault on the breastworks. When the Confederates breached the defenses, the brave artillerymen turned their guns on MacRae's infantry inside the breastworks. "The right piece was swung round and poured charge after charge of canister into the approaching column." MacRae recognized the danger of the enfilade fire and ordered his troops to seize the cannons. The Union gunners were caught in a bad situation. Their infantry support had evaporated and the sharpshooters had killed all their horses. Left alone, they could not withdraw their guns, but they continued firing until the attackers overran each gun. "The cannoneers then fell back to their next piece, under the direction of their lieutenant, and fired that piece in like manner. So, falling back from piece to piece, firing each in succession, they did not leave their guns until all their supports had gone and the last round of ammunition had been expended." The courageous conduct of the Union artillery lieutenant not only inspired his men to fight gallantly, but also led to a chivalrous attempt by the Confederates "to save the life of this manly opponent. Unfortunately he was struck by a ball . . . and he fell from his horse mortally wounded, not more lamented by his own men than by those who combatted him."[52]

With the defense rapidly disintegrating, Hancock tried to retrieve the situation. He ordered Gibbon to counterattack with Smyth's Brigade to push the Confederates out of the position. "In the attempt to obey this order, that portion of the division with me did not sustain its reputation, and, demoralized . . . retired after a very feeble effort," Gibbon reported. Murphy's Brigade had its own troubles defending the southern breastworks. Broady's collapse left Murphy's right flank and rear exposed. About that time, Wade Hampton's dismounted cavalry struck the southern breastworks, including Murphy's sector. "I found the command much disorganized," Murphy admitted. His regiments faced the threat of Confederate cavalry attacks against the southern entrenchment, while MacRae's troops pressured him from inside the perimeter. "[Murphy's men] had to cross the rifle-pits as many as four times, being forced to do so by the enemy's fire, which at one time would come from the rear and then change again to the front. . . . The advance of the enemy on our front and flank made the capture of the greater part of the command very probable, if it had not retired, which was executed in any way but the best order."[53]

Heth followed through by committing two reserve brigades into the fight. The reinforcements helped MacRae, Cooke, and Lane push deeper into the Union position and consolidate their hold on Reams Station. Nonetheless, the Confederates ran out of steam, preoccupied with the large haul of prisoners. The three assault brigades had captured a force of Union soldiers nearly equal to their combined strength. Hancock assembled his disordered brigades in the woods east of the rail line. The Union corps commander ordered a counterattack with his full force, but Gibbon confessed that his men would not advance;

they had become too dispirited. Hancock canceled the counterattack and, much to his chagrin, gave up all hope of retaking Reams Station. He waited until dark and then withdrew his broken corps east to the Jerusalem Plank Road.

Hancock's Corps suffered a disaster at Reams Station. The losses reached staggering levels: 109 killed, 501 wounded and 1,762 missing! Yet, the humiliation of defeat stung worse than the casualties. The II Corps had been routed from an entrenched position and had retreated in panic. What had happened to the heroes of Cemetery Ridge, the stubborn fighters of the Wilderness, the veterans of Spotsylvania? Hancock had a ready explanation. "I attribute the bad conduct of some of my troops to their great fatigue . . . and their enormous losses during the campaign, especially in officers." The draft levies and recruiters had refilled the ranks but did not replace the experienced soldiers. Hancock noted, "The material compares very unfavorably with the veterans absent." Some of the responsibility for the calamity rested with Meade. He passed on another opportunity to crush an isolated Confederate force near two of his corps. Meade did provide reinforcements to help Hancock "thrash the enemy," but he sent them on a route that effectively took them out of the battle. An offensive-minded commander would have sent Mott and Willcox on a mission to find and attack the enemy. The lack of aggressiveness shown by the Union army commander contrasted sharply with the fighting spirit displayed by Lee, Hill, Heth, MacRae, and others.[54]

The clear victory at Reams Station gave the Confederacy a much needed boost. Lee's troops had whipped the Yankees, just like the glorious days of 1862 and 1863. Once again, the fighting prowess of the Confederate soldier won the day. Heth remarked, "This charge and its results, has proved to me that nothing is impossible to men determined to win." Reams Station marked the Confederate high point of the Petersburg campaign. The battles of the Mine, Globe Tavern, and Reams Station gave Lee his best score in the gruesome war of attrition. Lee penned a special letter of congratulations to Governor Vance to recognize the Tar Heel brigades. "I have frequently been called upon to mention the services of North Carolina soldiers in this army, but their gallantry and conduct were never more deserving of admiration than in the engagement at Reams' Station. . . . The brigades of Generals Cooke, MacRae, and Lane . . . advanced through a thick abatis of felled trees, under a heavy fire of musketry and artillery, and carried the enemy's works with a steady courage that elicited the warm commendation of their corps and division commanders and the admiration of the army."[55]

The Confederate army and Heth's troops felt euphoric over their impressive victory, although the final result tended to overshadow some genuine problems. Frankly, Lee had been very lucky. The Confederate senior commanders disregarded tactical maneuver and relied totally on their soldiers' fighting spirit to retake Reams Station. The decisive assault massed only 1,750 infantrymen against Hancock's defenses, a comparative strength that was worse than Cemetery Ridge. Had the Union troops held a little longer, the Confederates would have suffered a bloody repulse. It was too late in the war for Lee to risk heavy casualties for the single purpose of punishing an isolated Union corps.

The 11th N.C. endured its share of casualties at Reams Station. Lt. Col. Francis W. Bird, the brave officer who carried the colors at Cemetery Ridge, died the next day from his head wound. His death reduced the regiment to one field grade officer, again. Capt. James Young and 1st Lt. Duncan Waddell were both wounded. The regiment lost Waddell's services for good; he spent the rest of the war as the recruiting officer in Mecklenburg County. Still, the Bethel men relished their latest victory. Despite being wounded in the arm, Pvt. John C. Warlick of I Company called Reams Station "the prettiest fight we were ever in." The capture of so many enemy soldiers, cannons, and colors helped ease their pain.[56]

Jones Farm

September 1864, Petersburg

Flushed with their success at Reams Station, the 11th N.C. returned to the Petersburg trenches and reconstituted. Nothing could be done about the lieutenant colonel's slot after Frank Bird's death, but companies throughout the regiment tried to fill other leadership voids left by recent casualties. Company A asked Colonel Martin for permission to elect a new lieutenant after 3d Lt. James Montgomery died from wounds received at Reams Station. Montgomery had been the only commissioned officer with the company since June. Two of the company's officers were confined at the Union's Fort Delaware prison, and Lieutenant Taylor was in the hospital. The fighting had depleted the enlisted ranks, as well. At the time, only fifty-seven of the one hundred and seven men assigned to the company could be counted present for duty. The election of Richard B. Alexander helped improve the situation, as did the return of Billy Taylor. K Company seldom had an officer present for duty after Captain Young was wounded at Reams Station. Even after his return to duty, Young would spend most of his time commanding the regiment, not K Company. Jacob Bartlett had to take charge, once the company promoted him to the rank of first sergeant. 1st Lt. William Todd, of C Company, took Duncan Waddell's place as the leader of the regiment's worthy sharpshooters after he recovered from his latest wound (also at Reams Station). Company I had only Lieutenant Lemuel Hoyle and could elect no others because the captain and two lieutenants remained captives. The regiment's companies learned to operate with one or two officers instead of the normal complement of one captain and three lieutenants.[57]

The regiment had to deal with some unpleasantness concerning one of its officers, 3d Lt. Jones Watson of G Company. Watson had been suffering from deteriorating health for over a year after one of his lungs was "almost entirely destroyed." Watson told his father that his health would force him to resign, but he wanted to stay with the regiment until the fall campaign ended. When the regiment marched to Reams Station, Watson decided to follow. The young officer struggled to keep up with his company during their attack, but the rigors of combat thoroughly exhausted him. Once they had penetrated the Union defense, Lieutenant Watson turned around and started for the rear. While searching for the regimental surgeon for a medical pass, he ran into the assistant surgeon, James McCombs. McCombs refused to examine Watson and accused the officer of running from the fight. Watson ignored him and continued walking back to the rear. After the battle, McCombs swore out a charge of cowardice against Watson. Perhaps a more sympathetic commander would have taken some pity on

Watson, but Billy MacRae would never tolerate any shirking among his officers. After reading McCombs's report, the general immediately convened a court-martial against Watson. The court met on September 5 and convicted the feeble lieutenant of cowardice in the face of the enemy. MacRae cashiered Jones Watson and directed that notice of the verdict be distributed to newspapers throughout North Carolina. Watson's horrified father published a rebuttal of the court's proceedings, in an attempt to save some of his son's ruined reputation. Sick, discharged, and humiliated, the younger Watson somehow held onto his loyalty and dignity. He enlisted in the 3d N.C. Cavalry the next month and served as a private throughout the remainder of the war.[58]

After Reams Station, MacRae's Brigade manned its usual place on the far right (western) end of the trenches. The men did not appreciate the dreary duty in the breastworks under the constant strain of Union sharpshooters and mortar bombardments. Yet, their morale remained high, as Lee's inspector general (IG) discovered when he inspected Heth's Division. "MacRae's Brigade . . . I found in good order, in discipline, arms, accouterments, and clothing; police was fair." The IG went on to praise the leadership of Generals Cooke and MacRae. "Two brigades of Heth's division, Cooke's and MacRae's, it will be seen are in specially good order and commanded by two most excellent officers, who are strict disciplinarians, but who have great influence over their men in camp and on the field. Their spirits are specially good since the brilliant victory which they, under General Heth, achieved at Reams' on 25th of August."[59]

That victory boosted the Confederates' hopes for a political settlement to the war. One of MacRae's officers wrote expectantly about the Democratic Party's upcoming convention. "If the Rebels are still successful in repelling all their [Union army's] assaults . . . the Convention will nominate a candidate on the 'peace' platform, & the army & those at home who oppose the war, will rally around him & elect him."[60] This hope collapsed after Sherman's army captured Atlanta on September 2. The fall of Atlanta gave the Union its first major victory of the year and ended the political crisis that weighed so heavily on the Lincoln administration during the summer of 1864. After so many bloody and indecisive battles, Lincoln could now point to visible progress toward military victory, and his political opposition crumbled, as the dismal summer ended. The news took the wind out of the Democrats' sails, once they could no longer play up the military stalemate. The Republican political machine steamed ahead in the wake of Sherman's victory.

The situation in Virginia did not match the dramatic events in Georgia. Petersburg remained strangely quiet during the weeks following Reams Station, although the Confederates gained no relief from the siege. Grant's westward thrust across the Weldon Railroad posed a new threat to the Confederate supply lines. The roads southwest of Petersburg provided vital access to the Weldon Railroad south of Globe Tavern where the Confederates off-loaded supplies onto wagon trains short of the Union position. If Grant clamped down on these wagon routes, the flow of supplies to Richmond would dwindle dangerously. Lee ordered two new lines constructed, extending the entrenchments southwest to cover the Boydton Plank and Squirrel Level roads.

Grasping axes, shovels, and picks, the Tar Heels constructed new fortifications and improved the old ones. One of MacRae's soldiers recalled the busy days after Reams Station. "On reaching the city we were placed in line, the right of our brigade resting on the Petersburg & Weldon Railroad. Here we engaged in throwing up a new line of works in front of those at that time occupied. At this employment we continued until 16 September, when we were moved to a point about a half mile south of the Boydton plank road, and about three miles southwest of the city, where we were employed in constructing rifle-pits until the 20th. On this day we were moved about one mile further south of the Boydton road and engaged in constructing works of a more elaborate character until the 29th." MacRae's troops also extended the Boydton Plank breastworks as far west as the Harman Road. The brigade commander initially tasked his adjutant, Capt. Louis Young, to design these breastworks and plan their fields of fire, but Young's defensive plan led to a dispute with his boss. "General MacRae ordered me to lay out the works and make the details to construct them. This I did to the best of my ability, and when the work was fairly under way, the General came to see what was being done. To my chagrin he condemned and changed my lines, whereupon I retired." In this case, MacRae acted hastily. His altered design provided good fields of fire against the main enemy avenue of approach but overlooked a concealed approach through nearby woods. The former railroad engineer soon recognized his oversight and ordered the lines reworked more closely to Young's original layout. MacRae "generously acknowledged" his error to Young. Unfortunately, several days were required to fix the flaw in the breastworks. They did not get the chance to finish.[61]

The Union inactivity was deceptive; Grant had not forsaken the offensive. The Union commander used this time to prepare a massive effort to capture Richmond — his "Fifth Offensive." Once again, Grant planned mutually supporting attacks against the Confederate flanks to upset the balance of Lee's defense. The offensive would open with an attack by Butler's Army of the James directed at the Confederate capital. Butler optimistically predicted that his army could crack the Richmond defensive line and capture the city by storm. Grant had more realistic expectations, but he figured that a serious threat to Richmond would force Lee to weaken the Petersburg front. Once Lee had reinforced Richmond with troops from Petersburg, Grant intended to push Meade's army west around Lee's right flank. Grant hoped to seize the new Confederate trench line, cut the road network southwest of Petersburg, and interdict the Southside Railroad. At the least, Grant believed his powerful one-two punch to the flanks would allow Meade to overrun more of the Confederate supply lines. Grant gave specific guidance about permanently cutting the wagon and rail routes into Petersburg. "If the road is reached it, or a position commanding it, should be held at all hazards."[62]

The Army of the James delivered the opening blow on September 29. Butler's army scored an important tactical victory by capturing Fort Harrison, one of Richmond's defensive fortifications. Confederate intelligence had picked up the large-scale movement toward Richmond, and Lee reacted quickly. That morning, both of the reserve divisions at Petersburg departed for the north side of the James River. As news of the fall of Fort Harrison came in, Lee grasped the magnitude of the crisis.[63] Butler had penetrated the Richmond line and could capture the capital unless the Army of Northern Virginia sealed the breach. Lee sent a third division north from Petersburg and took precautionary measures to abandon Petersburg, if that became necessary to save Richmond. These movements nearly denuded the Petersburg trenches of infantry and risked the loss of the besieged city to direct assault. To compensate, Lee pulled MacRae's Brigade back from the new defensive lines and held it in reserve behind the Petersburg fortifications.

In the late afternoon of September 29, the officers ordered the troops of the 11th N.C. to halt work on the new breastworks and fall into formation. The soldiers picked up their rifles and ammunition pouches and then marched northeast along the Boydton Plank, leaving the partially constructed fort vacant. Heth's infantry abandoned the new trench lines along the Boydton Plank and Squirrel Level roads, as Confederate cavalry took their place in the incomplete trenches. Without defending infantry, however, the Confederate supply lines southwest of Petersburg lay exposed to a Union attack. The Confederates could not defend the supply routes, but they could contest a Union move into the area. A reserve force, which included the Bethel Regiment, lay poised to counterattack any Union advance west of the Weldon Railroad. Nevertheless, Lee had to shift his forces, abandon a fortified defensive line, and rely on a mobile defense to fight in the open field. Lee had reacted to the Union initiative just the way Grant had foreseen.

General Meade planned to attack with four divisions: two from Warren's V Corps (Griffin's and Ayres's) and two from Parke's IX Corps (Willcox's and Potter's). Warren would strike west from Globe Tavern along the Poplar Spring Road and then cross the Vaughan Road. Parke's Corps would follow Warren, deploy on his left flank, and cooperate in breaching the Confederate trench line at the Church Road–Squirrel Level Road intersection. Meade neglected to delineate any plan for exploiting a breach of the Squirrel Level defenses or for carrying the attack onto the Boydton Plank. The limited scope of Meade's battle plan revealed his misgivings over the operation.[64]

The constant shuffling of Confederate forces in and out of Petersburg on September 29 clouded Meade's picture of the situation, so he remained where he was until he received specific orders from Grant to move. After conferring with Butler on the morning of September 30, Grant affirmed his estimate of the situation and directed Meade to begin the attack. Warren's men sortied from Globe Tavern by 9:00 A.M. and then moved cautiously forward through the thick woodland. Warren's elongated column took nearly four hours to reach the Squirrel Level defenses and deploy. At 1:00 P.M. Griffin's Division finally stormed Fort Archer, which was an incomplete fortification at the Squirrel Level–Church Road intersection. Griffin's assault swept the

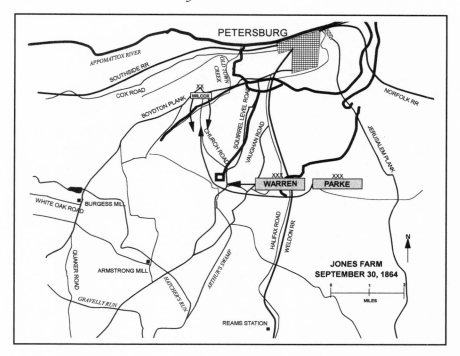

JONES FARM
SEPTEMBER 30, 1864

Confederate cavalry out of the fort. The horsemen fell back, leaving a large enemy force holding the flank of the new breastworks. A single Union division had broken the Squirrel Level defensive line.

Instead of exploiting their success with a bold advance toward the Boydton Plank, the Union commanders piddled away the next few hours carefully consolidating their positions around the breakthrough. Although Parke's two divisions had not engaged the enemy, the IX Corps did not follow up Warren's success, nor did Meade intervene to coordinate a general advance. When a reconnaissance failed to locate any significant Confederate force southwest of Petersburg, Meade worried that the Confederate cavalry might be marshaling to raid his rear. He spent some of his time making defensive preparations in the rear rather than pushing his two corps forward. Apparently, Lee's propensity for vigorous offensive action had the Union commanders searching for phantom counterattacks. Grant did not suffer his subordinates' anxiety. The Union general correctly perceived the precariousness of Lee's defense. Without enough strength to defend both flanks simultaneously, Lee would have to forsake Petersburg to save Richmond. The ease with which Meade's army had broken through the Squirrel

Level defensive line proved that Lee had pulled forces from Petersburg to concentrate against Butler. Around 3:00 P.M. Grant told Meade to press onward to seize the Boydton Plank trench line and the Southside Railroad while the opportunity lasted. Meade complied with the order, although he failed to move forward to coordinate the drive and left the two corps commanders to work in concert on their own.

Parke's IX Corps resumed the lethargic advance around 4:00 P.M. After leaving Fort Archer, Potter's Division led the advance up the Church Road through a clearing around the Pegram Farm with two brigades under Brig. Gen. Simon Griffin and Col. John Curtin. The woods on the north side of this clearing separated the Pegram Farm from a larger clearing around the Jones Farm. Griffin halted his brigade in the woods to allow Curtin's Brigade to deploy on his left (western) flank. Potter wanted security on his flank before continuing through the eastern end of the Jones Farm toward the Old Town Creek. The trailing division commander, Orlando Willcox, dispersed his three brigades behind Potter. While Potter crept forward, General Parke left his corps artillery in the rear to guard against the feared cavalry raid. Gouverneur Warren did not move either of his two divisions much beyond Fort Archer. He simply connected the V Corps right flank back to Globe Tavern and consolidated. Warren did come forward himself but only to urge Parke to attack with greater vigor. After exhorting Parke, Warren returned to his corps but did nothing to help the advance. Parke left the meeting with the mistaken belief that Warren would move Charles Griffin's Division forward to support the right flank of Potter's Division. With the army commander avoiding direct involvement and the two corps commanders operating independently, the Union attack suffered an ominous breakdown of command and control.[65]

The Confederate forces suffered no such confusion. General Lee departed the area for Richmond on September 29 and left Lt. Gen. A. P. Hill in command of Petersburg. Hill watched helplessly as the four Union divisions pushed through the Squirrel Level defensive line. Shortly thereafter, the Confederate high command released two brigades of Cadmus Wilcox's Division to return to Petersburg. As soon as Wilcox returned, a cavalry courier rode up and reported that a Union force was advancing up the Church Road. General Wilcox reacted to the report and, on his own authority, moved Lane's and

McGowan's brigades forward to Old Town Creek to forestall the Union advance. Hill, who approved Wilcox's move, ordered Heth to send MacRae and Archer to help Wilcox form a counterattack. Hill dispatched an artillery battalion with Heth and then ordered Hampton's cavalry to cooperate with the infantry force. When Harry Heth joined Wilcox, he assumed overall command of the counterattack. Heth graciously turned over control of all four infantry brigades, including MacRae's, to Wilcox, while he coordinated with the artillery and cavalry. Unlike their Union counterparts, the Confederate generals easily developed a command arrangement that preserved unity of command for the upcoming battle.[66]

Around 5:00 P.M. General Parke restarted his movement toward the Boydton Plank trenches. The lead division commander, Robert Potter, instructed his brigadiers on the plan of attack. "I ordered General [Simon] Griffin to form his brigade to attack and Curtin to form on the left to cover a road coming in from the left in my rear, understanding that a brigade of Willcox's division [McLaughlen's] would look after the right." Coordination among the Union commanders broke down at this point, caused by Parke's misunderstanding with Warren. General Parke, thinking that Charles Griffin's Division of the V Corps would move up to support Potter's right flank, shifted McLaughlen's Brigade of Willcox's Division to the left. However, Warren did not push Charles Griffin's Division forward. Finding no one on either of his flanks, Potter objected but was "ordered to push on with my whole force as rapidly as practicable, without reference to any one else." Simon Griffin, Potter's lead brigade, formed his unit into two echelons, each with three regiments abreast, preceded by a single regiment of skirmishers. As the Union forces approached the Boydton Plank defensive line, the formidable two corps attack envisioned by Grant had turned into a hesitant movement to contact. Only one corps moved past Fort Archer; only one division advanced beyond Pegram's Farm; only one brigade pushed forward to the Jones Farm and Simon Griffin led this attack with only three regiments in the forward line of battle. Between the Squirrel Level Road and Jones Farm, the Union attack had shrunk from four divisions to three regiments.[67]

At Jones Farm northern timidity ran afoul of southern temerity. Cadmus Wilcox observed Potter's skirmishers approaching Old Town Creek and decided to throw them back. "Skirmishers from the brigades were thrown forward and soon drove those of the enemy from Jones' House, capturing some twenty or thirty." The sudden counterpunch sent the Union skirmishers scurrying back to Griffin's forward line of battle. Griffin halted to reorganize his advance and let Curtin's Brigade close behind his left. Colonel Curtin sent his forward battle line (45th Pa., 58th Mass., and 51st N.Y.) into the clearing west of the Jones house, behind and to the left of Griffin's second line of battle. The confusion over right (east) flank security for Griffin's Brigade left the lead Union force dangerously exposed. Griffin reported, "No brigade came to the front where my right rested. While these formations were in progress, before there was any line of battle at all on my right or one completed on my left, orders came to advance."[68]

Wilcox decided to seize the initiative when he saw the small Union show of force and the weak reaction to his limited attack. He deployed Lane's and McGowan's brigades on the west and east side of Church Road, respectively. Archer's Brigade fell in behind and farther east of McGowan's. MacRae's troops, including the 11th N.C., moved behind and to the west of Lane's force. "Before these brigades had been formed in line, the enemy [Simon Griffin's first line of battle]

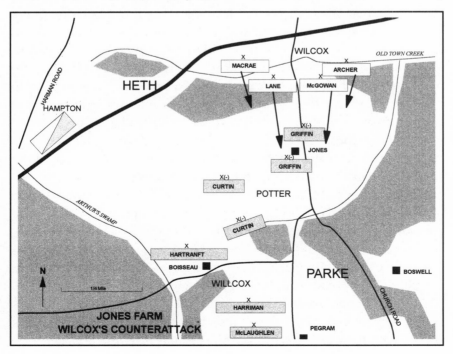

advanced, drove in our skirmishers, and their line of battle had nearly reached Jones' House. Not wishing to receive the attack whilst Heth's brigades were forming [I] ordered [my] two brigades, already in line, to advance." Wilcox enveloped both flanks of Griffin's leading battle line, using Lane to crush the west while McGowan hit the east. MacRae's Brigade had not gotten on line and had to follow Lane's men *en echelon* to their right and rear. The Bethel soldiers hardly had time to check their rifles and ammunition before they raced off to catch up with Lane. The Confederate counterattack smashed into Griffin, who bitterly recalled the clash. "On arriving at the Jones house we met the enemy also advancing, with a line of battle stronger than our own, and overlapping us on both flanks." Simon Griffin tried to reinforce his lead battle line with the other three regiments but to no avail. "Being furiously attacked on three sides by superior numbers they were compelled to abandon the place," he admitted. Before Griffin could concentrate his brigade and stem the oncoming tide of Confederate infantry, "the whole line was carried away."[69]

Lane and McGowan routed Griffin and pursued him down the Church Road. As Lane's Brigade swept south along the Church Road, MacRae deployed his brigade to supporting their right (west) flank. The 52d N.C., on the extreme right flank, moved into the clearing with the 11th N.C. alongside. The pursuit of Griffin's scattering force carried the Confederates past the position of Curtin's first line of battle, which had halted in the clearing. Curtin's three regiments spotted MacRae's Brigade to their right and boldly decided to attack. The Union regiments wheeled their line of battle to the east and charged into the exposed flank of the 52d N.C.

The unexpected Union assault on MacRae's right flank caught the Confederates by surprise. The Tar Heels were unaccustomed to such aggressiveness by the Union army on the open field. The attack began to roll up the 52d N.C. and threaten the entire brigade. Colonel Martin reacted quickly. "The situation was critical; there was no time for orders, and without orders I at once caused my own regiment and the one next to me, the Fifty-Second, . . . which was being thrown into disorder, to change front to the right and charge the Federal flanking party."[70] With a neat battlefield maneuver the 11th N.C. swung round to confront Curtin's three regiments. The years of practice drills paid off in the heat of battle, allowing the regiment to move quickly under enemy fire. The regiment aligned itself, lowered bayonets, and rushed forward. The 52d N.C. rallied and joined the charge of the Bethel Regiment. In an unexpected meeting engagement, three Union regiments collided head–on with two Confederate regiments. Once again, the *esprit de corps* and discipline of the Confederates' prevailed. Curtin's regiments broke and ran.

The Union troops fled west to escape the Tar Heel charge. They could not turn south, as Lane's, McGowan's, and the rest of MacRae's brigades were already sweeping through Curtin's second line of battle. Colonel Curtin tried to rally his men in the clearing by getting them to fire on Martin's assaulting force. Each time the Union soldiers started to reform, the Tar Heels lunged forward and kept driving them west. Suddenly, two regiments of dismounted Confederate cavalry appeared from the west to cut off Curtin's line of retreat. General Potter watched helplessly. "The enemy now advanced a considerable force to my left [west], attacking, impetuously, and their cavalry advanced and attacked to the left and rear, but I think not in much force. They succeeded in making a junction between the attacking forces on the right and left, and cut off a considerable portion of my First Brigade [Curtin's]." Blocked in the west and pursued vigorously from the east, the 45th Pa., 58th Mass., and the 51st N.Y. surrendered to William Martin's infantry and the cavalry. Three colors, three regimental commanders, and over 600 men fell into Confederate hands, more men than were in the 11th and 52d N.C. combined. Only Colonel Curtin and a handful of others escaped. Curtin had to suffer the indignity of being thrown headlong from his horse before he scampered away on foot to safety.[71]

While the Bethel men rounded up prisoners, Wilcox pursued the broken remnants of Potter's Division into Pegram's Farm. Parke organized a defensive front across the clearing of Pegram's Farm using Orlando Willcox's Division and the elements of Potter's that could be rallied. The IX Corps artillery finally got into the battle and hammered the Confederate force across the clearing. At last, Warren committed a part of his corps to help the IX Corps. Lane and McGowan struck the hasty Union defensive line, followed later by Archer's Brigade, but they had gotten disorganized from the rapid pursuit of Potter's troops. The Confederate attack reached its culminating point at the Pegram Farm where it failed to dislodge Parke's Corps.

Wilcox reformed the Confederate brigades in the woods at the north end of the clearing after the attack ground to a halt. In the twilight, William MacRae had to reorganize his dispersed but exhilarated troops for a possible Union night attack. He pulled the 11th and 52d N.C. south to the woods near the Pegram Farm where he set up a hasty defense. Union artillery gunners harassed the Confederates by firing across the clearing, but the fire lacked intensity. The random Union shelling did strike a hard blow to the regiment, though. William Martin recalled, "We . . . were in the act about dark of reforming the line when I was struck with a shell which carried away a large slice of my left thigh. I was with difficulty carried off the field in a blanket."[72] Martin's wound left the Bethel Regiment without any field grade officer and only four captains present to manage the unit. Capt. William Grier assumed temporary command of the regiment until Capt. James Young could return to duty. The loss of the colonel put a damper on the splendor of the day's accomplishments. For the second battle in a row, the regiment had crushed a Union force and captured a large number of enemy troops. The leadership of its senior officers and the solid fighting mettle of the troops earned another victory for Hill's Corps.

For the Confederates, the success of the counterattack may have eclipsed the strategic picture, but Powell Hill perceived the gravity of the Union advance. Meade's army held the Squirrel Level entrenchments and threatened the supply lines. Hill withdrew MacRae's and Archer's brigades, after a rain shower eliminated the danger of a Union night attack, to help form a strike force for the next day. He counted heavily on retaining the initiative gained on September 30 to drive Meade back and reclaim the Squirrel Level breastworks. General Mahone had scouted the gap between the Squirrel Level Road and Globe Tavern and reported that the Union defense looked weak. "It was supposed that here a successful blow might be struck." Hill planned to strike southwest from Petersburg along the Squirrel Level Road with all four of Heth's brigades. After crushing the Union flank, they would push forward to seize the Church Road intersection. Wilcox's Division would attack to fix Parke's IX Corps, already massed at Pegram's Farm. Whether he realized it or not, A. P. Hill nearly duplicated the chain of events at Globe Tavern six weeks earlier. The Confederates had stung the Union with a sharp counterattack the first day and then tried a more powerful blow against the inside flank of the Union line on the second day. These were sound tactics, but the plan suffered from the same lack of force that plagued the Globe Tavern battles.[73]

The Union corps commanders fully expected more counterattacks on October 1 and made defensive preparations throughout the rainy night. Warren positioned Ayres's Division on the Squirrel Level Road to stop any attack coming from the direction of Petersburg. These troops dug in and linked up with units on their flanks to form a cohesive defensive front. Meade ordered Parke's Corps to consolidate farther back on the breastworks already constructed by the Confederates along the Squirrel Level Road (formerly Fort Archer). This position offered the Union forces better fortifications and simplified tying the two corps together. Meade still planned to resume the offense on October 1, but the corps commanders preoccupied themselves with defending and made no effort to fulfill the army commander's desire to advance.

In the predawn hours, Heth gathered all four of his brigades near the Squirrel Level-Boydton Plank intersection and marched them south through the early morning rain. By 7:00 A.M., the division formed on the Squirrel Level Road northeast of Ayres's defenses. MacRae's Brigade held the frontline position on the right (west) side of the road. General Archer aligned his brigade on their left. Davis and Cooke marched in support behind the frontline units. MacRae's hand-picked sharpshooters moved forward, followed by the main line of battle. The sharpshooters ran into the Union pickets as they neared the Chappell House. The aggressive sharpshooters soon drove back the Union skirmish line, then ran into the forward position of the 140th N.Y., 10th U.S., and 12th U.S. After a brief but intense fight, the Union soldiers fell back to their main defensive line. Heth's men, believing they had collapsed the Union's flank, plunged ahead. They slammed into Ayres's breastworks, constructed the night before.[74]

Heth halted his advance to evaluate this unexpected Union obstacle. Artillery came forward to soften up the Union breastworks for an attack.[75] By 9:00 A.M., Heth decided to probe the defense using MacRae's Brigade. Emboldened by their success of the day before, two of MacRae's regiments, the 44th and 52d N.C., broke ranks and charged full speed toward the defenders. The overzealous troops apparently thought they could rout any enemy they faced. Billy MacRae tried to restrain their impulsive assault but failed to prevent it. Only a sudden rain shower slowed their spirited but ill-fated charge. The 44th and 52d N.C. stormed the Union defenses and were blasted by the disciplined fire of Ayres's troops. The Bethel Regiment and the rest of MacRae's men followed the two lead regiments into the cauldron but had no hope of overrunning the Union breastworks. The regiment's officers pulled the line of battle back before the ranks were badly cut up by the enemy's fire. As his units fell back from the breastworks, MacRae reorganized his brigade. The fiery general seethed with anger over the breakdown in discipline. Meanwhile, Archer's and Davis's brigades attempted to follow through on the assault but had no better luck. Despite his intent only to probe the Union position, Heth had delivered two uncoordinated attacks, which Ayres handily rebuffed.

The results of the attack convinced Heth that Hill's battle plan could not succeed against an obviously well-prepared Union defense. "I concluded not to make a determined assault, which, if successful would have been with such heavy loss, that no further attack could have been [made]." Heth wisely withdrew to Petersburg. Wilcox's supporting attack at Pegram's Farm did push back an advanced Union brigade but lacked the strength to break Parke's defensive line near Fort Archer. Like Heth, Wilcox concluded that the Union's grip on the Squirrel Level line could not be shaken loose with the limited forces at hand. Powell Hill had to accept the permanent loss of another supply route and the westward extension of Union fortifications.[76]

By this time, the corps commanders on both sides had their fill of offensive action, but General Meade still hoped to force a decisive battle before the Confederates retired behind their breastworks. Throughout the day, he urged Parke and Warren to advance, and he sent another division to reinforce the IX Corps. Still, the two corps commanders spent October 1 improving their fixed positions. Dissatisfied with the limited gains and eager to fight the Confederates in the open, Meade ordered a general attack for October 2, using the five divisions assembled along the Squirrel Level Road. Mott's Division of the II Corps, recently attached to Parke, would advance on the outside of a large wheeling movement that would swing the Union force to the north. Meade expected the wide swing of five divisions to dislodge the enemy around Pegram's Farm. He counted on a vigorous pursuit to overrun the Confederates before they could establish a stable defense on the Boydton Plank defensive line.[77]

The Union attack started at 7:00 A.M. on October 2 but moved slowly toward Pegram's Farm. The Union force crept forward, carefully maintaining tight formations to repel any sudden counterattacks; Parke and Warren did not want a repeat of the Jerusalem Plank fiasco. Cautiously, the attackers approached, then crossed the terrain where they had anticipated a fierce fight. They found only skirmishers there to harass them. Perplexed, the Union commanders halted and probed a little beyond Pegram's Farm. They learned that the Confederates had abandoned the ground south of the Boydton Plank entrenchments. General Meade realized that he had lost his chance to fight a decisive battle in open terrain. He saw no purpose in continuing the offensive, especially against an entrenched enemy. Before noon, Meade called off the attack and ordered his two corps to consolidate the ground gained over the past three days behind new breastworks.[78]

Meade's decision came too late to stop one last significant action. Gershom Mott's Division continued its movement to the Boydton Plank before word of Meade's decision reached him. At the time, only a Confederate cavalry unit held the western end of the fortifications. The cavalrymen knew they could not stop a Union infantry division, and they sent a courier off to A. P. Hill with an urgent appeal for help. Hill dispatched MacRae's Brigade to shore up the western end of the breastworks. While en route, Billy MacRae learned from couriers that Mott's Division was nearing the plank road and would soon breach the trench line near the Harman Road. MacRae understood the urgency of the situation and ordered the brigade to hurry toward the breastworks they had recently constructed and left unfinished. The 11th N.C. dashed down the Boydton Plank Road in a foot race with the Union troops. The Tar Heels knew the catastrophic consequences if Mott beat them to the Harman Road. The 11th N.C. and its sister regiments arrived at the unfinished fort simultaneously with the Union skirmishers. MacRae's soldiers charged into them from their march column and sent the skirmishers back to their line of battle. Mott moved forward to break through the resistance, while Captain Grier and the Bethel soldiers jumped into the incomplete fortifications. Luckily, Mott advanced against the Confederates over the open ground and not the concealed approach through nearby woods. The Bethel Regiment threw the Union troops back from their entrenchment with well-placed rifle fire. Capt. Louis Young remarked on the irony of

Mott's attack hitting the improperly constructed breastworks from the only avenue they could defend. "Thus did it providentially happen that had the lines been correctly laid out the works could not have been held by us for five minutes. As it was the attack was repelled." The rapid movement of the Tar Heel infantry kept Mott from turning the crucial trench line and gaining a stunning victory.[79]

Mott consolidated his position in front of the Boydton Plank breastworks and established a defensive line by mid-afternoon. General Parke still wanted to determine the strength of the Confederate breastworks, so he ordered a probe of the trench line near the Harman Road by a small force. At 3:00 P.M., three Union regiments, commanded by Lt. Col. George Zinn, advanced against the Boydton trenches. Zinn avoided a direct assault on the fort constructed by MacRae's Brigade and tried to envelop the fortification by charging from a nearby ravine on the northeast side. The three Union regiments ran into Davis's Brigade, which had reinforced MacRae's left. Zinn's thin attack force bravely advanced into "a severe concentrated fire from musketry and artillery." Davis's and MacRae's soldiers easily repelled Zinn, who withdrew to safer ground. Mott and Parke made no effort to follow up the brief attack, satisfied that the Confederate breastworks were defended in strength. They had no idea how close they had come to breaking the Boydton entrenchments and turning the entire Petersburg defensive line. After the fighting died down, both sides occupied themselves by extending their breastworks southwest of Petersburg.[80]

The men of the Bethel Regiment had performed bravely during Grant's Fifth Offensive. Colonel Martin's quick thinking and the soldiers' heroic charge at Jones Farm saved at least MacRae's Brigade from a damaging flank attack and may have saved the tactical victory on September 30. The next day's debacle on the Squirrel Level Road revealed a breakdown in discipline within the brigade but not by the 11th N.C. The final engagement at the Boydton Plank trench line proved to be an easy rout of a feeble Union attack. The three-day battle cost the lives of eleven soldiers, including E Company's first sergeant, David W. McDonald. His brother John took his place and served until the end of the war. The regiment suffered twenty to thirty more wounded. Lewis Warlick wrote to his wife about Corp. Emmanuel Hennessa, one of the D Company soldiers. Hennessa "was shot through the head. . . . He is sure to die as he has lost part of his brain." Hennessa proved him wrong; he survived, though partially paralyzed. These were the most casualties in a single battle since Gettysburg. Yet, the Bethel Regiment survived in good shape, except for the wounding of Colonel Martin. Despite the months of steady fighting and cumulative casualties, the regiment still maintained good *esprit de corps* and discipline. William Martin later attributed this fact to the quality of the sergeants and enlisted men.[81]

The Confederates under A. P. Hill won a significant tactical success at Jones Farm. They foiled Grant's ambitious offensive with bold counterattacks delivered against a superior Union force and inflicted disproportionate losses on the Army of the Potomac. However, the strategic outlook did not look so comforting. Hill's Corps could not force Meade's army to retreat because they could not mount a sufficiently large strike force to turn their tactical success into a strategic victory. Warren and Parke consolidated their advance and had no difficulty in beating back the Confederate counterattack on October 1. Meade's advance on the following day accomplished nothing significant, although he had come desperately close to scoring a major coup. In the end, the Union army extended its line of fortifications farther west. Slowly, relentlessly, Grant strangled the Richmond supply lines and forced Lee's army to defend a greater and greater frontage. Lee could not retake the initiative, nor could he send any help to Johnston's army in Georgia. Since neither side scored a knockout blow during Grant's Fifth Offensive, the two commanding generals continued the grim siege around Petersburg and Richmond.

BURGESS MILL

October 1864, Petersburg

Generals Lee and Hill took steps to strengthen the vulnerable right (western) flank once the Fifth Offensive ended. The entrenchments along the Boydton Plank only ranged a short distance beyond the Harman Road. Because Parke's Corps lay within easy reach of this open flank, Lee decided to stretch the trenches to Hatcher's Run to anchor the defensive line on the small creek with thickly vegetated banks that could obstruct movement. The men of the 11th N.C. stacked their arms and picked up their shovels to dig more breastworks protecting the Boydton Plank Road. The road ran southwest to Hatcher's Run, where it spanned the creek at the Burgess Mill dam, and then continued south toward Dinwiddie. Upstream from the dam, a wide mill pond had formed. The run served as a convenient Confederate obstacle on the right flank. It channeled any westward attack from Pegram's Farm to the northwest and into the new trench line. If Grant wanted to turn the new Confederate defensive line, he would have to cross Hatcher's Run downstream at the Vaughan Road bridge, then swing far to the west around the mill pond. On the negative side, the greater frontage required more troops to guard the trenches.

Lee's concerns were justified because U. S. Grant remained committed to offensive operations, especially with the national elections in November drawing near. A military victory in Virginia would certainly improve President Lincoln's chances for reelection. By mid-October, prisoner interrogations and other sources alerted Union officers that the Confederates were constructing more fortifications along the Boydton Plank Road. From the information gathered, the Union concluded that the line was incomplete and weakly defended. George Meade saw a chance to elevate his sagging military reputation with a decisive victory over Lee. He formulated a plan to send a powerful multicorps force west from the Union entrenchments, turn the incomplete Confederate line, and fight Lee's army on the extreme western flank. Meade proposed his ideas to Grant who quickly approved the ambitious plan and added his own characteristic stamp to the operation. Once more, Grant wanted to pressure Lee's flanks to keep him off balance and prevent him from concentrating against Meade. Grant designated the Southside Railroad as Meade's primary objective. "Make preparations to march out at an early hour on the [October] 27th to gain possession of the South Side Railroad, and to hold it and fortify back to your present left." At the same time, Butler's army would demonstrate against the Richmond front.[82]

Meade planned to use a much larger force against the Boydton Plank than he had used at Pegram's Farm, twenty-five brigades, nearly thirty-five thousand soldiers, drawn from three corps. The rest of the army would stretch to cover the Petersburg front while Meade assembled his force. The attacking corps would move west from the fortifications to execute a wide envelopment of the Confederate flank. Parke's IX Corps would attack directly west from Pegram's Farm and then serve as the pivot for the wheeling maneuver. Warren's V Corps would march abreast of Parke's left and sweep the area just north of Hatcher's Run. The II Corps had the longest maneuver. Hancock would march down the Vaughan Road before dawn on October 27. His troops then had to cross Hatcher's Run by Armstrong Mill before turning west. Using the Dabney Mill Road on the south side of Hatcher's Run, Hancock's two divisions would attack to the Boydton Plank. Staying south of the run, Hancock intended to swing around the Burgess Mill pond on the White Oak Road before turning north to the railroad. This bold turning movement depended on Warren's and Parke's ability to break the incomplete breastworks and pin down the Confederates. Otherwise, Hancock's widely separated corps could be fixed and destroyed by the inevitable counterattack. If Warren and Parke encountered stiff resistance, Hancock would recross Hatcher's Run at Burgess Mill and then strike north. With Parke and Warren fixing the Confederates, Hancock's attack across Burgess Mill would still envelop the enemy's flank and accomplish the same purpose.

The Union army jumped off, as planned, on separate avenues. Parke and Warren moved cautiously and made disappointing progress. Their slow, deliberate movement held true to form, given the nature of the two commanders and the miserable weather. "The morning was dark and gloomy, a heavy rain was falling, the roads were muddy and obstructed, and tangled thickets, dense woods, and swampy streams confronted the troops at all points." Still, they pushed west toward the Boydton Plank against only modest opposition. Both corps reached the Confederate entrenchments around 9:00 A.M. only to find complete and well-defended breastworks. This startling discovery exposed the faulty intelligence on which Meade had constructed his plan. He had to abandon that plan early in the operation. Hancock's Corps would have to deliver the decisive stroke by itself, while the other two corps played a minor supporting role. The army chief of staff, Maj. Gen. Andrew Humphreys, tried to offset this problem. He ordered Crawford's Division of Warren's V Corps to cross Hatcher's Run and

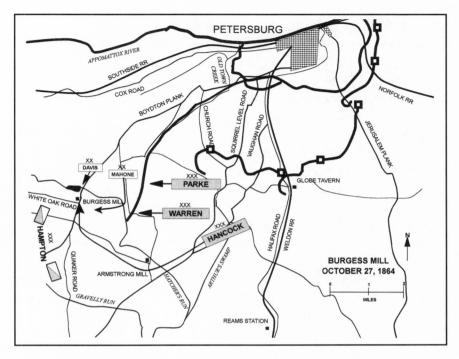

PETERSBURG

APPOMATTOX RIVER

SOUTHSIDE RR

COX ROAD

OLD TOWN CREEK

BOYDTON PLANK

CHURCH ROAD

SQUIRREL LEVEL ROAD

VAUGHAN ROAD

NORFOLK RR

JERUSALEM PLANK

XX DAVIS

XX MAHONE

XXX PARKE

GLOBE TAVERN

WHITE OAK ROAD

BURGESS MILL

XXX WARREN

HAMPTON

XXX

XXX HANCOCK

QUAKER ROAD

ARMSTRONG MILL

HATCHER'S RUN

ARTHUR'S SWAMP

HALIFAX ROAD

WELDON RR

N

BURGESS MILL
OCTOBER 27, 1864

0   1   2
MILES

GRAVELLY RUN

REAMS STATION

tie in Hancock to Warren's left flank to prevent the Confederates from isolating the II Corps.[83]

The II Corps had pushed aside the Confederate pickets on the Vaughan Road bridge at daybreak. Once across Hatcher's Run, Brig. Gen. Thomas Egan turned his division west on the Dabney Mill Road and headed for the Boydton Plank. Wade Hampton, the Confederate cavalry commander, fought a brisk delaying action while trying to ascertain Hancock's objective. To hold back the Union forces, Hampton posted his artillery and cavalry forces around Burgess Tavern. The tavern stood a quarter mile south of the mill where the White Oak Road terminated into the plank road. A quarter mile farther south the plank road intersected the Dabney Mill Road; it was little more than a cart path. Another quarter mile to the south, the Quaker Road entered the Boydton Plank from the southeast. Most of the area in the immediate vicinity of the tavern was cleared, except for woods on the west side of the plank road and the forest beyond the clearing to the east. Egan's Division debouched from the woods on the Dabney Mill Road and entered the large clearing at 10:30 A.M. Hancock reported the Confederate reaction. "As soon as we emerged into the clearing at the plank road the enemy opened fire on us from near Burgess' Tavern and from our left, having apparently a section of artillery at each place."[84] The appearance of Hancock's artillery and cavalry at the Quaker Road intersection drove off Hampton's artillery.

Bounding across the clearing with Rugg's, Willett's, and Smyth's brigades, General Egan overran Burgess Tavern. He consolidated his division in a wide arc from the White Oak Road to the clearing east of the tavern with its center oriented toward the mill. Hancock, pleased with his advance, got disturbing news from General Meade. "At this juncture, about 1 P.M., I received instructions from the major-general commanding to halt at the plank road."[85] The change in plans forced Hancock to change directions from a westward turning movement to a northward attack across Hatcher's Run. He had planned to attack up the White Oak Road with Mott's Division, but the change caused him to deploy Mott in support of Egan. At 1:00 P.M. Brig. Gen. Thomas Smyth started the action toward Hatcher's Run by driving back the Confederate pickets near the bridge. While the II Corps labored at Burgess Mill, Crawford's Division meandered through the dense underbrush toward Hancock.

The Confederates were busy, as well. Hampton redeployed his cavalry farther south on the plank road and west on the White Oak Road to contest any westward movement by Hancock. The cavalry officer reported the latest Union moves to A. P. Hill. Hill was too ill to take charge along the Boydton Plank, so he relinquished operational control to Harry Heth. Heth ordered Davis's Brigade and a cavalry unit to secure the bridge over Hatcher's Run. With Davis holding the extreme right flank of the entrenchments and his other brigades holding the other two Union corps in check, Heth gathered a strike force to throw back the Union threat south of Hatcher's Run. From his own division he pulled MacRae's Brigade, including the 11th N.C. At 2:00 P.M., General Mahone reported to Heth with two of his brigades, Weisiger's and Sanders's. Heth chose to hit Hancock with these three brigades, plus Davis. Davis would assault across the run at Burgess Mill in a supporting attack, while Mahone would lead the other brigades in the main attack against Hancock's right (eastern) flank. Following the pattern of Globe Tavern and Squirrel Level Road, the Confederates chose to strike the inside flank of the extended Union corps. Heth told Mahone to follow a little-used path through the dense woods east of Burgess Mill in order to surprise Hancock by approaching unobserved.[86] Hampton's cavalry would make supporting attacks from the Plank and White Oak roads. Once again, the 11th N.C. would do battle with its old foes, Hancock's II Corps. The regiment had crossed bayonets with the II Corps seven times before. Now, it had a chance to crush Hancock's Corps in an isolated position.

While Hancock reoriented his corps, U. S. Grant and George Meade arrived on the scene to confer with him. The success of the mission rested with Hancock, now that Warren and Parke had stopped short of the Boydton Plank. Grant wanted to check the situation for himself to gauge Hancock's chances for turning the Confederate line. With the election approaching, the political consequences of the campaign outweighed its military value. Grant hoped that Meade and Hancock could score a major victory, but he had to avoid a military defeat at all costs. He chose to see the battlefield for himself. The commanding general personally galloped down to the Burgess Mill bridge to reconnoiter the Confederate defenses across the run. By mid-afternoon Grant finished his estimate of the situation and concluded that Hancock had little chance of winning decisive results by attacking across Hatcher's Run. He figured that Meade's offensive would not pay any big political dividends, so he canceled the operation. Grant advised Hancock to hold his place for the rest of the day and then withdraw on October 28. Grant's guidance changed Hancock's mission to a tactical defense of a temporary forward position.[87]

Grant turned and departed. Horace Porter accompanied Grant as the general returned to the Union lines. "General Grant then took a narrow cross-road leading down to the Run to the right of Hancock's corps; but it was soon found that there were no troops between our party and the enemy, and that if we continued along this road it would probably not be many minutes before we should find ourselves prisoners in his lines. There was nothing to do but turn around and strike a road farther in the rear. This, as usual, was a great annoyance to the general, who expressed his objections, as he had done many a time before, to turning back."[88] Luckily, Grant agreed to retrace his steps.

A few hundred yards east of the general's party, the Bethel Regiment and Mahone's ad hoc division advanced through the dense underbrush toward the Union position. The situation followed a familiar pattern. The battle of Burgess Mill, like Jerusalem Plank, Globe Tavern, Reams Station, and Jones Farm, would come down to a late afternoon clash between a stalled Union offensive and a Confederate counterattack. Hancock busied himself by perfecting his defensive dispositions. His first concern, the gap between the II and V Corps, needed immediate attention. General Smyth received instructions from Hancock "to endeavor to make a connection with troops who were engaged on our right, supposed to be the Fifth Corps. . . . I deployed the Tenth New York Volunteers from the right of my line to the right at intervals of about ten paces, but this line failed to make the desired connection."[89] Despite Smyth's attempt to connect with Crawford, Hancock's eastern flank remained vulnerable, so the corps commander split Pierce's Brigade from Mott's Division and deployed it in the clearing behind and to the right of Smyth's Brigade. Pierce formed his brigade around a battery of artillery near the woods. De Trobriand's Brigade from Mott's Division faced west to protect against Hampton's cavalry. Mott later sent McAllister's Brigade to back up Egan's Division, which stayed poised at Burgess Tavern to repel any counterattacks from across Hatcher's Run. Hancock's defensive arrangement looked strong but had one major shortcoming; he relied on Warren's Corps to cover his exposed eastern flank.

The Confederate artillery subjected the Union troops to annoying, though ineffective, fire through much of the afternoon. Hancock's men ignored the incoming shells and continued digging their positions. Hancock may have been satisfied with his own dispositions, but he became increasingly worried about the failure to link up with Crawford's Division. While waiting, the II Corps' officers heard small arms fire to the east and sent some of their skirmishers to investigate. Hancock hoped the shooting heralded the arrival of Crawford's Division, but the force coming from the east was Mahone's, instead. Mahone's troops, including the 11th N.C., found the forest track leading toward Burgess Tavern and pushed ahead. The Confederates proved better able to traverse the woodland than Crawford's tardy division. Mahone's Division had troubles of their own, however, because Sanders's Brigade did not keep up with Weisiger's and MacRae's troops.

Back at Burgess Tavern, Brig. Gen. Byron Pierce prepared his brigade to secure the eastern flank. He placed the 5th Mich. and 93d N.Y. at the eastern edge of the clearing and had them face east. The 5th Mich.

commander, Col. John Pulford, sent a skirmish line well forward into the forest to provide early warning and, hopefully, make contact with Crawford. "I deployed three companies of the Fifth Michigan as skirmishers to the front [east], with orders to advance about 1,500 yards." The rest of the Brigade remained in the clearing alongside the artillery battery, oriented to the north. Shortly before 4:00 P.M., Pierce became uneasy over the firing coming from the woods. He decided to reinforce the two regiments inside the woodline with a battalion of the 1st U.S. Sharpshooters. These troops had barely gotten into position when Colonel Pulford saw MacRae's sharpshooters. "The enemy's skirmishers were seen advancing, and brisk skirmishing commenced on both sides." The sudden increase in rifle fire alerted the Union field commanders to the storm breaking upon their eastern flank.[90]

The skirmish line did not delay the Confederates for long. MacRae's aggressive sharpshooters drove in the Union picket line. The 1st U.S. Sharpshooters observed, "The enemy charged upon the Fifth Michigan with a line of battle, striking the left flank of my line, the enemy cutting their way through the line." General Pierce reacted by moving the 105th Pa. from the clearing into the woods "to support [the]

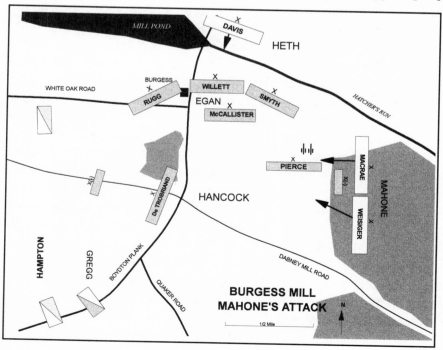

skirmish line, which was then being driven back." Pierce's battle line confronted the Confederate vanguard inside the woods. "At the first volley from the three regiments I had in line, the enemy was handsomely repulsed, and was held in check in their front." The small Union force "kept up this fire for ten minutes" and exchanged several volleys with MacRae's troops. Although Pierce thought he had stopped the Confederates, General MacRae took this time to reconnoiter and deploy his line of battle after the sharpshooters had located the Union flank. Meanwhile Pierce shifted his brigade to meet the Confederate attack on his right (eastern) flank. The commander of the 141st Pa. on Pierce's left flank wrote, "[I] changed front by filing my command to the right and then moved forward in line of battle toward the woods and in the direction of the enemy's attack." Pierce hurried his three remaining regiments to support those in the woods, but he never completed the movement.[91]

Before the Union troops could get set, MacRae and Weisiger formed their lines of battle and launched their attack against Pierce's regiments. K Company first sergeant, Jacob Bartlett, recalled, "We found them [Pierce's Brigade] behind an old rail fence at the edge of a field, and our rifles and the rebel yell both began to ring at the same time." One of MacRae's officers confirmed, "With a yell we charged the enemy's lines, which were broken by the impetuosity of our attack, and were driven rapidly before us." Weisiger hit the south side while MacRae overwhelmed the 5th Mich. and 93d N.Y. on the north end. Colonel Pulford reported, "The line of battle to my right and left gave way and I was compelled to fall back." Pierce's regiments could not hold back the Confederate drive. "They came around each flank and completely enveloped them, so much so that three regiments had to cut their way out." Pierce's other regiments, which tried to reach the woods in time to help, ran into trouble, instead. One Union commander wrote, "The right of the regiment had just reached the woods when a heavy fire was opened on them and the regiments in the woods fell back, making it impossible to form the line." The commander of the 57th Pa. reported, "The enemy charged as our column was trying to change position, which threw our line into confusion, so that it was impossible to rally the men in the field."[92]

Pierce's command collapsed as the 105th Pa., 141st Pa., and the 1st U.S. Sharpshooters fell back under pressure from Weisiger's troops in the south. Weisiger soon ran into stiffer resistance as the 141st Pa. boldly counterattacked his southern flank. On the north side, MacRae's Brigade chased the other five regiments across the clearing toward the Boydton Plank. Just like Jones Farm and Reams Station, the Bethel infantrymen enjoyed the exhilarating sight of the enemy infantry fleeing before their bayonets. MacRae's spirited attack swept across the clearing and seized the battery of the 5th U.S. Artillery that had been posted in the clearing. "While crossing the field, we passed a field battery of six guns . . . they had failed to take away one caisson—so two of Company K—mounted the horses and soon landed it on the other side of the creek," Bartlett related.[93] With the enemy on the run, MacRae's soldiers pursued relentlessly. The Tar Heels continued pushing all the way to the plank road south of the White Oak Road intersection, effectively cutting off Egan's Division from the rest of the II Corps.

As MacRae dashed across the clearing, his bright blue eyes locked onto a thrilling sight. A short distance to the south, just across the Dabney Mill Road, stood the wagon trains of the II Corps. Hancock's troops could not sustain themselves in the field without the supplies riding on those wagons. The possibilities dazzled MacRae. If his force overran the wagon train and kept Hancock isolated from the rest of Meade's army, they could bag Hancock's whole corps. MacRae halted the westward charge and reoriented his regiments against the lucrative target on the other side of Dabney Mill Road.

Hancock faced a critical situation. Mahone's attack nearly cut his corps in two. MacRae's Brigade had reached the Boydton Plank Road, and Weisiger's Brigade threatened to sever the Dabney Mill Road, Hancock's only supply line and escape route. Hampton's cavalry and artillery fired on the II Corps from the south and west, while Davis poured in fire from across Hatcher's Run. Fortunately for Hancock, the Confederates had some problems of their own. Sanders's Brigade had not joined the attack, which left no support force to follow through on MacRae's success. After the rush across the clearing, MacRae's regiments were all tangled together. The Tar Heel regiments tried to sort out the snarl as they prepared to launch their attack. Despite the confusion, the Confederates seemed ready to seize the II Corps trains. The Union teetered on the brink of the very military disaster Grant wanted to avoid.

Although prospects looked bleak, Hancock "the Superb" and his veterans turned the tables on Mahone with clearheaded actions. Brig. Gen. Regis De Trobriand moved quickly to protect the Dabney Mill Road. "I at once ordered a change of front to the rear by counter-marching my six regiments at hand so as to face the enemy and . . . formed a new line along the road we came by [Dabney Mill], which I had to defend at all hazards." Hancock dispatched a staff officer to Egan to advise him of the danger and order a counterattack by his division. Egan responded with McAllister's Brigade from Mott's Division, which had just been attached to him. Col. Robert McAllister, already well positioned on the northern flank, simply ordered his troops to "about face" and "move on the enemy with my rear rank in front." Meanwhile, Pierce rallied his disjointed regiments where they had taken refuge in the woods west of the Boydton Plank.[94]

Hampton and Davis had launched their supporting attacks on the cue given by Mahone's heavy firing, but these supporting attacks did not achieve a breakthrough, nor did they provide relief for MacRae. MacRae and Weisiger held their ground hoping for reinforcements or a complete collapse of the II Corps. MacRae had no intention of calling off his attack, although he could see De Trobriand and Pierce forming their lines of battle. Hancock may have had a better understanding of the Confederate's true situation than Mahone or MacRae. Hancock perceptively noted, "I do not think the enemy comprehended the situation precisely."[95] The movements of Hancock's forces put Mahone in a box. De Trobriand held his ground in the south, Pierce had rallied his men in the west, McAllister bore down from the north, and Crawford's Division approached from somewhere off to the east. Without immediate support, Mahone's force was itself in danger of being cut off. The Union forces soon struck back to do just that.

McAllister's four regiments hit MacRae's troops in the rear. "A charge was now ordered and made. . . . We moved down the hill on the charge over the gulleys [sic] and through the thick hazel-brush under a severe flank fire." The startled Bethel soldiers craned their necks to see where the surprise fire came from and observed McAllister's Brigade bearing down on them from the north. This sudden attack from an unexpected direction revealed their danger. Jacob Bartlett described their predicament: "We discovered that we had only knocked a gap out of the Yankee line and that the two ends were clos-

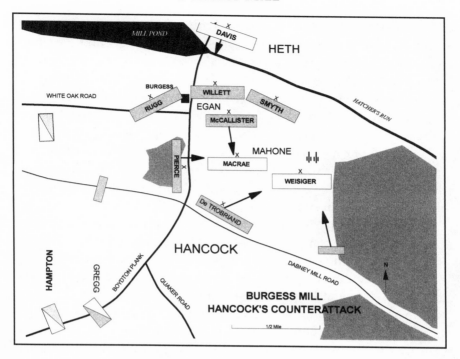

ing together behind us." The Tar Heel infantrymen remembered MacRae's reaction. "Undismayed by the large force which surrounded him, and unwilling to surrender the prize of victory already in his grasp, MacRae formed a portion of his command obliquely to his main line of battle, driving back the foe at every point." McAllister's relatively green New Jersey troops got a full taste of southern tenacity as they closed with MacRae's veterans. "On reaching the high ground on the opposite side I received a severe fire in our front, which was too much for our raw recruits to stand and they broke." McAllister reformed his brigade in the north and fired back at the Tar Heels who countercharged his troops. This time they were ready to fight. "The enemy [MacRae's men] again advanced in our front, when our line opened a destructive fire upon them."[96]

MacRae had other attacks to ward off. Pierce's regiments west of the plank road, reinforced by the 1st Me., counterattacked MacRae's front (if such a distinction could still be made). The bulk of De Trobriand's Brigade and a dismounted cavalry brigade struck MacRae and Weisiger from the south. The triple blows from opposite directions by McAllister, De Trobriand, and Pierce threatened to destroy

MacRae's Brigade. Minié balls ripped through the ranks from all directions as the troops fought back. In the vain hope of obtaining support, MacRae "held his vantage ground at all hazards, and against enormous odds." MacRae's obstinate stand in the clearing failed to save the victory that seemed so close. The II Corps troops, far from collapsing, aggressively counterattacked from all directions and the help he expected from Sanders and Davis failed to appear. "No help came while his men toiled, bled and died." Finally, MacRae ordered the troops to fight their way out of the perilous situation. One Bethel soldier wrote, "[We] were perfectly surrounded but we did not falter; we about faced and cut our way out."[97]

This time Pierce's men drove MacRae's across the clearing. The Bethel Regiment charged its way out of the trap as 1st Sgt. Bartlett saw one of his buddies fall. "We had not gone far on the second charge until one of Company K—was wounded, and being near me he asked me to help him and I assisted him a short distance and found that we were passing the cannons the second time. I turned him loose, got a sassafras sprout from which I took a piece with which I spiked one of the cannons and took my place again in the ranks, and my wounded comrade got out all right." Pierce's soldiers drove MacRae across the field and recovered the Union artillery battery. They also captured numerous Confederates who could not get out of the Union vise. MacRae's remaining troops reached the woods and then battled back fiercely. Bartlett and the rest of the regiment still had plenty of fight left. "Just before reaching the old rail fence where we first struck the Yankees, one of their artillery officers rode up behind us carrying the Artillery Flag and trying to rally his men to their guns again; a shower of bullets from our rifles cut the flag staff in two just above his hand." The Union counterattack petered out once MacRae's troops gained the cover of the woods. The commander of one of Pierce's regiments acknowledged, "Owing to the confusion along the line we were again compelled to fall back."[98]

Pierce's Brigade retired to the Boydton Plank Road, then turned its attention to an isolated pocket of Confederates. A large part of MacRae's brigade had been separated and pulled into the woods on the west side of the plank road. Pierce's Brigade attacked this Confederate pocket just as the 36th Wis. from Rugg's Brigade charged down the plank road from the north. Trapped between these converging attacks, the isolated troops were captured along with the colors from the 26th and 47th N.C. A large number of Bethel soldiers fell into enemy hands during the confused fight. Weisiger had his share of troubles along the southern and eastern flanks where De Trobriand's six regiments charged his line of battle. The 141st Pa., 105th Pa., and the 1st U.S. Sharpshooters pitched in to help drive Weisiger back into the woods. De Trobriand had to suspend his counterattack because Hancock recalled his brigade to stabilize the far western flank; Hampton's cavalry was putting heavy pressure on De Trobriand's skirmish line.[99]

MacRae had been pushed back but he had not given up. After shaking off Pierce's counterattack, he concentrated on McAllister's Brigade. McAllister had received reinforcements from Egan and he held an advantageous position on MacRae's northern flank that could counteract any Confederate move. MacRae sent part of his force north to turn McAllister's eastern flank. The Union generals countered by shifting their line of battle linking McAllister's flank with Smyth's Brigade. Possibly, the sight of Egan's Division behind McAllister dissuaded MacRae from launching another attack, or he realized that the onset of darkness made any additional attacks pointless. Whatever the reason, MacRae pulled back to the woods and began to prepare a defense for the night. The fighting on October 27 ended with the two Confederate brigades clinging to the woods on the eastern edge of the clearing.[100]

The regiment's infantrymen settled down in the dark and wondered how they could get out of the II Corps' grasp. The troops knew they were nearly surrounded south of Hatcher's Run, but they had faith that Billy MacRae would somehow get them out the next day. Furthermore, they realized that they had missed a chance to score a huge victory. Second Lt. Lewis Warlick, who had followed the regiment despite a serious illness, regretted the lost opportunity. "If we had had more troops to support when the attack was made I think we could have captured the whole concern." The Confederates lacked the resources to capitalize on their tactical successes. "Being too weak to accomplish the design the plan was abandoned." The elusive victory and heavy losses left Billy MacRae feeling angry. "MacRae complained bitterly about his superiors in command [Mahone] allowing him to be cut to pieces when it could have been prevented."[101]

For the Union, the day's fighting accomplished far less than planned.

Instead of turning the Confederates' flank, Hancock finished the day worried about his own survival. Hancock assessed the situation grimly. The near brush with disaster, the inability of the other corps to fix the enemy in their entrenchments, Crawford's failure to link up, and the depleted state of his ammunition stocks played on Hancock's mind. The corps commander noted, "Quite a heavy rain was falling, and the wood road to Dabney's Mill, my only communication with the rest of the army, was seriously threatened by the enemy, and was becoming very bad." The memory of Reams Station must have haunted him, as well. When Meade offered him the choice of staying until morning or withdrawing at night, Hancock chose the latter option. "I was of the opinion that the necessary preparations to meet successfully the enemy's attack in the morning could not be made, and . . . I felt compelled to order a withdrawal rather than risk disaster by awaiting an attack in the morning only partly prepared."[102]

That night the II Corps troops regrouped in the dark and filed back over the muddy Dabney Mill Road. The rain provided good cover from the Confederate pickets, who did not detect the movement, but the Union soldiers did not appreciate that fact as they slogged their way back. The confusion of the battle and the difficulties of moving at night forced the Union to abandon some of their own wounded men. General McAllister wrote to his wife of the traumatic experience. "Oh, how my heart thrilled for these poor, dying soldiers! They were far from home and friends; and they were soon to be left in the hands of the enemy, for our ambulances were but few and all full."[103] The next morning Mahone's men found a battlefield strewn with debris, weapons, equipment, the dead, and many Union wounded. The chaotic scene testified to the precipitousness of Hancock's withdrawal. The Union retreat greatly relieved the Confederates who had decided that they had to resume the offensive on October 28. From a strategic point of view, the Confederates were victorious this time.

Tactically speaking, the battle of Burgess Mill could not be called a clear Confederate victory. Mahone held a worse position at the end of the fighting than Hancock. Both sides suffered heavy casualties — the Union more so than the Confederates — but proportionately not so much. Lewis Warlick acknowledged the loss of 114 men in the desperate battle, more than one hundred of them prisoners. The II Corps even captured the dauntless Woodston Garrett and sent him off to prison at Point Lookout, Maryland. Fortunately, only a handful of troops had been killed or wounded during the mêlée. Nevertheless, the Bethel Regiment had its worst day since the ill-fated Gettysburg campaign. Despite the recent addition of some recruits, MacRae's Brigade had declined to the strength of a regiment. Warlick noted, "We still have about five hundred arms bearing men in the brigade after all our hard fighting this campaign." The brigade had fought in nearly every battle around Petersburg and had endured 1,647 casualties since the beginning of the 1864 campaign. Lee, Hill, and Heth showed sympathy for them and decided not to use the brigade in any additional counterattacks. By this stage of the war, however, the Bethel Regiment and the other units could not bounce back after absorbing the heavy losses at Burgess Mill. Other problems would soon add to the woes of the regiment and prevent the command's full recovery.[104]

If the battle did not have a clear winner, it did have a clear loser. General Winfield Scott Hancock had attacked south of Hatcher's Run in the hopes of redeeming his military reputation and erasing the humiliation of Reams Station. He could take no solace from the action at Burgess Mill. His corps did not get to execute the bold turning movement against the Southside Railroad and then could not hold its intermediate position south of Hatcher's Run. No blame could be attached to Hancock for his performance. Once again, he had demonstrated his mastery of a critical situation. But, there was certainly no redemption, either. The disappointment broke his spirit. Within thirty days, Hancock took a leave of absence from the army, blaming his earlier wounds. He never returned to his corps.

6

Honor Answering Honor

HATCHER'S RUN

Winter 1864–65, Petersburg

After Burgess Mill, both sides resumed the tiresome siege. The endless work on breastworks and the stress of close enemy contact made the duty an ordeal for the infantry-men. "From then until the close of the year the Eleventh was contin-uously on duty and daily (and nightly, too) under fire."[1] The battles at Reams Station, Jones Farm, and Burgess Mill certainly proved that the men retained their fighting spirit, but the ever-lengthening reach of the Union trenches contributed to their increasing stress. The Bethel soldiers could see that Grant's slow, agonizing squeeze on the supply lines nullified their past tactical successes. Despite their sacrifices and hard fighting, the men sensed that they were losing ground and could not elude the Union army's clutches.

On November 8, 1864, the Confederacy lost its best hope when President Lincoln won reelection by a decisive margin. The Ameri-can people voted on the course of the war, and they chose to prose-cute it to a complete military victory. There would be no negotiated peace, no compromise. The election caused dismay in the South. With the Mississippi Valley in Union hands, Atlanta demolished, the naval blockade cutting imports to a dribble, and Lee's magnificent army pinned down at Petersburg, everyone knew the Confederacy could not last another four years. Back in North Carolina, William Holden still agitated for peace. The majority of North Carolinians and the troops still supported the cause, but political divisions chipped away at one of the regiment's original strengths, the motivation of the men.

The conditions around Petersburg continued to deteriorate. The cold autumn rains made the roads difficult to travel and forced a suspension of active operations. Except for a brief expedition to Belfield in early December, the regiment remained in the gloomy trenches. The soaking winter rains brought another invader to the Petersburg entrenchments — mud. Mud pervaded the lives of the soldiers. The bombproofs, their places of refuge from enemy mortar fire, filled with muddy water from the constant leaking of the dirt roofs. Each time the Union mortars and artillery fired into their trenches, the troops had to dive for cover in the mire. One Confederate soldier recalled that even the senior generals had to accustom themselves to the muck. "General Lee came through every few days, wading sometimes almost to his boot tops, but he never said a word about the mud. He knew we couldn't keep it out."[2]

The poor roads slowed the movement of supplies into Petersburg, so rations declined in quality and quantity. With no unspoiled land to forage, the troops seldom ate any meat. The Confederate cavalry dispersed their horses to the countryside beyond the lines because they could not feed them near Petersburg. The citizens of Richmond tried their best to maintain morale by treating the army to a decent Christmas meal, including meat, vegetables, and bread. The soldiers in the Petersburg trenches anxiously awaited the distribution of the holiday meal, but the rations petered out before they reached the western part of the line where the Bethel Regiment served. "It hardly paid to throw the tobacco out of our mouths for what we got." Naturally, they grumbled that troops in the rear must have stuffed themselves at their expense. In January, Brig. Gen. Joseph Finegan forwarded an official complaint through channels about the lack of nourishment for his men. "Sometime in November last I brought [up] . . . the subject of the insufficiency of the bread ration issued to the troops of my brigade, and recommended that the amount be increased to one and one-quarter pounds of meal or eighteen ounces of flour per man daily. The fact that there is now six months' pay due the troops is another serious subject of complaint, and should be removed at the earliest practicable moment." His letter drew a mildly sympathetic rejection from A. P. Hill. "I believe that the ration is insufficient, yet nevertheless other troops bear without complaint these evils they know we cannot help." The poor diet did not exempt them from working on the fortifications nor fatigue duty. The troops built crude mud and wood cabins to protect themselves from the elements, but these did nothing to relieve the constant pressure of the siege. In February 1865, General Lee reported, "some of the men were suffering from reduced rations and scant clothing, exposed to battle, cold, hail and sleet. . . . If some change is not made . . . I apprehend dire results. The physical strength of the men, their courage, services, must fail under this treatment."[3]

The first real cracks in the regiment's *esprit de corps* appeared in the fall of 1864. During this burdensome time, Pvt. John Q. Taylor from Mecklenburg County fell into despair and killed himself. Union pickets began bringing in deserters from every Confederate unit, including the 11th N.C., in record numbers. The Union army detected the Confederates' growing weariness and sent over propaganda to encourage desertions with promises of paroles, safe civilian jobs, and bounties for bringing over Confederate rifles. The significance of these desertions was not lost on Grant. He later wrote, "I knew from the great number of desertions, that the men who had fought so bravely, so gallantly and so long for the cause which they believed in . . . had lost hope and become despondent." On December 4, 1864, the Bethel Regiment performed its only execution. Pvt. Joshua Starney, a recent recruit from Burke County, deserted shortly after arriving in Petersburg. The Confederates apprehended Starney and sentenced him to death by firing squad. Pvt. John C. Warlick, recently returned after recovering from his wound, served on the detail. The assignment did not please Warlick, but he showed no pity for the deserter. "It was my sad lot to help shoot him. I aimed a bullet at his heart."[4]

The cruel winter wore down the enlisted and officer ranks. In January 1865, Heth's Division reported a drop of 565 soldiers present for duty, nearly 11 percent of the division. The command structure of the regiment suffered during the winter, as well. The regiment still could not appoint a major or lieutenant colonel, even while Colonel Martin stayed on convalescent leave. Capt. James Young, the senior captain, assumed command, but Capt. William Grier had to take over near the end of December when Captain Young went home on sick leave. Capt. William Kerr also served as regimental commander in January 1865. As they had only six captains on the active roles, the officers present for duty had to work doubly hard throughout the winter. Second Lt. Lewis Warlick, whose letters in 1861 and 1862 had been filled with patriotic statements, now wrote mostly about his repeated requests for furloughs and their inevitable denials. He added that every officer in the brigade had submitted a request for a furlough.[5]

The declining morale and worsening military situation moved the Confederate government to send a peace feeler to Lincoln. The high-level Confederate commissioners met with Lincoln and Secretary of State Seward on a steamer lying off Fort Monroe on February 3, 1865. Lincoln acted cordially but insisted that the southern states accept the laws of the United States, including the Emancipation Proclamation. The commissioners could not approve these terms, as they effectively terminated southern independence and slavery, two central causes of the Confederacy. Lincoln could not be tempted to relax his terms in exchange for an early cessation of the fighting. Obviously, after years of frustration, the president could afford to stand firm and wait. He felt confident that the spring campaign would bring an end to the war on his terms, so the Confederate commissioners returned empty-handed. U. S. Grant decided to end the winter respite once the peace negotiations ended. On February 4, he ordered a powerful multicorps attack to interdict the Boydton Plank Road. Although the weather was bitterly cold, a dry spell permitted the use of the roads, and Grant took advantage of the favorable traffic conditions. Clearly, Grant wanted to send his own message about the prospects for peace; the Union army would attack relentlessly until the South surrendered.

Meade's plan resembled the operation of late October, with a less ambitious objective. Gregg's Cavalry Division would attack Dinwiddie Court House to destroy the wagon trains using the Boydton Plank Road. The V and II infantry corps would support the cavalry by pushing out to the plank road. This time, Warren's V Corps would move south of Hatcher's Run, while the II Corps, now commanded by Maj. Gen. Andrew A. Humphreys, would cover the Confederate trenches north of the run. Meade reversed the roles of the two corps from those in October, most likely because of Hancock's loud complaints about the failure to contain Mahone's counterattack. General Humphreys took precautions to prevent a similar attack against Warren. He wanted to pin the defenders in their trenches, although he would avoid attacking them directly. After the advance, the II Corps would entrench a solid front from the Duncan Road back to Peebles Farm.

On February 5, the Union men marched out of their fortifications into the predawn cold. Humphreys used part of Mott's Division to secure the Vaughan Road crossing over Hatcher's Run. He then sent Smyth's Division northwest along the north bank of Hatcher's Run. Smyth advanced beyond Duncan Road after crossing over Rocky Branch, a small tributary that flowed into Hatcher's Run. Smyth immediately prepared a defensive arc extending from Hatcher's Run on the left to Rocky Branch on his right, facing the Confederate entrenchments to the northwest. Meanwhile, Mott established a position on the south side of Hatcher's Run with two brigades. His third brigade, commanded by General McAllister, defended north of the run near the Vaughan Road to repel a possible counterattack. McAllister's flanks were supposed to rest on the Rocky Branch on the left (west) and another swamp on the right (east). As soon as McAllister moved into position, he ordered his men to throw up breastworks. "On giving the order to my men, they jumped at it with a will. Rails and timber were carried with dispatch and dirt was thrown up with an unparaleled [sic] rapidity." By 1865, all soldiers understood the value of breastworks.[6]

General Humphreys inspected the defensive array shortly after the troops began to entrench. Although Smyth anchored his flanks securely on swampy terrain, a dangerous gap split his right from McAllister's left. Humphreys feared that the gap would invite a counterattack. Mott's Division had only one brigade north of the run, McAllister's, to connect Smyth's Division with the Union trenches. Humphreys judged that one brigade could not cover the interval properly, so he ordered Brig. Gen. Nelson Miles to pull a brigade out of the trenches to relieve McAllister. Humphreys instructed Mott to shift McAllister west to cover the existing gap between him and Smyth. By 3:30 P.M. Brig. Gen. John Ramsey reported to McAllister that his brigade would assume responsibility for McAllister's portion of the line. Owing to a delay in receiving his orders, McAllister pulled his brigade to the rear and did not begin moving into the gap until 4:00 P.M.[7]

Humphreys's alertness may have saved his corps because Harry Heth's scouts also detected the vulnerable gap separating Smyth and McAllister. Initially, the Confederates concentrated on Warren's movement south of Hatcher's Run, but they soon realized that Warren did not intend to push as far west as Hancock had in October. Powell Hill turned his attention to the weak spot in the II Corps sector. Hill shuffled the divisions around Petersburg to allow Heth to gather a three-brigade strike force by using MacRae's, Cooke's, and McComb's brigades. The Bethel troops emerged from the relative comfort of their earthen bombproofs into the midst of a biting sleet storm and moved to a position north of Smyth, east of the Rocky Branch. The little stream could serve as a guide for the counterattack force as they headed south into the gap. Heth put Cooke's and McComb's brigades in the front with Cooke on the western (right) flank. MacRae's Brigade provided the support force for the lead brigades. Heth and Hill wanted to spare MacRae's Brigade any additional combat, but events forced them to commit the Tar Heels. At least, they gave the brigade a supporting role. The fact that Billy MacRae was away on leave gave Heth more reason to keep the brigade in reserve. By 4:00 P.M. the division

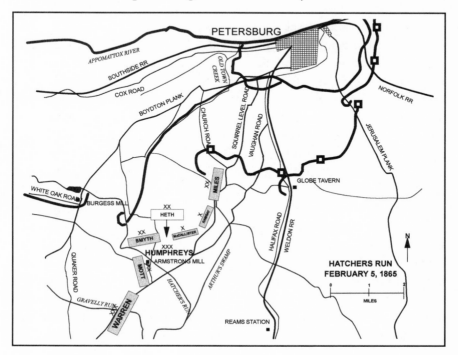

formed its battle lines and began to advance. Following the usual pattern, the 11th N.C. launched a late afternoon counterattack against their old foes, the II Corps.[8]

The Union troops did not idly await the expected counterattack; they worked diligently to correct the defect in their line. Smyth had noticed the gap on his eastern (right) flank and threw a skirmish line across the Rocky Branch to cover it. Before long, the Confederates probed the skirmish line but could not elicit a reply from the Union pickets who wisely held their fire. Smyth ignored a feint on the western flank and stayed focused on the threatened area.[9] Meanwhile, McAllister had already positioned one regiment in the gap to extend the breastworks closer to the Rocky Branch. Once his orders became clear, he moved the rest of the brigade forward to occupy the line on Ramsey's left, including part of the breastworks built by his troops earlier.

The Confederate skirmishers ran into Smyth's pickets east of the Rocky Branch by 4:15 P.M. The brisk exchange of fire alerted McAllister to the coming attack, and he rushed his troops forward. "Double quick, and on the right by file into line!" McAllister's troops dashed into the breastworks just as Heth's three brigades chased the skirmishers to the rear. McAllister described the action: "The fire was taken up all along the line as fast as my troops were formed. The pickets in my new front having come running in without firing a shot, left the enemy right on us before I had my line completed. Regiment after regiment opened on the rebels as fast as they wheeled into position, causing their line to halt and lie down. The left regiment, the Eighth New Jersey Volunteers, under command of Major Hartford, or the left wing of it, had no works, and were exposed to a terrible fire in this unprotected position." Maj. Henry Hartford observed the Confederates' reaction when they charged into his defensive line. "They were greeted with a terrific volley of musketry from our men, and thrown into confusion."[10]

The heavy fire caught the Confederates by surprise, causing a few to break and run for the rear. MacRae's adjutant, Capt. Louis Young, saw them flee: "The effect of the first volley from the enemy was to cause a stampede in the command in our front [part of McComb's]." General Lee, who had followed behind Heth's force, tried to restrain some of the terrified men. Even Lee's commanding presence could not restore order to the frightened troops. One demoralized soldier screamed at him, "Great God, old man, get out of the way, you don't know nothing!" Thankfully, the Confederates could count on MacRae's Brigade. "As soon as [the panicked soldiers] had broken through our lines, we closed up and the brigade advanced to the front line." Although Heth and Hill had intended to keep MacRae's Brigade out of the fighting, the Tar Heels found themselves nose to nose with the enemy. McAllister's prepared defense bitterly disappointed Heth and his brigadiers who had hoped to blast through an undefended gap. The gap had vanished, and now they had locked into close combat with an entrenched enemy. The situation must have reminded the Bethel veterans of the sudden appearance of the II Corps behind the railroad embankment at Bristoe Station, a painful memory. The stout Union defense may have surprised Heth, but he would not give up easily. He ordered the attack to continue.[11]

"The well known Rebel Yell rolled out on the evening breeze and on rushed their massed columns," McAllister recorded. He had made an adjustment to his fire distribution to help repel the Confederate assault. Taking advantage of a forward angle in his breastworks, McAllister directed the 7th N.J. to fire obliquely to the left, across the defensive line, to achieve enfilade fires against Cooke's Brigade on the western flank. The Confederate brigades surged forward into the deadly Union fires, pressing hardest against Hartford's exposed line. "Again they [Heth's troops] advanced in strong force, and, notwithstanding the destructive fire poured into them, succeeded in gaining the shelter of stumps and fallen timber on our left front, and for a time kept up a fatal fire on the exposed wing of the battalion."[12]

While victory hung in the balance, Chaplain Henry Hopkins of the 120th N.Y. took up a rifle and fired away at the Confederates. The chaplain, flushed with the fervor of combat, began singing lustily "The Battle Cry of Freedom." The Union troops caught the spirit from the chaplain and joined in song. Above the din of the raging fire, the combatants heard the familiar refrain, "Rally round the flag, boys." Not to be outdone, the Tar Heels loudly retorted in song, "WE will rally round YOUR flag, boys." The two sides exchanged rifle fire at close range, but McAllister's troops held firm. The attackers took a terrible pounding from the Union artillery and the enfilade fires of the 7th N.J. Finally, the Confederates recoiled for a second time, but they were not yet finished. McAllister recalled, "The heavy firing had now ceased for the time being, but the pause was of short duration. . . . Once more we heard that unwelcome yell resounding, which told us plainly that they were again charging our lines. But our boys were ready for them." The three brigades pressed forward to break through McAllister's defense, concentrating on Hartford's end of the line. "They again made their appearance, seemingly determined upon carrying the line, but the well-directed fire checked them when within eighty yards of our works."[13]

The three Confederate brigades lined up for a final attempt to penetrate at dusk, but the attack did not get off the ground. McComb's Brigade, in the center, balked. They had lost their fighting spirit and did not get up to advance. Giving up on the center brigade, Louis Young rode over to General Cooke on the right to suggest that his brigade and MacRae's attack without McComb. Cooke refused to strike without the full force. Young rejoined the brigade with a dejected look on his face. The exasperated commander of the 44th N.C. confronted the adjutant with sword in hand. "We but await the word to attack!" Captain Young could only shake his head in response. Without MacRae's fiery presence, Heth's Division failed to make the final charge.[14]

Robert McAllister beamed with pride as the battle ebbed. "As the darkness of night had closed in upon us, the discharge of musketry and burning, flashing powder illuminated the battle scene. This, together with the roaring of small arms and the loud thundering of artillery, made the scene one of more than ordinary grandue [grandeur]. We thus rolled back the Rebel columns for the last time, and the victory was ours. Cheer after cheer resounded along our lines."[15]

Something had changed over the cold winter months. McAllister's green troops from October had learned how to stand their ground. A single Union brigade withstood the mighty blow of Heth's Division, the same blow that had sent previous Union offensives reeling. McAllister's effective fire planning and the fighting spirit of his soldiers whipped Heth's veterans. Congress later awarded Chaplain Hopkins the Medal of Honor for his part in animating the Union soldiers at the height of the battle. The Union corps commander, Andrew Humphreys, also deserved credit for his sharp survey of the defensive line and the quick action to plug the gap. The battle also exposed a distressing decline of spirit within the Confederate infantry. They had lost the killer instinct that had won the day at McPherson's Ridge, Reams Station, and Jones Farm. A Confederate force had refused to attack, a chilling indication of their waning *esprit de corps*. Heth pulled his battered division back to the trenches — this time, with their heads hung down.

Although the Confederate counterattack failed, the fury of Heth's blow impressed General Meade. He suspected that Warren might be the target of another counterattack, so he ordered the V Corps to pull back from the Boydton Plank Road and prepare a tighter defensive line. His caution was timely. A. P. Hill massed his forces south of the run on February 6 and was drawn into a savage, indecisive fight. Another sleet storm helped to suppress the fighting that evening but left the soldiers on the field to endure a miserable night in the cold. After more indecisive action on February 7, Meade withdrew Warren's Corps to the north side of the run and directed the Union troops to entrench the recently advanced Union line. The net result of the operation was another westward extension of the Union trenches. Meade's army now occupied a continuous front from Hatcher's Run to the fortifications around Richmond.

The action at Hatcher's Run produced no major change in the military situation — only another measure of strain on the overstretched Confederates. Although they could not replace their losses, they had to defend more frontage. Grant's "anaconda process" slowly reached toward the decisive point when he could envelop Petersburg "preparatory to swallowing it and Lee's army."[16]

No Man's Land

March 1865, Petersburg

The stalemate around Petersburg continued for six more weeks with neither army making any dramatic movements, though both worked to improve their fortifications. The opposing trenches along the Boydton Plank sector were one and a half to two and a half miles apart but came closest where Heth's Division defended because of the projection of the Union position around Pegram's Farm. Here, the Army of the Potomac built two earthen works, forts Welch and Fisher. The forward thrust of the forts protected the Union salient and improved its ability to attack across the Jones Farm against Heth. A. P. Hill's Corps established a strong picket line in the "no man's land" between the two trenches to buffer such an assault. "Our picket posts were half a mile or more in front of the breastworks, being a succession of small earthworks at about twenty-yard intervals, called rifle pits," one of Heth's sharpshooters stated. "Still, beyond these, videttes were posted at night, as close as it was necessary to the enemy."[17] The strong picket line could quickly engage any Union move beyond their forts and sound an early warning. Each night, soldiers rotated on picket duty to keep a fresh force between the trenches. The Confederate officers also relied on the pickets to discourage desertions.

While the men languished in the trenches, their three-year term of enlistment expired. The officers tried to reenlist the troops by appealing to their patriotism and *esprit de corps*. The appeal fell flat, overwhelmed by the miserable conditions and the forlorn plight of the Confederacy. Jacob Bartlett described the sad spectacle. "The 11th Regiment was formed in regular order on the parade ground, the colors were placed a few paces in front and the regiment was called by companies to form on the colors, that is, all who were willing to reenlist. The conscript law had been enforced some time in the Confederate states. . . . When Company K was called to form on the colors, I was the only boy to go. I am not writing this to make the impression that I was the only brave boy in the company, for I was not, but I did prefer the name volunteer to that of conscript."[18] Even the sight of their venerable colors could not stir their spirits. There had been too much fighting, too many losses, too little hope.

For the Confederates, the inactivity in Virginia offered little comfort because the military situation in North Carolina deteriorated rapidly. Maj. Gen. John Schofield's army captured Wilmington on February 22, followed by Sherman's entry into the state in early March. Johnston's Confederate army could not prevent Sherman from destroying the logistical base that supported Lee's army. The Union advance into the state seriously alarmed the Tar Heel soldiers in Virginia. "O how my heart sinks within me as I think of the desolation of my own sweet little cottage, & the terror & alarm & anxiety of my dear loved little family," one soldier wailed.[19]

The *esprit* *corps* and discipline that had served the Bethel Regiment so well throughout the war unraveled under the strain of the political shift toward peace, and the invasion of the home state. Events in North Carolina aggravated the vexing problem of desertions. William W. Holden's peace movement gained ground and eroded the soldiers' motivation, while Sherman's entry into the state made them worry about their homes. Many soldiers gave up and crossed the picket line to the Union trenches where they could swear an oath of allegiance before being paroled. The soldiers who stayed appeared to sympathize with the ones heading home. "What speaks worse for the spirit of the army, is that the men on the picket line fire off their guns into the air & will not try to shoot down those who are in the act of deserting to the enemy." On March 3, six men from G Company deserted. Eleven days later, twelve men from E, G, and K companies gave up the cause and turned themselves in to Union authorities. The regiment lost forty-six men to desertion during the months of February and March. Another sign of sagging morale involved Capt. William Kerr, the E Company commander, and one of the regiment's senior officers. Confederate authorities forced him to resign in disgrace on March 16, after charging him with unauthorized absence and drunkenness. The regiment missed the strong core of leaders that had once infused it with discipline: Leventhorpe, Martin, Ross, Bird, Lucas, Haynes, Armfield, Waddell, McCorkle, McDonald, Parker, Jetton, and many others. The regiment — indeed the entire army — was in poor shape to begin another season of campaigning.[20]

After examining the bleak situation, Lee concluded that holding Richmond served no purpose if he were to lose North Carolina. The only solution required a massing of Lee's and Johnston's armies to deliver a shattering blow to Sherman. One obvious obstacle remained in the way. How could Lee slip away from Grant's army? Grasping for a military miracle, Lee looked for a point in the Union entrenchments that could be penetrated by a surprise assault. Lee optimistically reasoned that a breach of the Union line would cause Grant to lift the siege to protect the Union supply base at City Point. As soon as Grant pulled back, the Army of Northern Virginia could withdraw to join Johnston's army. This desperate plan set off a disastrous chain of events.

Lee was not the only general examining the Confederates' strategic dilemma. From his headquarters at City Point, Grant anticipated

Lee's attempt to break away from his grasp. Grant planned to make yet another movement to the west around Lee's right flank to squeeze tighter on the Confederate supply line and, more important, to squeeze a position that would keep Lee pinned down at Petersburg. Again another ace in the hole. Maj. Gen. Philip Sheridan's cavalry corps had defeated Jubal Early's Confederate force in the Shenandoah Valley and was en route to Petersburg to reinforce the siege. Grant hoped to strike farther to the west than ever before with the additional cavalry force. He intended either to turn the Confederate flank or to compel Lee to stretch his force beyond the breaking point. As the month of March 1865 entered its last week, both Lee and Grant had decided to take the offensive against the other.

Maj. Gen. John B. Gordon reported to Lee that he had found a suitable point to attack to fulfill Lee's plan — Fort Stedman. This battlement, rising above the Union entrenchments east of Petersburg, stood on an axis that could lead Gordon's assault forces into the vital Union logistical base. Gordon selected this point because the two trenches came very close together in this sector, so a surprise attack could cross no man's land before the defender had time to react. Lee approved Gordon's daring attack plan and promised to support him with every unit he could scrape from the defensive line. At 4:00 A.M. on March 25, 1865, Gordon overwhelmed the Union defenders with a sudden rush and Fort Stedman fell into his hands. That was the extent of the success. Attempts to widen the breach failed, and by daybreak the Union artillery and adjacent units poured heavy fire into the fallen fort. The Union commanders reacted vigorously with a quick counterattack that sealed the break in the line. More Union units swarmed to the endangered part of the fortifications. By 8:00 A.M. Gordon abandoned all hope of achieving a decisive victory at Fort Stedman. He withdrew to the safety of the Confederate entrenchments through blistering fire.

The Union army then exacted a stiff price for the daring attack. The Army of the Potomac had not collapsed around the breach as Lee had planned or, rather, hoped. The II and VI corps remained in place while the IX Corps restored the line at Fort Stedman. Two Union corps commanders, Humphreys and Wright, astutely surmised that Lee had massed much of his army at Fort Stedman and left the rest of the entrenchments weakly defended. They asked Meade to sanction a counterstrike in the Boydton Plank sector to drive back the Confederate pickets.[21] Meade approved their request by 10:00 A.M.

The VI Corps attack began poorly. General Wright organized a makeshift assault force by reinforcing his own skirmishers with two regiments from Brig. Gen. Joseph Kiefer's Brigade. The selection of the officer to command the assault upset General Kiefer. "General Seymour [Kiefer's commander] thought he would give a Lt. Col. on his staff an opportunity to distinguish himself, he according[ly] directed me to order two regiments to report to him and I was told to look on & see them do the work." Kiefer did not like turning over two of his regiments to the untested staff officer and voiced his objections. "I protested, but obeyed."[22]

Across no man's land, the Confederates reinforced their picket line with a few troops they scraped from the trenches. Second Lt. James Saville of H Company led the detached pickets from the Bethel Regiment in the rifle pits. Saville and his men watched the Union soldiers file forward through ravines and gullies, then form into lines of battle. As soon as the blue lines advanced, the Confederate pickets pelted them with rifle fire. The VI Corps troops charged bravely but could not withstand the fire and broke off the attack. Kiefer blamed the failure on "want of proper direction and in consequence of an improper selection of the place of attack." Upset by the setback, he went over Seymour's head to General Wright. "I at once offered a bitter protest to the useless slaughter of men under incompetent officers." Wright agreed with the brigadier and directed Seymour to let Kiefer select the leader for the next assault. Kiefer decided to lead it himself. Meanwhile, Wright beefed up the attack with two brigades from Getty's Division.[23]

Getty's assistant adjutant general, Hazard Stevens, described the second Union effort. "[Getty's Division and Kiefer's Brigade] filed over the works, and rapidly deployed in front and to the left of Fort Fisher. . . . A brigade flag waved the signal to advance, the line moved forward. . . . The enemy from their intrenched picket line poured in a hot fire, their artillery from the left doubled its storm of shell, and flanked and almost enfiladed our ranks." Barry Benson, a Confederate sharpshooter, watched the Union assault from a vantage point in the trench.

On they came, shoulder to shoulder, the stars and stripes flying over their heads. Again the fire broke from one of our rifle pits, extending to the right and left till the whole line, as far as rifles could reach, was cackling and sputtering. But forward still swept the line of blue, heeding neither their dead nor their wounded. Forward still with a rush and a shout, the flag well to the front, and our hearts sink with the fear that they will go over the works at the first charge. But no, they have stopped! They stand still and fire, reload and fire. And our men, kneeling in the pits, take good aim and we can see how busy they are. It is but a minute before the enemy's line falters, appears about to break and flee. But look, the color bearer runs forward alone with his flag. With a shout that rings again, the blue line follows in a swift charge through our deadliest fire. They reach the works and turning rapidly to the right and left, they sweep the line in both directions for a long distance, taking possession of half a mile of rifle pits.[24]

The II and VI corps troops seized the picket line in the fields of the Jones Farm, and they quickly entrenched to retain the forward position. The Confederates did not give up easily, and soon a brigade-size force sortied from the east to hit the VI Corps troops on their right (eastern) flank. General Getty, anticipating the Confederate counterstrike, shifted two regiments to his right and had them hide just behind the crest of a small rise. Getty's tactics caught the Confederates by surprise. "The two regiments still lie crouching under the crest, but as the opposing [Confederate] line steadily advances nearer and nearer, they straighten up in the ranks, burst over the crest in well-dressed line, pour in a close and destructive volley, and charge the enemy, who break and fall back in disorder to the shelter of their main line of works." The victorious VI Corps troops guarded their hard-won line the rest of the day, then dug in their own rifle pits that night. The 11th N.C. lost twenty-five soldiers during the fight in no man's land; the casualties were irreplaceable. Lieutenant Saville was caught on the picket line when the Union attacked. Saville had enlisted in the original Bethel Regiment, risen in rank and survived wounds at Gettysburg and Jones Farm, only to fall captive in no man's land.[25]

Without the picket line, the Confederates had no one in front of the Boydton Plank line to provide early warning of an attack. The loss of this security would have terrible consequences. The Union commanders quickly realized the benefit of holding the ground between the trenches. Hazard Stevens noted, "The advanced positions thus gained were of incalculable advantage. From them all the intervening ground to the enemy's [Confederate] main line could be closely scanned, as well as his works themselves, and room was afforded to form an attacking column in front of our works and within striking distance of the enemy's. . . . Many eager eyes were searching the enemy's intrenchments to find a weak spot, and many earnest discussions took place as to the feasibility of this or that point," Stevens remembered. "Getty soon convinced himself that he could force one part of their line opposite Fort Welch. The ground here was nearly level, dropping off on the left into a shallow marshy hollow [Arthur's Swamp], which narrowed to a ravine next [to] their works." Getty passed the word to the senior officers that he believed he could penetrate the Boydton Plank line.[26]

On the opposite side, Harry Heth wanted to reestablish security, although he knew he could not restore the former picket line. He noticed one advanced position of the Union rifle pits on a "slight knoll" near the Squirrel Level Road that afforded the Union soldiers excellent observation up and down the Confederates' front. Heth could not leave such a valuable position in enemy hands, so he formed a special assault force of sharpshooters and one Mississippi regiment to retake the small hill. MacRae's elite company of eighty sharpshooters reported to Colonel Stone, the commander of Davis's Mississippi Brigade, who led the attacking force. General MacRae decided to accompany his cherished sharpshooters on this dangerous assignment, although the expedition was commanded by a lower-ranking officer.[27] Billy MacRae seldom missed a fight.

Before dawn on March 27, Colonel Stone ordered the makeshift force to file silently out of the breastworks, cross over the Confederates' own obstacles, and form a line of battle in no man's land. Using stealth, the Confederates crept forward in the dark to catch the Union pickets off-guard. Sharpshooter Barry Benson took part in the brief action. "As we drew nearer the enemy, the snapping of sticks, the rustling of brush seemed to me so loud that I could not understand how we went so far undiscovered. We could see the low mounds looming ahead of us in the gloom, when silence was broken by the first cry of 'Halt!' and the ring of a rifle. In the same instant a wild Confederate yell split the air. A solid rush, and we leaped over the works amongst the half awakened foe, who barely fired a score of shots as they fled in confusion. To the right and left we swept, clearing the line as we went. A few scattering shots, and our surprise and victory were complete." The sharpshooters captured two officers and forty enlisted men from the Union picket line. They spent the next day sniping with the Union skirmishers, while other troops rapidly constructed rifle pits closer to the Confederate entrenchments. When night finally provided some concealment, the sharpshooters retired behind their new picket line. The minor victory came at a price; every officer in MacRae's elite force was wounded. The leader of the Bethel sharpshooters, 1st Lt. William Todd, suffered his third wound of the war. The commanding captain of the sharpshooters was killed and had to be replaced. Capt. John Thorp from the 47th N.C., one of the volunteers who charged with Henry Lawson Wyatt at Bethel, took over the elite outfit.[28]

The events following the assault on Fort Stedman disappointed General Lee. His ambitious, optimistic effort to lift the Petersburg siege failed to accomplish anything and cost the Confederates their picket line. Worse yet, the Union army had regained its fighting spirit. Since the presidential election, they seemed to fight with renewed resolve. Surveying the situation, Lee reached a sad but undeniable conclusion. Lee advised Jefferson Davis on March 26, 1865, that the Confederate capital could not be saved.[29] The Confederate high command drew up plans to retreat to North Carolina with Meade's army, presumably, in hot pursuit.

The attack on Fort Stedman did not disrupt Grant's plans to turn Lee's western flank. Grant put the Union army in motion as soon as Sheridan's force arrived on March 26. Grant shifted several of his corps to the left to relieve Humphreys's II Corps and Warren's V Corps from trench duty, permitting them to maneuver. Grant planned to use the cavalry to tear up the Southside Railroad, while the infantry would fight the Confederate counterattack force after sallying from the trenches. On March 29, Sheridan's powerful cavalry corps swung well to the south and west to seize Dinwiddie Court House. Simultaneously, the two infantry corps crossed Hatcher's Run on the Vaughan Road, then turned northwest. Humphreys's II Corps advanced to a position between Hatcher's Run and Quaker Road, while Warren's V Corps made a wider turn along the Quaker Road just beyond Gravelly Run.

As expected, the Confederates sent Maj. Gen. Bushrod Johnson's Division to meet the advance. Johnson had limited success against the Union drive, so Lee reinforced the defense south of Hatcher's Run with Scales's and McGowan's brigades of Wilcox's Division. Humphreys and Warren continued their advance on March 30, pushing the Confederates back to Burgess Mill and the White Oak Road entrenchments. During the night of March 30, Meade shifted Miles's Division of the II Corps over to the left (west) to permit Warren's Corps to confront the White Oak Road. The swelling Union offensive forced Lee to send MacRae's Brigade to augment the White Oak Road defensive line. "My Brigade was withdrawn from the works [Boydton Plank trench line] near the Hart House and directed to report at Burgess Mill," Billy MacRae wrote.[30] The 11th N.C. occupied a portion of the White Oak Road line by the morning of March 31.

The fighting heated up considerably on March 31. At ten in the morning, Warren decided to test the Confederate defenses on the far west flank with Ayres's Division. Ayres failed to dislodge the defending Confederates who responded by counterattacking with three brigades — McGowan's, Hunton's, and Gracie's. The three Confederate brigades threw Ayres backwards onto Crawford's Division, which also gave way under the Confederate pressure. Word came down to MacRae to prepare his brigade to join the battle and, hopefully, convert the success into a general attack against Warren's Corps. "I was directed to hold my command in readiness to participate as soon as his [Warren's] left should be driven back as far as my front. The enemy was driven as far as the front of the Brigade on my right (Wise's) . . . at which point the attacking party finding the enemy too strongly entrenched to be dislodged was withdrawn to the works [White Oak Road line]," MacRae reported.[31] General Humphreys sent Miles's Division to help drive the sudden Confederate attack back to the White Oak Road. Meanwhile, Warren reorganized a steady defense. As with many previous assaults, the Confederates proved capable of winning a tactical success against a larger Union force but could not expand their gains into decisive results.

While the two infantry forces clashed along the White Oak Road, Grant changed the objective of his offensive. He directed Sheridan to make a joint cavalry-infantry sweep westward to draw Lee's infantry out of the trenches and crush them in a decisive battle west of the

White Oak Road entrenchments. Sheridan, having been given operational control over Warren's Corps, moved his cavalry northwest toward Five Forks, where they encountered Pickett's Division, supported by a cavalry division. The V Corps moved west toward Five Forks, while Humphreys's Corps shifted west to cover the White Oak Road front. The following day, April 1, Sheridan's combined force smashed Pickett's eastern (left) flank and forced thousands of his men to surrender. Those Confederates who could escape withdrew to the northwest, away from the rest of Lee's defensive line. The immortal hero of Gettysburg had suffered a disastrous defeat while he had been away from his command attending a shadbake. The crushing victory over Pickett allowed Sheridan to interpose his force between Pickett's retreating troops and the main Confederate western (right) flank. At last, the Union army had turned the flank of the Petersburg entrenchments. The Union soldiers at Five Forks sealed the fate of Richmond as they celebrated their decisive win.

For Maj. Gen. Gouverneur K. Warren, a personal humiliation cut short the joy of the moment. General Sheridan abruptly relieved him of command at the end of the battle, apparently dissatisfied with the speed of Warren's movement and the energy he displayed in the attack. Another old foe of the 11th N.C. ended his career on a bitter note. The regiment first encountered Warren at Bethel where he was one of the few Union officers to perform competently on the war's first battlefield. After Bethel, the regiment never had any luck against the Union corps commander. He proved to be a skillful, if somewhat overly cautious, opponent who worked best in defensive situations. Warren had commanded the troops that beat the Bethel Regiment at Bristoe Station, Globe Tavern, and Squirrel Level Road. Now, just as the war drew to a close, the Union army discarded Warren as if he were just another one of their many failed generals. He spent the rest of his life pleading with the army to reverse this stain on his military record. Finally, in 1882, an army court of inquiry declared that Sheridan had no cause for relieving Warren at Five Forks. The verdict came three months after Warren died.

Col. Horace Porter raced back to Dabney's Mill to report the victory to Grant. Porter's description of Sheridan's success sent Grant's headquarters into joyful celebrations. The normally abstemious Porter was so carried away that he thumped the impassive commanding general on the back. Grant then queried Porter about the particulars of the engagement. Porter poured out details of the battle, as he watched for Grant's reaction. "The general, with scarcely a word of comment, walked into his tent, and by light of a flickering candle took up his 'manifold writer,' and after finishing several despatches [sic] handed them to an orderly to be sent over the field wires, came out and joined our group at the camp-fire, and said as coolly as if remarking upon the state of the weather; 'I have ordered a general assault along the lines.' "32

The long-awaited moment had come. The next day, April 2, the Army of the Potomac would throw its full weight against the Confederate entrenchments around Petersburg. These lines had held the Union army at bay for nine months. The tedious process of stretching the Confederate defenses thin and squeezing their supply lines came to a close with a few calm strokes of Grant's pen. The time had come to break the Confederate line with one climactic assault.

BREAKTHROUGH

April 2, 1865, Petersburg

Although the Confederates had little idea of the calamity that had befallen Pickett, they feared he had suffered a reversal. Bushrod Johnson pulled back from the White Oak Road to reestablish contact with Pickett and preserve the integrity of the western flank. Harry Heth took control of the remaining brigades south of Hatcher's Run. Heth asked General Wilcox, the commander of the forces between the run and Petersburg, for troops to help replace Johnson's Division. Wilcox declined the request and expressed his alarm over the situation along the Boydton Plank line. He had only five brigades to defend seven miles of trenches. He also thought that the heavy skirmishing on March 31 and April 1 indicated a growing aggressiveness on the part of the Union forces across his front. Union sharpshooters had even shot his horse twice from a distance of six hundred yards. Heth looked at the situation and realized that a rupture along the Boydton Plank spelled disaster for Petersburg and his position on the White Oak Road. That night, April 1, he sent all the men that he could spare, half of a brigade, to help shore up the Boydton line. Billy MacRae drew the assignment. "Shortly after dark two of my regiments the 11th and 52nd N.C. under command of Lt. Col. Erson of the latter were sent by order of Maj. Gen. Heth to report to Brig. Gen. Cooke. This, together with 220 men left on picket near the Claypole House, left me with only 280 men." Lt. Col. Eric Erson, another veteran of the 1st N.C. Volunteers, claimed his force had a total strength of only 280 men. The small number under MacRae and Erson actually manning the breastworks showed how far the brigade's pool of fighting men had dwindled.[33]

Trudging across Hatcher's Run, the men of the 11th N.C. headed back to the Boydton Plank entrenchments and, unbeknownst to them, into the approaching storm. Eric Erson reported to General Cooke who must have been disappointed with the slim reinforcement. Cooke had responsibility for the three brigades of Heth's Division north of Hatcher's Run and for half the length of the trench line. He, in turn, reported to Cadmus Wilcox who had overall command along the Boydton Plank. Cooke's own brigade straddled the run and connected with the Mississippi Brigade on its left (north) flank. McComb's Tennessee Brigade held the far left of Cooke's portion of the line. Brig. Gen. James Lane's Brigade from Wilcox's Division occupied the line in front of the Jones Farm. Thomas's Brigade held the eastern flank and tied into the Petersburg breastworks near Battery Gregg. Cooke slid Erson's two regiments into the line near the center. Erson later reported, "I was ordered by General Cooke to relieve a portion of McComb's Brigade occupying from the right of McComb's winter quarters on the left, to the battery in front of McComb's winter quarters on the right." Erson positioned the Bethel Regiment on his left, adjacent to a ravine that flowed into Arthur's Swamp. The 52d N.C. occupied the line on their right. The men of the Bethel Regiment occupied their position in the trenches around 1:00 A.M. on April 2 and nervously waited for morning.[34]

April 1 did have one bright moment for the Bethel Regiment. That night Colonel William Martin rejoined the regiment after returning from convalescent leave. After six months without a field grade officer, the regiment had its colonel back in command! His leg wound had not completely healed, but the Confederates needed every officer they could muster in the field. Colonel Martin had recently been appointed as the chief of the Nitric and Mining Bureau, undoubtedly because of his background in chemistry.[35] The urgency of the situation around Petersburg apparently convinced him to forgo his job in the Richmond bureaucracy and rejoin the regiment, despite his poor medical condition.

William Martin's return was a bittersweet experience for the veteran officer. Certainly, the sight of his troops filled him with joy, but a quick survey of the situation caused dismay; the regiment had deteriorated since he had left. Apart from the obvious decline in strength, the customary fighting spirit of the regiment had waned over the cold winter, sapped by the pervasive sense of hopelessness. Martin was alarmed by the dispositions of his soldiers in the trenches. "The works . . . which would have been impregnable if defended by an adequate force . . . in fact were occupied by a mere skirmish line." The regimental commander saw, firsthand, the effects Grant's strategy had on the Confederates. "His [Grant's] programme was to bear down on our right with crushing force, and in case Lee reinforced his right with troops from the trenches at Petersburg, to assault the weakened lines at any practicable point and carry them. The plan was a complete success. Lee did carry every available soldier to the right." Only 4,100 men remained to defend the seven-mile frontage of the Boydton Plank trenches. Martin bitterly noted how attenuated the defenders had become: "The men were five to six feet apart!" Actually, Wilcox had only one soldier for every nine feet of frontage along the Boydton Plank. That compares with a figure of one soldier for every half foot of frontage during the battle of Spotsylvania. Furthermore, Martin could deploy skirmishers only a short distance to the front for early warning, as the Union forces had seized control of the rifle pits in no man's land.[36]

Martin's anxiety would have been greater still, had he known of the tempest gathering across no man's land. Horatio Wright, the Union VI Corps commander, prepared his men for the grand assault against the Petersburg trenches. Wright had carefully examined the defensive line after March 25 with the help of Brig. Gen. L. A. Grant and Maj. Gen. George Getty. The VI Corps officers selected the point where their men could attack "over ground perfectly cleared of trees [Jones Farm] and offering few natural obstructions," the spot defended by

Lane's Brigade and the demibrigade commanded by Erson. The Bethel Regiment had the misfortune of defending directly in the path of Wright's planned assault.[37]

Wright developed an elaborate but well-conceived plan to hack through the Confederate obstacles and penetrate the trench line. He massed his entire corps on a narrow front and arrayed his three divisions in a wedge formation, Getty's Division in the center with Seymour's and Wheaton's echeloned behind him from left to right, respectively. Each of the seven brigades formed in columns of regiments, which gave them excellent depth and the frontage of a single regiment. Wright figured that the regiments would require some time to position their formations properly in the dark. Because these formations had to be aligned forward of the Union trenches, his corps would be exposed and vulnerable during this critical time. In his order, Wright admonished his men, "The necessity of perfect silence in this movement up to the time of making the assault cannot be too strongly impressed upon the command." Wright further instructed, "Pioneers should be distributed along the front of the assaulting columns, to clear away abatis and other obstructions." In addition, a special detachment of Union artillery crews accompanied the infantry for the purpose of turning captured guns against the defenders. Wright risked nothing in the preparation for the attack. He insisted that every soldier understand the plan before the assault. "These orders . . . were read at the head of every company before the movement began." The veteran VI Corps soldiers recalled the horrors of Spotsylvania and Cold Harbor, as they listened. Hazard Stevens later wrote of their reaction. "The remark was frequent among the men, 'Well, good-by, boys that means death.' Full well the officers and veterans realized that they were undertaking a forlorn hope with the chances greatly against them, but they did not flinch."[38]

Starting at 9:00 P.M. on April 1, Wright's artillery pounded the Confederates for three hours to soften up the objective for the assaulting infantry. Once the fire lifted, Wright's three divisions quietly filed out of forts Fisher and Welch to form in the forward positions. The men had shed their haversacks and canteens to avoid making noise as they milled about in the dark. They had to move quietly because they were within range of the Confederate fortifications. The capture of the Confederate rifle pits on March 25 assumed added significance. Horatio

Wright remarked on its importance, "The position then gained was an indispensable one to the operations upon the main lines, by affording a place for the assembling of assaulting columns within striking distance of the enemy's main intrenchments." Wright's Corps endured an anxious moment around 2:00 A.M. "While the troops were moving into position, the pickets commenced firing to cover, it is said, the movement. The enemy's [Confederate] pickets replied vigorously, and a number of brave officers and men were killed or wounded." With so many troops packed into a confined space, the VI Corps could have suffered terrible casualties, but they maintained discipline. Wright later reported, "Everything was soon quieted down. . . . The men behaved well during the whole of the severe fire, without returning a shot or uttering a word to indicate their presence to the enemy."[39]

The stage was set for the decisive attack. Wright had fourteen thousand soldiers positioned to charge through the predawn twilight against the breastworks. The Confederates had two thousand soldiers manning the trenches near the point of attack. Fewer than 300 belonged to the 11th and 52d N.C., who stood in the way of Wright's left flank. The attackers lay down in neat regimental rows, mere yards separat-

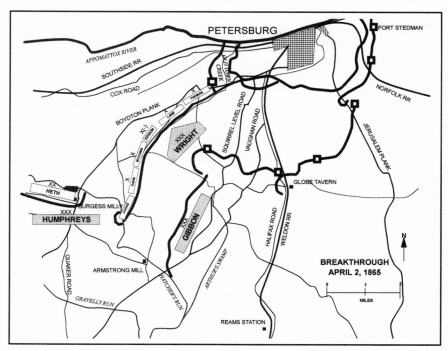

ing the rows, and waited for the signal to advance. The attack had been set to start at four in the morning, but Wright shook his head as he scanned the predawn sky. He let the departure time pass because conditions were too dark for an orderly movement. By 4:40 A.M., there was enough illumination to allow the infantry to see where they stepped but not enough to expose them to the Confederate pickets. Satisfied with the visibility, Wright ordered a cannon fired from Fort Fisher to signal the attack. "At the command the men rose to their feet, leaped over the rifle-pits, and moved forward." Officers and sergeants had to make "many a prod with boot or sword" to get some of the more reluctant troops going. "The lines, being massed close together, advanced successively, each [regiment] moving forward as the preceding gained a distance of 100 yards. For several moments nothing was heard but the tramp and rustle of the advancing columns." A short distance to the front, anxious Confederate skirmishers peered into the twilight for any signs of movement. Close behind them the Bethel soldiers stood ready in the trenches, forewarned of the attack by the signal cannon.[40]

Staring through the predawn darkness, Confederate pickets spotted shadowy figures sneaking toward them. They responded with a "scattering volley" that did little more than alert the main defensive line that the attack was upon them. The attackers' need for stealth disappeared once the Confederate pickets opened fire. "The troops instantly responded with a ringing cheer and pushed on in the face of the enemy's fire, which was now spitting along the whole line." Although the defenders, including the 11th N.C., fired intensely against the onrushing Union soldiers, the mass and close approach of the attackers allowed them to maintain their momentum through the Confederate obstacles. One attacking commander admired the Confederate abatis even as his men hacked their way through them. "All were astonished to find these obstructions such serious obstacles and so difficult to remove; openings were made in them, however, under a severe canister and musketry fire . . . and men pushed through." Sadly, the Confederates lacked the infantrymen to defend the obstacles properly, and the attackers quickly reduced the abatis.[41]

The weak Confederate fire could not deter the waves of storming Union infantry. "Resolute men from every regiment in the division rushed gallantly forward, forced aside the abatis and swarmed over the works," exclaimed George Getty, the lead division commander. The Confederates put up a savage but brief struggle. One Union chronicler described the ordeal of the first man to leap into the Confederate trenches, Capt. Charles Gould of the 5th Vermont. "Upon mounting the works he received a severe bayonet wound in the face and was struck several times with clubbed muskets, but bravely stood his ground, killing with his saber the man who bayoneted him." He was saved when the rest of his brigade swept over the parapet. "His comrades came to his assistance and routed the enemy from their lines."[42]

At this critical moment, Wright's clever use of a wedge formation helped widen the puncture. The Bethel soldiers, including 1st Sgt. Jacob Bartlett, concentrated against Getty's Division at the point of Wright's wedge, as it struck the breastworks to the regiment's left. "On our left they came with a tremendous yell, while in our front they were advancing without noise. We directed our fire toward the noise, it not being light enough to see those in front. My attention was so much attracted to the left the Yankees were coming over the breastworks, about four rods to my right, before I knew they were there." General Kiefer, one of Seymour's brigadiers, reported fierce combat in the trenches defended by the Tar Heels. "A hand-to-hand fight ensued within the main works, in which many gallant officers and men fell killed and wounded." The attackers decided the issue once they plunged into the trenches. "The enemy [11th N.C.] in our front was soon killed, wounded, captured, or dispersed." Jacob Bartlett suddenly realized that the breastworks had been lost. "I looked around and saw that there was no one there except myself and the Yankees. I might not have known that they were there had they not been yelling and shooting at the boys who ran before I did . . . so I set out for a foot race." Pushed by fear, Bartlett streaked for safety. "I know I ran fast, for the balls they shot at me never overtook me."[43]

As the Union wedge drove deeper into the Confederate defense, Seymour's Division ripped the hole wider on the Bethel Regiment's left side. Pvt. John C. Warlick in I Company was still fighting off attackers to his front when the Union troops rolled up the flank. "I was shooting at Yanks in front of me where they were as thick as black birds. They had broke our line on our left & come on us on our left flank. I had seen them, but thought it was our own men until a Cap't who was in front of his men with sword drawn whacked me over the head twice. Before I realized my situation his men were right at his heels with fixed bayonets."[44] The VI Corps attack crushed the regiment under the weight and violence of its attack. Nearly two thirds of the regiment's troops shared Private Warlick's fate, as Wright's force swarmed over the breastworks.

The VI Corps had done it! They broke the Petersburg defensive line and sliced Lee's army in half. The entire Confederate line ruptured between Erson's two regiments and Lane's Brigade. James Lane pulled the remnants of his broken brigade east toward Petersburg. The fragments of Cooke's force, including the Bethel Regiment, peeled back to the west and tried to organize a coherent defense against the breakthrough. Lt. Col. Eric Erson wrote of the Tar Heels' efforts to stem the Union tide, "We fought him [the enemy] for some length of time, when finding that he greatly outnumbered us, and was flanking us on our left, we were compelled to withdraw."[45] Hundreds of troops defending the line fell into enemy hands, along with several regimental colors. Colonel Martin and a fragment of the regiment barely avoided capture, but they continued to fight. Some defenders, who could not withdraw to either flank, simply fell back to the Boydton Plank Road but had no command structure left to organize a defense. These scattered bands were powerless to stop the vigorous pursuit. Union soldiers rounded up many of them the next day as they tried to escape across the Appomattox River.

Initially, the Union commanders found it impossible to control their men who were "perfectly wild with delight at their success in this grand assault." "The troops, after breaking through the enemy's works, pressed forward with the greatest dash and enthusiasm, and without order or formation, until at length they were halted with great difficulty and the lines reformed at a point on the Boydton plank road over a mile from the Rebel lines." General Wright confessed, "In the ardor of the movement it was quite impossible to check the advance of the troops." As they gained control of their overzealous men, the Union commanders tried to reorient their units to drive toward Hatcher's Run. First Seymour's Division on the left, then Getty's Division, swung around to bear down on the exposed flank of Heth's Division that held the western end of the defensive line. Brig. Gen. Kiefer described the situation of Seymour's left flank brigade. "The troops of the brigade were in some confusion after entering the enemy's works, but the main

body was at once directed along the enemy's fortifications to the left."
Once Getty and Seymour formed on line at a right angle to the Confederate trenches, Wright ordered them to attack.[46]

The Union ground up Heth's men as they stormed down the length of the breastworks. William Martin witnessed the onslaught. "The Federals swung around to the left and swept down the trenches, turning our own artillery against us as it was captured." Troops from Getty's Division used Confederate artillery to their advantage despite some difficulties. "Being unable to procure primers the pieces were discharged by firing a musket into the vent of the piece." Before long, an artillery gun crew took over and fired into Heth's troops, to the dismay of Martin and his men. The Confederates rallied for a brief time at a fort west of the breakthrough. The defenders used four artillery guns to hold off the attackers, but Seymour's men soon overran the fort. In a last desperate effort, McComb's Brigade mounted a local counterattack to recapture the redan. McComb reported, "[I had] formed the remainder of my Brigade perpendicular to the works and charged the enemy." Giving Seymour's troops a last taste of southern tenacity, McComb's force pushed the Union soldiers out of the fort and recaptured the guns but not for long. Kiefer's Brigade turned several captured cannons against the fort and then launched a coordinated attack that finally overpowered the stubborn Confederates. By 7:45 A.M. no organized resistance stood between the VI Corps and Hatcher's Run.[47]

Once Kiefer's men seized the last fort, the Confederate defense crumbled. One Vermont officer described the final sweep. "The whole command pushed forward vigorously through the thickets, swamps and pine woods, soon losing all organization again in the eagerness of the men to surpass each other in the pursuit of the enemy, who were being pressed so closely they could scarcely fire a shot." The breakthrough turned into a rout. Triumphantly, General Getty reported, "For over two miles the line moved forward over a wooded and difficult country, capturing flags, guns, and prisoners at every step." The VI Corps flowed into the rear area and overran the Confederates' winter quarters. Even Heth's division colors fell into the hands of the victorious VI Corps. The Union seized the regiment's camps and captured hundreds of soldiers on sick call or fatigue duty in the rear.[48]

General Cooke tried to save Heth's brigades from the attackers' grasp. As soon as he got word that McComb's Tennessee Brigade could not hold back the assault, Cooke decided to withdraw. "I then sent orders to Colonel Nelson, commanding Davis's Brigade, to withdraw at once. . . . Colonel Nelson was very slow in obeying the order and in consequence I think, very unnecessarily, surrendered his command." Cooke's own brigade slipped over Hatcher's Run where they held the line. To escape the pursuers, Colonel Martin and his men had to cross the run near Burgess Mill or fall straight back from the trenches to the northwest. Those who tried to link up with General Heth at White Oak Road sped southwest with McComb's Brigade to the mill bridge. Getty's and Seymour's divisions had already flanked McComb's men and pursued them vigorously. William McComb reached Hatcher's Run but ran into more trouble. "I found the enemy had possession of the bridge at Burgess Mill. My Brigade at this time was very much scattered & General Cooke said the only chance for escape was to swim." Forced to swim the swollen creek, many of the men had to abandon their weapons and equipment. VI Corps troops caught eight men from the 11th N.C. as they tried unsuccessfully to get across the run. Command and control fell apart as the Confederates fled from the triumphant Union assault.[49]

The Confederates lost another senior officer that fateful morning. Lt. Gen. A. P. Hill had been conferring with General Lee when news came of the Union assault. Hill jumped on his horse and raced off with his escort to make contact with the western flank. Lee sent a courier after Hill with a warning to be mindful of his own safety, a wise precaution that Hill should have taken more to heart. Soon the Confederate riders encountered two Union soldiers wandering around in the Confederate rear area and captured them. Leaving two of his couriers to take care of the prisoners, Hill and the other rider tried to skirt around the Union penetration. The two riders ran into two more enemy infantrymen while trying to get back to the Boydton Plank Road. Hill again attempted to capture the stray troops. Instead of surrendering, the Union soldiers from the 138th Pa. shot Hill from his horse, killing him. The Bethel Regiment had fought under Powell Hill's command for nearly the entire time it had served with the Army of Northern Virginia. His loss, so late in the war, must have stung them deeply. After years of fighting through dozens of fierce conflicts, Hill died just a week before Lee's surrender.[50]

Hill's futile effort to retrieve the situation along the Boydton Plank line was too late to do any good. The VI Corps sweep did not stop until it reached Hatcher's Run. After a rest, the corps retraced its steps and marched east to the Petersburg trenches. Horatio Wright called off the attack on Petersburg that evening because of the exhausted state of his troops; they had already done a full day's worth of fighting.

News of the breakthrough soon reached Harry Heth in the White Oak Road trenches. He held his position until Cooke's Brigade rejoined him, but he had to give up on Davis's Brigade and most of McComb's, which did not survive as organized units. With the Boydton Plank severed, Heth knew that his command risked capture if it remained. "My position no longer being tenable, I gave orders to withdraw to Sutherland's Station on the Southside Railroad, crossing Hatcher's Run at Watkins Bridge." This route of withdrawal moved Heth's force west then north on the Claiborne Road. The troops had a three-mile march on the Claiborne Road to reach Sutherland Station, which lay eight miles west of Petersburg. Heth had no time to spare because Humphreys, the II Corps commander, decided to capitalize on the VI Corps' success. "At 8:30 A.M. Major-General Mott reported to me that the enemy in his front were moving quickly to our left [west] inside their intrenchments, and subsequently that they were withdrawing their artillery from the redoubts. I ordered him to press forward on the enemy and attack," Humphreys recorded. Humphreys's left (western) flank division, commanded by Nelson Miles, also reacted quickly to the Confederate withdrawal. "At 9 A.M. the enemy abandoned his works, and they were immediately occupied by my men. The pursuit of the enemy was at once commenced, and he was followed closely to a point near Sutherland's Station."[51]

While Heth withdrew to Sutherland Station, a messenger brought word from Lee that Powell Hill had been shot and that he must assume command of the fractured corps. Lee directed that Heth report in person to receive instructions. "On reaching Sutherland's Station I placed my command in line of battle in order to cover the withdrawal of our wagon trains which I found parked at that point," Heth reported. "I then turned over the command to Brig. Gen. John R. Cooke and directed him as soon as the wagon train withdrew to push on after it, that my desire was not to fight a battle if it could be avoided." Heth rode to Petersburg to meet Lee but never got there. He ran into Union forces that blocked the way. Turning back to Sutherland Station, he discovered that the II Corps had cut off the road he had just used. Trapped between Union forces on three sides, Heth crossed the Appomattox River to the north side. The acting corps commander avoided capture, but he also removed himself from his command at Sutherland Station. Harry Heth became one more Confederate fugitive.[52]

General Cooke did his best to follow Heth's guidance. He deployed McGowan's Brigade on the left (eastern) flank, MacRae's Brigade in the center, and Scales's Brigade on MacRae's right. How many of the 11th N.C. had rejoined MacRae is unknown, probably no more than a handful. MacRae reported his total strength at Sutherland Station as under three hundred infantrymen. Obviously, the Confederates under Cooke's command could not expect to stop Humphreys's Corps, but they still threw up breastworks to hold off their pursuers. Heth's instructions to avoid a fight, notwithstanding, Cooke's troops soon became embroiled in a savage battle. When Miles encountered the Confederates at Sutherland Station, he thought a quick, bold charge from the march could rout Cooke's force, but he learned that the Confederate spirit was not yet beaten. Cooke's troops "handsomely repulsed" the hasty Union attack. Miles quickly regrouped his two brigades for another assault. "At 12:30 P.M. a second assault was made by the Third Brigade. . . . The artillery of the division had at this time come up, and being placed in position assisted in the attack by a vigorous shelling of the enemy's line. This attack was also repulsed, the enemy being able to concentrate his force opposite any threatened point."[53]

The Confederates had frustrated Miles's two frontal assaults, but Miles persisted. "I now determined to carry the position by an attack on the enemy's flank. A strong skirmish line was pushed forward upon the extreme right [western] flank of the enemy, overlapping it and threatened the railroad. . . . The attention of the enemy being thus diverted from his left [eastern] flank, the Fourth Brigade (Brevet Brigadier General Ramsey) was moved rapidly around it through a ravine and wood, and massed in the woods without being discovered by the enemy." Miles supported Ramsey's assault with another attack by the 2d and 3d brigades. Ramsey described the attack on the eastern flank against McGowan's Brigade, "The whole line pushed forward with resistless fury, determined for victory. While advancing the enemy used his artillery, giving us grape and canister, but its use was of short duration. The fire did not intimidate or retard our advance. . . . The men continued the advance cheering lustily, and when the right of the line struck the railroad the enemy commenced his retreat, my command pressing as rapidly as circumstances would permit." Miles's third attack won the field and more glory for his rising reputation. Sound tactics prevailed where momentum and massed fire failed. General Ramsey expressed the feelings of his men, "This success was eminently a happy, a glorious one."[54]

On the other side of the field, Billy MacRae fought for survival: "About 5 o'clock P.M. they [Miles's Division] succeeded in turning our left, where McGowan, the left Brigade gave way in confusion. I ordered up my sharpshooters at once to the support of his left, but they arrived too late to affect anything. In a few moments Scales's Brigade on my right gave way leaving me alone to confront the enemy with 280 men. Deeming it folly to attempt alone to make head against the vastly superior numbers confronting me [I] at length gave the order to fall back. The enemy pursued rapidly. I several times attempted to reform the line but without success." The defenders abandoned Sutherland Station, and Cooke's force dashed away to the Appomattox River to avoid being overrun. MacRae's, McGowan's, Scales's, and Cooke's brigades repeated the flight of McComb, Erson, and Lane earlier in the day. MacRae wrote, "My Brigade with the others was badly scattered and crossed the river at different points, in squads of three and four." Many troops could not find a way across the river and fell into enemy hands. Pvt. David M. Glenn of the Bethel Regiment's I Company had survived the collapse of the Boydton Plank line earlier in the day only to get captured at Sutherland Station in the afternoon. Fortunately, the victors did not pursue to the river, so hundreds of soldiers escaped on foot or crossed the river on rafts.[55]

By the end of April 2, the extent of the catastrophe was apparent. Between the battles of Five Forks, Boydton Plank, and Sutherland Station, Grant had annihilated Lee's entire army west of Petersburg. Heth's, Pickett's, and Johnson's divisions were reduced to disorganized bands of fleeing soldiers. Gordon's Corps and the remnants of Wilcox's Division barely hung on to the Petersburg breastworks but had no hope of holding another day. The long siege of Petersburg, the scene of so many of the Bethel Regiment's tactical victories, ended in a crushing defeat.

RETREAT

April 1865, Appomattox River Valley

Geneneral Lee knew the meaning of the April 2 collapse when he sent a discouraging assessment to the Secretary of War. "I see no prospect of doing more than holding our position here till night. I am not certain that I can do that [he did]. If I can I shall withdraw to-night north of the Appomattox, and, if possible, it will be better to withdraw the whole line to-night from James River. . . . Our only chance, then, of concentrating our forces, is to do so near the Danville railroad, which I shall endeavor to do at once." Lee wanted to regroup fifty-five miles to the west, where the railroad could be used to resupply the army. Lee issued his orders to abandon Petersburg and Richmond that evening, then notified the government of his decision. "It is absolutely necessary that we should abandon our position to-night, or run the risk of being cut off by morning. I have given all the orders to officers on both sides of the river, and have taken every precaution that I can to make the movement successful. It will be a difficult operation, but I hope not impracticable. . . . The troops will all be directed to Amelia Court-House." After suffering a dreadful defeat in the arduous siege, the Army of Northern Virginia had to flee for its life.[56]

The army evacuated under the worst set of circumstances. Lee's original plan had called for a sudden, surreptitious withdrawal, but Grant's massive attack ruined their opportunity for a head start. Lee had hoped that the Union would begin its pursuit from their trenches and follow a longer route. Instead, Sheridan's cavalry force already had an advantageous position on the western flank and would pursue Lee on a shorter line of march. Lee had assumed that the army could slip away from Petersburg in good order, but the army began the retreat badly disorganized and scattered. Lee intended to execute a well-planned retreat, but the confusion following the collapse crippled his army on its retreat to North Carolina. The cruel turn of events revealed the disastrous consequences of Lee's decision to storm Fort Stedman. He had declined an opportunity for an orderly withdrawal to gain an extra advantage from a daring offensive thrust. Once the assault against Fort Stedman failed, Grant seized the initiative and never let it go.

The rout at Sutherland Station left the remnants of MacRae's, McGowan's, and Cooke's brigades huddled along the Appomattox River. They could see their refuge on the far shore but found only one small boat to ferry them over. "There followed a sort of panic, the men asking questions which no one could answer. The Generals met in consultation and it was decided to push as rapidly as possible up the river until we reached some crossing—where or what it would be not even the generals knew." A few crossed the river on the boat, while the rest "turned our faces up the stream and in Indian file followed a footpath along its banks, hoping every minute to reach some bridge or ferry."[57] The band plodded on throughout the night. Whenever they came upon anything that floated, they paddled to the safety of the north bank.

The men of the Bethel Regiment, those who had evaded capture, began the long, gloomy retreat north of the river on April 3. Their early morning flight the day before had given them more daylight to find small boats and rafts than the rest of Heth's Division. At least on the north side, they could walk west without the immediate threat of Union cavalry running them down. Many had no weapon; few had any food. With only their pride and loyalty to keep them moving, they marched in small groups toward the designated rally point, Goode's Bridge. Most of Heth's men did get across sometime that day and joined the dispirited body of soldiers escaping from Petersburg and Richmond. Bit by bit, the men coalesced into larger clusters as troops recognized officers and sergeants from their unit. Still, much of Hill's Corps moved in a disorganized mass. Gnawed by hunger, the infantry scrounged for food in the farms they passed, as they slowly moved on roads clogged by wagons and artillery. A South Carolinian wrote that the survivors of the April 2 battles were "so crushed by the defeats of the last few days, that [we] straggled along without strength, and almost without thought. So we moved on in disorder, keeping no regular column, no regular pace. . . . An indescribable sadness weighed upon us."[58]

April 4 dawned more hopefully than the day before. The prospect of getting a meal at Amelia Court House helped to keep the men moving. Fighting off hunger and despair, the remnants of the 11th N.C. marched in scattered groups to the bridge where they had to recross the river to the south side. By noon, General MacRae "had succeeded in collecting about 150 men at Goode's Bridge." MacRae's Brigade had reported 1,174 men present for duty a month earlier in the Petersburg trenches. Now, the brigade commander felt pleased that he could gather a mere 150 soldiers. The determined general kept his small command moving, gathering more stragglers and lost troops as they marched to Amelia Court House. The tired band entered the town by 4:00 P.M., terribly hungry but still present for duty.[59]

The troops found disappointment, cruel disappointment, at Amelia Court House. In its haste to evacuate Richmond, army headquarters bungled the transportation arrangements for the rations. The staff failed to advise the commissary general to move the supplies to Amelia Court House, so the rations were left in Richmond. This fiasco led the army to rendezvous at a point without food. The regiment's famished troops could only catch some sleep and hope that the commissary could forage rations from the surrounding countryside. The army wasted a day waiting for the foraging parties to return with little food. Colonel Martin and General MacRae, at least, made use of the time to assemble the scattered groups into a unit. The brigade increased its numbers to those of a small regiment, which would again be a useful fighting force.

Lee spent the morning of April 5 at Amelia Court House, reorganizing his army and sorting out new command relationships following the death of A. P. Hill. Harry Heth and Cadmus Wilcox rode into town and found Lee seated with William Mahone next to an oat field. The three division commanders asked Lee "to whom they should report." Heth, the senior officer, waited breathlessly for Lee's decision as the army commander became momentarily distracted. Lee soon returned to the subject and responded, "Report to General Longstreet and I give notice of my purpose to diminish the number of Corps and division commanders in this army."[60] The announcement crushed Harry Heth. This command change denied him the chance to command a corps and indicated that Lee lacked confidence in his ability to lead a larger unit. Lee had neither forgotten nor forgiven the horrible panic in the Wilderness. Lee's decision consolidated Heth's, Mahone's, and Wilcox's divisions from Hill's Corps into Longstreet's Corps. Anderson and Gordon retained command of their own corps, while General Ewell took control over Kershaw's Division and a few miscellaneous units that joined the army. The Army of Northern Virginia would move to North Carolina organized into these four ad hoc infantry corps.

The ration mix-up may have been demoralizing, but an even more ominous problem gathered south and west of Amelia Court House. Sheridan's cavalry, accompanied by the V Corps, had traveled west along a direct route south of the Appomattox River to Jetersville. This move put Sheridan astride the Danville Railroad, Lee's intended route of withdrawal. Sheridan soon located Lee's army at Amelia Court House and quickly entrenched at Jetersville. Meade got news of Lee's location a short time later. "On the night of the 4th, receiving a dispatch from Major-General Sheridan that [Lee's] army was in position at Amelia Court House, immediate orders were given for the resumption of the march."[61] Grant's army had the inside track in the race and moved quickly to block Lee's retreat.

The Confederate command had no idea of this dangerous development. Unsure of the enemy situation, Lee issued instructions to strip the Confederate army of unnecessary ammunition, guns, and wagons to help speed the march to Danville. The Confederates blew up the excess equipment and ammunition on the morning of April 5, thoroughly startling the unsuspecting troops. Soon word came down the chain of command to resume the movement. The hungry soldiers got to their feet around midday and started marching southwest to Burkesville. They hoped to meet a supply train coming north with food, not knowing that Sheridan had already severed the rail line.

Sheridan's cavalry wasted little time in harassing the retreating Confederates. One Union cavalry brigade exploited a gap in the Confederate column and quickly attacked the wagon train. Wreaking havoc, the cavalry destroyed hundreds of wagons and rounded up a large herd of draft animals needed by the southerners for their march. Worse news followed. The head of the Confederate column ran into dug-in skirmishers, after traveling just a few miles. The Confederate infantry at the front of the column prepared for battle, while the senior officers awaited word from Lee. General Wilcox described the situation. "Some four or five miles from Amelia Court House we struck the railway and halted there till near dark, the enemy being close upon our left flank. Line of battle was formed, and slight skirmishing [occurred] between our and the enemy's cavalry."[62] Lee debated whether or not to attack. Wisely, he elected to bypass the position by shifting onto a westerly course toward Farmville where the western track of the Southside Railroad crossed the Appomattox River on its way to Lynchburg. The army could get provisions from Lynchburg using the Southside Railroad instead of the Danville line that Sheridan had interdicted. The weakened condition of his famished soldiers weighed on Lee; he rarely passed up a chance to attack. Had he attacked, the Confederates would have struck the Union V Corps in a prepared defense and then faced Meade's army that arrived at Jetersville shortly thereafter.

Lee's army resumed the march after dark on April 5 but shifted to roads heading west. Colonel Martin expressed the despairing attitude of the Bethel Regiment during the difficult march. "During this retreat MacRae's Brigade was often called upon for service, which it rendered with alacrity if not with hopefulness."[63] The night march severely tried the troops' patience. A heavy rain shower added to the agony of the men who were gnawed by hunger and fatigue. Cracks appeared in their discipline and weariness strained their nerves. The more alert soldiers noted that many men mumbled incoherently while they trudged along in the darkness. Startled by a breakaway horse, jittery troops fired indiscriminately into the dark, which caused several fratricidal casualties. Some troops drifted away in search of food; others were separated as they stumbled through the night. A few gave in to exhaustion and lay down by the side of the road, to be scooped up by the Union cavalry the next day. The pace became maddeningly slow as the sluggish wagon trains congested the muddy roads. The columns staggered through the night, robbing the men of much needed rest, yet they advanced only seven miles. The column strung out so far that Gordon's Corps, the rear guard, did not clear Amelia Court House until morning. When the sun rose on April 6, the army stretched out in a long, vulnerable march column.

In Jetersville, Meade's army lay in wait behind breastworks for the expected Confederate attack, knowing that they blocked Lee's avenue of escape. Curiously, the attack did not materialize. Meade described the Union reaction. "No attack being made, on the morning of the 6th of April the three corps were moved in the direction of Amelia Court House, with the intention of attacking the enemy if found there; but soon after moving intelligence was received that Lee had moved from Amelia Court House toward Farmville. The directions of the corps were changed." Meade's misguided move against Lee's assumed position at Amelia gave the Confederates a chance to slip away to the west. However, more problems arose for the Confederate high command. During the night, scouts captured and searched two Union soldiers dressed as Confederates. A captured message revealed that Maj. Gen. Edward Ord's army, consisting of the XXIV and XXV corps, had reached Burkesville. This placed Ord's two corps due south of the Confederate march column and moving on a parallel course. Deeply concerned about the noose closing around his army, Lee urged Longstreet to keep the head of the column moving as fast as possible to get clear of the Union pursuit.[64]

The Confederates made better progress on the crowded roads after daybreak. Passing through Deatonsville, Longstreet's column crossed Sayler's Creek on its way to Rice's Station and the Southside Railroad. MacRae's Brigade finally reached the station with Longstreet's wagon train about midday on April 6. Upon arriving, Longstreet learned that a Union raiding party had passed through the station earlier that morning. Based on accounts of the size and composition of the Union party, Longstreet concluded that they intended to destroy the bridges over the Appomattox River, so he dispatched a cavalry force to intercept the raiding party. After a savage fight, the Confederate cavalry troopers completely destroyed the raiding party. Meanwhile, Longstreet formed a line of battle to protect the station against an attack by Ord or Sheridan. Longstreet put MacRae's Brigade "in the second line," which kept the Bethel Regiment out of direct engagements with the Union cavalry that probed Longstreet's position incessantly.[65] Fortunately, the Union cavalry avoided assaulting Longstreet's force.

The lead corps had deflected a serious threat, but farther back in the long column command and control began to unravel. The order of march put Longstreet in front, followed by Anderson's and then Ewell's Corps. Gordon's Corps, the rear guard, had to protect the army from Meade's pursuit. While Lee went forward with Longstreet, the three trailing corps commanders began having problems coordinating their movements. Anderson, inexplicably, halted his move, which caused a gap to develop between himself and Longstreet. Sheridan's cavalry injected itself between the two corps and blocked Anderson's route. The rear of the Confederate column became disconnected simultaneously. Ewell sent his wagon train on a separate road from his infantry and then failed to tell Gordon that his wagons had taken a different road. Gordon's Corps followed the road taken by the wagon train, which uncovered Ewell's rear to the pursuing Union infantry. Even the generals had difficulty coping with the fatigue and stress. With Union cavalry blocking Anderson and Union infantry massing on Ewell's rear, the middle two corps got caught in a vise. The breakdown in the movement led to the tragic Battle of Sayler's Creek.

Meade described the action at Sayler's Creek in his official report. "The Second Corps soon came up with the enemy and commenced a rear-guard fight, which continued all day till evening, when the enemy was so crowded in attempting to cross [Sayler's] Creek. . . . The Sixth Corps, on the left [southeast] of the Second, came up with the enemy posted on Sayler's Creek [Ewell's Corps]. Major General Wright attacked with two divisions and completely routed the enemy. In this attack the cavalry, under Major General Sheridan, operated on the left of the Sixth Corps, while Humphreys was pressed on the right. The result of the combined operations was the capture of Lieutenant General Ewell and four other general officers, with most of Ewell's Corps." In fact, the Union army overwhelmed both Anderson's and Ewell's corps. Yet another disaster! Lee lost a third of his combat force in one sudden collapse in the middle of his column. Gordon managed to slip away from the Union trap and headed toward High Bridge northeast of Farmville while Lee tried to shore up the rear with Mahone's Division. Lee and Mahone rode to the rear to see the situation at Sayler's Creek for themselves, and they were greeted by the spectacle of mule teams dashing about without their wagons, refugee soldiers fleeing without their weapons, and Union infantry advancing without opposition. General Mahone recorded Lee's horrified response. "General Lee surveying the field straightened himself in the saddle looking more of the soldier than ever, exclaimed, as if talking to himself, 'My God! Has the army dissolved?' Recovering self control for the moment lost I replied, 'No, General, here are troops ready to do their duty.'" Lee regained his composure and answered Mahone, "Yes, General, there are some true men left."[66]

As the sun set on the disastrous day of April 6, Lee returned to Rice's Station and conferred with Longstreet. They prepared new movement orders in the hope of escaping from the aggressive Union army. The day's operations proved that the Confederates could not withdraw under constant pressure from Meade's infantry and Sheridan's cavalry. The Army of Northern Virginia, now only two corps, had to recross the Appomattox River to separate themselves from Grant. Longstreet's Corps, including the 11th N.C., would continue moving west from Rice's Station to Farmville, then cross the river on either the rail or wagon bridge. Gordon's Corps would cross the river at High Bridge, north of Rice's Station. All bridges over the river would be burned as soon as the troops crossed. Once it was safely on the north side of the river, the army could rest briefly before resuming its march west on the Lynchburg Pike. This route, though protected by the river, would carry the army out of its way because of a northward bend in the river. The Lynchburg Pike recrossed the river at Appomattox Court House before turning west toward Lynchburg. The longer route of march posed a risk, but Lee reasoned that the army could move faster once it was free of the Union army. He directed the movement to commence immediately after dark.

At 8:00 P.M., Longstreet started the march to Farmville with Field's Division leading, followed by Heth, and then Wilcox. The cavalry and skirmishers covered the rear of Longstreet's column. MacRae's Brigade accompanied the wagon train to help it negotiate the creek crossings. The slow-moving wagons proved to be a great hindrance on the retreat. Almost at once, the column halted owing to congestion on the road. General Wilcox wrote about the chaotic situation. "The troops (Heth's and Wilcox's Divisions) halted for the wagons to pass, the bridge had been injured by the breaking of a plank, the approach to it was over a muddy flat, covered with water in some parts, and there was but a narrow place on which the wagons could move with safety. Lights were made and men stationed to warn the teamsters when and how to drive. The bridge was steep and with some of the wagons there was much delay by balking of teams, one or two wagons were thrown from the bridge, not being able to cross loaded with ammunition." Leading by example, the Confederate senior officers helped deal with the frustrating wagons. "General Heth and myself attended personally to the crossing of the wagons at this bridge, and often with our hands and shoulders assisted in getting them over. It was broad daylight before the troops had passed, every wagon had been crossed first." The Bethel Regiment restarted its march to Farmville at dawn after enduring another weary night. The men had not slept since the night of April 4 and had not received rations since April 1. Many of them subsisted on the parched corn that was fodder for the draft animals. The soldiers who remained were, indeed, "true men."[67]

To reach Farmville, Longstreet had only to cover a distance of three to four miles. With the wagons out of the way and the sun up, the regiment moved rapidly to the town. Toward their right, the men could see Gordon's Corps and Mahone's Division crossing High Bridge. Shortly thereafter, they saw flames as Mahone's men burned the bridge behind them. Events seemed to be proceeding according to plan. The starved Tar Heels received their first good news upon entering Farmville. Food! A supply train waited in town with cornmeal and bacon. Those who got the chance filed by the train and picked up their rations on their way to the bridge. Because they were still on the south side of the river, the soldiers had to carry the rations across it before lighting their cooking fires. Savoring the thought of their first meal in six days, the Tar Heels hurried across the Farmville bridge to enjoy their meal north of the river.

Suddenly officers barked out new orders. Union infantry and cavalry were moving rapidly on Farmville, and Longstreet's troops had to be recalled to help save the rear guard. Regretfully, the men abandoned their cooking fires and wolfed down the uncooked cornmeal and bacon, while dashing into another fight. The Confederate rear guard managed to withdraw through the town, so Longstreet's men crossed the bridges once more to the north side. As soon as they cleared the bridge, the Confederates put the torch to it. The sudden alarm spoiled the meal the Bethel men had been dreaming about for several days. How disheartening! The retreat from Petersburg had brought the men nothing but a steady stream of disasters and hardships. Once back on the north side, the 11th N.C. did get the slight satisfaction of seeing some of the wagons burned. The need for rapid movement and the exhaustion of the malnourished draft animals forced the army to burn most of the wagons. Cadmus Wilcox expressed a common sentiment, "It was a great relief to many to see them burn, for they had caused much delay and inconvenience on the march."[68]

A new crisis developed late in the afternoon of April 7. A Union cavalry division commanded by Maj. Gen. George Crook forded the Appomattox River and lunged at the Confederate artillery train. The 11th N.C. was "taken at double-quick, with the remainder of Heth's

Division, to protect the artillery stalled in mud and menaced by a large force of cavalry." Colonel Martin wrote, "The division witnessed a cavalry charge that seemed to be bloody and terrific, but the retreat of the Federals disclosed the fact that although the two bodies of cavalry had violently assaulted each other with sword and pistol, the only man killed on the field was a Confederate lieutenant, whose head was shot off by our own guns."[69] Obviously, William Martin had more regard for the effectiveness of infantry than cavalry. While the cavalry and Heth threw back Crook's raid, more trouble grew on the eastern flank. Humphreys's II Corps had pressured Mahone's Division as it crossed High Bridge. The Confederates fired the High Bridge and the adjacent wagon bridge, but the Union troops saved the wagon bridge from the flames. Humphreys quickly shoved his divisions across the river and continued pursuing Gordon and Mahone. The approach of the Union II Corps forced the Confederates to deploy a hasty defense near Cumberland Church, three miles north of Farmville. Humphreys threw Miles's Division against Mahone's troops, hoping for another victory like Sayler's Creek, but Mahone's men did not fold. Instead, the defenders drove off the attack with some help from Longstreet. The Confederates may have been worn down by the last few days, but they were still not defeated. In this attack, Confederate Brig. Gen. William Gaston Lewis suffered a gunshot wound in the thigh. Lewis, a veteran of the 1st N.C. Volunteers, became the last Confederate general wounded in action. On the opposite side, Brig. Gen. Thomas Smyth became the last Union general killed in battle. Smyth had been wounded while fighting the Bethel Regiment at Cemetery Ridge and had fought against them at Bristoe Station, Wilderness, Reams Station, Burgess Mill, and Hatcher's Run. He fell for the last time two days before the end.

After the setback, Humphreys realized that he faced the entire Confederate army alone. He pulled back until he could be reinforced. The engagement kept Humphreys at bay, while Lee prepared the army for the march toward Lynchburg. However, the fact that a Union corps had crossed the river and remained in hot pursuit proved that Lee's revised plan had failed. Far from having an unmolested march, the Confederate army had been forced to repel an attack before it had properly linked up north of the river. That night, Wright's VI Corps completed a bridge over the river at Farmville. The Confederates would have to move quickly the next day, with Humphreys and Wright giving chase. They had to reach Appomattox Court House before the Union army cut off the route to Lynchburg. Lee did not know it, but Sheridan's cavalry was already riding to Appomattox on a direct route south of the river. Sheridan could easily outstrip the Confederates, but the real race was with the V and XXIV corps of Ord's Army of the James. If the Union infantry beat Lee to Appomattox, Lee's entire army could be trapped.

Ever since the battle of Five Forks, the Army of Northern Virginia had stumbled from one calamity to another. It had lost its ability to execute swift, sure maneuvers in the face of the enemy and displayed less aggressiveness than the Union soldiers. Weak march discipline, poor control, mismanagement, and listless execution marred the army's attempt to escape. Clearly, the nine-month siege of Petersburg had weakened the fighting spirit and operational skill of the army. Lee's remarks during the Spotsylvania campaign, *"This army cannot stand a siege,"* seemed hauntingly prophetic.

Surrender

April 1865, Appomattox

*L*t. Gen. U. S. Grant spent the night of April 7 relaxing at the Prince Edward Hotel in Farmville; Lee had stayed there the previous night. As he stood on the front porch of the hotel, he watched a long procession of VI Corps soldiers marching through the town to the Appomattox River bridge. The men paraded before their general singing and shouting till they became hoarse. Sensing victory, their spirits soared. The throng of Union soldiers surged forward with emotions in marked contrast to the bedraggled Confederate column that headed west on the Lynchburg Pike at that same hour. Grant stared at the jubilant multitude passing his impromptu reviewing stand and decided that the time had come to extend a peace overture. He composed a short note to Lee to persuade him to surrender by appealing to Lee's sense of humanity and pointing to the forlorn circumstances of his men. "The results of the last week must convince you of the hopelessness of further resistance. . . . I feel that it is so, and regard it as my duty to shift from myself the responsibility of any further effusion of blood."[70]

Grant's message passed to Lee's field headquarters during the night. Lee examined the letter when it arrived and then handed it to Longstreet. The corps commander read the message and replied, "Not yet." Longstreet's laconic response proved his willingness to continue the fight but also revealed his apprehension of the outcome. Lee wrote a brief reply to Grant denying the hopeless position of the Confederate army, while carefully pointing out that Grant's note contained no terms. "I reciprocate your desire to avoid useless effusion of blood, and therefore before considering your proposition, ask the terms you will offer on condition of [the army's] surrender." In his memoirs, Grant recorded his reaction, a reaction Lee's reply had been intended to generate. "This [Lee's response] was not satisfactory, but I regarded it as deserving another letter." The peace feelers would continue through another day of retreat.[71]

Throughout the night of April 7–8, the Bethel Regiment trudged along the road to Appomattox Court House, their third night on the march. The exhausted soldiers collapsed and slept at every halt, which made command and control even more difficult. Many succumbed to fatigue and neglected to get up when the march resumed. Officers and sergeants, too numb to care, did not bother to keep track of all their men. The army suffered heavily from straggling during the night, but it needed the cover of darkness to avoid the constant daylight harassment of the Union cavalry. The Confederates stopped to rest the weary troops in the early morning hours, after gaining a small lead on the pursuing Army of the Potomac. During the interval, several soldiers wandered off to forage for food; some never returned.

Colonel Martin and the other officers saw the dire circumstances of the army and decided to take special care of the regimental colors. "On the night of 7th April, in a consultation of the officers of the Eleventh Regiment, Captain Outlaw, of C Company, was advised to take charge of the flag and see that it was not lost. It was removed from the staff, the silk cover replaced, and during the 8th of April it was not unfurled and no one knew but that the flag was on the staff." Edward R. Outlaw had been a member of the 1st N.C. Volunteers and later succeeded

Frank Bird as C Company commander. Although he missed the Gettysburg campaign while on leave, he earned a reputation as a good officer and aggressive fighter. Officers were not supposed to carry rifles, but Outlaw preferred to shoot the enemy himself when the opportunity arose. On one occasion, he was so absorbed in shooting that he ordered a few of his men to load rifles for him while he fired away as fast as they could hand him the weapons. He also had a bloodthirsty streak. According to one camp story, he once confronted a Union soldier face to face when he realized that he was out of percussion caps. He bluffed the enemy soldier and demanded that the northerner hand over his ammunition pouch. The Union soldier, now a captive, complied. Outlaw took out a cap, loaded his rifle, then shot the unsuspecting soldier. Perhaps this reputation for fierceness made him the logical choice to guard the precious flag.[72]

The army moved out at noon on April 8, only slightly refreshed. Heth's Division drew the dangerous assignment of rear guard for the march column. Fortunately for the regiment, this day's march proceeded in much better fashion than the previous three. The ubiquitous Union cavalry, for some unknown reason, did not shadow nor harry the Confederates. Humphreys's and Wright's corps gave chase, but the Confederates made better progress on the Lynchburg Pike, especially as the excess wagons had been destroyed. The expectation of food at Appomattox and the balmy weather renewed their hope that they just might out-race Grant's army and escape. Lee felt more optimistic when another letter from Grant arrived. This time Grant spelled out just one condition for the surrender of the Army of Northern Virginia. "The men and officers surrendered shall be disqualified for taking up arms against the Government of the United States until properly exchanged." Lee did not accept Grant's simple yet generous offer. Instead, he countered with an offer to meet Grant at 10:00 A.M. the next day (April 9) to discuss the "restoration of peace," a subject that was beyond Grant's military authority.[73]

As evening descended on April 8, Gordon's Corps approached the outskirts of Appomattox Court House while Longstreet's Corps protected the army's rear. General MacRae formed his brigade "in a triangle across the road, the men six feet apart, the rear angle resting on the road." In this position the Tar Heels halted for a much deserved rest. April 8 did not pass pleasantly for all of the regiment; the Warlick family lost another son. The youngest of the five brothers, William Julius, died at Appomattox. The cause of his death is not known.[74]

The Confederates' respite was shattered that evening. A Union cavalry division, commanded by Brig. Gen. George A. Custer, rode through Appomattox Station and seized the supply train waiting on the tracks. Custer turned north toward Appomattox Court House where he discovered a large concentration of Lee's artillery that had moved in advance of the rest of the army. With help from nearby Confederate units and the approach of darkness, the artillery fought off Custer's attack and reorganized for a continuation of the retreat to Lynchburg.

Although Custer had been driven back to Appomattox Station, his appearance had a telling effect on the Confederate high command. Lee and his generals now understood why the Union cavalry had not molested their march. Sheridan had spent the day dashing forward on the parallel roads south of the river to cut off Lee's line of retreat through Appomattox. The Union cavalry had robbed the Army of Northern Virginia of its provisions and blocked its route of withdrawal. That night Lee and his generals conferred on their plight. The red glow of Union campfires illuminated the eastern, southern, and western skies as they gathered. The situation looked grim, but the Confederates still saw a faint glimmer of hope through the ominous red glow. If the Union defended Appomattox only with cavalry, a determined attack by infantry could push through and open the direct road to Lynchburg. Lee ordered General Gordon to launch an early morning attack toward Appomattox Station, while Longstreet's men defended the rear from attack by the Union infantry. After departing the conference, General Gordon sent a staff officer back to ask Lee, "Where should he halt tomorrow night?" The hopeful question brought a rare smile to Lee's face and elicited the whimsical response, "Just beyond the Tennessee line."[75] As long as there was hope, the army would keep fighting.

In the predawn hours of April 9, Maj. Gen. Bryan Grimes led an attack against Appomattox Station with his division of North Carolina troops and other elements of Gordon's Corps. Sounding the rebel yell for the last time, Grimes's assault plowed through the Union defenders who turned out to be only dismounted cavalrymen. Gordon's Corps wheeled to face south and cleared the Lynchburg Pike for the rest of the army. Just as Grimes completed his attack, General Gordon spotted a large formation of Union infantry closing on his right rear flank from the west and south. Ord's V and XXIV corps had reached Appomattox and prepared to block the escape route. This sealed the fate of the Army of Northern Virginia. Gordon knew he could push his way past a cavalry force, but a large infantry force was a different matter. Gordon gave a message to one of Lee's staff officers to take back to the commander. "I have fought my corps to a frazzle, and I fear I can do nothing unless I am heavily supported by Longstreet's Corps."[76] Such a message from his most pugnacious subordinate immediately convinced Lee that the situation had become hopeless. Lee knew that Longstreet already had his hands full fending off the advance of Humphreys and Wright; there was no one left to help Gordon. Lee called in his generals for a conference, most notably Longstreet, whose advice Lee always appreciated.

When Longstreet arrived at Lee's headquarters, he noted that the commanding general had put on his full dress uniform with sword, sash, and spurs. Lee described the situation facing the army and asked Longstreet what he thought. Longstreet, choosing his words carefully, asked Lee whether an additional sacrifice by the Army of Northern Virginia could help the Confederacy in some other theater. Lee replied, "I think not." Longstreet did not presume to tell Lee what to do, nor did he wish to advocate surrender. He simply stated, "Then your situation speaks for itself." Lee solicited opinions from the other generals present. Brig. Gen. Porter Alexander suggested that the army disperse and conduct guerrilla warfare. Lee rejected that idea by stating that the troops would be reduced to marauding the land they were supposed to protect. After hearing the opinion of his other generals, Lee sadly decided to seek terms from U. S. Grant.[77]

Lee rode to the rear to meet Grant at 10:00 A.M., as he had proposed in his letter of April 8. He found only a Union staff officer who informed him that Grant had refused his suggestion to discuss the "restoration of peace" and had not come. Lee immediately sent a message to Grant asking for "an interview in accordance with the offer contained in your letter of yesterday."[78] The staff officer dashed off to locate Grant who was on the road to Appomattox Station. Meanwhile, Lee arranged a cease-fire with both Meade and Sheridan after some tense moments. Lee passed a few anxious hours waiting under an apple tree for Grant's response, dreading his possible demands. Finally, at 12:30 P.M., a courier rode up with a message that Grant accepted Lee's offer to meet between the lines. General Lee mounted his horse and trotted off under a flag of truce to the house of Wilmer McLean in Appomattox.

Captain Outlaw recalled the sad moment when the Bethel Regiment watched Lee ride away under a white flag. The officers had one important duty to perform. "When General Lee rode to the front and through the lines to meet General Grant, every one knew that the hour of surrender had come. The officers present with the regiment at once retired to a secluded thicket, and raking up a pile of twigs and leaves, committed the flag to the flames. Before burning it, Captains Outlaw and J. M. Young tore out pieces of each color. Sincere tears have often been shed around funeral pyres, but never more bitter and sorrowful tears bedewed any ashes than were shed over their dead flag. It had been given by the Legislature of North Carolina to the Bethel Regiment, and then committed to the keeping of the Eleventh. It had never been dishonored and they could not bear to see it the trophy of an enemy."[79]

General Grant did extend generous terms at McLean's house, much to Lee's relief. The agreement contained the following conditions, "To wit: Rolls of all the officers and men to be made in duplicate. One copy to be given to an officer designated by me, the other to be retained by such officer or officers as you may designate. The officers to give their individual paroles not to take up arms against the Government of the United States until properly exchanged, and each company or regimental commander sign a like parole for the men of their commands . . . This done, each officer and man will be allowed to return to their homes, not to be disturbed by United States authority so long as they observe their paroles and the laws in force where they may reside." Lee, grateful that Grant offered magnanimous terms, wrote a short letter of acceptance to Grant. "I received your letter of this date containing the terms of the surrender of the Army of Northern Virginia as proposed by you. As they are substantially the same as those expressed in your letter of the 8th instant, they are accepted. I will proceed to designate the proper officers to carry the stipulations into effect." At the stroke of Lee's pen, the Army of Northern Virginia ended its bloody struggle.[80]

In mid-afternoon, Lee rode back to the Confederate lines where his soldiers waited for word of his meeting with Grant. "Are we surrendered?" the troops cried out. The normally impassive general could no longer control his emotions. With tears filling his eyes he apologized, "Men, we have fought through the war together. I have done the best I could for you. My heart is too full to say more."[81] Out of compassion for the condition of Lee's troops, Grant ordered the Union commissary to issue rations to the starved and depressed former Confederates. They gratefully accepted the kindness and ate their fill without disturbance. But no meal could overcome the dismay felt by soldiers who had to surrender after fighting so valiantly.

Rain and cold swept into Appomattox the next day, which added to the somber disposition of the troops. Throughout the day, William Martin had to fulfill one of the stipulations of the surrender by signing the paroles of the remaining men of the 11th N.C. He paroled seven officers and seventy-four enlisted men at Appomattox. Over the next few days, Martin paroled ten more soldiers who surfaced in the area, some of them stragglers and others reluctant parolees. The Bethel Regiment surrendered a total of ninety-one men at the conclusion of the war. Several veterans of the 1st N.C. Volunteers were among the parolees. They had served throughout the war under the Bethel Regiment's colors. James M. Young, Edward R. Outlaw, Thomas R. Parks, John F. Freeland, and William B. Taylor had risen through the ranks to become the regiment's remaining senior officers at the time of the surrender. First Sgt. Jacob Bartlett served in the Buncombe Rifles for the length of the war and lived to write about his experiences many years later. Second Lt. Lewis Warlick was not so fortunate. He survived the war and was paroled from the Farmville Hospital in April. He returned to Burke County and the young wife he had courted and corresponded with for so long. Sadly, he died shortly after his return. His health had failed over the winter and he never recovered. He was the last of the five Warlick brothers, all of whom gave their lives while serving in the Bethel Regiment.[82]

The Warlick boys were among the 492 soldiers who died during the four-year existence of the regiment. Of these fatalities, 318 died of disease and ten by other causes. Poor sanitation, hostile climates, and an epidemic took a huge toll during the first two summers. After that, the men adapted better to camp life and the death rate moderated. However, the deaths in northern prisons offset whatever improvement the regiment had in controlling disease. The horrible prison conditions and the large number of internees from the regiment produced a steady number of prison deaths from the summer of 1863 to June 1865. Pneumonia, typhoid, yellow fever, and a host of other afflictions killed far more than did Union fire. The regiment lost 164 men in battle between Bethel and Appomattox. The majority of them fell at Gettysburg. The bloodiest battle of the war taught the Confederates to be more sparing with the lives of their soldiers. The regiment fought in several sharp clashes after Gettysburg but avoided the toe-to-toe slaughter of McPherson's Ridge and the rash assault of Cemetery Ridge. The wily veterans of 1864 averted disaster at the Wilderness and Globe Tavern, when continuing the fight could have cost them dearly. They invariably defended behind the protection of breastworks and never again pressed a hopeless attack to the point of senseless sacrifice. The 11th N.C. launched repeated attacks against the Union army during 1864, including assaults on enemy breastworks, but the leaders relied more on sound tactics than brute force. These precautions paid off for the Bethel Regiment. Only thirty-eight soldiers died in battle during the 1864 campaigns. The regiment retained its combat power until the battle of Burgess Mill when the II Corps captured 104 men in the confused struggle. The regiment could not recover before the disastrous campaign of 1865.

On the day following the surrender, General Lee wrote his farewell address to the Army of Northern Virginia. The melancholy task pained the commander who was so devoted to and loved by the soldiers he had to surrender. With heartfelt words, he expressed his appreciation to the men and offered them his best wishes. "I earnestly pray that a merciful God will extend to you his blessing and protection." Then he bade them farewell.

One final act had to be played out before the men could be released to return to their homes. At General Grant's insistence, the Army of Northern Virginia had to march through a formal surrender ceremony, to include the stacking of arms and laying down of battle flags. The Confederate commissioners had tried repeatedly to waive the necessity of a ceremony that would certainly be a painful ordeal for the humbled Confederates. Yet Grant himself, who had otherwise been very accommodating to Confederate sensibilities, stuck to the demand for a surrender ceremony. Grant's implacability on this point revealed his conviction that the southerners had to acknowledge their defeat openly in a formal, substantive manner. The commissioners agreed to conduct a simple ceremony on April 12. The Union commissioners appointed Brig. Gen. Joshua L. Chamberlain to receive the surrender from the Confederates as they passed his reviewing stand.[83]

Chamberlain lined both sides of the Lynchburg Pike with two Union brigades that the Confederates had to pass on their way to the point where arms would be stacked. The southern column moved out from its bivouac site, crossed the river, and advanced up the pike to the parade ground. The troops marched in dignified order with neatly dressed formations; the army's old march discipline was evident even in its last movement. The men still projected a sense of order despite their tattered, emaciated appearance. Chamberlain observed the red battle flags flapping above the formations "crowded so thick by the thinning out of men that the whole column seemed crowned with red."[84] Of course, one regiment marched under a bare staff covered by its silk shroud. At the head of the column rode Maj. Gen. John B. Gordon, tall and erect in the saddle but with downcast countenance. The soldiers of the Army of Northern Virginia marched behind him to the surrender with dejected expressions, struggling to endure one final humiliation.

Chamberlain watched the solemn formation approach. He had decided, on his own initiative, to add a final gesture of respect to the simple ceremony. As Gordon came abreast of the Union brigades, Chamberlain motioned to his men.

> Our bugle sounds the signal and instantly our whole line from right to left, regiment by regiment in succession, gives the soldier's salutation, from the "order arms" to the old "carry" — the marching salute. Gordon at the head of the column, riding with heavy spirit and downcast face, catches the sound of shifting arms, looks up, and taking the meaning, wheels superbly, making himself and his horse one uplifted figure, with profound salutation as he drops the point of his sword to the boot toe; then facing to his own command, gives word for his successive brigades to pass us with the same position of the manual, honor answering honor. On our part not a sound of trumpet more, nor the roll of drum,

not a cheer, nor word nor whisper of vain-glorying, nor motion of men standing again at the order, but an awed stillness rather, and breath-holding, as if it were the passing of the dead![85]

When they reached the honor guard, the 11th N.C. came to carry arms and marched silently past the Union troops. The men stopped at the designated point, quietly stacked their arms and the bare flagstaff, and then marched off. Once clear of the parade ground, William Martin dismissed the formation and released the men to go their separate ways. The next several days would call for a long mournful walk to Morganton, Bertie County, Charlotte, or Chapel Hill for the veterans of the Bethel Regiment. They had been a strong, disciplined body of soldiers; now they were only a collection of lonely men heading home. "The gallant regiment ceased to exist. Different parties took different routes to their desolate homes, and we bade each other a sad, in many cases a tearful, farewell."[86]

Epilogue

Spring 1867, Chapel Hill, N.C.

A palpable tension swept across the University of North Carolina campus, stirred by rumors of a student demonstration. Several underclassmen, some of whom were Confederate veterans and others southern patriots, had decided to protest publicly the recent Reconstruction Acts passed by Congress and imposed on the state by the military government. Relations between the university and the military government were already strained by the defiant attitude of the collegians whom many considered to be reactionary and aristocratic. For their part, the small, tightly knit student body felt bitter over the military occupation of the state and the loss of their cherished "southern rights." The creation of a Republican Party in North Carolina under William Woods Holden and the activities of the Union League in organizing Negro voters thoroughly alarmed the young college men. The Old North State stood on the brink of political and social upheaval. Members of one group of students could not let these "outrages to southern honor" continue unopposed, so they chose to defy the authorities by proclaiming their undying allegiance to the Confederate cause.

As students and faculty started for their classes on the spring morning, they were greeted by a large Confederate flag hanging unabashedly from the garret window of the South Building. The brazen protest quickly drew a crowd of sympathizers who began chanting and shouting loudly. Some of the faculty hurried over to quell the potentially embarrassing disturbance. The university president, D. L. Swain, asked the students to remove the flag before the military regime heard about the protest, but the rebellious students shouted him down. They ignored his plea not to draw down the wrath of the "powers that be."

Finally, Prof. William J. Martin approached the throng, determined to end the incident. The popular chemistry professor had sworn an oath of allegiance to the federal government at Appomattox, and he would not be part of any demonstration that undermined his sacred oath. Martin ordered one of the underclassmen to remove the flag. Before the young man could make a move, the others threatened to "demolish" him if he tried. Professor Martin then stated, "I'll take it down myself." The students quickly barred his way and told him they would not let him touch the flag. Martin stared down the defiant students and calmly explained, "Young men, I fought four years for that flag, and I carry evidences of the fact on my person, in the scars of wounds scarcely healed. I think you might trust me to say whether any good purpose is served by this crazy demonstration. . . . I say it must come down, and that at once."

The moral force of Martin's manner, military service, and personal suffering overwhelmed the obdurate students. How could they defy someone who had served the cause with such courage and distinction? Sheepishly, they pulled down the flag, and calm returned to the campus, though feelings of animosity toward the authorities remained.[1]

Sadly, the efforts of Martin, other faculty members, and the university president could not save the University of North Carolina. The next year, the state elected a new governor, W. W. Holden, under a new constitution approved by the military governor. Governor Holden cleaned out the incumbent university trustees and denied funding for the troublesome campus; the university soon closed its doors. Anticipating the closure, Professor Martin had previously resigned from the university's faculty and had left Chapel Hill in search of new employment. He accepted a position at Davidson College, D. H. Hill's former school, where he became its most popular professor. Eventually,

Martin rose to the presidency of the college and presided over its growth in size and stature as an institution. The widely admired educator died in 1896.

Daniel Harvey Hill took an entirely different view of Reconstruction than William Martin. After the war, he applied his energies to reviving southern literature and the memories of the Lost Cause, as editor of *The Land We Love* and *The Southern Home*. His strident expressions and recalcitrant themes helped pave the way for a Conservative resurgence across North Carolina in 1876. In all of his time as editor, Hill never repudiated the Confederate cause nor resolved his hatred of the Yankees. D. H. Hill resumed his career as an educator after 1877, first as president of Arkansas Industrial University (now the University of Arkansas) and later as President of Middle Georgia Military and Agricultural College at Milledgeville. He succumbed to cancer in 1889, after a full and productive career that earned the lasting respect of friends and foes.[2]

Collett Leventhorpe, the English giant, never lost his fondness for the ideal of a southern gentry. He opposed the social changes sweeping over North Carolina and secretly sympathized with the Ku Klux Klan. Leventhorpe did not actively obstruct the new sociopolitical order; rather, he preoccupied himself with several business ventures, undoubtedly supported by his family's financial holdings in the old country. He moved to New York briefly to manage a shipping firm and then returned to Rutherfordton, North Carolina, to oversee a mining operation. Leventhorpe's real interests, however, lay outside the business world. He ran for the office of state auditor in 1871 but lost to a "carpetbagger." His chances for popular election may have suffered from his reputation as an enforcer of conscription while he commanded the state's home guard in 1864. Throughout the years, he published poetry, collected art, traveled extensively, and, apparently, neglected his businesses. His fortune appears to have dwindled by the mid-1880s, when he moved in with his sister-in-law on her Caldwell County estate. Nevertheless, he had led a dramatic and fruitful life by the time he died in 1889.[3]

The number of surviving Bethel soldiers also dwindled after the Reconstruction years. The veterans would occasionally gather at local Confederate reunions where they could greet one another, chat about their livelihoods, and complain about the scurrilous histories, written by Virginians, demeaning their assault on Cemetery Ridge. As the years passed, North Carolina veterans became concerned about the loss of the history of their once proud regiments. William Martin tried to preserve some of the Bethel Regiment's story by publishing an article in the Southern Historical Society Papers before he died. Edward R. Outlaw, the captain who tore out part of the Bethel flag, embellished this brief history when Walter Clark asked for contributions to a monumental history of every regiment mustered by North Carolina. Outlaw was the obvious choice for the task. He held onto his precious memories of the Bethel Regiment with the same ardor he had demonstrated on the battlefield. He still treasured and preserved his remnant of the regimental flag, which he loaned to the state's Museum of History in 1920, so that it could be displayed to younger generations. When Outlaw died in 1921, the museum returned the flag to his family who, presumably, buried it with him.

The last remnant of the Bethel flag may have been interred with Edward Outlaw but not the "colors" of the Bethel Regiment. In 1877, the state legislature departed from the old discredited militia system and created the North Carolina State Guard. Two regiments of the new State Guard were formed around nineteen companies of volunteer citizen-soldiers; over half were separately enrolled black units. The newly organized regiments marched in their inaugural parade before Gov. Zebulon B. Vance at the state fair grounds where D. H. Hill had drilled their predecessors in 1861. The volunteer companies of the 2d Regiment included such distinguished units as the Fayetteville Independent Light Infantry, Lafayette Light Infantry, Hornets Nest Riflemen, and the Charlotte Greys. Because of their linkage to the companies of the Bethel Regiment, the army conferred the lineage and battle honors of the old regiment upon the North Carolina State Guard's 2d Regiment of Infantry. This unit evolved into the combat battalions of the North Carolina National Guard and carried its fighting traditions into the twentieth century. Battle streamers with the names of Ypres–Lys, Bellicourt, Flanders, Normandy, Mortain, Duffescheide, Ardennes, and Stoumont grace the regimental flags alongside the blue-gray streamers of Appomattox, Petersburg, Wilderness, Gettysburg, and Bethel.

Notes

LIST OF ABBREVIATIONS

DU	Duke University
NA	National Archives
NCDAH	North Carolina Department of Archives and History
NCT	North Carolina Troops
OR	War of the Rebellion: A Compilation of the Official Records of the Union and Confederate Armies
SHC	Southern Historical Collection, University of North Carolina
SHSP	Southern Historical Society Papers
UNC	University of North Carolina
VHS	Virginia Historical Society

CHAPTER ONE

SECESSION

1. W. Buck Yearns and John G. Barrett, eds., *North Carolina Civil War Documentary* (Chapel Hill: UNC Press, 1980), 5–6.
2. Daniel W. Crofts, *Reluctant Confederates: Upper South Unionists in the Secession Crisis* (Chapel Hill: UNC Press, 1989), 60; William C. Harris, *North Carolina and the Coming of the Civil War* (Raleigh: NCDAH, 1988), 23.
3. Joseph Carlyle Sitterson, *The Secession Movement in North Carolina* (Chapel Hill: UNC Press, 1939), 150.
4. James C. MacRae, "Address Delivered by Major James C. MacRae to the Fayetteville Independent Light Infantry Company, on the Occasion of Its 81st Anniversary," *Our Living and Our Dead* 1 (Sept. 1874): 33–4.
5. Emily Semple Austin, "History of the Edgecombe Guards During the War Between the States," Joyner Library, East Carolina University.

6. Hal Bridges, *Lee's Maverick General: Daniel Harvey Hill* (New York: McGraw-Hill, 1961), 20–1, 27; Douglas Southall Freeman, *Lee's Lieutenants* (New York: Charles Scribner's Sons, 1944), 1:20–1.

7. Crofts, *Reluctant Confederates,* 147–8; Marc Wayne Kruman, "Parties and Politics in North Carolina 1846–1865," (Thesis, Yale University, 1978), 223.

8. *Hillsborough Recorder,* 1 January 1861; Yearns and Barrett, *Documentary,* 9, 13.

9. Richard W. Iobst, "North Carolina Mobilizes: Nine Crucial Months December 1860–August 1861" (Thesis, University of North Carolina, 1968), 17–43; William S. Powell, *North Carolina Through Four Centuries* (Chapel Hill: UNC Press, 1989), 346–7.

10. Iobst, "North Carolina Mobilizes," 143. Quoted from the *Wilmington Journal;* MacRae, "Fayetteville Independent Light Infantry," *Our Living and Our Dead* 1: 34; Harold Scott Painter, "The Edgecombe Guards," Edgecombe Community College, Tarboro, N.C., 4–6.

11. S. A. Ashe, *History of North Carolina* (Raleigh: Edwards & Broughton Co., 1925), 558–9.

12. Henry Gilliam Parker, "The History of a Confederate Casualty," VHS, Richmond, Virginia, 7; Crofts, *Reluctant Confederates,* 180–1.

13. Walter Waightstill Lenoir to Vance, February 5, 1861, *The Papers of Zebulon Baird Vance,* ed. Frontis W. Johnston (Raleigh: NCDAH, 1963), 1:97; Ashe, *History of North Carolina,* 573.

14. Crofts, *Reluctant Confederates,* 341; Sitterson, *Secession in North Carolina,* 241; *Hillsborough Recorder,* 8 May 1861. Quoted from the *North Carolina Standard.*

15. U.S. War Department, *War of the Rebellion: A Compilation of the Official Records of the Union and Confederate Armies* (Washington, D.C.: GPO, 1880–1901), 1:486 (hereafter cited as OR).

16. Austin, "Edgecombe Guards," ECU; Manly Wade Wellman, *Rebel Boast: First at Bethel—Last at Appomattox* (New York: Henry Holt & Co., 1956), 28; William R. Trotter, *Ironclads and Columbiads: The Civil War in North Carolina: The Coast* (Winston-Salem, N.C.: John F. Blair, 1989), 10; Louis Leon, *Diary of a Tar Heel Confederate Soldier* (Charlotte, N.C.: Stone Publishing Co., 1913), 1; Sarah Parks Bryan, "Taking of the Fayetteville Arsenal," Military Collection, NCDAH, Raleigh, N.C.; OR, 1:480.

17. Iobst, "North Carolina Mobilizes," 63–4. Quoted from the *Wilmington Daily Herald;* Walter Clark, *Histories of the Several Regiments and Battalions from North Carolina in the Great War 1861–'65* (Goldsboro, N.C.: Nash Brothers, 1901), 1:74 (hereafter cited as Clark); "The First North Carolina Volunteers and the Battle of Bethel," *Southern Historical Society Papers* (herafter cited as SHSP) 19 (1891): 221; J. Lewis Warlick Letter June 12, 1861, Cornelia McGimsey Papers, SHC, University of North Carolina, Chapel Hill, N.C. (hereafter cited as Warlick Letters); Egbert Ross Letter May 13, 1861, Egbert A. Ross Letters, SHC (hereafter cited as Ross Letters).

18. SHSP, 19:212–3.

19. OR, 1:486–7.

20. Clark, 1:130–1; F. A. Sondley, *A History of Buncombe County North Carolina* (Spartanburg, S.C.: The Reprint Co., 1977), 814; *North Carolina Whig,* 30 April 1861; Sitterson, *Secession in North Carolina,* 242. Quoted from Frank Parker Papers, NCDAH; Leon, *Diary of a Tar Heel,* 1.

21. Leon, *Diary of a Tar Heel*, 1; Iobst, "North Carolina Mobilizes," 237. Quoted from *Raleigh State Journal;* John T. Jones Letter, May 8, 1861, Edmund Walter Jones Papers, SHC, (hereafter cited as Jones Letters).

22. Warlick Letters, May 12, 1861; Wellman, *Rebel Boast,* 37; Ross Letters, May 13, 1861.

23. Warlick Letters, May 12 and 29, 1861; Iobst, "North Carolina Mobilizes," 237. Quoted from George Wills Papers, SHC, Letter dated April 30, 1861; *North Carolina Whig,* 7 May 1861.

24. Iobst, "North Carolina Mobilizes," 344. Quoted from *Raleigh State Journal.*

25. Iobst, "North Carolina Mobilizes," 98–101.

26. SHSP, 19:214–7.

27. Clark, 1:131–3; SHSP, 19:221.

28. Wellman, *Rebel Boast,* 26–7; Edward William Phifer, Jr., *Burke: The History of a North Carolina County, 1777–1920* (Morganton, N.C.: N.p., 1977), 77, 319–21.

29. D. H. Hill, Jr., *Confederate Military History: North Carolina* (Atlanta: Confederate Publishing Co., 1899), 8–9; D. H. Hill, Jr., *Bethel to Sharpsburg* (Raleigh: Edwards & Broughton Co., 1926), 44.

30. MacRae, "Fayetteville Independent Light Infantry," *Our Living and Our Dead* 1:35–6.

31. SHSP, 19:218. Quoted from the *Western Democrat.*

BETHEL

32. SHSP, 19:218–9; Warlick Letters, May 23, 1861.

33. SHSP, 19:219–20. Quoted from the *Western Democrat.*

34. Leon, *Diary of a Tar Heel,* 2.

35. Warlick Letters, May 29, 1861; Wellman, *Rebel Boast,* 47–8; Clark, 1:83.

36. Clark, 1:83; Wellman, *Rebel Boast,* 49; Bridges, *Maverick General,* 28.

37. OR, 2:93.

38. *North Carolina Whig,* 18 June 1861. Quoted from the *Richmond Dispatch;* OR, 2:94.

39. OR, 2:77–8.

40. OR, 2:86, 2:79.

41. OR, 2:84.

42. Warlick Letters, June 11, 1861; Benjamin Huske, "Account of the Battle of Bethel," Military Collection, NCDAH; Clark, 1:86; *North Carolina Whig,* 29 September 1861; OR, 1:91.

43. SHSP, 19:232; Elam B. Bristol Letter, July 6, 1861, Bristol Letters, Burke County Public Library, Morganton, N.C.; OR, 2:94–5; Clark, 1:90–1; "Battle of Bethel," SHSP 29 (1901): 198.

44. Henry Lawson Wyatt Sketch, Military Collection, NCDAH; OR, 2:84, 89; Gouverneur Warren to Butler, June 15, 1861, *Private and Official Correspondence of Gen. Benjamin F. Butler During the Period of the Civil War* (Norwood, Mass.: N.p., 1917), 1:144–5.

45. SHSP, 19:224; Clark, 1:90; Benjamin Huske, "Account of Bethel," NCDAH.

46. Bridges, *Maverick General,* 29.

47. OR, 2:89, 103; Clark, 1:93; D. H. Hill, *Bethel to Sharpsburg,* 52; Henry E. Benton Letter, June 1861, Private Collection, NCDAH; OR, 2:87.

48. SHSP, 29:199; OR 2:90–1, 94.

49. *Hillsborough Recorder,* 19 June 1861. Quoted from the *Richmond Examiner;* OR, 2:90–5.
50. OR, 2:87.
51. Clark, 1:101.
52. OR, 2:94–5; Benjamin Huske, "Account of Bethel," NCDAH.
53. SHSP, 19:225; OR, 2:88, 95.
54. Charles F. Johnson, *The Long Roll: One of the Hawkins Zouaves* (N.p., N.d.), 23; Warren to Butler, June 15, 1861, *Butler Correspondence,* 1:145–6.
55. SHSP, 19:225; Benjamin Huske, "Account of Bethel," NCDAH.
56. OR, 2:91–2.
57. Warlick Letters, June 11, 1861; Ross Letters, June 20, 1861; Benjamin Huske, "Account of Bethel." NCDAH.
58. OR, 2:82.
59. SHSP, 19:222–3, 229–30; 29:198. Magruder's initial estimate of 3,500 Union troops at Bethel did not include the two reinforcing regiments.
60. OR, 2:92. Wyatt was the first Confederate soldier killed in a battle but not the first one killed in action. Nine days before Bethel a Union cavalry reconnaissance ran into Confederate cavalry pickets at Fairfax Court House, Virginia. Captain John Q. Marr of the Virginia cavalry was killed during the ensuing exchange.

YORKTOWN

61. Jones Letters, June 12, 1861; Warlick Letters, June 23, 1861.
62. Wellman, *Rebel Boast* 61–2; Warlick Letters, June 23, 1861; Louis Manarin and Weymouth T. Jordan, comp., *North Carolina Troops 1861–65* (hereafter cited as Manarin and Jordan), vol. 3 (Raleigh: NCDAH, 1971), 57–62.
63. SHSP, 19:241; MacRae, "Fayetteville Independent Light Infantry," *Our Living and Our Dead* 1:36; *North Carolina Whig,* 30 July and 20 August 1861.
64. Warlick Letters, June 16 and August 3, 1861; Leon, *Diary of a Tar Heel,* 3; Ross Letters, August 8, 1861.
65. Iobst, "North Carolina Mobilizes," 329, 340–1.
66. Ross Letters, June 25, 1861; Warlick Letters, August 31, 1861; Wellman, *Rebel Boast,* 66.
67. Warlick Letters, August 3, 1861; Ross Letters, August 8, 1861; J. M. Cutchins, Reminiscences, Military Collection, NCDAH; Manarin and Jordan, 3:1–64.
68. Ross Letters, August 8, 1861; Warlick Letters, August 31, 1861; Henry Huske Letter, September 1, 1861, Private Collection, NCDAH.
69. Henry Huske Letter, September 1, 1861, NCDAH; Warlick Letters, August 31, 1861.
70. Archie Davis, *Boy Colonel of the Confederacy: The Life and Times of Henry King Burgwyn, Jr.* (Chapel Hill: UNC Press, 1987) 76–7.
71. Warlick Letter, September 11, 1861.
72. SHSP, 19:240; *North Carolina Whig,* 24 September 1861.
73. *North Carolina Whig,* 24 September 1861.
74. SHSP, 19:245–6.
75. Ibid.
76. Warlick Letters, October 7, 1861.
77. Clark, 1:117–21.

CHAPTER TWO

WILMINGTON

1. Ashe, *History of North Carolina,* 735; Parker, "Confederate Casualty," VHS, 8–9.
2. Ashe, *History of North Carolina,* 691–2; Clark, 1:9.
3. Manarin and Jordan, NCT, 5:91; Bell I. Wiley, *The Life of Johnny Reb: The Common Soldier of the Confederacy* (Indianapolis: Bobbs-Merrill, 1943), 336.
4. Warlick Letters, June 3, 1862.
5. Collett Leventhorpe Collection, Special Collections Library, DU (see also Clark, 1:132–3); William J. Martin and E. R. Outlaw, "Eleventh Regiment," in *Histories of the Several Regiments and Battalions from North Carolina in the Great War, 1861–'65,* 1:583–6 (hereafter cited as Martin).
6. Leventhorpe Scrapbook, Private Collection, NCDAH; Kemp P. Battle, *History of the University of North Carolina* (Spartanburg, S.C.: The Reprint Co., 1974), 763.
7. Martin, 586–7.
8. Leventhorpe Collection, DU; Compiled Service Records, 11th Regiment NCT, NA; Leventhorpe Collection, DU.
9. Leventhorpe Collection, DU.
10. Collett Leventhorpe Letter, May 6, 1862, Military Collection, NCDAH (hereafter cited as Leventhorpe Letters); Martin, 586.
11. Leventhorpe Collection, DU.
12. Martin, 586; Francis W. Bird Letter, May 26, 1862, Robert Watson Winston Papers, SHC (hereafter cited as Bird Letters); Leventhorpe Collection, DU.
13. W. H. Neave Letter, April 21, 1863, The Regiment Band of the 11th North Carolina Troops, Inc., Fayetteville, N.C.
14. Clark, 1:11–13; Bird Letters, June 16 and September 17, 1862.
15. Warlick Letters, June 17 and 24, 1862.
16. Kruman, "Parties and Politics," 273–4.
17. Neave Letters, August 29, 1862; Ross Letters, July 5, 1862.
18. James Sprunt, *Chronicles of the Cape Fear River 1660–1916* (Raleigh: Edwards & Broughton Co., 1916), 284; Warlick Letters, August 17, 1862.
19. Warlick Letters, July 26, 1862; Manarin and Jordan NCT, 5:6–105.
20. Leventhorpe Letters, (eighth page of manuscript); Warlick Letters, September 20, 1862; Sprunt, *Cape Fear River,* 284–5; Warlick Letters, September 20, 1862.

WHITE HALL

21. Bird Letters, October 28, 1862; Martin, 587.
22. Elam Bristol Letter, November 23, 1862, Bristol Letters, Burke County Public Library; Leventhorpe Letters, November 22, 1862.
23. Warlick Letters, November 19, 1862.
24. Leventhorpe Letters, November 22 and December 1862; OR, 18:144–5.
25. Robert M. Browning, Jr., *From Cape Charles to Cape Fear* (Tuscaloosa: University of Alabama Press, 1993), 91; Trotter, *Ironclads,* 175.
26. OR, 18:106–7.
27. Collett Leventhorpe to Marcus Wright May 30, 1888, Marcus Wright Papers, Special Collections Library, DU.
28. OR, 18:56, 18:113.

29. John C. Warlick, "Battle of White Hall, N.C.," *Confederate Veteran* 12 (January 1904):178; W. W. Howe, *Kinston, Whitehall and Goldsboro* (New York: W. W. Howe, 1890) 25–6; Charles H. Woodwell, "Journal of a Private Soldier," Manuscript Division, Library of Congress, 34–5; Trotter, *Ironclads,* 184; OR, 18:121; Bird Letters, December 23, 1862.
30. Clark, 5:87–8; Howe, *Kinston, Whitehall and Goldsboro,* 28; OR, 18:57.
31. OR, 18:121–2; John C. Warlick, "White Hall," *Confederate Veteran* 12:178.
32. OR, 18:61–2, 122.
33. Leventhorpe to Marcus Wright, DU; OR, 18:122.
34. Warlick Letters, December 30, 1862.
35. OR, 18:57, 122; Leventhorpe to Marcus Wright, DU; Martin, 1:587–8.
36. OR, 18:110; Archie K. Davis, *Boy Colonel,* 221.

SIEGE OF WASHINGTON, N.C.
37. Warlick Letters, December 30, 1862.
38. Collett Leventhorpe to Mary Pettigrew, May 14, 1867, Private Collection, Pettigrew Papers 13:18, NCDAH; Leventhorpe Letters, June 9, 1862; Clyde N. Wilson, *Carolina Cavalier: The Life and Mind of James Johnston Pettigrew* (Athens: University of Georgia, 1990), 158–9, 203; Archie K. Davis, *Boy Colonel,* 191.
39. Warlick Letters, December 30, 1862; William G. Parker Letter, January 4, 1863, Private Collection, NCDAH (hereafter cited as Parker Letters).
40. Leventhorpe Letters, January 14, 1863.
41. Robert M. Browning, Jr., "The Blockade of Wilmington, North Carolina" (Thesis, East Carolina University, 1980), 109–10; Browning, *From Cape Charles,* 92.
42. Leventhorpe Letters, January 18, 20, February 2, 1863.
43. Warlick Letters, January 25, 1863; Parker Letters, February 11, 1863.
44. Parker Letters, February 22, 1863.
45. Leventhorpe Letters, February 22, 1863; OR, 51:Pt. 2:830–3; North Carolina Literary and Historical Society, *Five Points in the Record of North Carolina in the Great War of 1861–5* (Goldsboro, N.C.: Nash Brothers, 1904), 10.
46. OR, 18:907.
47. Randolph Abbott Shotwell, *The Papers of Randolph Abbott Shotwell,* ed. J. G. de Roulhac Hamilton (Raleigh: North Carolina Historical Commission, 1929), 1:455–7.
48. Parker Letters, March 24, 1863; Shotwell, *Shotwell Papers,* 1:458–9.
49. Archie K. Davis, *Boy Colonel,* 252; Leventhorpe Letters, April 2, 1863.
50. OR, 18:244, 247.
51. OR, 18:245.
52. Leventhorpe Letters, April 10, 1863.
53. Mrs. Archbell, "Battle of Blount's Creek Mill," Military Collection, NCDAH; OR, 18:246; Manarin and Jordan NCT, 5:97; OR, 18:246.
54. Trotter, *Ironclads,* 200–1.
55. OR, 18:246; Leventhorpe Letters, April 10, 1863.
56. Trotter, *Ironclads,* 201–2.
57. Warlick Letters, April 26, 1863; Wilson, *Carolina Cavalier,* 186; Archie K. Davis, *Boy Colonel,* 256.
58. Proclamation of North Carolina Department, Leventhorpe Collection, DU.
59. Warlick Letters, June 3, 1862.

60. Parker Letters, April 19, 1863.
61. Parker Letters, April 20, 1863; Warlick Letters, April 26, 1863.

CHAPTER THREE

GENERAL LEE'S ARMY

1. Archie K. Davis, *Boy Colonel,* 258–62; Parker Letters, May 4, 1863.
2. Jacob S. Bartlett, Reminiscences, SHC (hereafter cited as Bartlett Reminiscences); Parker Letters, May 4 and May 6, 1863.
3. Parker Letters, May 24 and May 29, 1863; Bird Letters, May 16, 1863.
4. Leventhorpe Letters, May 28, 1863; Parker Letters, June 17, 1863.
5. Clifford Dowdey, *Death of a Nation: The Story of Lee and His Men at Gettysburg* (New York: Alfred A. Knopf, 1958), 31, 34–5; Leventhorpe Letters, June 4, 1863.
6. Parker Letters, June 11, 1863.
7. Parker Letters, June 15 and June 17, 1863; Archie K. Davis, *Boy Colonel,* 270–1.
8. Archie K. Davis, *Boy Colonel,* 272.
9. Manarin and Jordan, vol. 5.
10. Collett Leventhorpe, Compiled Service Record, 11th NCT, NA; G. J. Fiebeger, *The Campaign and Battle of Gettysburg* (West Point: Military Academy Printing Office, 1915), 40.
11. Lt. William B. Taylor Letter, June 22, 1863, William B. Floyd Papers, Gettysburg National Military Park (hereafter cited as Taylor Letters).
12. Jacob Hoke, *The Great Invasion* (reprint, New York: Thomas Yoseloff, 1959), 160; Leventhorpe to Pettigrew, May 14, 1867, Pettigrew Papers, NCDAH.

McPHERSON'S RIDGE

13. Randolph A. Shotwell, "Virginia and North Carolina in the Battle of Gettysburg," *Our Living and Our Dead* 4 (March, 1876): 82; Glenn Tucker, *High Tide at Gettysburg* (Indianapolis: Bobbs-Merrill, 1973), 98–9; Clark, 5:115.
14. Shotwell, "Virginia and North Carolina," *Our Living and Our Dead* 4: 92.
15. SHSP, 4:157; Clark, 5:115–7.
16. Archie K. Davis, *Boy Colonel,* 308–9.
17. Warren W. Hassler, Jr., *Crisis at the Crossroads: The First Day at Gettysburg* (reprint, Gettysburg, Pa.: Stan Clark Military Books, 1970), 52.
18. Freeman, *Lee's Lieutenants,* 3:81.
19. OR, 27:Pt. 1:244.
20. Leventhorpe to Pettigrew, May 14, 1867, Pettigrew Papers, NCDAH.
21. Henry Heth to William Jones, June 1877, "Causes of Lee's Defeat at Gettysburg," SHSP 4 (1877): 158.
22. OR, 27:Pt. 1:268; Leventhorpe to Pettigrew, May 14, 1867, Pettigrew Papers, NCDAH.
23. OR, 27:Pt. 1:643; Leventhorpe Letters, Address by Edmund Jones, 28; John W. Busey and David G. Martin, *Regimental Strengths and Losses at Gettysburg* (Hightstown, New York: Longstreet House, 1986), 174; Louis G. Young, Account of Gettysburg, F. D. Winston Papers, Private Collection, NCDAH (hereafter cited as Young, Account of Gettysburg). Busey and Martin calculate a figure of 617, which includes 575 enlisted men engaged, based on the regimental muster of June 30th and some assumed figures for soldiers not present for duty that day.

Lt. Young quotes a figure of 550 men engaged. This figure does not include officers and staff enlisted men, which would add another 43 soldiers to the count.

24. Clark, 3:56–8; OR, 27:Pt. 1:268.

25. Taylor Letters, July 29, 1863.

26. OR, 27:Pt. 1:327; Pt. 2:638; Young, Account of Gettysburg.

27. Clark, footnote 5:119.

28. OR, 27:Pt. 1:173–4, 269; Young, Account of Gettysburg.

29. Taylor Letters, July 29, 1863; Young, Account of Gettysburg; Manarin and Jordan, vol. 5. Lt. Young puts the regiment's loss at 250. This figure cannot be firmly established but appears to be within reason. See also, Busey and Martin for total casualties during the entire battle; Parker, Confederate Casualty, VHS, 14.

CEMETERY RIDGE

30. Julius Lineback, Diary, SHC.

31. William Garrett Piston, "Cross Purposes," *The Third Day of Gettysburg & Beyond,* comp. Gary Gallagher (Chapel Hill: UNC Press, 1994), 31–55.

32. B. D. Fry, "Pettigrew's Charge at Gettysburg," SHSP 7 (1879): 92.

33. Edward Porter Alexander, *Fighting for the Confederacy,* ed. Gary Gallagher (Chapel Hill: UNC Press, 1989), 251–2.

34. *North Carolina Whig,* 19 November 1861.

35. OR, 27:Pt. 1:237–40; Fairfax Downey, *The Guns at Gettysburg* (New York: Collier Books, 1962).

36. Young, Account of Gettysburg; Clark, 5:124; Taylor Letters, July 29, 1863.

37. Robert Johnson and Clarence Buel, *Battles and Leaders of the Civil War* (reprint, New York: Thomas Yoseloff, 1956) 3:355. Quoted from the March 1887 issue of *Southern Bivouac.* Estimates of the strength of the three divisions in the attack vary widely. Missing and imprecise beginning strength figures coupled with crude casualty estimates for the first two days of the battle make it impossible to arrive at an accurate figure. Based on the estimates of casualties and Busey and Martin's landmark study, I believe the 12,500 figure is a reasonable estimate.

38. Shotwell, "Virginia and North Carolina," *Our Living and Our Dead* (March 1876) 4:89; Robert L. Bee, "Ben Hirst's Narrative," *Third Day at Gettysburg,* 140; SHSP, 7:92.

39. Downey, *Guns at Gettysburg,* 160–2; OR, 27:Pt. 1:476.

40. John W. Moore, *History of North Carolina* (Raleigh, Alfred Williams & Co., 1880), 2:205. Quoted from a letter by Isaac Trimble. Taylor Letters, July 29, 1863.

41. Shotwell, "Virginia and North Carolina," *Our Living and Our Dead* 4:91; George R. Stewart, *Pickett's Charge* (Boston: Houghton Mifflin, 1959), 183.

42. Wilson, *Carolina Cavalier,* 197; Stewart, *Pickett's Charge,* 172; Moore, *North Carolina,* 216. Quoted from a letter by John T. Jones dated July 30, 1863.

43. SHSP, 7:93.

44. Johnson and Buel, *Battles and Leaders,* 3:392.

45. Young, Account of Gettysburg; Bruce Catton, *Gettysburg: The Final Fury* (Garden City, New York: Doubleday, 1974), 88.

46. OR, 27:Pt. 1:465, 467; Bee, "Ben Hirst Narrative," *Third Day at Gettysburg,* 142; John Purifoy, "Confederate Assault at Gettysburg, July 3," *Confederate Veteran* 32 (1925): 227–8; Moore, *North Carolina,* 207. Quoted from a letter by Joseph H. Saunders dated September, 22, 1877; James H. Lane, "History of

Lane's North Carolina Brigade," SHSP 9 (1881): 33. Quoted from a letter by Isaac Trimble dated October 15, 1875.

47. Stewart, *Pickett's Charge,* 225–6; H. S. Stevens, Papers, Private Collection, NCDAH; North Carolina Literary and Historical Society, *Five Points,* 32. Quoted from the February 1886 issue of *Southern Bivouac.*

48. OR, 27:Pt. 1:373; SHSP, 7:93, 9:35; Clark, 5:108; Wilson, *Carolina Cavalier,* 197.

49. Moore, *North Carolina,* 225. Quoted from a letter by A. S. Haynes dated October 8, 1877; Bird Letters, undated; P. H. Winston, Jr. to Francis W. Bird August 6, 1863, Robert W. Winston Papers, SHC. Quoted from a newspaper article; Clark, 1:590; Moore, *North Carolina,* 216. Quoted from a letter by John T. Jones dated July 20, 1863; SHSP, 9:35; Shotwell, "Virginia and North Carolina," *Our Living and Our Dead,* 4:94.

50. Moore, *North Carolina,* 224. Quoted from A. S. Haynes letter; Manarin and Jordan, vol. 5.

51. Taylor Letters, July 29, 1863; Robert K. Krick, *The Gettysburg Death Roster* (Dayton, Ohio: Morningside Bookshop, 1985), 40; Busey and Martin, *Regimental Strengths,* 299; Leventhorpe to Marcus Wright, DU.

52. Stewart, *Pickett's Charge,* 257; Purifoy, "Confederate Assault," *Confederate Veteran,* 32:229; Stewart, *Pickett's Charge,* 252–3.

FALLING WATERS

53. Leventhorpe to Marcus Wright, DU; Leventhorpe Letters, 27; Compiled Service Records, 11th NCT, NA.

54. Henry Heth, *The Memoirs of Henry Heth,* ed. James L. Morrison (Westport, Conn.: Greenwood Press, 1974), 178; Louis G. Young to Joseph Englehard, 18 August 1874, "Death of Brigadier General J. Johnston Pettigrew, of North Carolina," *Our Living and Our Dead* 1 (Sept. 1874): 29–31; Jones Letters, July 17, 1863.

55. Young, "Death of Pettigrew," *Our Living and Our Dead* 1:30; Jones Letters, July 17, 1863.

56. Heth, Memoirs, 179; Young, "Death of Pettigrew," *Our Living and Our Dead* 1:31; Wilson, *Carolina Cavalier,* 202; Jones Letters, July 17, 1863.

57. OR, 27:Pt. 2:641; William Blount Letter August 2, 1863, Steed and Phipps Family Papers (hereafter cited as Blount Letters), SHC; Jones Letters, July 17, 1863.

58. Jones Letters, July 17, 1863; Blount Letters, August 2, 1863.

59. *North Carolina Standard,* 19 August 1863; Wilson, *Carolina Cavalier,* 203; Bird Letters, undated fragment.

60. Young, Account of Gettysburg.

61. Cutler Andrews, *The South Reports the Civil War* (Princeton: Princeton University Press, 1970), 313–4.

62. Frank A. Haskell, *Haskell of Gettysburg: His Life and Civil War Papers,* ed. Frank L. Byrne and Andrew T. Weaver (Madison: State Historical Society of Wisconsin, 1970), 165.

63. Moore, *North Carolina,* 217. Quoted from a letter by John T. Jones dated July 30, 1863; Taylor Letters, July 29, 1863; Bird Letters, August 6, 1863; Jones Letters, August 17, 1863; North Carolina Literary and Historical Society, *Five Points,* 21–33.

64. Clark, 5:110; Krick, *Death Roster*, 7, 14. There is no means of accurately separating the regiment's casualties suffered on July 1 and July 3. Manarin and Jordan, vol. 5, lists forty men killed on July 1 and twenty men on July 3. The records of the remaining forty-eight fatalities do not specify on which day the soldier was mortally wounded.

65. Walter H. Taylor, *Four Years with General Lee* (New York: D. Appleton & Co., 1878), 105–8; A. L. Long, *Memoirs of Robert E. Lee* (Secaucus, N.J.: Blue and Grey Press, 1983), 289–90.

BRISTOE STATION

66. Leventhorpe later served as the commanding general of the state's Home Guard. Toward the end of the war, the Confederate government gave him a brigadier general's commission.

67. Memorial Number, *The Davidson Monthly*, April 1896, 263; Paul B. Means, Personal Sketch of William J. Martin April 24, 1905, William J. Martin Family Papers, Davidson College.

68. Martin, 590–1; Francis W. Bird, Compiled Service Records, 11th NCT, NA.

69. Bird Letters, July 30, 1863; Manarin and Jordan, vol. 5.

70. Bartlett Reminiscences; Taylor Letters, July 29, 1863; Duncan Waddell, Compiled Service Records, 11th NCT, NA; Warlick Letters.

71. Ashe, *History of North Carolina*, 858; Benjamin W. Justice Letters August 16, 1863, Emory University (hereafter cited as Justice Letters).

72. Ashe, *History of North Carolina*, 835–7; Kruman, "Parties and Politics," 297–9; Ashe, *History of North Carolina*, 843; Jones Letters, August 17, 1863.

73. Justice Letters, September 14, 1863; William S. Long Reminiscences, Breckinridge Long Papers, Library of Congress, 1207 (hereafter identified as Long Reminiscences).

74. Long Reminiscences, 1207–9.

75. Long Reminiscences, 1210; Bird Letters, October 9, 1863.

76. Andrew A. Humphreys, *From Gettysburg to the Rapidan* (New York: Charles Scribner's Sons, 1883), 14–19.

77. Long Reminiscences, 1210–3.

78. Long Reminiscences, 1214.

79. OR, 29:Pt. 1:426, 430.

80. Long Reminiscences, 1215–17, 1233.

81. OR, 29:Pt. 1:426, 430–1; *North Carolina Standard,* 28 October 1863.

82. Long Reminiscences, 1219, 1233.

83. Bartlett Reminiscences.

84. Martin, 593; *Davidson Monthly,* April 1896, 262; Martin, 593.

85. Haskell, *Haskell of Gettysburg*, 218, 222. Quoted from a letter October 31, 1863; Long Reminiscences, 1224.

86. Bird Letters, October 15, 1863; OR, 29:Pt. 1:248, 433.

87. OR, 29:Pt. 1:432; Freeman, *Lee's Lieutenants,* 3:246; *North Carolina Standard,* 28 October 1863.

88. *North Carolina Standard,* 28 October 1863.

89. Long Reminiscences, 1230.

90. Heth, *Memoirs,* 180.

91. Bellfield King Letter, January 18, 1864, Willis King Papers, DU; John M. Tate Letters, April 10, 1864, John L. Brown Papers, SHC.

92. L. A. Bristol Letters, January 1864, Burke County Public Library.
93. W. J. Kincaid to Calvin Brown, December 7, 1863, William J. Martin Family Papers, Davidson College; Phifer, *Burke,* 321; Manarin and Jordan, 5:21; Manarin and Jordan, vol. 5.
94. Ashe, *History of North Carolina,* 879–80. Quoted from the *North Carolina Standard,* 3 March 1864; Kruman, "Parties and Politics," 311; S. A. Ashe, "North Carolina in the War Between the States," *Confederate Veteran,* 37 (1930): 173.
95. Ashe, *History of North Carolina,* 880–1; John M. Tate Letters April 10, 1864, John L. Brown Papers, SHC.
96. Warlick Letters, March 22, 1864.

CHAPTER FOUR

WILDERNESS

1. Gordon C. Rhea, *The Battle of the Wilderness* (Baton Rouge: Louisiana State University Press, 1994), 25.
2. Justice Letters, May 4, 1864. This letter was started on the 4th but finished after the battle. Rhea, *Wilderness,* 83–5; Henry Heth, Official Report December 7, 1864, Eleanor S. Brockenbrough Library, Museum of the Confederacy, Richmond, Va. (hereafter cited as Heth Report).
3. Rhea, *Wilderness,* 121; Edward Steere, *The Wilderness Campaign* (Harrisburg, Pa.: Stackpole, 1960), 115; Justice Letters, May 4, 1864; Heth Report.
4. Rhea, *Wilderness,* 117; Justice Letter, May 4, 1864; Heth Report; OR, 36:Pt. 1:676; Military Historical Society of Massachusetts, Papers, vol. 4, "The Wilderness Campaign" (Boston, 1905), 190.
5. Heth Report; The deployment of Kirkland's Brigade is not stated. The published histories of the 26th, 44th, and 52d N.C. in Clark give their positions, but the 11th and 47th do not. However, the statements by Martin in Clark 1:595 place the 11th N.C. behind the 15th N.C. of Cooke's Brigade on the south side of the Plank Road.
6. Heth, *Memoirs,* 182; OR, 36:Pt. 1:697, 709–10; Charles H. Richardson, Diary, Library of Congress; Heth Report.
7. OR, 36:Pt. 1:682, 697; Heth Report.
8. OR, 36:Pt. 1:697, 714; Heth Report.
9. Martin, 594–5; OR, 36:Pt. 1:697.
10. OR, 36:Pt. 1:677; Martin, 595.
11. OR, 36:Pt. 1:492, 498.
12. Steere, *Wilderness Campaign,* 217. Quoted from *Letters of Theodore Lyman from the Wilderness to Appomattox.*
13. Martin, 595.
14. Heth Report.
15. Clark, 3:75.
16. Heth Report; Heth, *Memoirs,* 184; James I. Robertson, Jr., *General A. P. Hill: The Story of a Confederate Warrior* (New York: Vintage Books, 1987), 260–1.
17. Martin, 595; Heth Report. The precise position for the Bethel Regiment is not stated. Colonel Martin's vivid description of the initial contact on May 6 suggests that the 11th N.C. was on the left flank of Kirkland's Brigade in the morning. Clark, 1:744, 2:446.

18. Heth, *Memoirs,* 184.
19. Martin, 595; Foster Reminiscences, Alfred and John A. Foster Papers, DU; Martin, 595.
20. Clark, 4:245, 4:563; D. H. Hill, Jr., *Confederate Military History,* 235; Clark, 2:382.
21. Steere, *Wilderness Campaign,* 332.
22. Heth, *Memoirs,* 185; Clark, 2:382.
23. Samual Finley Harper Letter, May 6, 1864, Private Collection, NCDAH.

SPOTSYLVANIA
24. Warlick Letters, May 19, 1864; Bartlett Reminiscences.
25. Robertson, *A. P. Hill,* 269.
26. William D. Matter, *If It Takes All Summer: The Battle of Spotsylvania* (Chapel Hill: UNC Press, 1988), 141.
27. Foster Diary, DU; Matter, *If It Takes All Summer,* 141; *Hillsborough Recorder,* 1 June 1864.
28. Foster Diary, DU; Matter, *If It Takes All Summer,* 144; OR, 36:Pt. 1:332; Heth, *Memoirs,* 188. Union commanders record three unsuccessful Confederate attacks; Confederate sources disagree. Heth states that the attack was not stopped at any point until it reached the river. Other Confederates say Heth's attack overran a series of enemy breastworks. Foster's Diary suggests that the Confederate attack moved forward in separate stages. Most likely, the two sides became confused by actions on the skirmish lines and temporary halts in the action. Opposing sides often misinterpreted the actions of the other. A. H. B., *The Land We Love* 4 (March 1869): 415.
29. Foster Diary, DU; Matter, *If It Takes All Summer,* 145–6.
30. Martin, 596; *Hillsborough Recorder,* 1 June 1864; OR, 36:Pt. 1:357.
31. Memorial Number, *Davidson Monthly,* April 1896, 242; Heth Report; OR, 36:Pt. 1:333, 409.
32. Clark, 2:384–5.
33. Foster Diary, DU; Heth, *Memoirs,* 185–6.
34. Heth, *Memoirs,* 186.
35. Heth, *Memoirs,* 187.
36. OR, 36:Pt. 1:928; Bird Letters, May 13, 1864.
37. Martin, 596.
38. Bird Letters, May 21, 1864; *Hillsborough Recorder,* 1 June 1864; Warlick Letters, May 19, 1864.
39. OR, 36:Pt. 1:1046; Warlick Letters, May 19, 1864.
40. Warlick Letters, May 19, 1864; Bird Letters, May 21, 1864.

TOTOPOTOMOY
41. Foster Diary, DU.
42. Noah Andre Trudeau, *Bloody Roads South* (Boston: Little, Brown & Co., 1989), 230–1.
43. Heth Report; Jed Hotchkiss, *Confederate Military History: Virginia,* vol. 3 (Atlanta: Confederate Publishing Co., 1899), 460.
44. Warlick Letters, May 25, 1864; OR, 36:Pt. 1:9.
45. Douglas Southall Freeman, *R. E. Lee: A Biography* (New York: Charles Scribner's Sons, 1935), 3:337.

46. OR, 36:Pt. 1:9.
47. Foster Diary, DU; Heth Report.
48. Henry Albright, Diary, Private Collection, NCDAH.
49. OR, 51:Pt. 2:969; OR, 36:Pt. 3:399–402; OR, 36:Pt. 1:674, 707.
50. Martin, 597; James Wright Letter, May 31, 1864, John Wright Family Papers, Private Collection, NCDAH.
51. Heth Report.
52. Clark, 4:95; Long Reminiscences, Library of Congress, p. 1235b; Clark, 4:95. First Lt. Long attributes these events to the following day, June 2, but the description of the action closely fits Gibbon's attack on June 1. There is no evidence of a Union attack against Kirkland on June 2.

COLD HARBOR
53. OR, 36:Pt. 1:344.
54. OR, 36:Pt. 3:499.
55. OR, 36:Pt. 1:1032.
56. OR, 36:Pt. 3:501, 504; OR, 36:Pt. 1:926.
57. Heth, *Memoirs,* 188–9; Heth Report; Long Reminiscences, 1236.
58. Long Reminiscences, 1237; OR, 36:Pt. 1:926.
59. Long Reminiscences, 1237, 1238–8b; OR, 36:Pt. 1:926.
60. Long Reminiscences, 1238b–39.
61. OR, 36:Pt. 1:932; Long Reminiscences, 1241; Heth Report.
62. Heth Report; Heth, *Memoirs,* 189.
63. Colonel Martin's comments (Martin, 597) show that he might have been one of those who spoke up about Kirkland's weak leadership.
64. Albright Diary, Private Collection, NCDAH. The Foster Diary states that the 52d N.C. retired to the road, then stacked arms that night. Other testimony suggests that some of the brigade remained along the front line that night. Capt. Thorp of the 47th N.C. recorded in Clark, 3:96 that Heth's Division "remained on the ground taken that night." Nevertheless, Heth did shuffle Cooke's and Kirkland's brigades that night, which suggests that Kirkland was pulled out of the line. All the sources agree that Kirkland's Brigade was back on the front line when Burnside attacked the next morning. Clark, 1:746.
65. Clark, 1:746, 3:96; Albright Diary, NCDAH; OR, 36:Pt. 1:930.
66. Clark, 1:746; OR, 36:Pt. 3:547.
67. Albright Diary, NCDAH and Heth Report.
68. OR, 36:Pt. 3:551.
69. OR, 36:Pt. 1:930, 933; OR, 51:Pt. 2:982; Clark, 1:746; Heth Report.
70. OR, 36:Pt. 1:882, 914.
71. Clark, 3:96; OR, 36:Pt. 1:901.
72. Gregory Jaynes, *The Killing Ground: Wilderness to Cold Harbor* (Alexandria, Va.: Time-Life Books, 1986), 158; U. S. Grant, *Personal Memoirs of U. S. Grant* (reprint, New York: Da Capo Press, 1982), 444.

CHAPTER FIVE

PETERSBURG
1. Foster Diary, DU; Albright Diary, NCDAH.

2. Bird Letters, June 4, 1864; Foster Diary, DU; Warlick Letters, May 25, 1864; OR, 36:Pt. 1:434.
3. OR, 36:Pt. 1:680.
4. Warlick Letters, June 12, 16, 1864.
5. OR, 36:Pt. 1:11.
6. Warlick Letters, June 12, 1864; Heth Report.
7. Warlick Letters, June 16, 1864; Bird Letters, June 17, 1864.
8. Albright Diary, NCDAH.
9. OR, 40:Pt. 2:258.
10. Martin, 597; Justice Letters, July 11, 1864.
11. Martin, 598–9.
12. OR, 40:Pt. 2:307.
13. OR, 40:Pt. 2:343, 375–6; OR 40:Pt. 1:502.
14. OR, 40:Pt. 2:355–9.
15. Justice Letters, June 27, 1864; OR, 40:Pt. 2:694–5; Robert MacRae Letter July 4, 1864, Hugh MacRae Papers, DU.
16. Charles M. Stedman, "Memorial Address," Fredericksburg and Spotsylvania National Military Park, Fredericksburg, Va., 1890.
17. Clark, 4:563–4.
18. Stedman, Memorial Address.
19. Woodson Garrett, Personal Sketch by Duncan C. Waddell, Military Collection, NCDAH (hereafter cited as Waddell, Sketch of Woodson Garrett).

GLOBE TAVERN

20. Justice Letters, June 27 and July 11, 1864; OR, 40:Pt. 3:38, 76; Bird Letters, July 9, 1864. See also, OR, 40:Pt. 3:145, 192, 207.
21. Warlick Letters, July 8, 21, 1864.
22. Warlick Letters, July 21, 1864.
23. *Wilmington Daily Journal,* 2 August 1864; OR, 40:Pt. 3:598.
24. OR, 40:Pt. 3:809; Martin, 598.
25. Wright Diary, NCDAH; Foster Diary, DU; OR, 42:Pt. 2:4–5; Bartlett Reminiscences; Clark, 4:564.
26. Heth, *Memoirs,* 191.
27. John Horn, *The Destruction of the Weldon Railroad: Deep Bottom, Globe Tavern, and Reams Station, August 14–15, 1864* (Lynchburg, Va.: H. E. Howard, 1991), 92.
28. Bartlett Reminiscences; Foster Diary, DU.
29. Horn, *Weldon Railroad,* 97.
30. Bartlett Reminiscences; Horn, *Weldon Railroad,* 96; OR, 42:Pt. 1:472; Martin, 599.
31. Horn, *Weldon Railroad,* 97.
32. Clark, 2:388–9. The historian of the 26th N.C. quotes Duncan Waddell as the source of this story, but he identifies the incident with the battle of Reams Station on August 25. However, the attacking brigades at Reams Station began their advance at different times, and the terrain would have prevented Heth from signaling the attack from MacRae's skirmish line. The facts behind the story strongly suggest that the event took place at Davis Farm on August 21. The attacks at Davis Farm and Reams Station are the only possible sites for this incident.
33. Martin, 599; Waddell, Sketch of Woodston Garrett; Horn, *Weldon Railroad,* 100.

34. Clark, 4:564; Bartlett Reminiscences.
35. OR, 42:Pt. 1:431: Horn, *Weldon Railroad,* 106–7.
36. Martin, 599; Bartlett Reminiscences.
37. OR, 42:Pt. 1:475; Waddell, Sketch of Woodston Garrett.
38. Waddell, Sketch of Woodston Garrett.
39. OR, 42:Pt. 1:542–3.

REAMS STATION
40. Bird Letters, August 24, 1864; Heth Report; Justice Letters, August 30, 1864.
41. OR, 42:Pt. 1:222.
42. Noah Andre Trudeau, *The Last Citadel* (Boston: Little, Brown & Co. 1991), 185; OR, 42:Pt. 1:252.
43. OR, 42:Pt. 1:225.
44. Clark, 4:565.
45. John C. Warlick to Edward R. Outlaw, December 1, 1901, DU. Warlick's letter mentioned that he passed over the cut in the rail bed. This places the 11th N.C. on the left flank because the rest of the regiments passed over the embankment. See also Clark, 3:30; Horn, *Weldon Raiload,* 133, 138; Heth Report.
46. OR, 42:Pt. 1:289.
47. OR, 42:Pt. 1:253; Stedman, Memorial Address, 21; Clark, 3:30, 4:565–6.
48. Bird Letters, newspaper obituary; Compiled Service Records, 11th NCT, NA; *Davidson Monthly,* April 1896, 242; OR, 42:Pt. 1:253.
49. Heth Report; Stedman, Memorial Address, 20. See also Clark, 3:30; OR, 42:Pt. 1:287–9.
50. OR, 42:Pt. 1:302; F. A. Walker, "Reams Station," Military Historical Society of Massachusetts, Papers, vol. 5 (Boston, 1906), 289; Heth Report.
51. OR, 42:Pt. 1:253.
52. OR, 42:Pt. 1:285; Stedman, Memorial Address, 21–2; OR, 42:Pt. 1:415.
53. OR, 42:Pt. 1:293, 318.
54. OR, 42:Pt. 1:227–8.
55. Heth Report. See also Justice Letters, August 30, 1864; OR, 42:Pt. 2:1207.
56. James Young and Duncan Waddell, Compiled Service Records, 11th NCT, NA; James C. Warlick to Edward R. Outlaw, December 1, 1901, DU.

JONES FARM
57. William Martin, Compiled Service Records, 11th NCT, NA; Bartlett Reminiscences; Stedman, Memorial Address, 12.
58. *Hillsborough Recorder,* 5 October 1864; Manarin and Jordan, 5:75; Jones Watson, Compiled Service Records, 3d N.C. Cavalry, NA.
59. OR, 42:Pt. 2:1274–5.
60. Justice Letters, August 19, 1864.
61. Clark, 3:249, 4:566–7.
62. Richard J. Sommers, *Richmond Redeemed* (Garden City, N.Y.: Doubleday, 1981), 182.
63. Sommers, *Richmond Redeemed,* 208–9.
64. Ibid., 238.
65. OR, 42:Pt. 1:546; Sommers, *Richmond Redeemed,* 259–60.
66. Cadmus M. Wilcox, Papers, Notes on the Richmond Campaign, Library of Congress.

67. OR, 42:Pt. 1:546, 579.
68. Wilcox Papers, Notes on the Richmond Campaign; OR, 42:Pt. 1:587.
69. Ibid., 587–8.
70. Martin, 600.
71. Sommers, *Richmond Redeemed,* 288–9; Heth Report; OR, 42:Pt. 1:142, 579.
72. Martin, 600.
73. Heth Report; Sommers, *Richmond Redeemed,* 307–8.
74. Ibid., 328.
75. Sommers, *Richmond Redeemed,* 328–9.
76. Heth Report.
77. Sommers, *Richmond Redeemed,* 369–70.
78. Ibid., 386–8.
79. Ibid., 393–4; Clark, 4:567; Heth Report.
80. OR, 42:Pt. 1:366.
81. Warlick Letters, October 6, 1864; Manarin and Jordan, 5:43.

BURGESS MILL
82. Trudeau, *Last Citadel,* 222.
83. Horace Porter, *Campaigning with Grant* (reprint, New York: Da Capo Press, 1986), 309; Trudeau, *Last Citadel,* 231–2
84. OR, 42:Pt. 1:231.
85. Ibid.
86. Francis A. Walker, "The Expedition to the Boydton Plank Road," Military Historical Society of Massachusetts, Papers, vol. 5 (Boston, 1906): 335f.
87. Porter, *Campaigning with Grant,* 310–1.
88. Ibid., 311.
89. OR, 42:Pt. 1:326.
90. Ibid.,367–8, 374.
91. OR, 42:Pt. 1:368, 374, 382, 386, 388; Clark, 3:31.
92. Bartlett Reminiscences; Clark, 3:250; OR, 42:Pt. 1:368, 372, 374, 378.
93. Bartlett Reminiscences.
94. OR, 42:Pt. 1:359, 396.
95. OR, 42:Pt. 1:234.
96. OR, 42:Pt. 1:396; Bartlett Reminiscences; Clark, 3:32.
97. OR, 42:Pt. 1:359; Clark, 2:411–2, 3:32; Trudeau, *Last Citadel,* 247. Quoted from the *Charlotte Bulletin.*
98. Bartlett Reminiscences; OR, 42:Pt. 1:380.
99. OR, 42:Pt. 1:304, 360.
100.James I. Robertson, Jr. ed., *The Civil War Letters of General Robert McAllister* (New Brunswick, N.J.: Rutgers University Press, 1965), 529; OR, 42:Pt. 1:396; Clark, 3:250.
101.Warlick Letters, October 29, 1864; Clark, 3:98.
102.OR, 42:Pt. 1:235.
103.Robertson, *McAllister Letters,* 529.
104.Warlick Letters, October 29, 1864; Manarin and Jordan, 5:69; Heth Report; Clark, 4:567.

CHAPTER SIX

HATCHERS RUN

1. Martin, 601.
2. W. A. Day, "Life Among Bullets—In the Rifle Pits," *Confederate Veteran* 29 (1921): 217.
3. Day, "Life Among Bullets," *Confederate Veteran,* 29:217; OR, 46:Pt. 1:382, Pt. 2:1145.
4. Manarin and Jordan, 5:19, 47; Grant, *Personal Memoirs,* 525; John C. Warlick to Edward R. Outlaw December 1, 1901, DU.
5. OR, 46:Pt. 1:383–5; James Young, Compiled Service Records, 11th NCT, NA; Warlick Letters, January 27, 1865.
6. OR, 46:Pt. 1:191–2, 212; Robertson, ed., *General Robert McAllister,* 581.
7. OR, 46:Pt. 1:192; Robertson, ed., *General Robert McAllister,* 581
8. Trudeau, *Last Citadel,* 315; Clark, 4:567–8.
9. OR, 46:Pt. 1:212.
10. Robertson, ed., *General Robert McAllister,* 582; OR, 46:Pt. 1:238–9, 245.
11. Trudeau, *Last Citadel,* 316; Clark, 4:567.
12. Robertson, ed., *General Robert McAllister,* 583–4; OR, 46:Pt. 1:245.
13. Ibid.
14. Clark, 4:567–8. Louis Young's account of the battle does not match the Union official reports. McAllister witnessed three distinct charges against his position, while Young claims that Heth's force failed to attack after the first assault. McAllister may have mistaken local actions and rebel yells for concerted attacks. Once again, opposing forces viewed the action in different terms.
15. Robertson, ed., *General Robert McAllister,* 583–4.
16. Martin, 601.

NO MAN'S LAND

17. Barry Benson, *Berry Benson's Civil War Book: Memoirs of a Confederate Scout and Sharpshooter,* ed. Susan Williams Benson (Athens: University of Georgia Press, 1993), 174.
18. Bartlett Reminiscences.
19. Justice Letters, March 15, 1865.
20. Justice Letters, March 15, 1865; Manarin and Jordan, 5:49.
21. OR, 46:Pt. 3:139–45.
22. Joesph Warren Kiefer Letters, March 25, 1865, Library of Congress (hereafter cited as Kiefer Letters).
23. Benson, *Civil War Book,* 176; Kiefer Letters, March 25, 1865.
24. Hazard Stevens, "The Storming of the Lines of Petersburg by the Sixth Corps, April 2, 1865," Military Historical Society of Massachusetts, Papers, vol. 6 (Boston, 1907) 415; Benson, *Civil War Book,* 177.
25. Stevens, "Storming Petersburg," 6:415–6; Manarin and Jordan, 5:76.
26. Stevens, "Storming Petersburg," 6:417.
27. Stedman, Memorial Address, p. 12–3.
28. Benson, *Civil War Book,* 177; Stedman, Memorial Address, 13.
29. Trudeau, *Last Citadel,* 353.
30. William MacRae, Official Report, April 11, 1865, Lee Headquarters Papers, VHS.

31. MacRae Report, Lee Headquarters Papers, VHS.
32. Porter, *Campaigning with Grant,* 443.

BREAKTHROUGH

33. Cadmus Wilcox, Official Report, March 29–April 9, 1865 Lee Headquarters Papers, VHS, 70; MacRae Report, Lee Headquarters Papers, VHS.
34. John R. Cooke, Official Report, April 11, 1865, Lee Headquarters Papers, VHS; Eric Erson, Official Report, April 11, 1865, Lee Headquarters Papers, VHS. Most histories state that the 26th N.C. defended next to the 11th N.C. This is based on an erroneous statement by Colonel Martin in Clark, 1:602. Erson's and MacRae's reports prove that the 26th N.C. was south of Hatcher's Run with the rest of MacRae's Brigade.
35. William J. Martin, Compiled Service Records, 11th NCT, NA.
36. Martin, 602.
37. Stevens, "Storming Petersburg," 6:418–9; OR, 46:Pt. 1:903.
38. OR, 46:Pt. 1:902; Stevens, "Storming Petersburg," 6:422.
39. OR, 46:Pt. 1:903, 954.
40. Stevens, "Storming Petersburg," 6:421, 423; OR, 46:Pt. 1:903, 954.
41. OR, 46:Pt. 1:954, 910.
42. OR, 46:Pt. 1:954, 969.
43. Bartlett Reminiscences; OR, 46:Pt. 1:993.
44. John C. Warlick to Edward R. Outlaw December 1, 1901, DU.
45. Erson Report, Lee Headquarters Papers, VHS.
46. OR, 46:Pt. 1:910, 955, 903, 993.
47. Martin, 602; OR, 46:Pt. 1:970; William McComb, Official Report, April 11, 1865, Lee Headquarters Papers, VHS. McComb states that he was driven from the fort at 7:40 A.M.
48. OR, 46:Pt. 1:969, 955.
49. Cooke Report, Lee Headquarters Papers, VHS; McComb Report, Lee Headquarters Papers, VHS; Manarin and Jordan, vol. 5.
50. G. W. Tucker, "Death of General A. P. Hill," SHSP, 11:564–9; "Further Details of the Death of General A. P. Hill," SHSP, 12:183–7; OR, 46:Pt. 1:993.
51. Henry Heth, Official Report, April 11, 1865, Lee Headquarters Papers, VHS; OR, 46:Pt. 1:679, 711.
52. Heth Report, Lee Headquarters Papers, VHS.
53. MacRae Report, Lee Headquarters Papers, VHS; OR, 46:Pt. 1:711.
54. OR, 46:Pt. 1:711, 746.
55. MacRae Report, Lee Headquarters Papers, VHS; Manarin and Jordan, 5:89.

RETREAT

56. OR, 46:Pt. 1:1264–5.
57. Benson, *Civil War Book,* 190–1.
58. Richard Wheeler, *Witness to Appomattox* (New York: Harper & Row, 1989), 143.
59. MacRae Report, Lee Headquarters Papers, VHS; OR, 46:Pt. 1:389.
60. William Mahone, "On the Road to Appomattox," *Civil War Times Illustrated* 9 (January 1971): 8.
61. OR, 46:Pt. 1:604.

62. Wilcox Report, Lee Headquarters Papers, VHS.
63. Martin, 603.
64. OR, 46:Pt. 1:604; Burleigh Cushing Rodick, *Appomattox: The Last Campaign* (New York: Philosophical Library, 1965), 58.
65. MacRae Report, Lee Headquarters Papers, VHS.
66. OR, 46:Pt. 1:604; Mahone, "On the Road to Appomattox," 9.
67. MacRae Report, Lee Headquarters Papers, VHS. MacRae's report gives the date of April 5, but the description of the problems with wagons suggests that this event occurred on April 6. Wilcox Report, Lee Headquarters Papers, VHS.
68. Wilcox Report, Lee Headquarters Papers, VHS.
69. Martin, 603.

SURRENDER
70. Porter, *Campaigning with Grant*, 458–9; Rodick, *Appomattox*, 89; Grant, *Personal Memoirs*, 550.
71. Wheeler, *Witness to Appomattox*, p. 202; Grant, *Personal Memoirs*, 551.
72. Martin, 603; John C. Warlick to Edward Outlaw, December 1, 1901, DU.
73. MacRae Report, Lee Headquarters Papers, VHS; Grant, *Personal Memoirs*, 551.
74. Martin, 603; Rachel Warlick Dunn, *Daniel Warlick of Lincoln County and His Descendants* (N.p., 1983), 356.
75. Wheeler, *Witness to Appomattox*, 212–3.
76. Ibid., 216–7.
77. Ibid., 217; Alexander, *Fighting for the Confederacy*, 531–3.
78. Grant, *Personal Memoirs*, 554.
79. Martin, 603.
80. Grant, *Personal Memoirs*, 556–8.
81. Wheeler, *Witness to Appomattox*, 231.
82. "Paroles of the Army of Northern Virginia," SHSP 15 (1887): 295–7; Manarin and Jordan, 5:21; Rachel Warlick Dunn, *Warlick Descendants*, 356.
83. OR, 46:Pt. 1:1267.
84. Joshua L. Chamberlain, *The Passing of the Armies* (New York: J. L. Chamberlain, 1915), 258.
85. Chamberlain, *The Passing of the Armies*, 258–60.
86. Martin, 604.

EPILOGUE

1. Edmund Jones to Paul B. Means, November 11, 1905, William J. Martin Family Papers, Davidson College.
2. Bridges, *Lee's Maverick General*, 273–9.
3. Clarence W. Griffin, *History of Old Tryon and Rutherford Counties North Carolina* (Asheville, N.C.: Miller Printing Co., 1937) 293–4 n.

Bibliography

MANUSCRIPTS

Burke County Public Library, Morganton, N.C.
Bristol, Lambert A. and Elam B. Bristol. Letters.

Davidson College Library, Davidson, N.C.
Martin, William J. Family Papers.
Davidson Monthly. Memorial Number. April 1896.

Duke University, Special Collections Library, Durham, N.C. (DU)
Foster, Alfred and John Foster. Papers. John A. Foster Diary.
King, Willis. Papers. Bellfield King Letters.
Leventhorpe, Collett. Collection.
MacRae, Hugh. Papers. William MacRae Letters.
Warlick, John C. Letter.
Wright, Marcus. Papers. Collett Leventhorpe Letter.

East Carolina University, Joyner Library, Greenville, N.C.
Austin, Emily Semple. "History of the Edgecombe Guards During the War Between
    the States."

Edgecombe Community College, Tarboro, N.C.
Painter, Harold Scott. "The Edgecombe Guard." Tarboro, N.C. 1992.

Emory University, Robert A. Woodruff Library, Atlanta, Georgia
Justice, Benjamin W. Letters.

Fredericksburg and Spotsylvania National Military Park, Fredericksburg, Virginia

Stedman, Charles M. "Memorial Address: A Sketch of the Life and Character of General William MacRae, With an Account of the Battle of Reams' Station," Wilmington, N.C., 1890.

Gettysburg National Military Park, Gettysburg, Pa.

William B. Taylor. Letters (photocopies).

Library of Congress, Manuscript Division, Washington, D.C.

Kiefer, Joseph Warren. Letters.
Long, Breckinridge. Papers. William S. Long Reminiscences.
Richardson, Charles H. Diary.
Wilcox, Cadmus M. Papers. Notes on the Richmond Campaign.
Woodwell, Charles H. "Journal of a Private Soldier."

Museum of the Confederacy, Eleanor S. Brockenbrough Library, Richmond, Virginia

Heth, Henry. Official Report. December 7, 1864.

National Archives, Washington, D.C. (NA)

Compiled Service Records. 11th Regiment North Carolina Troops.

New Hanover County Library, Wilmington, N.C.

Gerdes, Susan. "General William MacRae."

North Carolina Department of Archives and History, Raleigh, N.C. (NCDAH)

Angley, Wilson. "A Brief History of the North Carolina Militia and National Guard," 1985.

Military Collection

Archbell, Mrs. "Battle of Blount's Creek Mill."
Bridgers, John L. Personal Sketch.
Bryan, Sarah Parks. "Taking of the Fayetteville Arsenal."
Cutchins, J. M. Reminiscences.
Garrett, Woodson. Personal Sketch by Duncan C. Waddell.
Huske, Benjamin. "Account of the Battle of Bethel."
Leventhorpe, Collett. Letters.
Lloyd, C. Whit. Personal Sketch.
Lloyd, Whitmel Pugh. Personal Sketch.
Parker, Francis. Personal Sketch.
Unknown. "Fight at Big Bethel."
Unknown. Rough Sketch of Plan of the Battle of Bethel.
Wyatt, Henry Lawson. Personal Sketch.

Private Collection

Albright, Henry. Diary and Letters.
Benton, Henry E. Letter.
Harper, Samuel Finley. Letters.

BIBLIOGRAPHY

Huske, Henry. Letter.
King, James A. Letter.
Leventhorpe, Collett. Scrapbook.
Parker, William G. Letters.
Pettigrew Papers (13.18). Collett Leventhorpe to Mary Pettigrew, May 14, 1867.
Stevens, H. S. Papers.
Winston F. D. Louis G. Young. Account of Gettysburg.
Wright, John. Family Papers. Letters of Cpl. James W. Wright.

Petersburg National Battlefield, National Park Service, Petersburg, Virginia
Detailed Map of Boydton Entrenchments.

The Regiment Band of the 11th North Carolina Troops, Inc. Fayetteville, N.C.
Neave, W. H. Letters.

United States Army Military History Institute, Carlisle Barracks, Pa.
Civil War Times Illustrated Collection
Nuttall, Charles A. Summary of Service.
Patterson, W. D. Letter. May 5, 1863.
War College Papers
Cabell, Maj. DeR. C. "The Operations about Spotsylvania." 1913.
Murphy, Maj. Truman O. "Campaign in Virginia: Movements from the North Anna to Include the Battle of Cold Harbor." 1914.
Ruckman, Col. John W. "Operations from Cold Harbor 1864 to Include the Siege Operations up to July 31, 1864." 1915.
Wyllie, Maj. Robert E. "The Battle and Campaign of Cold Harbor." 1916.

University of North Carolina. Southern Historical Collection. Chapel Hill, N.C. (SHC)
Bartlett, Jacob S. Reminiscences.
Beavans, William. Diary.
Brown, John L. Papers. John M. Tate Letters.
Bryan, Edmund. Papers.
Jones, Edmund. Papers. John T. Jones Letters.
Lineback, Julius. Diary and Papers.
Little, Benjamin F. Letters.
Martin, William J. Letter.
McDowell, W. W. Microfilm Collection.
McGimsey, Cornelia. Lewis Warlick Letters.
Polk, Leonidas Lafayette. Collection.
Ross, Egbert A. Letters.
Steed and Phipps Papers. William H. Blount Letters.
Winston, Robert Watson. Papers. Francis W. Bird Letters.

Virginia Historical Society, Richmond, Virginia. (VHS)
Parker, Henry Gillam. "The History of a Confederate Casualty."
Lee Headquarters Papers
    Cooke, Brig. Gen. John R. Official Report. April 11, 1865.
    Erson, Lt. Col. Eric. Official Report. April 11, 1865.
    Heth, Maj. Gen. Henry. Official Report. April 11, 1865.
    MacRae, Brig. Gen. William; Official Report. April 11, 1865.
    McComb, Brig. Gen. William. Official Report. April 11, 1865.
    Petition of several officers to Gen. Robert E. Lee. April 29, 1865.
    Wilcox, Maj. Gen. Cadmus M. Official Report. March 29–April 9, 1865.

THESES

Browning, Robert M. "The Blockade of Wilmington, North Carolina: 1861–65." ECU, 1980.
Iobst, Richard W. "North Carolina Mobilizes: Nine Crucial Months, December, 1860–August, 1861." UNC, 1968.
Kruman, Marc Wayne. "Parties and Politics in North Carolina, 1846–1865," Yale University, 1978.
Raper, Horace Wilson. "William Woods Holden: A Political Biography." UNC, 1951.

NEWSPAPERS

Daily Confederate, Raleigh, N.C. 1864.
Hillsborough Recorder, Hillsborough, N.C. 1861–65.
North Carolina Standard, William W. Holden, Ed., Raleigh, N.C. 1861–65.
North Carolina Whig, R. R. Holton, Ed. Charlotte, N.C. 1861–63.
Wilmington Daily Journal, Wilmington, N.C. 1861–62.

PERIODICALS

Civil War Times Illustrated, Harrisburg, Pennsylvania.
Confederate Veteran, S. A. Cunningham, Founder, Nashville, Tennessee.
North Carolina Historical Review, State Department of Achives and History, Raleigh, N.C.
Our Living and Our Dead, N.C. Branch Southern Historical Society, Raleigh, N.C.
Southern Historical Society Papers. 49 vols. Richmond, Virginia, 1876–1944. (SHSP).
The Land We Love, D. H. Hill, ed. vol. 6, Charlotte, N.C., March 1869.
The Military Engineer, vol. 39, January 1939.
The North Carolina Booklet, vol. 7, April 1908.

BOOKS

Adams, Michael C. C. *Our Masters the Rebels: A Speculation on Union Military Failure in the East 1861–1865.* Cambridge: Harvard University Press, 1978.
Alexander, Edward Porter. *Fighting for the Confederacy.* Ed. Gary W. Gallagher. Chapel Hill: UNC Press, 1989.

Ammen, Daniel. *The Atlantic Coast.* New York: Charles Scribner's Sons, 1883.

Anderson, Jean Bradley. *The Kirklands of Ayr Mount.* Chapel Hill: UNC Press, 1991.

Andrews, J. Cutler. *The South Reports the Civil War.* Princeton: Princeton University Press, 1970.

Ashe, S. A. *The Charge at Gettysburg.* Raleigh: Capital Printing, 1902.

———. *History of North Carolina.* Raleigh: Edwards & Broughton Co., 1925.

Barrett, John G. *The Civil War in North Carolina.* Chapel Hill: UNC Press, 1963.

Battine, Cecil. *The Crisis of the Confederacy.* New York: Longman, Greens, & Co., 1905.

Battle, Kemp P. *History of the University of North Carolina,* vol. 1. Spartanburg, S.C.: The Reprint Company, 1974.

Benson, Berry. *Berry Benson's Civil War Book: Memoirs of a Confederate Scout and Sharpshooter.* Edited by Susan Williams Benson. Athens: University of Georgia Press, 1993.

Blythe, LeGette, and Charles Raven Brockman. *Hornet's Nest: The Story of Charlotte and Mecklenburg County.* Charlotte: McNally, 1961.

Bonds, W. R. *Pickett or Pettigrew? An Historical Essay.* Weldon, N.C.: Hall & Sledge, 1888.

Bridges, Hal. *Lee's Maverick General: Daniel Harvey Hill.* New York: McGraw-Hill, 1961.

Browning, Robert M., Jr. *From Cape Charles to Cape Fear.* Tuscaloosa: University of Alabama Press, 1993.

Busey, John W., and David G. Martin. *Regimental Strengths and Losses at Gettysburg.* Hightstown, New York: Longstreet House, 1986.

Butler, Benjamin F. *Private and Official Correspondence of Gen. Benjamin F. Butler During the Civil War Period,* vol. 1. Norwood, Massachusetts, N.p., 1917.

Catton, Bruce. *A Stillness at Appomattox.* Garden City, New York: Doubleday, 1955.

———. *Gettysburg: The Final Fury.* Garden City, New York: Doubleday, 1974.

Chamberlain, Joshua Lawerence. *The Passing of the Armies.* New York: J. L. Chamberlain, 1915.

Clark, Champ. *Gettysburg: The Confederate High Tide.* Alexandria, Va.: Time-Life Books, 1987.

Clark, Walter, Comp. *Histories of the Several Regiments and Battalions from North Carolina in the Great War, 1861–'65.* 5 vols. Goldsboro, N.C.: Nash Brothers, 1901.

Crofts, Daniel W. *Reluctant Confederates: Upper South Unionists in the Secession Crisis.* Chapel Hill: UNC Press, 1989.

Cromie, Alice. *A Tour Guide to the Civil War.* Nashville, Tenn.: Rutledge Hill Press, 1964.

Davis, Archie K. *Boy Colonel of the Confederacy: The Life and Times of Henry King Burgwyn, Jr.* Chapel Hill: UNC Press, 1985.

Davis, Burke. *To Appomattox: Nine April Days 1865.* New York: Rinehart & Co., 1959.

Davis, William C. *First Blood: Fort Sumter to Bull Run.* Alexandria, Va.: Time-Life Books, 1983.

———. *Death in the Trenches: Grant at Petersburg.* Alexandria, Va.: Time-Life Books, 1986.

de Peyster, J. Watts. *La Royale! The Grand Hunt of the Army of the Potomac.* New York: Citizen and Round Table, 1872.

Dornbusch, C. E. Comp. *Military Bibliography of the Civil War.* 3 vols. Reprint. New York: New York Public Library, 1989.

Doubleday, Abner. *Chancellorsville and Gettysburg.* New York: Charles Scribner's Sons, 1882.

Dowdey, Clifford. *Death of a Nation: The Story of Lee and His Men at Gettysburg.* New York: Alfred A. Knopf, 1958.

———. *Lee's Last Campaign.* Boston: Little, Brown & Co., 1960.

Downey, Fairfax. *The Guns at Gettysburg.* New York: Collier Books, 1962.

Dunn, Rachel Warlick. *Daniel Warlick of Lincoln County and His Descendants.* N.p., 1983.

Early, Jubal A. *The Last Year of the War for Independence.* Lynchburg, Va.: Charles W. Button, 1867.

Fiebeger, G. J. *The Campaign and Battle of Gettysburg.* West Point: Military Academy Printing Office, 1915.

Fox, William F. *Regimental Losses in the American Civil War, 1861–1865.* Albany, N.Y.: Brandow, 1898.

Freeman, Douglas Southall. *R. E. Lee: A Biography,* vol. 3. New York: Charles Scribner's Sons, 1935.

———. *Lee's Lieutenants,* 3 vols. New York: Charles Scribner's Sons, 1944.

Gallagher, Gary W. Comp. *The Third Day at Gettysburg & Beyond.* Chapel Hill: UNC Press, 1994.

Grant, U. S. *Personal Memoirs of U. S. Grant.* Reprint, New York: Da Capo Press, 1982.

Griffin, Clarence W. *History of Old Tryon and Rutherford Counties North Carolina.* Asheville, N.C.: Miller Printing Co., 1937.

Griffith, Paddy. *Battle Tactics of the Civil War.* New Haven, Conn.: Yale University Press, 1989.

———. *Forward into Battle.* Novato, Calif.: Presidio Press, 1991.

Harris, William C. *North Carolina and the Coming of the Civil War.* Raleigh: NCDAH, 1988.

Haskel, Frank A. *Haskell of Gettysburg: His Life and Civil War Papers.* Edited by Frank L. Byrne and Andrew T. Weaver. Madison: State Historical Society of Wisconsin, 1970.

Hassler, Warren W., Jr. *Crisis at the Crossroads: The First Day at Gettysburg.* Reprint, Gettysburg: Stan Clark Military Books, 1991.

Heth, Henry. *The Memoirs of Henry Heth.* Edited by James L. Morrison. Westport, Conn.: Greenwood Press, 1974.

Hill, Daniel Harvey Jr. *Confederate Military History: North Carolina.* Atlanta: Confederate Publishing Co., 1899.

———. *Bethel to Sharpsburg.* Raleigh: Edwards & Broughton Co., 1926.

Hoke, Jacob. *The Great Invasion.* Reprint. New York: Thomas Yoseloff, 1959.

Horn, John. *The Destruction of the Weldon Railroad: Deep Bottom, Globe Tavern, and Reams Station, August 14–25, 1864.* Lynchburg, Va.: H. E. Howard, 1991.

Hotchkiss, Jed. *Confederate Military History: Virginia,* vol. 3. Atlanta: Confederate Publishing Co., 1899.

Howe, W. W. *Kinston, Whitehall and Goldsboro Expedition.* New York: W. W. Howe, 1890.

Humphreys, Andrew A. *From Gettysburg to the Rapidan: The Army of the Potomac from July 1863 to April 1864.* New York: Charles Scribner's Sons, 1883.

————. *The Virginia Campaign of '64 and '65: The Army of the Potomac and the Army of the James.* New York: Charles Scribner's Sons, 1883.

Jarratt's Hotel, Philip F. Brown, prop. *The Siege of Petersburg.* Petersburg: N.p., 1867.

Jaynes, Gregory. *The Killing Ground: Wilderness to Cold Harbor,* Alexandria, Va.: Time-Life Books, 1986.

Johnson, Charles F. *The Long Roll: One of the Hawkins Zouaves,* N.p., N.d.

Johnson, Robert Underwood, and Clarence Clough Buel, Eds. *Battles and Leaders of the Civil War,* vol. 3. Retreat from Gettysburg. Reprint. New York: Thomas Yoseloff, 1956.

Jones, Terry L. *Lee's Tigers: The Louisiana Infantry in the Army of Northern Virginia.* Baton Rouge: Louisiana State University Press, 1955.

Korn, Jerry. *Pursuit to Appomattox.* Alexandria, Va.: Time-Life Books, 1987.

Krick, Robert K. *The Gettysburg Death Roster.* Dayton, Ohio: Morningside Bookshop, 1985.

Leon, Louis. *Diary of a Tar Heel Confederate Soldier.* Charlotte: Stone Publishing Co., 1913.

Long, A. L. *Memoirs of Robert E. Lee.* Secaucus, N.J.: Blue and Grey Press, 1983.

Lykes, Richard Wayne. *Campaign for Petersburg, Official National Park Handbook.* Washington, D.C.: GPO, 1970.

Manarin, Louis H., and Weymouth T. Jordan, Comp. *North Carolina Troops 1861–65,* 13 vols. Raleigh: NCDAH, 1966–1994.

Martin, William J., and E. R. Outlaw. "Eleventh Regiment." In vol.1 *Histories of the Several Regiments and Battalions from North Carolina in the Great War, 1861–'65,* pp. 583–604. Goldsboro, N.C.: Nash Brothers, 1901.

Matter, William D. *If It Takes All Summer: The Battle of Spotsylvania.* Chapel Hill: UNC Press, 1988.

McWhiney, Grady, and Perry D. Jamieson. *Attack and Die: Civil War Military Tactics and the Southern Heritage.* Tuscaloosa: University of Alabama Press, 1982.

Military Historical Society of Massachusetts. Papers vol. 4; *The Wilderness Campaign.* Boston, 1905.

Military Historical Society of Massachusetts. Papers vol. 5; *Petersburg, Chancellorsville, Gettysburg.* Boston, 1906.

Military Historical Society of Massachusetts. Papers vol. 6; *The Shenandoah Campaigns of 1862 and 1864 and the Appomattox Campaign 1865.* Boston, 1907.

Moore, John W. *History of North Carolina,* vol. 2. Raleigh: Alfred Williams & Co., 1880.

North Carolina Literary and Historical Society. *Five Points in the Record of North Carolina in the Great War of 1861–5.* Goldsboro, N.C.: Nash Brothers, 1904.

The Official Military Atlas of the Civil War. Reprint. New York: Arno Press, 1978.

Patterson, Gerald A. *Rebels from West Point.* New York: Doubleday, 1987.

Phifer, Edward William. *Burke: The History of a North Carolina County.* Morganton, N.C.: N.p., 1977.

Pollard, Edward A. *Second Year of the War.* New York: Charles B. Richardson, 1864.

Porter, Horace. *Campaigning with Grant.* Reprint, New York: Da Capo Press, 1986.

Powell, William S. *North Carolina: A History.* Chapel Hill: UNC Press, 1977.

————. *North Carolina Through Four Centuries.* Chapel Hill: UNC Press, 1989.

Rhea, Gordon C. *The Battle of the Wilderness, May 5–6, 1864.* Baton Rouge: Louisiana State University Press, 1994.

Robertson, James I. Ed. *The Civil War Letters of General Robert McAllister*. New Brunswick, N.J.: Rutgers University Press, 1965.

———. *General A. P. Hill: The Story of a Confederate Warrior*. New York: Vintage Books, 1987.

Rodick, Burleigh Cushing. *Appomattox: The Last Campaign*. New York: Philosophical Library, 1965.

Shaara, Michael. *The Killer Angels*. New York: Ballantine Books, 1974.

Sheridan, Philip. *Civil War Memoirs* (edition). New York: Bantam Books, 1991.

Shotwell, Randolph Abbott. *The Papers of Randolph Abbott Shotwell*. Edited by J. G. de Roulhac Hamilton. Raleigh: North Carolina Historical Commission, 1929.

Sitterson, Joseph Carlyle. *The Secession Movement In North Carolina*. Chapel Hill: UNC Press, 1939.

Sommers, Richard J. *Richmond Redeemed*. Gardern City, N.Y.: Doubleday, 1981.

Sondley, F. A. *A History of Buncombe County North Carolina*. Spartanburg, S.C.: The Reprint Co., 1977.

Sprunt, James. *Chronicles of the Cape Fear River 1660–1916*. Raleigh: Edwards & Broughton Co., 1916.

Steere, Edward. *The Wilderness Campaign*. Harrisburg, Pa.: Stackpole, 1960.

Stern, Philip Van Doren. *An End to Valor: The Last Days of the Confederacy*. Boston: Houghton Mifflin, 1958.

Stewart, George R. *Pickett's Charge*. Boston: Houghton Mifflin, 1959.

Taylor, Walter H. *Four Years with General Lee*. New York: D. Appleton & Co., 1878.

Thomas, Benjamin P. *Abraham Lincoln: A Biography*. New York: Modern Library, 1952.

Trotter, William R. *Silk Flags and Cold Steel: The Civil War in North Carolina: The Piedmont*. Winston-Salem, N.C.: John F. Blair, 1988.

———. *Ironclads and Columbiads: The Civil War in North Carolina: The Coast*. Winston-Salem, N.C.: John F. Blair, 1989.

Trudeau, Noah Andre. *Bloody Roads South*. Boston: Little, Brown & Co., 1989.

———. *The Last Citadel*. Boston: Little, Brown & Co., 1991.

Tucker, Glenn. *High Tide at Gettysburg*. Indianapolis: Bobbs-Merrill, 1973.

U. S. War Department. *War of the Rebellion: A Compilation of the Official Records of the Union and Confederate Armies*. Washington, D.C.: GPO, 1880–1901.

Vance, Zebulon B. *The Papers of Zebulon Baird Vance,* vol. 1. Edited by Frontis W. Johnston. Raleigh: NCDAH, 1963.

Vanderslice, John M. *Gettysburg*. Philadelphia: G. W. Dillingham, 1897.

Wellman, Manly Wade. *Rebel Boast: First at Bethel—Last at Appomattox*. New York: Henry Holt & Co., 1956.

Wheeler, Richard. *Witness to Appomattox*. New York: Harper & Row, 1989.

———. *On Fields of Fury*. New York: HarperCollins, 1991.

Wiley, Bell I. *The Life of Johnny Reb: The Common Soldier of the Confederacy*. Indianapolis: Bobbs-Merrill, 1943.

Wilkinson, Warren. *Mother May You Never See the Sights I Have Seen*. New York: Quill, 1991.

Wilson, Clyde N. *Carolina Cavalier: The Life and Mind of James Johnston Pettigrew*. Athens: University of Georgia Press, 1990.

Yearns, W. Buck, and John G. Barrett, Comp. *North Carolina Civil War Documentary*. Chapel Hill: UNC Press, 1980.

Index